Descending from the Clouds

A Memoir of Combat in the 505 Parachute Infantry
Regiment, 82d Airborne Division

Where is the Prince who can afford so to cover his country with troops for its defense, as that ten thousand men descending from the clouds may not in many places do an infinite deal of mischief, before a force could be brought together to repel them?

— Benjamin Franklin, 1784

Descending from the Clouds

A Memoir of Combat in the 505 Parachute Infantry
Regiment, 82d Airborne Division

Spencer F. Wurst
and Gayle Wurst

CASEMATE
Havertown, PA

Published by
CASEMATE
2114 Darby Road, Havertown, PA
Phone: 610-853-9131

Typeset and design by
Savas Publishing & Consulting Group

ISBN 1-932033-31-9

First edition, first printing

Cataloging-in-Publication data is available
from the Library of Congress

Printed in the United States of America

To all the Company F, 505 Parachute Infantry Regiment World War II veterans, and especially to those among them who never had the opportunity to grow old in our wonderful nation. And to Millie, the most devoted, kind, and gentle wife a man could ever ask for.

Spencer F. Wurst

To the memory of my father, Vern Edward Wurst (1921–1959).

Gayle Wurst

On his way to war. Corporal Spencer Wurst, sitting for a
formal portrait in Alexandria, Louisiana, in March 1942. *Author*

Contents

Contents (continued)

Contents (continued)

Contents (continued)

Maps

Illustrations

Preface

The first time I went up in a plane I jumped out of it. It was late September 1942, and I was seventeen years old. I had lied about my age when I joined the military, so I had already served two years when I earned the right to blouse my trousers as a graduate of the Parachute School at Fort Benning. During most of World War II, I was a member of Company F, 505th Parachute Infantry Regiment, 82d Airborne Division, in which I served from July 1943 to August 1945 in the European Theater of Operations (ETO), where I made three of the regiment's four combat jumps, dropping in Italy, Normandy, and Holland.

Unlike the 101st Airborne and all other airborne units, the 82d had to develop very quickly under the pressure of crucial training directed at its early combat operations in Sicily and Italy. The training, tactics, organization and everything else that had to do with parachute troops were completely new, and we could not afford the time to perfect procedures before heading off for combat. The United States had no doctrine about airborne warfare, and the Army had never written anything about parachute operations: we wrote the book as we went along, and we added, changed, and deleted as we matured.

From the time I was assigned to the regiment in July 1943 up to VE-Day, the Allied victory in Europe on May 8, 1945, I was a rifleman in the 1st Squad, 3d Platoon of F Company, 2d Battalion, 505, where I moved up from private to squad leader, platoon sergeant, and platoon leader. Historians, biographers and generals have chronicled the proud history of the 505 and the 82d Airborne, their leaders' lives, decisions and military strategies, and I think it's fair to say that not many of these works have escaped me. More recently, a number of excellent books have at last begun to communicate the reality of the rank-and-file on the line, including memoirs by soldiers themselves. But to date, these memoirs have most often portrayed the experience of a single campaign. Never, to my knowledge, has anyone sat down to trace his evolution as a front-line parachute infantryman throughout the entire course of the war. This is what I have attempted to do in this memoir.

To the extent that my story is representative, it is the story of how the rapid evolution of airborne warfare during World War II shaped and was shaped by front-line parachute infantry soldiers. In showing how I fared through all the campaigns of the 505 from Sicily through the Ardennes, I've tried to convey the day-to-day reality, thoughts, hopes, fears, and fates of fellow paratroopers, as well as the abundant sense of irony and black humor present at the front. I felt it was especially crucial to show how we adapted and developed our fighting skills, and how we were transformed as individuals and human beings under the pressure of extensive periods of combat. On this ability to quickly adapt depended our survival, as illustrated by an epitaph in the mock cemetery at Fort Benning:

> *Here lie the bones of Lieutenant Jones*
> *A graduate of this institution,*
> *He died on the night of his very first fight,*
> *While using the school solution.*[1]

No matter how well we learned this lesson, facts beyond our control enormously influenced our casualty rates. Today almost nobody remembers that the practice of individual rotation did not begin until the Korean War, when the Army started developing a one-year policy that even included R&R leave. I first heard the word "rotation" in 1944, after I had been overseas for nineteen months straight, most of it on the front. For the entire 2d Battalion 505, the quota for our new so-called rotation policy was only two men. Based on statistics from November 1944, just 6 percent of all U.S. Army personnel in the ETO were riflemen, and yet we suffered most of the casualties. Think of it: there were 2,588,983 U.S. Army personnel in the ETO at the end of November 1944, but only 152,280 were in rifle platoons. We made up 68 percent of the total authorized strength of an infantry division, but our casualty rate was an incredible 95 percent. Few of us were lucky enough to survive, and every year fewer of us who did survive remain to tell the tale. This has added urgency to my desire to give another perspective, a bottom-up historical account of airborne warfare in the ETO.[2]

There is, of course, the problem of memory. Combat is an odd experience. Your point of view may differ from that of the person right next to you in the squad or even your fire team. One unit may have a much tougher time than another unit right next door. Experiences vary, and trying to reconstruct and articulate them so long after they occurred only complicates the problem. Rarely as a lowly private—or as a squad sergeant or even a platoon sergeant—did I have the full picture of what was going on. Our objectives were immediate: stay alive, assemble after a jump, get on with the duties at hand.

I do not pretend to recall all of my war-time experiences on a day-to-day basis. Yet I cannot get over the vividness of the experiences I do remember, and the way they remain so firmly fixed in my mind, as if they had happened only yesterday. During numerous reunions of the 505 Regimental Combat Team, I discovered friends and unit members often remembered the same events just as vividly, but very differently than I do. So where, I've so often asked myself, is the truth, the real definition of the experience? Surely, it is in the eyes of the beholder.

Then there is the problem of long silence. It has often been noted that most World War II veterans do not talk about their wartime experiences. This is the second reason I have undertaken this book. Immediately after the war, I was overwhelmed with a feeling of anger that probably had its roots in my first day of combat, grew until the last shot I fired, and then kept right on going. This anger, and the terrible sadness about what we had seen and done were typical of combat veterans immediately after the war. Long after we had made the transition back to civilian life, these emotions still made it stressful even to get into a discussion about the war. We all wanted to forget the experience.

Although it took me many years, I finally concluded that this inability or refusal to talk about the war amounted to a kind of collusion. My silence had deprived my children of a vital part of their heritage, and they had a right to know.

But how could I find the words to covey the unnamable? Combat veterans do not like to talk about their experiences because they mostly believe that no one who has not had to undergo combat can ever understand what it is like to be on the front line. We were different from all other soldiers; for us, killing and staying alive was not an emergency situation of limited duration, it was a full-time occupation for weeks or months on end. Among ourselves, at reunions, the talk is free and fast. Although the conversations are often humorous, they do get serious. It is when outsiders move in that combat veterans become silent.

This memoir, then, is written for our children. It is also written to honor the many soldiers who died on the line, and in the hope that other survivors might find themselves in my story.

Acknowledgments

I am very grateful to the many people who generously contributed advice, knowledge, criticism, encouragement, and moral support as this book gradually evolved from taped remembrances to its final form. Among former F Company members, I especially thank the following friends: Russell Brown, an original member of Company F and a four-jump trooper, for helpful advice as the book progressed and personal photographs; Don McKeage, former national president of the 82d Airborne Division Association, founding president of the 505th Regimental Combat Team Association, and long-time editor of *The Panther* (the 505 RCT publication), for advice, help in locating other Company F members, and photographs; Leonard DeFoggi, assistant machine gunner in the 3d Platoon, for photographs and help with the names of troopers I could not identify; and W. A. Jones (Sergeant Major, retired), a former member in my rifle squad, for reading the manuscript and refreshing my memory about some of our squad's combat actions. I am also grateful to Elmer Carlson, a close friend and fellow NCO in

Company H, 112th Infantry Regiment, who reviewed and made suggestions about the first few chapters, and to Rick Scalf and Jean Francisco Critelli for the photograph of my good friend Vernon Francisco.

Among those who provided a historical perspective, I wish to thank Phil Nordyke, who has done so much to compile the oral history of the 82d Airborne, for his interest in my story and his assistance in tracking down archival photographs; Barry Davis, who teaches history at my old high school, for his enthusiastic support and historian's eye; and Harold Burgard, Social Studies Department head at South Western High School, Jamestown, New York, who read an early draft and greatly encouraged me to keep on writing. Upon receiving the fruit of that process, a full 630 pages, our editor, Eric Hammel, had the experience and vision to recognize the *book* that has here emerged, and the faith to see the project through many revisions.   Gratitude also goes to Bud Atherton, the Business Director of the North East School District (PA), for his insightful critique of an early draft; Ellen Nas, for enthusiastically reading the manuscript and circulating it among other Dutch friends; Ellen Hawley, for helping us do the painful cutting of a long draft; Don Vandergrift and Shelly Allen, for their excellent transcriptions; and Walter H. Bell, for help with all things technical and bedrock moral and practical support.

In the research department, Star Jorgensen provided timely expertise to solve a thorny problem, and librarians Susan Darkhosh (Princeton Public Library) and Brenda Nickerson (Clymer-French Creek Library) both went beyond the call of duty with cheerful and efficient assistance. A special thank you is due to Harry Yeide, who graciously allowed me to use several maps from his new book, *The Tank Killers* (Casemate, 2004), and Karel Margry, editor at *After the Battle* publishers (London), who generously helped us track down sources for photographs.

Finally, I extend a very special thanks to my children, Chris Wurst, Carolyn Fialkowski, and Spencer Wurst, who did so much along the way, from critiquing drafts to offering emotional and practical support. I also wish especially to thank my niece and co-author, Gayle Wurst, whose help was so essential from start to finish. But above all, I am grateful to my patient and understanding wife, Mildred Wurst, who supported, helped, and endured me in our daily life though all the long years of the "book project."

Chapter 1

Enlistment and Premobilization Training, 112th Infantry, Pennsylvania Army National Guard

The first time I thought about joining the Army was in tenth grade chemistry class, when I spied a classmate reading a machine-gun manual. I showed interest, we talked, and the outcome was that I went to the Armory and joined up. I don't know if I talked it over with anyone, or if I just went and did it. I'd turned fifteen a few months earlier, on December 19, 1939. The legal age for enlisting was eighteen, so of course I had to lie about my age. I gave my new birthday as April 2, 1922. I figured I could remember 2/22, and hoped I'd remember April, the month of my enlistment.

I enlisted in the Pennsylvania Army National Guard on April 19, 1940, in my hometown of Erie, Pennsylvania. I discovered that eight or ten students from my school, for the most part underage, were already in the Guard. We were in Company H of the 2d Battalion of the 112th Infantry Regiment in the 28th Infantry Division. This was a heavy weapons company consisting of two platoons of water-cooled .30-caliber machine guns: the antitank platoon and the 81mm mortar platoon. The battalion anti-tank platoon was supposed to have .50-caliber machine guns as their antitank weapon. I mention this only because it's so ridiculous.

I had always been interested in the military, and World War II was starting to heat up. I remember pouring over books about the Civil War at my Great Aunt Myra's in Kennedy, New York. Aunt Myra's relatives had fought in that war, and her library was full of first-person accounts. When England and France declared war on Germany in September 1939, I spent study hall and any other free time I had reading *Time, Life* and *Newsweek*. Following the course of the war in my high school library, I thought we would soon become involved.

Because my mother and father were divorced, I guess I was seeking something to anchor my life as well as the spirit of adventure. My sister Vangie and her husband Ronnie, with whom I was living, weren't too happy with me for enlisting. My older brother Vern wasn't around at the time. My dad didn't object, because the Guard was paying us a dollar for every drill. That amounted to $12.00 to $14.00 a quarter, a significant amount of money for a fifteen-year-old in 1940, when the average laborer was earning $15.00 to $20.00 a week. When my mother found out, she was very upset. She either visited the Armory or wrote a letter to the battalion commander, LtCol Momeyer, protesting my enlistment. No one told me about this at the time; I only found out long after the fact.

The distance from my sister's home to the Armory in Erie was at least eight miles, and I walked or hitchhiked to and from drills, which took place on Friday evenings. Guards received all their training from the instructors within their parent company. My first sergeant for my first two years was Sergeant Rohaly, who looked to me like a grandfather. I think he was of Russian origin—at least we called him "the mad Russian" behind his back—and his vocabulary was very limited, except for military terms. He was quite a character, a real hard-nosed first sergeant.

We didn't receive the best training. In addition to drilling two hours a week, we went to the Armory for unpaid range firing. We used .22-caliber rifles for marksmanship training and a sub-caliber firing device that we attached to the .30-caliber water-cooled machine gun to enable it to fire .22-caliber ammunition. This allowed us to fire on a range in the basement of the Armory. We also received instruction in close-order drill in the basement, and attended classes on basic military subjects taught by a sergeant or corporal who had probably been trained a couple of years earlier under the same conditions.

I remember parading in Erie wearing the old class-A uniform. The only part of it I ever liked was the spiffy campaign hat that looked like the hat worn by Smokey the Bear. Running around the brim was a bright blue cord, the color of the infantry, with a couple of doodads hanging from it. I shelled out $14.00 for that hat, a fortune for a kid like me, but our uniforms changed before I had the chance to wear it.

In the very beginning, we had wrapped leggings. They were nothing but ribbons about an inch and a quarter wide that you had to wrap around your legs. Next we were issued leather leggings originally designed for the cavalry, because there weren't enough canvas leggings for the entire infantry. We did eventually get these and OD (olive drab) woolen trousers that we wore with a woolen coat or "blouse," but the uniform was hot and uncomfortable. During parades, we'd march over to State Street, up to the stadium, over 26th to Parade, and then back down to the Armory at 6th Street. It was a matter of fifty-two long blocks, a good six miles, quite a march for part-time civilian soldiers sweating in heavy wool.

Shortly after I enlisted, we were told that the 28th Division would participate in field army maneuvers at a base camp near Ogdensburg, in upstate New York. Annual training time was extended to three weeks from the usual two. We were billeted in six- or eight-man tents laid out in company streets. I was impressed with what I saw: the horse cavalry units, many large artillery guns, observation balloons, and Army planes. As I was only fifteen and had never been away from home for so long, I did feel homesick. The song "Sierra Sue" still sticks in my mind and reminds me of those days: Just like the song, I was full of sadness and loneliness. I went to town once but quickly returned to camp because the soldiers were so thick I could hardly walk on the streets.

I sometimes wonder if the Army maneuvers of 1940 weren't undertaken just to publicize the shortage of weapons and training. When we went on maneuvers in August, our only real weapons were the .45-caliber pistols we carried as individual weapons, and .30-caliber water-cooled machine guns dating from World War I. The antitank platoon built wooden mock-ups of the .50-caliber machine gun, and the 81mm mortar platoon carried lengths of stovepipe or steel pipe with a wooden base plate to simulate actual weapons.

Mobility was also a real problem. The machine gun platoon had a two-wheeled cart for each machine gun squad, with rubber-tired wheels and a draw bar so two men could pull the cart. We mounted the tripod on the cart, mounted the gun on the tripod, and then lugged away. If we were lucky, we got to pull the cart along a road; if we were unlucky, we would have to hand-carry the gun across rough terrain. This meant we had to carry either a 51-pound tripod or a 33-pound water-cooled gun or two 20-pound ammo boxes—quite a load for a kid like me at 5 feet 8 inches and 128 pounds. We also carried heavy-walled steel water cans used to cool the barrel of the .30-caliber machine guns. Once the guns started firing and heating up the barrels, the water moved from the jacket around the barrel into the water can and recirculated.

Thus was our condition when we participated in a parade of division-size or larger, where the honored guests were the President of the United States, Franklin Delano Roosevelt, and the Prime Minister of Canada. We marched a good number of miles to the parade grounds, all the while lugging those damn machine gun carts in the August sun. We were in our old class-A uniforms—wool trousers, khaki shirt, heavy blouse, issue shoes, canvas leggings, and World War I helmets—the round type seen in the British Army up into World War II. We must have looked downright silly marching in review in this get-up with relics and painted sticks for weapons, especially when we tried to perform the order "eyes right" while pulling a machine gun cart.

As for our training, the situation reminds me of a remark by a soldier I later had under my command, who was pretty dull about learning. The major general commanding our division dropped in on our training exercises and asked this soldier exactly what he thought he was doing. He replied, "Well, Sir, I think I'm just following them there fellers." That was about what a lot of us were doing in the Army maneuvers of 1940—just following them there fellers. Very seldom, if ever, did we understand the tactical situation or the types of maneuvers in which we were involved.

During this time, I was also learning (or not learning) how to handle my full-blown adolescent rebellion. I could not tolerate what I considered to be unfairness or stupidity on the part of my superiors. This regularly earned me the opportunity to reconsider the wisdom of my fifteen years while performing extra work details. One incident had to do with the garbage pit. The Army was leasing the land for maneuvers from private owners, and the leases protected the owners' rights. Each company had a garbage pit five to six feet deep, and one of the stipulations was that no *solid* matter would be buried in the ground above a certain depth. Once when we were cleaning camp, we threw some excess blocks of ice in the pit and covered them with dirt. That day, the owner came with a long metal rod, checking for buried solid material. He sank the rod into the garbage pit, and of course he had to hit an ice block. He just would not believe it was a chunk of ice. I got on the work detail to dig up the whole damn sloppy mess, while he stood over us and looked on. By the time we'd finished, I felt like burying him in the pit with the ice.

I also vividly remember the huge 30-gallon "piss cans" that were set up in the company street after dark, with an oil lantern marking each location. Every morning, a work detail carried the brimming, sloshing cans to a latrine dug some distance from the end of the company street. It was a bad duty, especially if some of the older men had had a beer party. The carrying detail served as punishment for soldiers who got on some NCO's list. I managed to get that detail a couple of times too.

My life, however, was soon to change in a very big way. When the Draft bill was passed in 1940, Congress gave the President the authority to call up the National Guard and bring it into Federal service, and FDR issued mobilization orders. I think all Guardsmen would have been called up sooner, but the Army had no camps or billeting areas for them, and hadn't yet developed the logistical support base to enlarge rapidly. As a result, the Guard divisions and some smaller units were ordered to active duty as the housing became available. Initially, soldiers were to serve one year on active duty, then return home to inactive duty status. In a popular song, a soldier sang farewell to his sweetheart. The lyrics were sad enough, but the idea was that he would be back in a year. I thought of those lyrics many times while soldiering throughout 1942, 1943, 1944, and 1945.

I quit school the day before I was inducted into the Army. My induction took place on a cold, blustery February 17, 1941. We fell into company formation, Sergeant Rohaly called the roll, and we each took one step forward and answered "Here!" At the end of roll call, we all raised our right hand, an officer read the oath of office to us, and we all repeated it. And so we went from being a National Guard unit to a unit of the Army of the United States.

Quitting high school to go into the Army as a sixteen-year-old was completely in keeping with my private circumstances and the larger social context. In those times, one did not plan the future in terms of years—high school, college, career, and so forth—but in terms of days, weeks, and months. We were in a long and hard depression; jobs were scarce, and young men went into Civilian Conservation Corps camps to send money home to feed their families. The percentage of youths completing high school was low because children had to quit school to help support their families. Only the rich could afford to send their children to college. Even families that maintained strong family ties and loyalties had difficulty keeping themselves together.

I had not been part of a family group for years; I had been living with others, more or less as an intruder. I mean no criticism of my sister or others who took me in; the fact is, I felt like a perpetual outsider. My brother Vern, who was three years older, was off in Florida much of the time, searching for our mother. He was having a hard enough time scrounging up jobs to take care of himself alone. He finally joined the Navy just to get something to eat, enlisting for a six-year stint in December 1940.

These were the bleak facts of my family life. Because of them, I might have romanticized the Army. The restlessness of youth and the possibility of being recognized as an individual certainly played a part in my enlistment.

The entire 2d Battalion, 112th Infantry, was stationed at the Armory in Erie, which is still in use at 6th and Parade Street. Everyone had to take a thorough physical examination to make sure he met the standards and didn't hide any defects or history of illnesses. An Army formation call, "short-arm inspection," was also my introduction to sex education. The uniform was raincoats only. A medical officer inspected our private parts for VD, body lice, and crabs. I had never heard of VD or body lice before this.

Once we were in the Army, all the under-age soldiers were especially eager to prove how adult we really were by indulging in excessive drinking. In civilian establishments, no one wearing a uniform was ever asked to show an ID. We could buy alcohol at any store that sold it, or step right up to a bar and be served. The surge of assurance this gave us made us think that drinking was one of the main benefits of enlisted life.

Starting with our first days at the Armory, for many of us under-age soldiers drinking simply became synonymous with fun.

In the beginning, of course, it didn't take much alcohol to make us lose control. I remember one under-age friend going to the PX for a drink. The entrance had a landing with six to eight steps. Coming out, he tripped on the first one, rolled head-over-heals to the bottom, got up, dusted himself off, and wobbled back to the barracks. I know he didn't have more than one beer. It is said that God looks after drunks and babies, and we were living proof that this is true.

Not long after we were inducted, we moved to Indiantown Gap, Pennsylvania where the new military reservation was still under construction. I arranged for my father to pick up a girl I'd been dating and bring her to the station so we could say our good-byes. My dad did pick my girlfriend up, but in the turmoil and commotion we couldn't find each other. I was bitterly disappointed as we reformed ranks and loaded onto the train. We had Pullman sleepers and were riding first-class now that we were in the Army, and I shed a few tears in the loneliness of my bunk that evening as the train made its way toward Indiantown Gap.

Chapter 2

Mobilization, Basic, and Small Unit Training

We arrived at Indiantown Gap Military Reservation the next day. Big packages in cardboard boxes were stacked in snowdrifts outside our barracks. These, we discovered, were our bunks and mattresses. Before we could go to bed, we had to break them out of the piles of snow and ice and set them up. We also had to make a fire, but we hadn't had much experience with coal-fired hot-air heating systems. It took a few days to get the technique, and we spent some pretty cold nights before we got the hang of it.

We immediately started on basic training, as if we'd been freshly inducted. At 5:00 or 5:30 A.M., we fell out for reveille, while the regimental band marched up and down the street playing snappy tunes like "Roll Out the Barrel" and "You Are My Sunshine." The reveille gun, a 105mm cannon on the top of a big hill, boomed out every morning, but First Sergeant Rohaly was usually into the squad rooms long before, blowing on his whistle to shock us out of bed.

Our training area was on a high point, Gobbler's Knob. We formed up in the company streets, marched out into a battalion column, and on past the band. Indiantown Gap still lacked sufficient accommodations to conduct large classes indoors, so regardless of snowstorms and blizzards, up the hill we marched to huddle together in the freezing weather to listen to basic training lectures on "military courtesy" and "customs of the service." Literally shivering in our boots, we learned when to salute officers, how to request permission to speak to the company commander, who should walk to the right or left in a group of mixed rank, and other such items of vital combat interest.

Many of our officers and NCOs were inexperienced, and we suffered from the lack of qualified instructors. And so I discovered field manuals. These were issued for every training subject, and I found I could get better information by studying on my own. Before long, I got the reputation of being a little smart ass. This didn't bother me. Maybe I wasn't too diplomatic in correcting my instructors, but afterward they hit the manuals themselves. I thought that having to learn the wrong way was twice as bad as learning the right way, because first you had to unlearn before you could learn.

After our morning lectures, we engaged in training until 5:30 P.M. At the end of the day, we always stood retreat, an honor ceremony conducted while the national colors were lowered. Preceding this, we underwent strict personal, uniform, and weapons inspection, during which we were often asked questions on military subjects. Some of the slower men had trouble remembering their serial numbers. The platoon leader always asked me: "Have you shaved today?" Being only sixteen, I didn't have a beard; let's just say I was a little fuzzy. The first time I answered, "No, I didn't think I had a beard, Sir." He instructed me to shave daily, whether I needed it or not. And so I came to grow a heavy beard in my youth.

It was a pretty full day for a sixteen-year-old. Many nights I went to bed around 8:00, and slept through until 5:00 the next morning. In addition to two heavy wool blankets, they issued us a good quality, single-size comforter. We did manage to sleep warm, after we got the knack of maintaining a good, hot fire in the coal boilers, but we experienced so many respiratory diseases that we were often placed in quarantine. Finally, we erected shelter halves between bunks in an attempt to block the spread of germs from coughing and sneezing.

Treatment did not include antibiotics; penicillin was yet to come as the wonder drug of the future.

Part of our basic training was learning to perform interior guard. This is the type of guard seen in movies, where the soldier marches back and forth with a rifle on his shoulder. Among the duties was guarding prisoners in the regimental guardhouse. Confinements lasted up to twenty-four hours while a prisoner's punishment was decided. Every regiment had a couple people who thought they knew everything about the military judicial system. We had one of these "guardhouse lawyers" in Company H who maintained that if a prisoner escaped from an interior guard, the guard would have to serve the prisoner's term.

I had a good scare about this early on when I was guarding a prisoner in the regimental area. I had an urgent call of nature, and informed the prisoner I was going to the barracks. I told him to stay close, and he gave me his word. I do not know why I did not take him in with me. I was certainly too pressed to go through the correct procedures, which required putting the prisoner under lock-and-key before going to the latrine, or calling for the corporal-of-the-guard. This would have meant hollering out, "Corporal-of-the-guard, post number five," then waiting as the guard at each post passed the call all the way up to the guardhouse, and the corporal came running to see what I needed.

When I came out of the latrine, my prisoner was nowhere in sight. I almost panicked; I was sure I would have to serve his sentence. As it turned out, he'd noted my inexperience, and decided to hide as a joke. Fortunately, he came out before I called the corporal-of-the-guard. This experience taught me two lessons right from the start: never trust a prisoner, and follow regulations.

I also pulled kitchen police duty. This was a very tough proposition. KP meant reporting to the mess hall at 3:30 or 4:00 A.M., and often working until 8:30 or 9:00 P.M. How bad it was depended on the mess sergeant, and ours was inexperienced and difficult. Being young and a bit of a rebel, I got into heated discussions with him. One day, in retaliation for some lip, he gave me the filthiest job of all, cleaning the grease trap for the kitchen sinks. This was a metal box about two and a half feet long, a foot and a half wide, and a good two feet deep, that caught all the greasy drainage from the kitchen.

It was a dirty, stinking job—and he ordered me to clean it out with my bare hands. I rebelled and said I wasn't about to do it without a tool.

When he retorted that he didn't have any tools, I said that in that case, they'd better call the first sergeant to escort me to the guardhouse. So they called Sergeant Rohaly, and a compromise was reached. I was provided with a long-handled dipper and was allowed to wear my gas mask. I didn't make many friends in the mess hall.

We trained from Monday morning until Saturday noon. When we started small-unit training, we added one or two periods of night training a week. Saturday morning was usually reserved for a thorough inspection of the barracks, grounds, weapons, and vehicles. Some inspecting officers wore white gloves and ran their hands over window sills and beams to find the smallest bit of dirt or dust.

In good weather, we marched out to an open field with full field packs, set up our pup tents in a row, and displayed our equipment in front of them. Even mess kits had to be laid out with knife, fork, and spoon properly aligned. The letters stamped on the knife had better be face up, or it was a gig. The clothes on the rack at the end of our bunk had to hang perfectly and in the right sequence; one button undone meant another gig. These minor discrepancies often resulted in company punishment for the offenders, or mass punishment to the entire company for the errors of individuals.

The limitations on administering company punishment were quite strict. A soldier could be confined to quarters on his off-duty training time or be punished with extra work details. This choice was the prerogative of the company commander only, and had to be administered on a formal basis. Nevertheless, between the wars, the Army was very small and the company officers had gotten into the habit of allowing the corporals, sergeants and first sergeant to run the company.

Further, if anyone did question the NCOs or first sergeant about administering punishment, there was nothing in the manual about additional training. Any NCO who wanted to punish a man could give him a pick and shovel after duty hours and say, "You didn't dig your last foxhole well enough on the last tactical training exercise, so dig a pit resembling a foxhole."

Anything that did not grow was policed up every morning, so if a soldier was caught throwing a cigarette butt on the ground, an NCO could make the offender dig a hole, say four feet deep and three feet across, toss the butt in, and cover it up. The first sergeants called this "extra training to learn the correct way of disposing of a cigarette butt." We called it chickenshit.

Rohaly had been indoctrinated in this system of discipline, and he ran the company with an iron hand. Technically, he needed to have the company commander's approval, and our first lieutenant, an ex-Marine officer, gave him a free rein.

By spring of 1941, we had several times been quarantined for a week or two because of respiratory illnesses. When we weren't quarantined, Rohaly punished us for minor discrepancies on Saturday inspections. For a total of six to eight gigs, the whole company would be stuck in camp without passes. He also gave out a lot of extra duty for small violations. We were then forming company streets, trying to get out of the mud by laying rock and shale from a pit about half a mile from our company area. I could often be seen on the shale pile after training hours.

One weekend, a large group of soldiers, NCOs and all, went over the hill. They left quietly without passes around Saturday noon and reported back for duty Monday morning. I didn't go: I was already on shale detail, and an AWOL charge would have been a double whammy. Rohaly reacted by submitting a request to the company commander for numerous NCOs to be reduced in rank. When the regimental commander got the request, he was smart enough to know that when NCOs go over the hill, a failure of leadership is the root cause. Following a brief investigation, he reduced the punishment for those who had gone AWOL and relieved the company commander. I learned a lesson I later used as an officer: never administer mass punishment.

Our new company commander, Capt. Gustav Hoffman, was ideal. He was very hard but also very fair. In my later career, I used him as a guide, and always looked up to him as a role model. One of the first things he did at company formation was make sure that everyone realized that *he* was the company commander, and that only he could administer company punishment under the regulations then in effect.

We began to get weekend passes. Leaving Indiantown Gap around noon on Saturday, we drove more than three hundred miles, cutting diagonally across Pennsylvania to get home by six or seven that evening, then started back around 2:00 P.M. on Sunday to arrive at base before midnight. If we had passes until Monday morning, we got back just in time for reveille. It was a fast, hard drive on curvy, two-lane roads though mountainous terrain. There were no bypasses or interstates; we went through every little town, often on the main streets or stuck behind a truck. When we got an open stretch, we really flew to make up for lost time. Very few of my friends had automobiles, and we paid those who did for the trip. The overloaded cars didn't improve the quality of the ride.

Around this time, I also had some learning experiences in areas outside of military training. Being a new Army post, Indiantown Gap Military Reservation hadn't entirely been cleared of brush and trees, and the word was that prostitutes were plying their trade between the regimental billet areas. I checked this out, and there was no doubt about it; the ladies had set up shop in the bushes. One of them, it was said, could take on the whole regiment. We called her Regimental Mary. I never did find out whether she was one woman or several. Of course, Regimental Marys have always existed. During the Civil War, General Joseph Hooker was so liberal in his policies about camp followers that we still use his name as a slang term for prostitute. In our case, the provost marshal soon added MP patrols and put an end to our adventures.

After completing basic training in April 1941, I was promoted to corporal. I was the leader of a machine gun squad, which at full strength consisted of eight men, including myself. That summer, the company received two groups of replacements from the Selective Service System. One was from Camp Wheeler, Georgia. I thought their training had been better than ours, and it was also much better than the training of the second group, from Camp Croft, South Carolina.

When the Draft first started, some draft boards took men in the highest age group first. The Camp Wheeler group contained a number of these soldiers who were assigned to my squad. There I was, a new corporal, sixteen years and five months old, with a group of fillers as old as thirty-seven, who were as well or even better trained than I was. I'll be the first to admit I had some difficulties handling men twice my age. On the other hand, several of the fillers were from rural Georgia and Alabama. They were easier to handle than the Camp Croft group, but it was the first time in my life I had ever encountered adult illiteracy. I had to read and answer letters for one member of my squad. I even had to teach him how to tie a necktie. But they all turned out to be good soldiers, and added a lot to the company. I learned a lot from them, and a lot from the experiences I had as their squad leader.

When any soldier started bitching and complaining about Army life and all of its inequities and hardships, the standard reply was, "Quit your bitching, you never had it so good. You struck a home in the Army." That was partly true for me, and even more so for some of the other men. Many had never had the opportunity to shower every day. I remember the weekly bath on Saturday night from my own childhood, when almost nobody could afford to keep a gas hot water heater going, and only started it up for laundry and bath day. Three hot meals a day was also a luxury for many of the men, although this was not my case. All these luxuries! And on the first of each month, they gave us money! For the time, it was a large amount—$21.00 to start and a raise to $30.00 after four months if we were good soldiers.

Chapter 3

Company, Battalion, Regimental, and First Army Maneuvers, 1941

After the German blitzkrieg of 1940, the Army made many structural changes in the infantry division organization, but the arrival of motorized weapons carriers most affected Company H, 112th Infantry. It was goodbye and good riddance to the hand-pulled carts. Each machine gun squad received a top-of-the-line, three-quarter-ton, four-wheel-drive truck. This meant each platoon had four trucks to carry the water-cooled .30-caliber machine guns, and the heavy weapons company had drivers, a maintenance platoon, and a larger company headquarters. The division as a whole was now called a motorized division. It wasn't possible to move everyone at once, because there were no trucks down in the rifle companies, but there were enough vehicles to move one battalion at a time.

With the new table of organization and equipment (TO&E), the M1 became the individual weapon for everyone not on a gun crew—those in company headquarters, and drivers, cooks, etc. Those of us in the heavy weapons squad were now supposed to carry the U.S. .30-caliber carbine, except for gunners and assistant gunners, who continued to carry .45-caliber pistols. The .30-caliber carbine was a much better close-in weapon than the pistol, but it couldn't compare to the M1. The carbine, however, was not yet available to us in 1941, so in lieu of it, they issued us the M1903 Springfield .30-caliber bolt-action rifle.

In the summer of 1941, we moved for about a month to A.P. Hill, Virginia, for company, battalion, and regimental unit training. It was a hot and dirty military reservation with very few roads. What roads there were were dust-covered dirt and gravel. Up until then, our field training had never lasted for more than a day or two at a time, but now we left base camp on Monday morning and participated in tactical exercises until Thursday or Friday of the same or even the following week. Everyone was more or less receiving on-the-job training, from division commander to squad leaders. We spent a lot of time in the field in very hot, dirty, dusty conditions.

We usually spent Saturday afternoon and Sunday at base camp, where we lived in pyramidal squad tents that housed six to eight soldiers. As soon as we got back from the field, the first order of business was the care, cleaning, and inspection of weapons and equipment, vehicle maintenance, and laundry. On Sunday, we wanted to relax, but our elderly regimental commander thought we should all go to church. There wasn't a very good turnout at the Protestant services the first week, so the following Sunday he ordered us to fall out in the company street and march to the service. There was much moaning and groaning about obligatory church. This was the first and last time I ever heard anything about forced church attendance in the Army.

As enlisted men, we slept with no bedrolls and took whatever cover we could find during rainstorms. Sleeping bags were not an item of issue until mid-1943 or later: the rank-and-file had one blanket and a shelter half to use as an outer cover. One thing we did have was quartermaster shower units, set up some distance from our base camp. Sometimes we were even lucky enough to get hot water if they had a portable heating system. The engineers also had purification units to provide safe drinking water.

After three or four very dirty days in the field, we'd walk to the showers in the evening, about three quarters of a mile away, then go to see a movie. There was a large screen set up in an open field where we saw the latest runs, sitting on whatever we could find. While we waited for darkness to settle, the PA system piped popular songs out over the field. I distinctly remember Helen O'Connel singing "Green Eyes" as I sat on a board in that field.

The excellent regimental band also put on concerts. In addition to marching music, it played all the popular songs of the day. In December 1944, the 112th Infantry Band was captured at the Battle of the Bulge, and so my memories of these early concerts are particularly nostalgic. There were also other recreations, like large craps and poker games, and I learned how to play both. My personal philosophy on gambling was to take X dollars, gamble with them, and quit when they were gone. I didn't go any deeper into my pockets if I lost.

I clearly remember an incident that occurred one payday that summer. We were lined up in the pay line outside the mess hall. The sun was beating down, so we changed configuration to take advantage of the shade offered by the mess hall wall. We had a couple of senior sergeants who were alcoholics, or very close to it. One of them, a bully of a man, about 6 feet 2 inches and 195 pounds, told us to straighten the line out. A friend of mine, Leslie Ford, murmured something under his breath. Without any warning, the sergeant hit Leslie right in the face with his fist and knocked him down. This was the first time I ever saw a man cold cocked.

The rest of us were in no position to defend Leslie. But he had a twin brother, Ed, a corporal and the company clerk, who was working at the pay table. After the pay line was over, he approached the sergeant. Now Ed was about 5 feet 9 inches and weighed about 140 pounds. He actually had to reach up to tap the sergeant on the shoulder. "I want to see you tonight in the rec hall," he said. "We're going to put on the gloves." He looked like a midget challenging Goliath.

Both men went to the rec hall after duty. They took their shirts off to fight on equal terms, not sergeant to company clerk. What the sergeant didn't know was that Ed and Les both had taken boxing lessons for years, and were very good at it. It ended up that Ed beat the shit out of that sergeant. He'd go down, then get up, and Ed would pound him some more. If Les had pressed charges, the sergeant would have been court-martialed. As it was, Les more or less forgave the sergeant, but his twin brother really did a job on him.

Later, as an officer, I applied a lesson from this—never look favorably on the physical enforcement of orders. I never touched a subordinate, to the point of never even straightening a shirt pocket when inspecting in ranks. I told the man to straighten his pocket himself. I felt that strongly about seniors being in physical contact with their juniors in rank.

After we returned to Indiantown Gap Military Reservation, we were given short furloughs. I went home and was introduced to my new stepmother. I hadn't even realized my father had remarried. I spent most of my furlough at the old farmhouse my sister and brother-in-law had bought in Belle Valley, southeast of Erie. Little did I know this was the last time I'd ever be able to visit with my sister.

On the evening of August 1, 1941, we had just been paid, and I was shooting craps, when the CQ handed me a telegram. It was a message from my father saying my sister had been in a serious accident and I should come home immediately. I packed a small suitcase and picked up my pass. Our duty officer drove me to the Harrisburg train station. The train to Erie was dubbed the milk run, because it stopped at every milk can across the state of Pennsylvania. The trip took almost twelve hours and was so trying I felt like getting out and pushing the train.

My brother Vern and I arrived home within hours of each other to discover that Vangie had been mortally wounded. Her husband had been sighting in a .32-caliber rifle, shooting off the back porch where he had a range set up on a dirt bank, then returning to the kitchen table where he had laid out tools to tinker with the scope. On one trip he accidentally discharged the rifle, hitting Vangie, who was sitting near the door. It was a hollow-point bullet, designed to fragment on impact. She received a low back wound that took out a kidney and part of her liver.

Vern and I did get to see our sister, although she was no longer conscious. I said goodbye to Vangie in a ward, behind a curtain a nurse had drawn for privacy. Afterward, I sat for a couple hours with my brother, neither of us saying a word, out on the lawn in front of the old St. Vincent's Hospital, waiting for her to die. My brother-in-law was very broken up about my sister's death. It was a long, sad affair attending her wake and burial.

When I returned to Indiantown Gap, many good friends tried to cheer me up and help me through this very hard time. A close group—Elmer Carlson, Dick Hertel, Alby Price, and several others—were very kind to me, and I really appreciated their efforts. Once they took me out to Lebanon, Pennsylvania, for a dinner at a good restaurant. I'd gone to a few lunch counters in high school, but this was one of the first times I'd ever eaten out in a restaurant. They all ordered steak, and so did I. I was sixteen, and it was the first steak I'd ever eaten. I'm sad and humbled to say I didn't know how to use the silverware. My friends quickly clued me in.

From late September through November 1941, the whole 28th Division and smaller units, along with most of the active Army divisions in the eastern United States, concentrated in North and South Carolina, where the famous First Army field maneuvers took place. Our base camp consisted of squad tents, but we didn't spend too much time there. We didn't have the luxury of cots, but we were allowed to cut tree limbs and saplings to construct our own beds.

Our base camp was near Wadesboro, North Carolina. We maneuvered through many a similar small southern town near the Pee Dee River. The main reason for these maneuvers was to ensure that commanders and their staffs were trained to plan for the movement, feeding, and logistical support of large bodies of troops. The larger unit staffs may have learned a lot, but down at our level, the most we got out of the maneuvers was the experience of living in the field without all the niceties of a base camp. They kept us out in the field for up to a month.

As usual, we didn't know what was going on most of the time. We'd go for two or three days at a crack with very little sleep, moving from one position to another, going into defensive positions, and trying to simulate the conditions of combat as closely as possible. Often, we'd get into position and start unloading in the dark, then suddenly have to change positions. The one thing I did learn was how to keep up with my personal equipment, my squad's equipment, and my squad members so I could put my hands on them in any condition of visibility and move in a hurry.

Motorization solved a lot of problems, but it created others. It was one of the first times that a unit as large as a field army had ever maneuvered with the motorized infantry configuration, and there were monumental traffic jams. Few people in the Army knew how to schedule large motorized units from one part of the front to the other, and no one had experience in getting the vehicles to move more quickly in the field. It was jokingly said that any lieutenant colonel who could stand out in the middle of the road and successfully direct motor traffic would get a promotion. We were all issued goggles for the dirty, dusty roads.

One of the problems of living in the field for such extended periods of time was personal sanitation. Whenever we had a few minutes near a source of water, we'd bathe and wash our clothes as best we could. I took lots of baths in the Pee Dee and whatever creeks we could find. For laundry, each squad had a canvas bucket. We often had to jump back in the truck and move before the laundry was done.

During one of the breaks, our battalion commander assembled us in a big open area and had a soldier demonstrate how to take a bath without the use of a bucket. He dug a hole, put in a shelter half to make a catch basin, then poured water into it. The man stripped and took a sponge bath out of the water in the hole, to the great catcalls of most of the men in the battalion. Later, when the Army issued the new steel helmets, we took out the liner and used our helmets to take a bath. We also used them as cooking pots to stew many a liberated chicken.

The Carolina maneuvers also introduced us to "tactical feeding." Especially in the rear areas near the front, we often took our meals in blackout conditions. Eating under cover of total darkness needed a lot of getting used to. We went through the chow line with five-yard intervals between men. It was necessary to take the cook's word for what we were getting, as he slopped it into our mess kits. We spread out as much as we could because a shell hitting a group could take many lives at once. It was challenging to eat in the dead of night, especially in the summer, when we ate sitting down in the field with grasshoppers, beetles, and other insects of every description whirring all around us. Without a doubt, we sometimes got an additional ration of meat. Our Thanksgiving dinner in 1941 was also served in the field, although not in blackout conditions. Our company commander even had a menu printed with all our names and the items in the meal—turkey, dressing, and all the fixings.

We were all up and down the Carolina woodlands and backwaters, and for us northern boys, this was our introduction to the rural poor in the South. It opened our eyes, especially to the abject poverty among black families, who lived in shanties two or three feet off the ground, supported by logs. There was a door and a few windows, and that was about it. Electricity and plumbing were unknown. A heavy, fetid odor hung over all, and I am sure the sanitary conditions were appalling. The crossroad general stores where black families went for supplies stocked only the bare necessities. Given these conditions, it is not surprising that

African-Americans tried to avoid us. They were very reluctant to approach or have a conversation.

The white civilians were mostly very friendly. If we had a break near their homes, whole families would come out to talk to us. Sometimes they brought guitars and banjos, gathered around, and treated us to homemade wine along the road. We'd get a couple boys playing guitars and have a pretty good time for an hour or two. They also had wine for sale, and I developed a taste for it. All in all, I thought they treated us as fairly as could be expected, given the fact they were being overrun by soldiers and military vehicles. I've heard that in other places in the South, civilians posted signs in their yards saying, "No Dogs or Soldiers Allowed." I imagine they removed them after Pearl Harbor.

When the word came down that the Carolina maneuvers were at an end, there was much shooting of blank ammunition and many shouts of joy. We soon received orders to halt the celebration and general carrying on. Oddly, the thing I remember most was laying my shelter half on the ground and crawling in under my blanket. It was a clear night, and there was a full moon that looked ten times larger than any I'd ever seen before. I lay there thinking of the past days, with the song "Carolina Moon" going through my mind. I fell asleep thinking how well that moon fit the song.

Chapter 4

Units in Turmoil: Pearl Harbor, Southern Training Camps, and War-time Expansion

On the morning of December 7, 1941, we were on route back to Indiantown Gap, riding in two-and-a-half ton trucks. Just before noon, we were given a ten-minute rest stop to relieve ourselves. Our platoon sergeant, who had been riding in the cab, must have had a portable radio. He came around the back of the truck and told us what had happened at Pearl Harbor: "Boys, you are now veterans of World War II." It was the first time I had ever heard the term "World War II" applied to me.

The first thing we asked was, "Where the hell is Pearl Harbor?" We were stunned that such a thing could happen to the United States. We rode the rest of the day full of gloomy thoughts, wondering what would happen to us, both individually and as a unit. Some soldiers who had been called up for only a year, myself included, had been looking forward to getting out in February. We knew this would all change.

At nightfall, the whole regiment disembarked in a huge pasture somewhere in Virginia. It started to snow as we moved into the field. We had started picking spots to sleep when the company commander called the NCOs and gave us the official word on Pearl Harbor. Usually, when a regiment assembles in a non-tactical bivouac area, there's plenty of talking, shouting, and joking. That night it was completely silent. By then, the snow was coming down steadily. There must have been two thousand men in that pasture, but you could have heard a pin drop anywhere.

We woke up with a layer of snow on our shelter halves. We brushed ourselves off and proceeded to Indiantown Gap. On our way to the Carolinas, our convoys had attracted little attention. But on December 8, our final day on the trip back, the streets and sidewalks of every community were crowded with shouting civilians. From the truck it looked like pandemonium; the population had no idea of how the attack would affect their personal lives. The crowds, clapping and cheering us on, thought we'd been mobilized in reaction to Pearl Harbor.

Back at the Gap, there were eight to ten inches of snow on the ground. They must have sent in an advance detail, because the barracks were warm. That first night, my cot seemed like the softest bed I'd ever slept in. I heard President Roosevelt declare war on the Axis powers. There would be no leaves and no early discharges. All periods of service were extended for the duration of the war plus six months.

We were constantly on some alert or another. Our battalion commander, Colonel Peterson, was an unusual character reputed to be a veteran of World War I. He was hard working and conscientious, and did everything possible to impress upon us the need to do the best job we could, no matter what it was.

The snow was deep on the ground. He often formed us up in the battalion area, and we fell out with full combat gear and marched into a square formation. In the middle was a platform six feet high on which Colonel Peterson stood. He then called a soldier out of the ranks: for example, "First scout in the 3d Platoon of Company E: fall out and come up here on the platform!" The soldier broke ranks, double timed, and got up with Colonel Peterson, who checked his equipment from helmet to shoelaces. He even made sure the man had his dog tags. If anything was missing, he called the soldier's squad leader up on the platform and chewed him out in front of the whole battalion. Then he maybe called up the platoon sergeant and did the same thing. Sometimes he even called the platoon leader to the platform. This certainly got our attention, and made us strict about inspection. His tactics were humiliating, but he instilled in us the responsibility to do our job, keep our weapons clean, and take care of our men. I can still hear Colonel Peterson up on that platform: "The Japs are knocking the hell out of us over on Bataan! Clean that weapon! They're closing in on Corregidor! Fix that vehicle!" He made us understand we needed to perform now that we were at war.

Another thing I can still see in my mind is our men from Alabama and Georgia, who had never experienced a real winter before, having snowball fights and carrying on like a bunch of kids. We were all happy when we heard that the Army was giving us furloughs after all. They were very short, but a whole lot better than nothing. Half the company got sent home for Christmas, but had to be back by New Year's, when the other half went home. I was one of the lucky ones to get home for Christmas.

Indiantown Gap was used as a staging area for overseas movement throughout the war, a place for the Army to move divisions for their pre-embarkation checks. This change in function meant the 28th Division had to move out. Just before the transfer, a directive was issued that all men who were still under eighteen could apply for discharge. I thought it was my duty to stay with the unit.

In January 1942, the division was transferred to Camp Livingston, Louisiana, but there wasn't enough room for all of us. The 32d Infantry Division was being sent from Livingston to the Pacific, but they hadn't entirely vacated the camp. The 112th Infantry always seemed to get the rawest deal when it came to living conditions, and this time we got stuck in Camp Beauregard, a regimental-size set-up with squad tents. It can get very cold in Louisiana in January, and all we had for heat was a Sibley stove, literally a leftover from the Civil War. It was a metal, wood-burning stove that sat on a large wooden box filled with sand or dirt. It wasn't safe to leave it burning at night, so we let it die out. The sanitation and other facilities weren't what they could have been either. It was three hundred feet to the nearest latrine. There were wooden buildings for mess halls, but no room to sit, so we placed our mess kits on a one by six foot board mounted between two poles, and ate standing up. Not a very nice arrangement.

Many of us had never been in Louisiana before, so our orientation included warnings about poisonous snakes, chiggers, and the huge mosquitoes that bred in the swamps. With typical Army humor, one joke had it that a soldier woke up to discover two enormous mosquitoes sitting on his chest. One of them was holding up his dog tags and reading them off while the other checked out his blood type to see if it was a match.

We fell out for reveille before daylight. Our old Sibley stove would have long gone out, and it would be freezing in the tent. Typically, we stayed in our cots as long as possible, then, at the very last minute, we jumped out, put on our shoes, and threw on our overcoats without the rest of our uniforms. After the sergeants took account of their units, they dismissed us, and we went back in to try to warm up by getting dressed. Rohaly got wind of this trick. One morning, instead of dismissing us after the reveille report, he walked down the ranks with a flashlight and made every one of us open up his overcoat. This put an end to our stunts.

The combat effectiveness of the 28th Division and all its organic units took a nosedive immediately after we entered the war. The Army had gone into high-gear expansion, and our division experienced a huge attrition of key personnel because we were providing cadres for new units. It got so bad that one newly assigned second lieutenant was signing the morning report for two different companies. Now, too, on some occasions, it was Sergeant Rohaly, the senior first sergeant in the battalion, who led the company and battalion out for training. Out of five company units, not one officer was present for duty.

NCOs were all but ordered to go before an examining board and apply for Officers' Candidate School (OCS). The Army was also expanding its Air Corps, asking for volunteers to be aviation cadets, and forming new divisions for which many of our officers and NCOs would serve as cadres. To say the least, our unit was in a state of turmoil. I did not apply to OCS, because I thought I was too young. I also knew the Army might run a tight security check on applicants. I was still underage, and thus afraid they might discharge me.

Throughout this situation, First Sergeant Rohaly remained a holy terror, flaunting his authority and trying to rule by an iron hand, but he was somewhat subdued by Captain Hoffman. I remember one close encounter, when he stood me at attention and chewed me out for half an hour for asking a simple question about the guard duty roster. I replied that I would like to see the company commander together, which we did, and the dispute was resolved in my favor. Rohaly in his prime was quite a character.

In April 1942, I received a promotion from corporal squad leader to section sergeant. This made me a three-stripe buck sergeant at the ripe old age of seventeen. I was responsible for two machine gun squads in the .30-caliber water-cooled machine gun platoon. I considered myself to be earning a very good wage, $78.00 a month—almost four times the amount I'd been earning when I had joined the Army two years earlier.

About the time I received my promotion, the other units bound for overseas moved out, and the 112th moved into Camp Livingston. This was a much better billeting area, with winterized tents housing six to eight men. For the first time, we enjoyed the luxury of a gas stove in every tent. They even had wooden floors! At last we had regular mess halls, too, and much better latrine and sanitation facilities. To make things even better, our mess sergeant left us; the cooks finally got rid of him. I later learned they'd slipped half a cake of GI soap into the coffee urn, which created quite a diarrhea problem in the troops.

In the summer of 1942, I got another furlough and went to Erie. We had to make the trip by milk train, and the crowding was almost unimaginable. For hours and hours, there was standing room only; GI brides, girlfriends, and families were moving between the camps and home, and we were obliged to give mothers, fiancees, and wives of service men our seats. For the most part, we rode standing for the day and a half it took to get home.

The return from leave to camp was a sad affair. We all expected this to be our last furlough home before we were sent to war. It was bad enough for the single man, but married men and fathers with children had many moving scenes at the station. As the train pulled out amid desperate farewells, I was very glad I was single and did not have to go through those emotional departures.

Chapter 5

From the 112th Infantry to
Parachute School, Fort Benning

Major General Omar Bradley took over as our division commander in June 1942. After a few weeks of observation, he decided too many friendships or cliques had formed, and decreed that all company commanders had to divide their NCOs into three groups. They would retain one group and transfer out the other two, but they wouldn't know which of the groups they'd be allowed to keep. This prevented them from padding one group with their best NCOs and passing off the less efficient ones. I was in the third of H Company that went to M Company in the 3d Battalion.

To say the least, Bradley was not very complimentary about the condition of the 28th Division, but I don't think he gave us a fair shake. The National Guard divisions made a huge contribution to the war effort by providing so many people for cadres and new divisions, armor and parachute school, and officers' candidate schools. Our situation could not have been helped, since higher headquarters had required us to provide so much personnel for other units and branches of the service.

This rapid response to war-time mobilization left all the pre-Pearl Harbor infantry divisions in a state of turmoil from 1940 until they went overseas.

The strength of the 112th Infantry and the 28th Division got so low that it was eventually decided to fill the division up with draftees. We received them directly from the induction centers, and each regiment formed a training cadre responsible for basic infantry training. I was selected as a basic training NCO—what we now call a drill sergeant—for the first group of selective servicemen. When these people arrived at Camp Livingston, they were civilians. From the day they got into uniform, we took charge.

Physical training began from scratch. On the first day, even as we marched the inductees the half-mile from their billeting areas to their training areas, some men fell out. To make bad matters worse, the higher-ups now decided infantry troops had to go through speed marches of up to twenty-five miles a day with a single canteen of water. Twenty-five miles may not seem like much, but when you're carrying a full field pack with limited water in the hot, humid, Louisiana climate, it becomes a real task. People who fell out had to complete the march on their own time, or start again and take it for its full length in the evening or on the weekend.

After December 1941, and starting with basic training in 1942, the quality of training programs greatly improved. For example, we now had gas identification kits. These contained small samples of each kind of gas, which came equipped with explosive caps. We'd go out in the field and explode one cap at a time. Each produced a small, low-density cloud. The trainees then rapidly moved through the area for a sniff test, which taught them to identify the odors of different gasses. Once they got the first whiff, they were supposed to stop inhaling and clear out to minimize exposure.

Numerous periods of instruction were devoted to the use of gas masks. After many drills, we took the men into a tent where, at a certain point, gas was released. At the command "Gas!" they had to whip out their masks and put them on. If the mask did not fit correctly, they got whiffs of tear gas. This exercise was designed to approximate conditions a soldier could likely encounter, as well as test the fit of every mask.

The military also now contracted out to the motion picture industry to produce lengthy training films. Some of the producers and executives took on "dollar a year" employment in the Army, donating their services to make movies against the injustices of Fascism. And so we marched into the huge post theater to watch films with titles like *Why We Fight* and *The Enemy*. So it was, too, that we were treated to graphic training films about venereal disease that showed all the terrible things that could happen to a soldier who contracted even the most common type of sexually transmitted disease. These were often shown right after lunch, and the close-ups of hideous canker sores and displays of deformed body parts did not exactly help our digestion.

My duties as a drill instructor involved numerous other tasks such as teaching the M1, at which I became quite proficient, although this still was not my primary individual weapon. Even when preparing my lesson plans, I continued to learn, and as our officers returned from officer training at Fort Benning, where they had followed classes in methods of instruction, they, in turn, passed on their knowledge to the NCOs. Slowly, then, the quality of our training increased. They used to say, "If the student fails to learn, the instructor failed to teach." I don't agree 100 percent, but there's a lot of truth to the saying.

I also became a better NCO because I learned to evaluate men, and I became seasoned in sizing up a man's character and leadership capacity. But a man's real leadership qualities cannot be determined until he is in combat, in a stay-alive, minute-to-minute situation. There are no more snappy orders in these conditions; leadership is often quiet, even mute. But soldiers always sense the real leaders after the first days of combat, and leadership qualities come out at all levels, from privates as well as solders in the higher grades. I learned very early on that you cannot pull a bluff on the soldiers under you—not as an instructor, and certainly not in combat. The American soldier is always smart enough to recognize the real thing.

All this said, by the early summer of 1942, I had had my fill of basic training. I'd been soldiering for a year and a half. I was well aware of the combat readiness of the 112th and the 28th Division as a whole, and knew we would not be entering a combat zone for some time. I wanted to get into an outfit where I would see some action.

If I had to soldier, I wanted to soldier in an elite unit, not in an average infantry regiment. I went through the thirteen-week training cycle with the first group of selective service people, but when the rumors started that we were going to receive a second group, I objected—to myself, of course. I made up my mind to get out of the unit. I knew that when I was vetted, my true age might come to light, and that Personnel flagged the file of anyone who applied for a transfer, and would not approve a second request. But I was so eager to get out of my current situation that I applied for OCS and the parachute troops simultaneously. I don't how they let me get away with it, but they did. I said I would take the first transfer to come in.

My application to the parachute troops came in first. This was a completely volunteer, elite unit. All transfers had to be in the grade of private, but I was so eager that I was willing to accept the reduction as the price of admission. A huge expansion of the parachute troops was taking place, and the Parachute School at Fort Benning was the only one in the Army at the time. The parachute troops had started there with a test platoon in the summer of 1940, and by the time I entered in 1942, they had already formed at least three parachute infantry regiments and four independent battalions.

Three or four of us from the 112th Infantry Regiment traveled from Camp Livingston to Fort Benning, Georgia, on the same set of orders. We boarded the train on the post at Camp Livingston and shuttled off onto the main track. I can tell you this: the trip from Louisiana to Columbus in hot, old coaches was a slow, tedious, filthy ride. And I emphasize *slow*. I don't think they'd improved on the locomotive system since the Civil War. They still had a steam engine pulling the train. It was so hot we were forced to open the windows, only to be assaulted with a cloud of cinders billowing out of the old coal-fired locomotive.

When I reported to Parachute School, the 505th Parachute Infantry Regiment had been filled up for about a month, and they were beginning to assign graduates to the 507 PIR. We were assigned to a student company with three or four platoons, with at least one platoon of officers for every class. They were billeted separately but went through the same training we did and took the same harassment.

The school consisted of A, B, C, and D stages, which each lasted for one week. In "A stage," everyone endured four hours of solid physical training daily—one hour of running, one hour of jujitsu, one hour of endurance calisthenics, and one hour of gym or other physical training. The goal was to screen out the soldiers who would not have enough guts and motivation to jump out of a plane.

Our jujitsu instruction took place in a large sawdust pit where we learned hand-to-hand unarmed fighting tactics—how to throw our opponents and so on. It was September 1942, and very hot. The instructors took delight in picking out smaller, lighter students like myself for demonstration purposes. Many times, we hit face down and got a mouth full of sawdust. We had to choke back our normal reaction to spit it out, because the instructors, who worked in the sawdust pit day in and day out, tried to keep it as clean as possible. Anyone caught spitting had to run around the pit with his arms held high as possible, repeating the chant, "I will not spit in the sawdust pit. I will not spit in the sawdust pit." We soon learned to keep our mouths shut on a hard fall.

The last instruction period for my platoon was always calisthenics, which took place around noon, the hottest time of the day. All sergeant instructors seemed to look like Jack Armstrong, the all-American boy. They wore jump boots, trousers and white T-shirts that showed their bulging muscles and slim waists to good advantage. We started calisthenics with a platoon of about forty-five men, and by the end of the hour, if ten or fifteen of us were still on our feet, it was considered a good day for the instructors. The rest would have passed out from heat or physical exhaustion. After a physically hard training period, we lined up at the drinking fountain. When we got up to it, we opened our mouths and the instructors popped in a salt tablet. We had to take a drink of water and swallow it. Some students got sick on them, but there was always a second instructor to insure that the tablets went down.

During "A Stage" we also practiced exiting the plane door. This taught us how to be in the correct position when the parachute opened. A plane fuselage was mounted about six feet off the ground, with steps leading up to the open front, or pilot's end. We climbed up the steps, shuffled to the rear side door, turned right through the door, and jumped out, turning to the left after leaving the fuselage. On leaving, we counted: "One thousand, two thousand, three thousand." Although we hit the ground before we reached three thousand, this taught us the interval needed for the main chute to open. If it didn't open, we were instructed to pull the ripcord on our reserve chute. We started practice at a low tempo and increased to a very fast pace as we repeatedly jumped, ran back to the front end, and jumped again.

It was repetition, repetition, repetition. Two or three instructors were positioned to correct and constantly harass us. The officers' platoon trained as a separate group and took even more verbal abuse than we did. Their ranks weren't recognized as long as they were assigned as students, which gave free reign to the sergeant instructors. In other areas, too, it seemed that the officers received a lot more push-ups for any infraction of the rules. We were often close enough to observe their jujitsu instruction, and it appeared that the instructors always picked the most senior officers to demonstrate the throws, and threw them harder than they did the rest of us. They especially enjoyed making officers run around with their hands in the air, repeating the ridiculous spitting chant. Some of these sergeants later regretted their deeds when they were transferred from the Parachute School to tactical units and ended up serving under the very same officers they had ridiculed.

By the end of four hours of physical training, we were drenched in sweat, soaked from the collar to the hem of our coveralls. We went back to the barracks on the double, emptied our pockets, and stepped into the showers fully clothed. We tried to wash ourselves and our coveralls at the same time, because they had to be clean for the next morning. We changed into clean khaki pants and shirts, then fell out and double-timed down to Lawson Field, where we learned to pack our parachutes.

The buildings were hangars filled with long, narrow packing tables. We spent four hours a day in these packing sheds in each stage of the school. The first three weeks we learned how to pack a chute, and the last week we packed the chutes we actually used on our qualifying jumps. We all had to pack our own chutes for the first five jumps. That way, we would be confident the chute had been correctly packed, and so would correctly open. We also knew that we really *had* to learn how to do it, because we were going to jump the chute we packed.

The buildings had high ceilings, but they were still very hot in the afternoon Georgia sun. There was strict discipline during instruction. If we didn't know the answer, or even murmured something under our breath, the instructor would say, "Give me five," "Give me ten," "Give me twenty-five," or "Give me fifty." This meant push-ups. We had to assume the push-up position immediately and do the designated number, all the while trying to keep up with the instruction of a very critical skill.

The "B Stage" of Parachute School taught correct landing procedure. We also practiced jumping from a ten-foot platform and were tested for reactions to jumping from a forty-foot tower. We learned landing procedures in a wide shed with a fifteen-foot platform at one end, where we stood and put on a harness. This was rigged to an apparatus with roller wheels and a quick-release mechanism; the whole was attached to an I-beam rail mounted at an angle running from fifteen to eight feet above the ground. We jumped from the platform with forward momentum and moved at quite a speed as we came down. We could be released at any time, so we always had to be ready to land. We were supposed to come down on the balls of both feet, then go into a left- or right-front tumble, and come up unscathed in the upright, standing position. Such a landing was hard enough to perform when we were not wearing combat equipment, but when we were combat-loaded, it was impossible.

The ten-foot platform was equipped with a set of stairs. We jumped off, went into a front tumble, immediately got up, double-timed around to the stairs, and climbed back up. An instructor constantly critiqued us. If the jumps weren't to his satisfaction we'd get fifteen to twenty push-ups.

On the forty-foot tower, we climbed up a ladder to a little shed built on a platform with a door at the edge. Outside, a heavy cable was fastened on both ends to poles about one hundred feet apart. The cable was about forty-five feet high at the cable end and angled down to about eight feet. The instructors rigged us up in a parachute harness with an eight- or ten-foot static line; we snapped the line on the cable, and stood in the door. When they hollered "Go!" we jumped. We assumed the correct body position and dropped free until we hit the end of the static line with a terrific jolt. We then slid down the cable, got out of the harness, and did the exercise again. Odd as it may seem, almost as many men refused the forty-foot tower as refused the first parachute jump. Just the *idea* of climbing forty feet into the air, standing in the door, and jumping was more than enough for some of them.

"C Stage" consisted of training on two types of 250-foot towers, a controlled tower and a free tower. This got us used to heights and taught us how to be in the correct position when we hit the ground. Each tower had four arms extending from the top of its center. On the controlled tower, four cables served to rig open parachute canopies, holding them on the outer edge. We climbed into the harness on the ground and were mechanically lifted by a cable running through the apex of our parachute. Once we got to the top they released us, and we dropped straight down. We hit bottom fast, and had to land on the balls of both feet if we wanted to escape injury. We also learned to pull down on all four risers on impact, an action that was supposed to reduce the stress of landing.

I much preferred the free tower. Most often, only two of the arms extending out at the top could be used at one time. The number depended on the velocity and direction of the wind, which could blow a man right into the tower. A cable attached to a winch on the ground ran up the vertical part of the tower, then horizontally to the end of the arm and down to the ground. That end of the cable was attached to a 28-foot-diameter ring. The chute was attached to the ring with quick releases. We got into the chute, were pulled up by the winch, and then automatically released when we got to the top.

We drifted rather than fell straight down. On our way down, the instructors would tell us to perform various procedures like slipping and preparing for landing, giving their commands through a bullhorn. We hit the ground with about the same speed as on a real jump. The instructors checked our names off and constantly harassed us. Everything was always on the double. Again, the slightest error resulted in fifteen or twenty-five push-ups.

Another exercise during this stage used the wind machine, a propeller about five feet in diameter enclosed in a safety wire cage and driven by a gasoline engine. It was mounted on a chassis with four rubber tires. We lay down in front of it, rigged in our complete parachute, while students picked up the canopy so it would fill with wind. Next they started the machine up, and the air caught and fully extend the canopy. As we were dragged along, students pushed the machine after us, keeping it close in order to maintain wind velocity. We had to learn how to get to our feet while being dragged. The trick was to get enough slack in our lines so we could run around and get in front of the chute and collapse it. If we landed in high winds, it was probable we would be dragged and hurt, so it was crucial to learn how to get out of our chute in these conditions.

Of course, our weight had a lot to do with how hard we were dragged. A big man was never blown around as fast as someone like me. I had difficulty, but I managed to get to my feet, run around, and collapse my chute after many attempts. The exercise left me with many scrapes, scratches, and bruises from head to foot. The instructors showed no mercy and accepted no excuses; we just had to do it. At the same time, they kept feeding us the old line of BS that ran, "One paratrooper can easily handle five men." They'd say this to build up our morale and keep us making progress.

This theme was kept up all throughout our schooling. The instructors always presented the toughness of our training as a personal challenge: "What are ya gonna be, a wimp or a man? Are ya good enough to be a trooper or not?" Sometimes when we groaned with pain and discomfort, they yelled, "What am I hearing? Crying and whimpering! What are ya? A man or an aging baby?" In the early 1940s, we were not exposed to any of the modern-day ideas about challenging authority, nor had we become cynical at an early age. We responded to their propaganda fully by pushing ourselves beyond our limits. It was a good thing we did. Once we got into battle, we would need every ounce of that extra strength, endurance, know-how, and confidence.

On the last day of "C Stage" we packed our parachutes. Bright and early Monday morning, "D Stage" would begin. We picked up the chute we had packed, moved to a hanger, and waited our turn to make our first qualifying jump. They assigned us into "sticks," a group of men who occupied one plane and jumped together. For qualifying jumps, the stick was divided in half. First one half would jump, then the plane would circle the field, and the other half would go out.

I didn't get much sleep the night before my first jump. I always had doubts about being successful. I told myself, "You've taken all the crap so far without quitting, even though others have failed." My main motivation was to not become less than the men around me. Personal pride, ego, self-esteem—all of it entered into it. What would my friends think if I failed? I had to succeed, I told myself, because failure would be more than I could handle. I *wanted* to be a paratrooper, to walk with the pride and self-confidence of a man who had proven himself to be a notch or two above the ordinary. But I was scared, very scared. I believe 95 percent of us were, and the other 5 percent were maybe liars.

Chapter 6

First Assignment:
507 Parachute Infantry Regiment

In "D Stage" we made one jump a day. All we had to do was pack our parachutes and jump out of an airplane for five days in a row. A truck picked us up and returned us to the packing shed where we packed our chutes for the next day's jump. "D Stage" thus was comparatively easy—except for one little thing. Most of us had never flown before. Here I was, going up in a plane for the first time, and I had to jump *out*. I think I made eighteen jumps in my life, including three combat jumps, and I was scared on every one of them.

The night jumps at Fort Benning were particularly problematic because it was so difficult to judge the distance to the ground. Even more seriously, it was hard to tell ground from water. The Chattahoochee River divided the military reservation, running close to a blacktopped road. If we were dropped to one side of the drop zone on a moonlit night and weren't real careful as we descended, we could mistake the moonlight shining off the blacktop for the river. There were cases where people made a water landing, releasing their straps at a height of twenty to one hundred feet, and hit the road instead of water, resulting in serious injury.

For the life of me, I cannot remember the specific experience of my first qualifying jump. We had received so much training, and it had been so repetitious, that the first actual jump just blended into the process. All I can figure out is that I, like all my fellow soldiers making that first jump, was completely on automatic. If anything, the first jump may have been the easiest, because we acted almost like robots.

The procedures, though, are indelibly engraved on my memory. We were seated in the plane approaching the drop zone when the jump master hollered, "Stand up and hook up!" We stood, grabbed our large metal fastener on the static line, and snapped it onto the anchor cable that ran overhead the length of the plane. The next command was: "Check equipment!" We then checked the jumper in front of us, making sure he was holding the static line correctly in his left hand, and wasn't in danger of entangling his arm in it. Next, we made sure the static line was in place, strapped crisscross with rubber bands across our main chute pack, and checked the other equipment. The "push out," the last man in the stick, turned around, and the man ahead of him checked his equipment. At the third command, "Sound off for equipment check," the last man in the stick hollered out his number: "Sixteen okay!" And on it went, right on down the line.

There was a light panel on the right side of the door that almost everyone could see. A red light came on about four minutes from the drop zone. Green was the signal to go. Shortly before, the jump master ordered, "Close up and stand in the door!" At this, we shuffled forward. We were taught not to lift our feet, for anyone who tripped would slow down the jump. The number-one man stood with his right hand on the right doorjamb, his left hand on the left jamb, and got ready to exit the plane. Then came the green light. The jump master shouted "Go!" and we started jumping, counting "one thousand, two thousand, three thousand" as we went out the door.

Safety regulations now require intervals of a specific number of seconds between jumpers. But in our day, they got us out as fast as they could. If you were the fifth man, when the command to go was given there was *immediately* an empty space four men deep in front of you. Those first four men went out the door like a compressed spring.

As soon as we started out, the prop blast caught us. The first thing we saw was the tail of the plane going over our head. Procedure called for the pilot to slow down to about 90 miles an hour, and go into a slight descent that raised the tail of the plane to give us more clearance. If the main chute didn't open by the count of three thousand, it meant we had a "streamer." We then pulled the ripcord on the reserve chute strapped across our torso, caught the chute, and cast it out in front of us to ensure it filled with air and deployed properly. Any trooper who got panicky and pulled the ripcord prematurely was in trouble. There would be two chutes trying to open, the main chute overhead and the reserve coming out in front, and one would steal the air from the other.

The opening shock was something else. In a good position, it wasn't too bad, but in a bad one—with our feet up and our head down, for example—the shock was unbelievable. It was even worse when we were heavily loaded, as we always were in any tactical or combat jump. Yet no matter how bad it was, we always welcomed the shock, because at least we knew our chute had opened.

Then there was the shock of landing. They used to say it was the equivalent of jumping from a height of fifteen to twenty feet. Even though I was in good physical condition, this caused me considerable pain in my joints and lower back. I suffered from lot of back pain because of my days as a trooper, and eventually had to have two operations. That said, I was lucky enough never to break any bones.

I was up in a plane seven or eight times before I ever landed in one. I'll always remember the heavy odor of aviation gas and oil we got when we started loading. Even the smell of it raised my fears. After we sat down in the bucket seats and the plane taxied to the end of the runway, the pilot checked his engines by revving them up to maximum RPM, then slowly released the brake and started off. When I heard the engines revving up, and knew I was about to go into takeoff, my fears mounted higher still. We did have refusals on all of the first five jumps. The policy was that we could refuse at any time up to the fifth jump without being court-martialed. Those who did refuse were hurried back and out of the company barracks before the rest of us returned from our successful jumps.

I don't think we had too many hot-shot pilots. Given the efficiency and training of the Air Transport and Troop Carrier commands, the experience of landing in a plane was almost as exciting as jumping out of one. I made a vow to myself that if I survived the war, I would never climb into another plane. I flew home after VE Day, then kept this vow until my youngest child was born on August 26, 1953, while I was at Indiantown Gap Military Reservation. The regimental commander graciously offered the services of a two-seater plane to fly me home to Erie.

Because of the inherent danger of what we did, and the fear we all had to master on a daily basis, we typically developed a cynical, black humor about ourselves and the tasks ahead. We had some grimly humorous songs like "Blood on the Risers" and "The Paratrooper's Lament," that we sang to the tune of the "Battle Hymn of the Republic." Then there were the jokes, like the old standard about the soldier getting ready for his first qualifying jump. He'd gone through all the pre-jump training, and memorized all the instructions: if his chute didn't open, he was to pull his reserve chute; then he'd land, climb on the truck, and go back to the packing shed. Well, our hero jumped and started counting, "one thousand, two thousand, three thousand," but his main chute didn't open up. So he pulled his reserve chute, and waited for it to open. But again, nothing happened. Then he said to himself, "I bet the damn truck won't be there either."

I graduated from Parachute School on October 3, 1942. Once we had our wings, we were qualified to wear our jump boots with the trousers bloused. We wore our boots and wings with tremendous pride, tucking our cuffs into our boot tops and folding our trousers over them, thus fully exposing the boots. Back then, the only people allowed to wear jump boots were qualified paratroopers; if anyone else was caught wearing them, the trousers were quickly cut off the man, and his boots were removed as a warning. We were top dogs in the Army.

After graduation, I went back to Erie on leave, intent on having the time of my life. Looking back, I think I probably made a horse's ass out of myself. At least one classmate had preceded me into the parachute troops, but that October I was the only trooper from my school in town. It was forbidden to wear our jump uniforms in civilian situations, but I did it anyway. Military police were rare, and as there were so few paratroopers and the uniform was so new, I figured even if I did run into an MP, he wouldn't know the regulations.

My father and stepmom were very proud of me, and I was proud to make them proud. I would not turn eighteen for another two months.

I spent my leave showing off. I got together with former classmates and demonstrated my skills at unarmed combat. I spouted off a lot of the BS our instructors had fed us about paratroopers being able to take on five ordinary men. Best of all, even though were all still underage, I took my friends to bars and got them served, because I was in uniform.

For once in my life, I received more invitations than I had time for. This might also have had to do with the fact that I was dating not one, but two girls. Those wings on my breast entitled me to a lot of privileges, but I hadn't yet learned to drive a car. I turned this to my hotshot advantage too, and took cabs. One of the girls lived way out in the country, and her mother was very impressed when I pulled up to the house in a taxi. It raised a lot of eyebrows to see a young paratrooper getting out of a cab. Imagine the difference if I'd had to ask my father to drive us on a date!

When I reported back to Fort Benning, I was assigned to I Company, 3d Battalion, 507th Parachute Infantry Regiment. Being assigned to the 507 that late in the organization of the regiment had its disadvantages. Even though I was a former NCO, I did not get my stripes back because the full quota of NCOs in I Company had already been met. The very day I was assigned, I was put on a cadre list, a skeleton force of NCOs and officers—first sergeant, supply sergeant, and at least three platoon sergeants—kept in readiness to supply the cadre for the next regiment to be formed.

We trained very hard in the 507, conducting squad-level, platoon-level, and weapons qualification training. Company I was a rifle company, which meant the M1 was now my primary individual weapon. We had more extensive cross-training in weapons than in the regular infantry; almost everyone in a parachute rifle company got the chance to fire every weapon in the TO&E, including the .45-caliber tommy gun, the Browning automatic rifle (BAR), and a light .30-caliber machine gun that was exactly the same as the water-cooled machine gun I had used in the 112th, except that it was air-cooled.

I now saw the new .30-caliber carbine for the first time. The paratroops had a specially designed carbine with a pistol grip and a folding, heavy wire stock. The grip was at the hinge of the stock, which folded onto the side of the carbine, so we could fire it one-handed when necessary. I received preliminary training on the carbine, but was never issued one; the TO&E changed too fast. At one time, we were supposed to have both a carbine and a rifle, because we could jump with the carbine in one piece and use it before assembling our M1. Then we were to carry a rifle only. Later on, they thought about giving us a pistol as well as a rifle, but that idea was cancelled too, at least for the 82d Airborne. I'm not sure how the TO&E ended up for the 101st.

Most of the platoon leaders in the 507 were good, well-rounded officers. I never got promoted in I Company, though, because I ran into difficulties with an inexperienced officer who was our instructor for marksmanship training. I had a natural flair for shooting, and by the time I came to the 507, I had already developed my skills. I'd started hunting in the mountains of Pennsylvania at eleven, and had shot several bucks, so I knew something about rifles before I entered the Army. I had completed marksmanship training as a private in 1941, taught the M1 course as a drill instructor in 1942, and fired numerous times on a range since then, including one instance where I'd shot the highest score in I Company. (The prize was a three-day pass, a couple of cartons of cigarettes and a steak dinner.) Our green lieutenant was not the best instructor, and I corrected him in class. Unfortunately, this conduct did not help me much as far as promotions were concerned. I don't think I ever did get off his list.

Our training in the 507 was even more physical than that to which I was accustomed. There was much more emphasis on squad, platoon, and company tactical training, and a lot of endurance training, which required us to be in the field for extended periods, going for long hours without rest. We also had realistic live-fire exercises. We did more shooting on tactical problems than the regular infantry. We concentrated a lot on night training, which is always tough, but helped us greatly in future operations.

The 507 finally moved to the Alabama area, way out in the boonies in the pine forest. It was very difficult to get to town. There wasn't even a bridge; men and vehicles alike had to cross the river by ferry. We were literally crammed into tarpaper shacks, double-bunked in flimsy, unheated buildings with very low ceilings, about twenty-four feet wide by thirty-five feet long, where we also had to store our field equipment and clothing. Northerners may *think* the South is always warm, but I spent some of the coldest nights of my life in the swamps of Georgia and Alabama in November and December 1942. The conditions in modern prisons are far better than the housing in most military camps during World War II.

Not surprisingly, we had trouble with the AWOL rate in Company I. Our company commander decided to make an example of one of the soldiers who returned late from his furlough. He tied a jump rope around the soldier's neck and led him around the company and training areas, saying, "If I can't trust you to come back from furlough on time, I'll keep you tied so you can't leave." The first officer senior to our commander to observe this disgusting example of improper treatment stopped it. This was the worst case of the misuse of command authority and discipline that I ever encountered throughout my military career.

I had a lot of furloughs and leaves in 1942, and when the 507th granted furloughs for Christmas that year, I took another one without complaint. That Christmas, I made sure to see my Great-Aunt Myra, whose library had all those stories about the Civil War that had fascinated me as a kid. In 1942, she must have been close to seventy. Public transportation had been cut way back, and the only way to get to Kennedy, New York, was to stick out my thumb. We had the kind of reunion you have when you return to the person who has loved you more than anyone else in your childhood. I don't know who was prouder—me to show her my wings, or her to see me wearing them.

My holiday, however, was threatened with being cut short by a telegram stating my furlough had been cancelled. Shortly after, I received another canceling the first one. I thought that second telegram was just about the best present I'd ever received. After Christmas, I had more good news when I returned to Alabama and discovered why I'd almost been recalled. The Army had issued activation papers for a new parachute infantry regiment, and I was to report as part of the cadre.

Chapter 7

Second Assignment: Cadre, 513 Parachute Infantry Regiment; Volunteering for Overseas Duty

When I got back to Fort Benning, I was transferred to Headquarters Company, 2d Battalion of the Parachute School, on the main post, where I eagerly waited assignment to the next regiment to be formed. I felt irritated at having to wait around through most of January as a private first class, but I was finally transferred to Headquarters Company, 2d Battalion, 513th PIR, at the end of the month. In February I was promoted to sergeant, the same grade I had made before volunteering for the parachute troops, and I was made a platoon sergeant. I was now eighteen years and two months old.

Although I was glad to get my promotion, I had a hard time of it emotionally after I left the 507. I had only been in the regiment a few months, but I had made friends, and the unit had become my home. In the 513th, I had to start making friends all over again. I didn't immediately have a full-sized platoon. Men were assigned as they came out of Parachute School, and it took some time for the unit to fill up. As a result, I was billeted in a tarpaper shanty by myself, or with only one or two other NCOs, for what seemed to me a long while. Even after the unit filled up, I didn't make many close friends in the 513. I was only in the unit four months, and as a platoon sergeant, I didn't want to become too friendly with the men in my platoon, at least not until I could feel comfortable with them.

I was young, the other NCOs didn't stick around after duty, and I often found myself alone. My mother had sent me a fine portable radio for Christmas, and I lay on my bunk night after night trying to find stations with music. I particularly remember listening in the dark to "As Time Goes By" from *Casablanca,* but many other tunes of the day remain deeply embedded in my memory: "I'll Walk Alone," "Fools Rush In," "I'll Never Smile Again," "We'll Meet Again," "There Are Such Things." These songs still evoke the loneliness of being far from home and the uncertainty of what was to come.

The late winter and early spring of 1943 found me training new men for a fledgling regiment. The soldiers had completed their basic infantry training prior to Parachute School, so we began with squad and platoon unit training. As far as I was concerned, this was getting very repetitious.

The airborne units were expanding at a hectic rate. No sooner had a regiment been formed than a tremendous push began to groom officers, NCOs, and potential NCOs for the next one. In March, I was transferred to Regimental Headquarters and Headquarters Company of the 513, where, in addition to training a platoon of men, I was assigned to a group of officers and NCOs who were taking extra classroom training and instructions at least three nights a week. Some of us, myself included, were also instructing yet another group of NCOs and potential NCOs for assignment to the next PIR. The hardest thing was that I was now confined to a unit that was not expected to go overseas for six or eight more months.

I did get weekend passes for Atlanta, but most often I went on my own. There wasn't much to do other than go to the movies, booze it up, and look for female companionship. The more I drank, the sadder I became. We also got passes to Columbus, Georgia, and Phenix City, Alabama, its sister city across the Chattahoochee, but there was very little transportation into town. Both had some pretty rough honky tonks, with poker, craps, and other games going in the back rooms, especially in Phoenix City. Paratroopers were paid an extra $50 per month, a lot of money for the time, and we could make some big wins when our luck was running well. This resulted in a conspiracy between the gambling operators and the taxi drivers hired to take men back to base. It got so that every payday we were pulling a drowned trooper out of the Chattahoochee River who had been taken for a ride after he had started home with his winnings.

These deaths created very high tensions between paratroopers and the locals, and more than once a full-scale riot was only avoided through the exercise of overwhelming police authority. Paratroopers were awfully clannish, and when one of us got into trouble, we could always count on help from our comrades. There was heavy rivalry between the armored divisions and the paratroopers, both of which considered themselves to be undoubtedly the best organization in the Army, and this also led to quite a few skirmishes. To alleviate the tension, our commanders sent details of troopers into town as a "city patrol" to supplement the MPs and police. Paratroopers were much more likely to take orders from their own kind.

In April, I was twice selected as sergeant in charge of this detail, and I rapidly gained an education in areas of life I had never known existed. The main job of the city patrol was to protect our troopers from the brutality of the MPs and the civilian police. All of these latter carried a "sap" or black-jack, a leather-covered weapon filled with lead balls or shot, which they were quick to use on a trooper's head. Not that the troopers didn't need it at times—a drunken paratrooper could quickly become very obnoxious—but as CPs, our most important duty was to get to trouble spots as fast as we could to take charge of our own people.

I was assigned a command car to patrol the streets, keeping a check on troopers on the sidewalks and on disturbances in the outlying honky tonks. I also spent time in the police station at Columbus, where I saw a lot of things that opened my eyes. The jail had horizontal cells stacked three or four deep, with just enough room in each cell for a man to crawl into it. Most of the people who ended up in these cages were black. It also had a large holding tank, usually filled with drunks and prostitutes. I learned a lot of new language and behavior at the tender age of eighteen during my duty at the Columbus police station.

In mid-April, the rumor started that the 513 was to provide a "replacement packet" for overseas shipment, which was how replacements for parachute units were designated. The levy was going to a combat area. No NCOs were supposed to be included, but I was young and eager and had certainly had my fill of basic and small-unit training, so I requested permission to go with the packet.

Anyone who asks why a soldier would volunteer for overseas combat would also probably wonder why in hell anyone would volunteer to jump out of a perfectly good airplane in mid-flight. But many other soldiers in World War II shared my desire to get into combat. In the American Civil War they called it "seeing the elephant"—seeing combat for the first time. Of course, most soldiers like myself, eager to get into war, quickly change their minds once they're there. After seeing the first artillery and mortar rounds fall about them, and hearing the sharp crack of MGs and rifle fire close about their ears, they'll tell you they daily prayed for a quick peace and wondered privately to themselves, "Why in hell did I rush into this?"

Initially, my transfer request was denied. There was, I was told, a critical need for experienced NCOs to train the 513th Parachute Infantry. But I kept making a nuisance of myself until the company commander reluctantly agreed to approve my request.

And so it happened that when the 82d Airborne went overseas in April 1943, I was in one of the two replacement groups it carried with it to North Africa. Two packets went with the 82d because it was estimated that training accidents in the rough, rocky terrain would be much higher than usual. It was also thought that illness would be considerable because of sanitation problems and the reliance on canned foods without fresh meat, vegetables, or fruit.

Unit designations for those going overseas were not allowed to be publicly displayed. When we packed to leave, we stenciled EGB447 or EGB448 on our duffel bags. This identified them as part of a particular shipment, "EGB" being nothing more than a shipping code. Over time, not only our bags, but also we, ourselves, became so designated. I was an EGB448, the last group assigned to the 82d Airborne Division. The first packet brought the 82d up to strength after their losses in North Africa so they could go into Sicily for their first combat jump, but we, the EGB448s, were assigned after that jump.

We moved from Fort Benning, Georgia to our embarkation point at Camp Shanks, New York. The EGBs weren't immediately assigned, but we moved along with the unit in order to be readily assigned whenever men were needed. The worst possible assignment in the Army, at least in World War II, was as a replacement to another unit. At first, even our

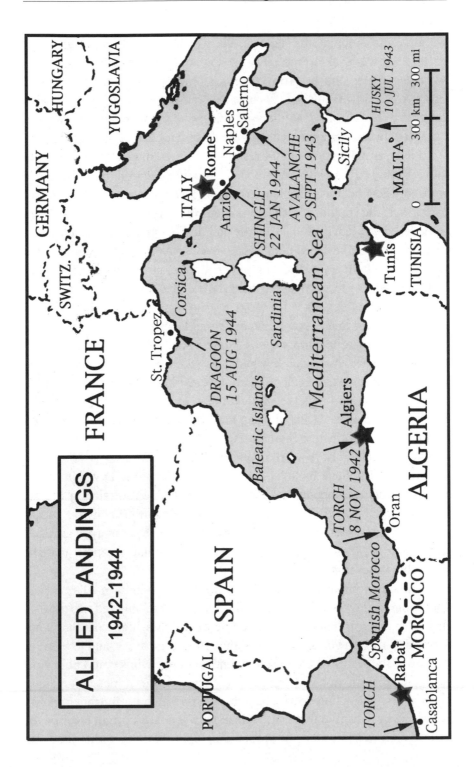

name, "replacement," was negative. The word had a bad ring: it reminded us that we were taking the place of someone who had been killed or wounded. Later on, the Army tried to come up with something more positive, and so all replacements became "reinforcements." We were also referred to as "casuals," soldiers or officers not attached to any unit and often without assignment, who were only temporarily at a location.

I left Camp Shanks with the rest of my packet, moved by rail down to New York Harbor, and was loaded onto the *George Washington*, a transport headed for Casablanca. Our ship was a converted passenger liner. All the civilian niceties, including dining rooms, had been removed. They just loaded the whole hull down with cots and made room to feed and handle large numbers of troops. And when I say "loaded down," I really mean it. The cots were similar to stretchers—nothing but a frame with a piece of canvas laced to it. The frame was attached to vertical poles, which made for easy stacking. And stack us they did, four to six cots high, to use every inch of available space.

Prior to boarding ship, we each were issued two .30-caliber M1903 bolt-action rifles. As usual, they had been stored in a wooden box full of cosmoline, and it was a heck of a hard job cleaning them. As we found out at the end of our journey, the whole process was just a way of getting the rifles over to North Africa in clean and workable condition. We turned them over to be issued to the Free French forces.

We left New York Harbor on April 29, 1943, as part of a huge convoy that I believe included the whole 82d Airborne Division. Navy escort vessels accompanied us, including at least one baby flattop aircraft carrier. Aerial surveillance was a big plus in escorting convoys. It not only gave early warnings of submarines, it kept them submerged as much as possible, at least during daylight. The convoy had weapons to fight any submarines that were spotted.

The ship companies set up to feed the men for ten days on a twenty-four- hour- a-day basis, and even at this rate we were only fed two meals a day. It was my rotten luck to have one of the four high cots that were stacked against the bulkheads throughout the cargo areas, and to be right on one of the aisles where the chow line went by. I thus could not avoid seeing that it was just was one long, continuous file of men. We passed through the chow line down one side of a one inch by four inch plank, which was about five feet off the deck between two upright steel posts, placed our mess kits on it and ate standing up. In rough weather food and liquids slopped over onto the deck, and we were usually wading around in messes. Then, too, some people would get seasick as they smelled the kitchen.

The odor in the troop compartments wasn't the best. No showers were provided, so body odor was horrendous. Add to this people getting seasick, and you have a pretty good idea of the unpleasantness of the troop compartments. They tried to rotate us up on deck to give us some exercise and fresh air, but time was limited. We would try to sneak up past the guards.

I think they made an honest effort to keep things cleaned up, but it was a losing battle. The latrine area was the worst case of stench and contamination, what with the overpowering smell of shit and the vomit from those who couldn't make it to the latrines. I'll never forget the command that periodically, day and night, came over the PA system: "Sweepers, man your brooms! Clean, sweep, fore and aft!" What the hell that meant, I don't know. I don't know who the sweepers were or what they were sweeping, because I never saw them. They must have been up on the main deck.

We were required to wear our life preservers twenty-four hours a day. We slept with them on, ate with them on, everything. Everyone knew that if the ship was torpedoed, it would go down fast. They attempted to carry out fire, evacuation, and abandon-ship drills, but anyone in his right mind could see there weren't enough lifeboats. The whole situation got darkly humorous, but we went through the drill anyway. In retrospect, I think it actually was meant to lay out a plan to empty the troop compartments and get us up on the open deck, where we stood a better chance of surviving a sinking.

We had a pretty good crossing as far as weather was concerned, and we arrived in the battle-scarred harbor at Casablanca, French Morocco, on May 10, 1943. The land campaign in North Africa ended three days later.

Chapter 8

French Morocco: Fifth Army Mines
and Demolition School

The day we landed at Casablanca, we were trucked to Fort Marshal Lyautey near Rabat, French Morocco. As we lined up for roll call, the commander came out of his orderly tent, looked at me intently, and said, "What the hell are you doing here, Sergeant Wurst?" Much to my amazement, I discovered I had reported to one of the selective service men I had trained as a recruit the previous spring. Here he was again, standing in front of me as the commander of my replacement company.

The EGBs had better living conditions than the 82d itself. We stayed behind on the coast at Rabat, while the division went about 400 miles straight east, into the dessert at Oujda. Even so, our training took place in 100 degree heat, although we did have fresh water and could occasionally go for a swim. It was interesting for a while, for this was our introduction to soldiers from various foreign armies, encampments of French Foreign Legion troops, and native French military organizations. We even had boxing matches with the Legionnaires.

We only had contact with the rural lower class of the native population, and the areas where we bivouacked were desperately poor. Soldiers who had fought in the North Africa campaign said the Arabs came into their firing positions to pick up the brass while shots were still being exchanged, ignoring the danger to themselves from both sides in their eagerness to get the cartridges. They were a real problem while a fight was going on, for their presence gave away our firing positions.

We had to keep a close watch on all our personal equipment and possessions, and the interior guard was exceptionally issued live ammunition as a last resort to keep the Arabs out of our camp. Not a night went by when I happened to be awake that I didn't hear a guard quickly challenge, rapidly followed by the sound of shots. Arab villages were within earshot, and after the shooting, especially on quiet nights, we could hear the sound of strange, disturbing chanting. It was hauntingly foreign to our ears, and went on for hours at a time. There were many nerve-wracking nights when I lay awake in my sack listening to the funeral chants coming from the villages.

The Arabs were also famous as traders, and I still have a large wallet that I bought from a street vendor and carried throughout the war. They also wanted to buy things we had, and we always haggled a long time over prices. Two especially hot items were our mattress covers and barracks bags. The mattress covers were sewn together at one end: the Arabs cut a hole in the middle of the closed end and another on either side, then slipped the mattress cover over their head for use as a tunic.

Barracks bags at the time were still made of cloth and had a drawstring top. Each man had two barracks bags, one labeled "A" and the other "B." The latter bags contained regulation items and were shipped as soon as we were off the front lines; A bags arrived when we got to a rear area. Both had quite a bit of stenciling: our name and serial number, shipping number, and other information, but never our unit number.

The Arabs cut two holes in the bottom of the bag, slipped it on and pulled it up like a pair of pantaloons, then pulled the drawstrings tightly around the waist and tied them. They were very ingenious, but we thought it was hilarious. To us, they looked like big diapers. We mostly sold them "B" bags, which meant they would walk around with something like: "'B' Bag, John Jones, serial number so-and-so" stenciled across the ass.

Of course, all this activity was strictly black market, and was frowned on by the authorities. The men who sold their barracks bags quickly learned to tell the buyers to turn them inside out so the lettering wouldn't show. I forget how much the bags were going for, but mattress covers were bringing at least $20.00 each, which was a good sum of money.

It was on the rifle ranges at Rabat that I became a life-long tobacco chewer, much to my future wife's dismay. Every time we fired a round, the muzzle blast kicked up a cloud of dust that drifted back over our heads. Before long, we had dry mouths and were spitting dirt. One of the fellows alongside me on the firing line was chewing tobacco. I asked him for a chew, and the rest is history. Of course, chewing was a lot safer on the front line than smoking. No matter how hard we tried to conceal a flaming match, we were never sure we managed it. The superstition about being third on a match is well founded in the facts of trench warfare in World War I. By the time the second man lit up, a sniper would have had time to locate the position and zero in on the third.

We also got the chance to shoot a new weapon in Rabat, a hand-held antitank rocket launcher with a diameter of 2.36 inches. The propellant consisted of thin sticks of slow-burning powder inserted into the rear body of the projectile. We named it the bazooka, after the musical instrument played by the comedian Bob Burns, whose act featured a home-made slide trombone he had put together from a bunch of pipes.

The first time we set about shooting a bazooka, I was acting as gunner. I placed it on my shoulder, and the assistant gunner put a rocket into the rear end of the tube. He then stood clear and tapped me on the shoulder, signifying it was ready to fire. I squeezed the trigger and was instantly stunned by an explosion that blew a hole right out of the tube. Luckily, the metal flew out away from my face, but I was momentarily dazed and dropped the bazooka. I bent over and started spitting, and the lieutenant in charge came running in a panic, thinking it was blood. He was greatly relieved to discover it was only tobacco juice.

As it turned out, the powder in the bazooka rocket I had fired had been stored in the hot African sun, which dried it out and made the rocket faster burning—so fast, that it exploded in the tube itself. The ordnance department responsible for designing the bazooka later reinforced the tube by tightly winding wire around the circumference of the back end, where the gunner's face touched the launcher. Later yet, I discovered the manuals stated that for training exercises, people had to wear a gas mask for extra protection against explosions in the launcher.

During my stay at Camp Marshal Lyautey, I only got one pass to Casablanca, much to my sorrow. We were warned about going into the Medina, the native quarters. I had started drinking early, and had gotten quite a nose full before joining up with a French Foreign Legionnaire. He couldn't speak much English and I couldn't speak much French, but I know now he took me to the Medina to roll me. He soon realized, however, that I wasn't drunk enough for him to knock me out and steal my money without a real struggle. So he left me there, stranded deep in the native quarter in black-out conditions.

I think I was as close to being KIA right there and then as I ever was in combat. I finally managed to get onto the main drag in the European section, but even then it was rough going under blackout. Eventually, I saw a light coming from around a doorjamb and heard voices speaking English behind the door. So I opened the door and walked in. Lo and behold, I was in the Allied Officers' Club. As a lowly sergeant, I was strictly off limits, but being in the mood I was in, I went right up to the bar and proceeded to order a drink. The bartender gave me a hard time, but it was about two deep at the bar and some of the junior officers stuck up for me. I managed to down a couple drinks before the MPs arrived.

The last thing I remember is being thrown on a two-and-a-half-ton truck. When I woke up, I was lying on the ground in an old POW stockade, with machine-gun towers in each corner. I had a very tough hangover.

The MPs assembled all the occupants and marched us into a building where I met a famous gentleman by the name of Major Fry, the provost marshal of the Casablanca area. I heard he had been a master sergeant in the peacetime Army who had run a very hard, brutal Army prison. Word had it he was the toughest provost marshal in the Army. Not only was he reputed to give the roughest sentences, he was said to have a strong prejudice against paratroopers.

I stood before him, headache banging, expecting the worst. He began by asking me a few questions, and of course I couldn't deny I had stormed an officers' club in a drunken condition. So the major gave me my choice. He said, "As you are an NCO, you can ask for a special court martial, or you can take a summary court martial." Then he told me the conditions: "I'm the summary court officer," he said. "If you go before a special court martial you could get six months and two-thirds of six months' pay withheld, and if I take your case you can get thirty days and two-thirds of thirty days' pay withheld. Which do you want?"

I didn't exactly have much choice. But after he'd completed his summary court martial, Major Fry made me a little proposition. "Sergeant," he said, "I can't order you to do this because you are an NCO, but if you can work for me out on the rock pile for a couple, three days, maybe we can tear up these court martial papers."

I thought it over and figured I probably had earned a couple of hard days on the rock pile. So I agreed to do the work for him. And thus it was that for some very hard, hot days, I broke rocks along with about twenty-five or thirty other gentlemen who were in the same position as me.

The major was constructing a racetrack and riding paths for senior officers. All day long, we made smaller rocks out of bigger ones and transported them to make lanes lined with stone walls. After I had put in two or three days of hard labor, Major Fry, true to his word, tore up my court martial papers, and they were never entered on my service record. I won't go so far as to say he used slave labor. Let's just say he used unwilling labor to get things done. Thus I learned the lesson that trouble never pays, but you always pay for trouble.

Within a few days of reporting back to the replacement company, I got a set of orders from the Fifth Army headquarters. I had been selected to attend the Fifth Army Mines and Demolition School, where demolition procedures and all the details about mines and booby-traps were taught to engineers and selected infantrymen. The school was situated back in the desert, and classes contained English, American, and French students, all mixed together. It was standard procedure to stand retreat in the rear areas, when inspection was followed by the bugle call "to the colors." Because three nations were represented, the end of the day was a colorful affair. We had to stand retreat through three national anthems, holding our salutes through the "Star-Spangled Banner," "God Save the King," and the "Marseillaise." To this day, whenever I hear the National Anthem, I associate it with standing retreat in some far-off place like North Africa.

Our chief instructor (and, I believe, the commandant of the school) was a very interesting English character by the name of Colonel Stevenson, who had long been the division engineer officer in the North

Africa campaign for the famous "Desert Rats," the British 7th Armoured Division. Colonel Stevenson knew everything worth knowing about mine warfare, and he set his school up to great advantage to teach us the basic facts. Classroom work was kept to a minimum and emphasis was put on practical application. We were taught to identify and disarm all kinds of mines, and how to safely handle explosives—TNT, plastic explosive blasting caps, and primer cord. First we used scale models, calculating the amount of demolitions needed and where to place them, then blowing them up. When we went out to the field to practice what we had been taught, we did not use dummy materials—we used live mines and live explosives. Believe me, we learned very quickly.

I vividly remember a night mine-clearing exercise where a man was accidentally killed by gunfire. We had to cut and clear a lane through a minefield containing barbed-wire obstacles, clearing it in the prone position, probing for the mines with a knife or bayonet. For once we were not using live mines. This time the danger was elsewhere: throughout the exercise, water-cooled .30-caliber machine guns fired real ammunition two to three feet over our heads.

We worked in teams, digging underneath the mines, lifting them up from their positions, removing the fuses, and moving them out of the lane. The lead man probed and found the mine, the next man lifted it, and so on. As the "lift" man, I checked for booby-traps, dug around the mines, removed the fuses, and set them to the side. We did all of this while crawling on our stomachs.

We had advanced part-way down the field when disaster struck. A tripod leg on a machine gun collapsed, sending a burst of gunfire down through the minefield. The bullets plowed into the lead man in my team, an engineer from the 36th Infantry Division, hitting him multiple times. He was working the field directly in front of me. This man later died of his wounds. He was the first man I ever saw killed by gunfire, and it was my own first narrow escape from death. It was truly a case of, "There but for the grace of God go I."

Shortly after I completed my course and returned to the Replacement Company, the EGB448s moved further east near Oujda, a small town crowded with soldiers of different nationalities. The flies and the insects were thick, and water was in short supply; as hard as we tried to keep clean and prepare our food in a sanitary manner, our efforts were usually defeated. The latrines were far from what they should have been. Our diet also contributed to health problems, as there was very little fresh meat or fresh vegetables. There were a lot of cases of the GI trots and dysentery.

We got passes into town, where the government sponsored a house of prostitution. There was a main center with two large courtyards leading from it—French prostitutes on one side, Arab on the other. Soldiers had to pass through the center going in and out, and it was impossible to leave without taking a prophylactic as a precaution against venereal disease. And when I say prophylactic, I mean a chemical liquid inserted into the penis.

The Army encouraged abstinence in North Africa, but failing that, we were told to take every possible precaution against disease. Supposedly, the prostitutes in the government-sponsored houses were examined weekly, or even daily, by Army medical authorities. The Army claimed there was a particularly virulent strain of venereal disease prevalent in North Africa called "the black syphilis," and that anyone who contracted it would not be allowed to return to the States. Believe me when I say this scared a lot of us away from having sex in North Africa.

Otherwise, there wasn't much to do in Oujda, so I mostly spent my time at camp. We did discover a supply of dry, very potent red wine in one of the nearby villages. Whenever we got particularly bored, we sent someone out with a five-gallon can to buy some wine, then sat around the can in a circle, and repeatedly filled our canteen cups until we were thoroughly inebriated. Then we rolled over and went to sleep. Eventually, we crawled back to our cots and finished the night off. This practice left us with some crippling hangovers, but they never deterred us from sending out for yet another can of red wine.

One morning, after one of these wine-guzzling sessions, I was assigned as an assistant instructor for bayonet training. The instructing officer explained the various jabs, and I was supposed to demonstrate each of the techniques. I was so hung over I could hardly bear to stand up. Finally, the long thrust did me in. I managed to perform it the first time, but I pitched forward the second time, and fell flat on my face in the dust. To say the least, I was one sheepish platoon sergeant.

In June 1943, the 82d Airborne Division moved east to Kairouan, French Tunisia, and the EGBs followed shortly thereafter. As our convoy proceeded east, we had to go through the Atlas Mountains. I distinctly remember their beauty—they were large mountain ranges, with roads winding up and over them. Unfortunately, I was distracted from higher things along the way.

Here we were, speeding down the road on a two-and-a-half-ton truck with a ton-and-a half trailer coupled to it, and I had a bad case of diarrhea. The convoy stopped only once every two hours for a break. But when ya gotta go, ya gotta go. I actually crawled out of the truck, got down on the tongue of the trailer, and responded to the call of nature, holding onto the tailgate with one hand and my pants with the other, at a speed of 40 miles an hour. And I wasn't the only one. It was interesting, to say the least.

Chapter 9

Permanent Assignment: Company F,
505 Parachute Infantry Regiment; the Move to Sicily

Kairouan was close to the bivouac areas of the 82d Airborne Division. I had been an infantryman for three years, and fully expected to be assigned to a parachute infantry company. But because I had attended the Fifth Army Mines and Demolition school, I found myself assigned to Company B of the 82d Airborne Division's 307th Airborne Engineer Battalion.

I did not like this at all. I felt I was much better qualified as an infantryman, so I made it my business to find the most senior officer in the area and request a transfer to the parachute infantry. For once I got some action. Without much delay, I was transferred and assigned to Company F of the 505 PIR. By this time, however, the 505 had already been committed to combat in Sicily.

One thing is sure—the 505 had no time to go stale. The regiment celebrated its first birthday in North Africa on July 6, 1943, with a steer roast, beer, and a rousing pep talk from Col. James Gavin, and was already in combat three days later in Sicily. By this time, fifteen generals had visited the division, from Eisenhower on down. I would join the 505 along with the other EGB448s after the fighting finished and the regiment came back to Kairouan. The EGB448s would not see Sicily until early September 1943, when the 505 returned there after leaving North Africa. But because we had been assigned as replacements in July, our members later received the Combat Infantry Badge and the Bronze Star Medal for meritorious service in Sicily, even though we hadn't jumped with the regiment.

While I was waiting in Kairouan, my life was less than glorious. You could smell the town for a good two, three, even five miles away, depending on the wind. The inhabitants believed that the dead must be buried in extremely shallow graves, and vented the caskets up to the surface. The air was polluted with the smell of rotting corpses. Add to this the stench from very primitive sanitation facilities. In the 100 degree weather, the odor was horrific.

The olive grove where the 505 was bivouacked afforded the only shade for miles and miles around. Each platoon or squad was assigned a certain number of trees to live under. The flies and other insects were horrible, and our mosquito nets were totally inefficient when we attempted to hang them over our blanket rolls from the branches of the olive trees.

Water, always in short supply in North Africa, was rationed. We were allowed one full helmet each day. First we bathed with it, then we shaved with it, and then we started to wash our clothes. By the time we got down to our socks, it wasn't much more than a helmet full of mud. The British Army ran a shower point about ten miles away, so we often loaded on the trucks and drove through the desert to enjoy a very limited time under the showerhead. By the time we retraced the ten dusty miles back to the bivouac area, we were just about as bad as when we started.

The high rate of dysentery, diarrhea, and digestive-tract problems was not exactly helped by our diet of canned food. It was here that Spam first became famous—or infamous. It was used in huge quantities, some days for breakfast, lunch, *and* dinner. I spent time in the hospital because of dysentery and a high fever. Of course, there was no running water, and the latrines were nothing but pits. There was an unsuccessful attempt to keep a washbasin of water handy so we could wash our hands after using the latrines.

Many troopers also picked up malaria. The rate got so high that they put us on anti-malaria medication, a bitter pill called Atabrine. An officer would stand at the end of the chow line, throw the pill down our throats, and make sure we swallowed it. Even then, some of the fellows managed to hold the pill in their mouths and spit it out later. The garbage cans were full of Atabrine, and their contents soon turned a sickening greenish yellow as the pills dissolved in the slops and trash.

Despite their appalling state, these garbage cans provided nourishment for the local population. From the time we arrived in North Africa in May 1943 until we left, children would come into camp for food whenever we were anywhere near an Arab settlement. Sometimes they would sneak in, and sometimes we let them in ourselves. They would head for the garbage cans, take the garbage out, and eat it on the spot, or put it in cans to take home for their families. Witnessing this gave us much more appreciation for our American way of life.

On August 20, the 505 was airlifted back to North Africa from Sicily, where it had made the first American regimental combat jump of World War II. Although I was unaware of it then, a major event in the Sicily operation concerning our sister regiment, the 504 PIR, had thrown the entire future of airborne warfare into question. The 504, minus its 3d Battalion, which had jumped with the 505 on D-day, had flown into friendly territory near Gela as reinforcements. Their arrival shortly followed a Luftwaffe attack on the U.S. naval invasion fleet situated just off the coast, which had received a pounding by thirty Ju 88 bombers. The last of the German fighters had barely left the area before our C-47s full of troopers appeared in the sky.

To come in over the beaches, the Air Corps had to fly over the naval convoy. The Navy had received strict orders that there be no firing. Maybe the word did not get all the way down, or the antiaircraft gunners on the ships got nervous. Either way, they opened fire on the low-flying troop transport planes. Ship after ship, and even gunners on shore, joined in the attack. By the time the massacre was over, twenty-three of the 144 C-47s in the armada had been shot down. Within minutes, 318 American paratroopers and many C-47 crew members lost their lives.

When the 505 returned from Sicily, I was assigned to the 1st Squad of the 3d Platoon of Company F, 2d Battalion. None of us knew anything about the 82d Airborne's baptism by fire; I was only very relieved to be assigned to a permanent unit and finally find a home after three long months as a "casual." Nevertheless, even after assignment, the EGB448s were still kept segregated as a group. We were not allowed to move our belongings to the area designated to our new unit, and the so-called "older" members looked down their noses at us. Even a few days of "seeing the elephant" in Sicily made the "old" men of Company F feel superior to the "new" men.

At one point, there was a regimental parade. The EGB448s were integrated into the 505 as part of the ceremony, undergoing the formal passage from replacement status. Never again did the 505 treat new men as badly as they had treated us. Subsequent replacements were quickly integrated into squads and platoons through training, and also on a personal level as friends and fellow troopers. Later, many of the men in the company who had made the Sicily mission would tell me that the first *real* combat for Company F was in Italy at Arnone on the Volturno River.

Meanwhile, I had to put up with second-class status. Being an NCO did not help my situation. In fact, our company commander, along with some of the other officers who had been in the 505 for a while, took a dim view of receiving NCOs as replacements. They would have preferred to promote soldiers to the NCO spots who had been with the company all along, although they also received officer replacements, and the officers, unlike the NCOs, were assigned to their normal leadership positions. I was a sergeant acting as a private, a simple rifleman under the authority of my squad leader. Further, our captain was constantly on the lookout for any violation of procedures or orders. Company commanders were allowed to make and break NCOs, and every legal means was used to reduce the EGB NCOs in rank.

Shortly after I was assigned to the 505 in August, Bob Hope and Frances Langford came to our bivouac area with the U.S.O. group. The 505 decided to have a show for them, too, and the new EGB448 replacements, myself included, were selected to make a demonstration jump. It was a late-evening jump, made in the dessert just beyond the stage area. After the jump, we all had to gather up our chutes and do everything else on the double in order to make the show. I did manage to make it on time—there was no way I was going to miss Frances Langford in the flesh, singing "Put Your Arms Around Me, Honey." I remember reading much later that at one point in her North Africa tour, this same song cost Frances Langford a lot of embarrassment. She sang it in an

Army hospital without realizing it was the amputee ward and some of the men she was singing to had just lost both their arms.

Other than the Bob Hope show, not much happened while we were waiting in Kairouan. We thought we would never get out of there. The 505ers who had seen better things in Sicily—not only fighting, but plentiful wine, good food, and women—were feeling pretty fed up with training exercises and Spam. Then, on September 5, the 505 was ordered to return to Sicily, where we bivouacked at three different airfields. My battalion, the 2d, was based at Comiso; Regimental Headquarters and the 3d Battalion were at Castelvetrano; and the 1st Battalion was at Barizzo, along with Company B of the 307th Engineers. We had no idea what our mission would be.[3]

While we were waiting for the next operation, we continued to train and did a lot of detail work. By this time, the enemy had been cleared off the island, but we were still subject to air raids, and we all had slit trenches dug as protection against the air raids and other enemy activity. One day, while I was on a work detail at the airfield, a little Sicilian boy came by with a couple bottles of wine. Alcohol was strictly forbidden in the bivouac area, although none of us was above sneaking in a little whenever we could manage it. We all chipped in to buy a bottle, and stowed it for future use. That evening, after chow, the squad passed the bottle around as we were shooting the breeze. The long and the short of it is that the empty bottle ended up in my slit trench.

The next morning, when we left for training, one of the squad members, a fellow named Zunda, stayed behind because he was running a fever. Our company commander walked through the bivouac area, spotted the wine bottle in the slit trench, and immediately asked Zunda, who was the only person around, who the trench belonged to. Zunda answered truthfully, and thus gave the captain the golden opportunity I believe he had been seeking for some time.

When I got in from training, the captain called me to the company CP. It was a matter of "sit down, Sergeant, stand up, Private." I felt that the reduction was unfair. Although I had violated the order, I had not drunk an entire bottle of wine: it had simply ended up in my trench. But the only protest I made was that I would only accept the bust if it read "reduced without prejudice." And so it was in the early days of September 1943 that I was once again back to the grade of private, albeit "reduced without prejudice."

Ever since we had arrived in Sicily, a lot of guessing had been going on about where the 505 would go for our next operation. Unbeknownst to us, the Italian government was teetering on the edge of collapse. Italy and Germany were still allies and the German Army heavily occupied the Italian peninsula. After a number of secret meetings among General Eisenhower's representatives, Italian political leaders appointed by the king, and the Italian Army high commander, it was agreed that Italy would surrender. But the Allies wanted more—they wanted the Italians to turn *against* the Germans and help us in the war.

As part of this negotiation, it was decided that the 82d Airborne would deploy to the mainland. The plan was to drop one or two regiments of troopers around the airfields at Rome, and depend on the Italian Army for logistical support (communication, transportation, trucks, fuel, food, and water) until the beachhead forces landed. Even under the best of conditions, it would have been a pretty tricky operation.

Very luckily for the 505, the plan was canceled. Even as it was, we had a very close call. The pathfinders of the 504 PIR took off, as scheduled, on September 8. They were actually in the air when they got the word to postpone. The mission was definitively called off on September 9, the very day the 505 was scheduled to make the jump. As it turned out, the Italians had backed down. Their excuse was that the Germans had reinforced the area around Rome with mechanized and armored troops, which made the German position much stronger than it had been when the Italians had agreed to the operation. And so the saying goes, "With friends like that, who needs enemies?"

The enlisted men were never told anything about this operation, called "Giant II," although officers had already been briefed on it. I remember marching along on a training exercise when the guesses and rumors were flying about. "Where do you think we'll go?" and "What are we gonna do?" was all you heard. Off the top of my head, I said, "I'll bet those dumb bastards are going to send us up to the airfields at Rome." I got a very quick double take from my platoon leader, which I didn't understand at the time. It was not until much later that I realized I had hit it right on the head. As it turned out, Rome was not taken until early June 1944, ten months later.

While Giant II was being planned, a halt was put to all medical evacuations from the unit. As soon as the operation was canceled, men who were seriously ill, people with malaria like Zunda, for example, reported to sick call. Our doctor and battalion surgeon, Lieutenant Stein, loaded up orders for men to be sent to the hospital. They were long overdue for hospitalization, but their absence soon was sorely felt when the regiment was committed to its second combat mission. The 505 had picked up many EGBs, but it was still understrength on the jump at Salerno, Italy.

Chapter 10

First Combat Jump: Salerno, Italy

Italy capitulated on September 8, 1943, and the Germans took control of many Italian military units, making prisoners of their former allies. Meanwhile, many missions for the 82d Airborne were planned and abandoned, including the one at Rome and another that called for a landing north of Naples at the outlet of the Volturno River. The objective area was too far north for the Allied air forces to provide air cover for the Navy; because of the great distance from their airfields to operation areas, they would have run out of fuel.

The plan that finally went into effect aimed to establish a beachhead about fifty miles south of Naples in the Bay of Salerno, where a small projection of the mountainous peninsula stuck out to form a wide, sheltered bay. The Allies were going to try something different at Salerno. There would be no preliminary naval bombardment, an effort to keep the mission secret and thereby catch the Germans by surprise. The Fifth Army, commanded by LtGen Mark Clark, was the American headquarters controlling the Salerno invasion force. The beachhead was coordinated with the British Eighth Army, which had already crossed the Strait of Messina at the toe of Italy and was working its way up from the toe toward Naples.

The Fifth Army landed at Salerno on September 9. The landing area was quite large, but around five miles inland the bay was surrounded by very high hills and mountain ranges. The terrain vastly favored defense over offense—and on September 9, the Germans were waiting. Far from being surprised, they had figured out the most likely spots for a beachhead, and had moved reinforcements down to Naples and points

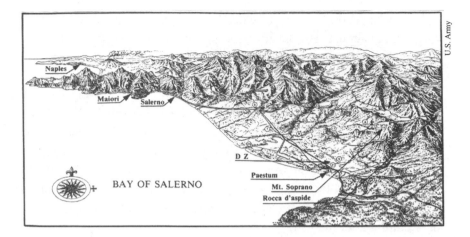

Naples

Maiori   Salerno

D Z

BAY OF SALERNO

Paestum
Mt. Soprano
Rocca d'aspide

south. Their observation of the landing beaches from the mountains and high hills inland was perfect: it was like looking down onto a stage at the theater. They had the right kind of units to counterattack the beachhead, and they had amassed a whole lot of artillery.

Salerno turned out to be as close as the Allies ever came to losing a beachhead in all the battles of World War II. On D+4 and D+5 the situation became so critical that plans were made to evacuate. General Clark moved to commit his available reserve, and decided to use the 82d Airborne. On September 13, MajGen Matthew Ridgway received his orders: the 504 and the 505 were to drop just behind friendly lines as quick reinforcements to help secure the beachhead. The independent 509 Parachute Infantry Battalion was to drop behind the lines near Avellino, twenty miles north of Salerno, to harass the enemy and prevent the flow of German reinforcements to the beachhead. Ridgway's first thought was to avoid a recurrence of the tragic airborne incident at Sicily. He insisted that all ground and naval forces be ordered to hold their fire the night of the 13th. Clark sent staff officers to all the antiaircraft battalions to insure these orders were carried out, and strict orders were given to the naval force as well.

Just nine hours after receiving the order, Ridgway had the 504 in the air, using loading plans that had previously been made for other jump locations. Ninety planes dropped 1,300 paratroopers on the beachhead within thirteen hours of General Clark's order. This included the entire regiment except for the 3d Battalion, which came in by sea with the division's artillery battalions and the 325th Glider Infantry Regiment.

Salerno was the first time pathfinders were used, and they were employed to good advantage. By the time the 504 came in, the pathfinders had marked the drop zone with a large "T" made of flaming oil drums.

The 509 and the 505 jumped into Italy on September 14. It was my first combat jump. It was a bright, moonlit night. Everyone was high-strung and nervous. We flew over water from the airfields of Sicily, guided along the Italian coast by new Eureka radar sets. In most cases, the Air Corps dropped us on the DZ, right on the beaches themselves. The first thing I saw going out of the plane was the blazing drums below. We landed and assembled in good order, then moved to the southeast portion of the beachhead. It was the easiest of any of the combat jumps I would make throughout the war.

The 504 and the 505 initially moved to the Mount Soprano area of the beachhead to relieve units from the 36th Infantry Division. I mainly remember how heavily loaded we were. I was carrying my own weight, nearly 150 pounds—my individual weapon, a rocket launcher, several rockets, a can of MG ammunition, and my personal gear. Our heavier equipment was dropped in equipment bundles. The real problem was how to transport it once we were assembled. The recent medical evacuations had made the regiment way understrength, yet every squad had to carry the same armament as if it had all its members. This meant a far heavier load for every one of us.

On September 16, the 504 was given the mission of taking the high ground around Altavilla. Now very heavily defended by the Germans, this area had already changed hands several times. The 505 was to set up roadblocks on Mount Soprano and the surrounding foothills to preclude any movement of German forces from that end of the beachhead. Company F's position was not too high up on the range. We were to wait there for contact with the British, who were still working their way northward to Naples.

British lorries took us to our initial position. We didn't meet any resistance. Our elevation offered us a ringside seat to observe the fireworks of aerial and naval warfare. A hasty airfield had been set up as one of our first objectives. The Army Air Corps, using P-38s, a twin-fuselage fighter aircraft, attempted to schedule constant air cover, but at times the scheduling was off. The Germans had very close observation over the beachhead, and the minute the P-38s hit the airstrip, their fighters and fighter-bombers came in over the mountain ranges and gave the naval flotilla a working over. This is the first time I had ever seen a direct hit on an oil tanker or an ammo freighter. They went up with a tremendous bang.

By this time, I had been in my squad for about five weeks, and I was getting to know the men. At eighteen, I was the youngest, although they thought I was twenty-one. I doubt that anyone in the squad was over twenty-three. There was J. E. Jones, whom I particularly liked, an easy-going, happy-go-lucky guy from Alabama or Georgia; George Paris, a Regular Army man; Charles Blankenship, another Southerner, a big, friendly fellow who was in the Army before Pearl Harbor and transferred to the troopers; our BAR man, Angus Reedy; Robert L. Smith, a married soldier we always kidded because he was so faithful to his wife; and Tommy Watro, our sniper, an original 505er from Johnson City, New York. I'm pretty sure they were all privates first class. They were all "old" men who had made the jump in Sicily, as did our sergeant, John P. Gore, who came from Indianapolis, I believe. The only other "new" man I can recall was Hubert Pack, who had been an EGB448 like myself.

I give full credit to everyone who jumped in Sicily, but we still didn't have too many battle-wise, seasoned veterans in the 2d Battalion. Everyone from battalion commander on down was still receiving much needed on-the-job training in Italy. Our company commander, Capt. Neal McRoberts, for example, was a university graduate, but he had little battle experience. Sergeant Gore had gone straight to parachute school after thirteen weeks of basic training, and I noticed he still was none too sure of himself.

This situation was partly due to the fact that the 1st and 3d battalions had seen most of the heavier fighting in Sicily. In combat, everything depends on the factors of a *particular* action. You can't always rigidly follow the rules. Arnone, especially, gave us the chance to learn to adapt our tactics in the heat of battle, with relatively little loss of life. But Italy served as one big training experience for the entire 505, not only for the 2d Battalion. The whole 82d Airborne Division was very fortunate to have experienced combat prior to Normandy.

The first couple days on Mount Soprano, we were in roadblock positions, mainly waiting for the Brits to move up to us. We received artillery fire, but there were no close engagements.

During this time, I began to have trouble eating. If there was one weakness in the parachute infantry units, it was feeding the troops. Unlike other kinds of troops, we never received a hot meal once we were committed. Our regiments were meant to be lean, mean, and swift. We were lean all right, but we were so overloaded that we couldn't move as quickly as the organizers intended. We carried in everything we ate.

In a combat situation, this meant we were never more than one or two meals ahead. We never sat down or had regular meal hours; we ate on the go, as food was needed. In Italy, I think I jumped with a day of K rations and two or three days of D rations, which were used strictly for emergencies. D rations consisted of a single semi-sweet chocolate bar, heavily wrapped in waterproof paper. K rations came in waxed, waterproof boxes that each contained one meal.

Usually after we made contact with the sea-borne forces or the main body, they would issue C rations, which were much better, but bulkier, than K rations. Each meal had two cans—one containing hash, stew, or beans, and the other biscuits. Otherwise, we tried to make out by scrounging, so I have had my fill of boiled chicken-in-a-helmet. But early on in Italy, when we were in isolated, mountainous terrain far from any villages, with no one or nothing to pilfer, living off the land was not an option.

Moreover, the rations just weren't getting down to us. We often went without eating for part of the day, and would sometimes go a full day or more without eating at all. When we did have C rations, they normally weren't too bad if we could get them near a fire and heat them up to get the grease mixed in, or pour it off, but this was rarely possible on the front lines. They weren't all that appetizing cold, and the grease was hell on the system. The trouble I began to have stomaching them now would lead to real problems later on.

The British made contact at our roadblock. We were relieved of duty about five days later, and marched down to the beachhead. We loaded onto trucks and moved northeast to Rocca d'Aspide, in a mountainous area south of Naples. Our main activity there was to go out on combat patrols. I remember being out in advance of the main body on one of these, a long, hard patrol over rugged terrain.

We stuck more or less to the roads and the trails, but whenever we did move into a settled area, the natives were all out, cheering us and greeting us as liberators. Every third or fourth person could speak some broken

English, and would tell us they had relatives living in the United States. More often than not it was in Brooklyn. This astonished me, because only a few days earlier these same people had been our enemies, yet here they were, obviously proud to have family members in the States. There were even American flags flying from some of the houses. I always wondered if their relatives sent them.

I particularly remember a funny incident when we entered one of these villages full of cheering people. It was a hot afternoon, and a priest stepped out of the crowd and handed me a glass of water. Without thinking, I downed it in one large gulp. Suddenly, I had a sputtering hot throat and mouth, and my stomach was on fire. I had just been introduced to grappa—a colorless liqueur of pure distilled spirits. After that, no matter how hot the day, I usually took a tentative first sip of any drink that people in the crowd handed out to me.

We had a lot of Americans of Italian descent in Company F who could speak Italian, so we were able to communicate pretty well with the natives. One of our Italian speakers was Richard Tedeschi, called "Teddy," a dark, wiry guy from the Bronx, who was so small I don't know how he made the weight requirement to get into the troopers. Teddy and others told us many things that made us realize why the villagers were cheering our arrival. There were lots of stories of German atrocities, which had especially occurred in the last few days. The villagers said, for example, that when the Germans were moving, they sometimes tossed grenades from their truck out into the crowds on the roads just for the hell of it, causing casualties among the civilians.

Moving northward, the 505 reached Castellamare and the Sarno plain by the evening of September 29. Our own group never made contact with the Germans, but our patrols were extremely fatiguing because of the mountainous terrain. I marched in the rain through a number of nights, but the dates and locations all run together.

I do remember September 29 because of a terrible accident that happened on the road. At that point we were being transported by British lorries. Company F, or at least my platoon, had been lucky enough not to encounter much resistance along the way. We had been strafed once or twice, but we hadn't sustained any casualties. When we loaded up, we folded down what seats there were, then stacked our weapons in the right front corner of the lorry bed to make more room to lie down in the back. We all were exhausted and grateful to get some rest.

We were moving along with most of us asleep when suddenly the lorry stopped. The order came to de-truck fast. We all sat up and instantly reached for our weapons. Reedy reached over to grab his BAR. Like all of us, he was scurrying to get out of the truck, and he pulled the BAR towards him, muzzle first. In a split second, the weapon went off, firing three rounds rapid fire. Reedy fell over right on top of me. I was just getting up, and the muzzle of the BAR was a matter of inches from my head.

Reedy was dead before he landed on me. The others pulled him off, and we opened his shirt. I will never forget the sight of the three little round, blue .30-caliber holes in his chest. When he pulled his BAR towards him muzzle first, the safety must have been off and the trigger probably caught on the bolt handle of an M1 rifle stacked up with the BAR. We very sorrowfully laid his body along the side of the road and marched forward on our mission. There was nothing else we could do.

The next event I can recall occurred during combat patrol in the mountainous terrain around Castellamare. We had marched all day and were high in the mountains when the 3d Platoon was ordered to go down to reconnoiter and clear the area so the company could advance the next morning. It was pitch dark, raining heavily, and there was no time for orientation. Our lieutenant was the patrol leader. He was a great big 6 foot 2 inch, heavy, tough individual. But although he looked the part, he was actually one of the weakest platoon leaders I ever observed in the war.

It soon developed that there were two ways to get killed that night: get shot by the enemy or drop off a mountain ledge. After a number of close calls, we were told to employ flashlights. When it came down to it, our platoon leader must have decided that he would just as soon get killed by Germans as lead his men off a cliff.

Coming down the mountain, I sometimes looked off into the far distance. It was impossible to put things in perspective, but at one point I observed what looked like a huge fire. I thought to myself, "Well, we're not the only dumb so-and-sos; the Germans don't have very good light discipline either!" This fire turned out to be my first view of the volcano on Mount Vesuvius.

We finally hit a road, moved down it for a ways in combat formation, and eventually came to a cluster of houses sometime after midnight. The patrol leader decided to investigate one of them, a villa surrounded by a tall wall with an entrance gate. We took the proper precautions, going

Italian Campaign
505 PIR Advance to the
Volturno River

(September 14 - October 8, 1943)

into all-around firing positions, and he had one of our Italian-speaking soldiers rattle the gate and call out in Italian. To our surprise, the owner answered, came out and opened the gate, welcomed us into the house, and offered to fix us a big spaghetti dinner. Our lieutenant consented, and around 2:00 A.M. I had my first Italian-made spaghetti dinner. Our hosts apologized for the meal, saying it was poor because of wartime shortages. It was one of the worst spaghetti dinners I ever ate, but I was so hungry it tasted damn good.

I don't know what the lieutenant's orders said about the duration of the patrol or how we should report, but he decided to spend the rest of the night there. I'm sure none of us gave him a very bad argument. Our platoon leader was the only officer in the platoon at the time, and our platoon sergeant, whom many of us had noticed was never around when the firing got hot, was not the man to protest.

The next morning, at the crack of dawn, our outpost security spotted a jeep coming down the road and stopped it. Lo and behold it was

Colonel Gavin, who immediately asked to speak to our platoon leader. I'm sure that Gavin was quite unhappy with what he found. He ordered us to keep patrolling until we made contact with the enemy. Our lieutenant wasn't with us for very long after that.

We continued the patrol until we got to a town that seemed to be a suburb of Naples. I later realized this was probably Torre del Annuziata. We held up there until the rest of the company and battalion caught up with us. This must have been September 30. That night, the 3d Battalion of the 505 was attached to the British 23d Mechanized Brigade. They entered Naples on October 1, following a British reconnaissance unit. The 1st and the 2d Battalions followed shortly behind.

Thanks to the 3d Battalion, the 505 can make a claim to liberating the first major city in Europe. The 3d Battalion guarded General Clark when he made his "Triumphal Entry" into Naples accompanied by General Ridgway. They were the first American troops to enter the city. Their commander, Maj. "Cannonball" Krause, was a real showman with a mind to getting his name in the history books. He raised the American flag in Naples, and would later raise this same flag again when the 505 liberated the first town in France, Ste. Mère-Eglise in Normandy.

By the time the 1st and 2d battalions closed in on Naples, the city had been secured. Company F found no resistance; we were greeted as liberators. It was the first time I saw a large city that had been subjected to heavy raids by Allied bombers. The devastation was incredible. The infrastructure was badly damaged. There was no running water, no sewers, very little food, and the streets were choked with debris.

What impressed me most of all was the complete, absolute, 100 percent destruction of the harbor, which the Allies had been planning to use for logistical support. The Germans understood this, so they subjected it to a thorough and very efficient job of destruction. They blew the huge cranes used for loading and unloading, and then dropped them into the water to block the passages. They sunk all the older ships and boats in the most strategic locations, and then they blew the piers themselves. It would require the Allies many months of engineering work to clear the harbor.

Chapter II

Baptism by Fire: The Battle of Arnone

I remember the next step in the Italian campaign differently from some of my fellow troopers, who recall laying over in Naples for a while. Fatigue, lack of food, and what I later discovered were symptoms of jaundice and malaria were beginning to affect me. It seems to me that the 2d Battalion moved right into the city and out again on foot, heading north in pursuit of the German Army. The 1st Battalion followed on October 5, and participated in the following battle. The 3d Battalion stayed in Naples to cover for the regiment.

Our battalion moved out of Naples around ten o'clock on October 4. We marched in tactical formation through what must have been the largest cemetery in the city. There were thousands of above-ground vaults and mausoleums. Many had had their sides or fronts blown off, and the bombs had blown open hundreds of graves and coffins, exposing the remains. That city of the mangled, desecrated dead seemed to stretch out forever. It must have taken us an hour to march through it. It is one of my starkest and most gruesome memories of the war.

I also remember marching in "route step," five yards or five paces between men, along a road on higher ground, probably not too far outside Villa Liturno. Company F was the advance guard with the 2d Platoon as point, screened ahead by a British light-armored reconnaissance unit. The road, like many others in the region, was lined with ditches that provided some natural cover, and holes similar to foxholes that the Germans or forced labor had dug as extra air raid protection.

We passed through units of the 36th Infantry Division, and then encountered German interdiction fire. It came in steadily, two to three rounds every fifteen minutes or so. As darkness fell, the order was passed to observe strict light and noise discipline. We couldn't talk or light a match; we had to remain absolutely silent.

Sometime after dark, we noticed lights not too far up ahead. We were quite confused until we discovered it was the British reconnaissance unit, which had stopped for the night. The Brits were busy brewing their tea over one-gallon cans, filled with dirt or sand and gasoline. I couldn't believe my eyes! Here we were, on the road, under strict light and noise discipline, forbidden even to have a smoke; and there sat the Limeys, sipping their tea and nicely cooking their dinners over a huge fire.

As I later discovered, the 2d Battalion's objective was to take five bridges that crossed canals south of Arnone and then take the town itself. If possible, we were also to seize intact the bridge over the Volturno River. I could only guess that our orders were to keep moving until we made contact, because that is what we did.

I was getting awfully tired, everyone was tired, but my own fatigue had worsened because I had not been getting nearly enough to eat. For about four days, ever since Castellamare, the only things I had been able to keep down were hard biscuits and the cocoa I prepared from my C ration packet. It was hot, wet and sweet was all I knew.

I trudged along, head down, only occasionally checking the distance to the man in front of me. Any shred of romance that my eighteen-year old brain might still have attached to combat had disappeared. My mind was a complete blank, wiped out by exhaustion. I had done everything humanly possible to get myself into this damn situation—trained hard for years, jumped out of airplanes, accepted demotions, transferred to the parachute infantry—yet now that I was finally about to face real combat, I hardly had any energy.

At one moment, I must have fallen asleep on my feet even as we marched. The next thing I knew, I looked up and discovered I was all alone. In the flick of an eye, the point men had evidently seen something and given the signal—I didn't hear any command—to go into the ditches that lined the road. So there I was, standing in the open, with not one soul around me. I dived into a ditch and vowed to remain more alert.

I don't remember taking the first bridge. It may be that we crossed it without opposition, never realizing it was one of our objectives. History records that we took it by 9:00 P.M. on October 4. The fog of war is always much thicker for infantry combat soldiers than for any other branch of the Army, and my own experience on the way to Arnone certainly attests to this truth.

I vividly remember the battle for one of the other four bridges, however; it was here that I came under machine-gun fire in combat for the first time. As Company F approached the bridge towards midnight, the point discovered it was already partially destroyed. Suddenly, two, or maybe three, German machine guns took us under fire from across the canal. It wasn't a split second before we were all in the ditch with tracers whizzing two or three feet over us. Fortunately for us, they were shooting high. Their guns were close, positioned forward, from twenty-five to fifty yards off to the left and right of the road, and they really poured it onto us.

Training, adrenalin, and fear kicked in, snapping my mind and body to attention. We didn't return much fire. Our SOP said we were to await orders. So there we lay in the ditch, getting shot at. Talk about frustration! Finally, the MGs stopped.

The 2d Platoon, on point, dug in on the south side of the bridge. The 1st and 3d Platoons went into all-around circular positions and dug in, the 1st Platoon moving off to the left of the road and the 3d Platoon, which was mine, moving to the right a couple hundred yards. Sergeant Gore ordered us to string out and dig individual foxholes. I was critical of this because I thought we should pair off. Soldiers perform much better when they have someone with them, and in two-man fighting positions, we could also take turns sleeping. But that night, no one got any sleep; we all remained on 100 percent alert, waiting to attack at first light.

At the break of dawn on October 5, a tremendous fire fight broke out in the 2d Platoon's area, close to the road by the bridge. The canal was about twenty feet across, and the Germans were still in position on the other side, or had moved back in undetected through the night. Our platoon was close enough to hear the fight, but not close enough to see or participate in it. The 2d Platoon lost a number of men, and so did the Germans, who didn't hold us up long. Evidently, these enemy troops were conducting a delaying action. By the afternoon, the 2d Battalion had advanced far enough to take all five bridges that made up our original objective.

When we continued forward, Company F was no longer the advance guard. It was like all combat situations—stop and go, hurry up and wait—as we moved toward Arnone. A quarter-ton jeep sped up the road towards the head of the column with the battalion communications officer, 2dLt Richard Janney, and his driver, Cpl Francis August. The jeep hit a land mine, and was blown to pieces before my eyes, resulting in the deaths of both men. It was tragedies like this that made us battle-wise. We later placed as many sand bags as we could collect on the floors of front line vehicles, to take up some of the shock if they hit a mine.

We went into another hasty defense position within a mile or a mile and a half of Arnone, and held up for the night again. During the day we'd been subjected to intermittent artillery fire, which told us the Germans knew we were approaching. We no sooner got situated than we received orders to go out on another night combat patrol. My platoon had been on the go now for three or four days and most nights.

We left on patrol shortly after dark, moving out in combat-patrol formation. We were to move forward to the bank of the Volturno River, and set up an ambush or take action to capture prisoners. When we got to the riverbank, our platoon leader decided to lay an ambush rather than move up and down the bank and draw fire or attempt to capture prisoners. Let's just say he was no more aggressive than when he had decided to lay over in the villa after that late spaghetti dinner.

Our lieutenant did make one heroic proposition that night that is legend in 505 lore. Our patrol included members from other platoons, and Richard Tedeschi was one of them. Because Teddy both spoke and looked like a native Italian, the lieutenant got the bright idea of sending him into Arnone. He told Teddy to find some civilian clothes, swim across the river, and check out the Germans. "Lieutenant," Teddy answered, "I'll go across if you come with me."

All of us spent the better part of the night on the riverbank in ambush position, including Teddy. We were on 100 percent alert. I was exhausted and shaking with cold, and I'm sure my comrades were in the same condition. When we did not get a prisoner by three or four in the morning, the lieutenant decided to return to our company defensive position.

We had gone out on patrol so soon after our arrival that we hadn't had time to dig our individual slit trenches. In my exhausted state, I had to argue myself into digging my trench. I finally dug a very shallow hole. I got below the surface of the ground, but that's about it. It was an extremely quiet night. I could hear the German artillery fire on the north bank of the Volturno River, and then hear the shells coming in. I had just settled down in my trench to catch some sleep, when I heard a shell coming my way. It was going to land very, very near.

That shell hit so close that the crater almost connected with my slit trench. The concussion from the explosion actually lifted the lower part of my body up out of the trench. I had never experienced anything like it; one moment I was in my trench, and the next thing I knew, I was halfway out of it. I heard yells and sounds of confusion, and people came running over. They wiped the dirt off of me, and discovered I wasn't injured, only badly shaken. Evidently, the shrapnel had already preceded the shock force. And so I survived my first close encounter with artillery fire, thanks to a little luck and the argument I'd had with myself to dig that slit trench, no matter how shallow.

According to the regimental history, all companies in the 2d Battalion sent out patrols on the night of October 5, but discovered very little sign of the Germans. The next morning, around 9:00 A.M., one of the other Company F platoons moved into Arnone and discovered the Germans had abandoned it. The rest of us then advanced, deployed in combat formation. The closer we got to town, the more resistance we encountered, not so much in small arms but in artillery fire from across the river. As our 1st and 2d platoons entered the town, they did receive small arms fire, and a fire fight developed.

The 3d Platoon was to the rear of the 1st and 2d platoons, on the outskirts of the town, about two hundred yards from where the fighting began. We were in support of the company, and sat out a lot of the battle. This was in accordance with tactics at the time, which taught that a commander should keep at least one-third of his force in reserve or support. At our level, we had no idea of the tactics employed; we simply wondered why we weren't in the fight.

We were lucky to be close to a well-traveled road with a lot of ditches, German-dug foxholes, and a short stretch of trench just off the berms. One end of the trench was covered with boards for about eighteen feet, similar to a dugout. The Germans stepped up the artillery, and shells burst all around us. A round hit close, and the whole squad piled into the trench. It was one mad scramble to get under the boards, with Jones, Blankenship, and Smith in the lead. Arms were flailing and legs were kicking; we did everything but pull each other out by the seat of the pants. It was nothing but one big logjam.

There was just no way we all were going to fit. We were scared as hell, but it turned into a joke. Laughingly, Jones proposed a deal. "Those of us here will get in the dugout, and you-all stay outside," he said. "And then, after a while, we'll switch off." This roused up a vocal protest. We all saw the point, but how did we know when to take turns? Did we use a unit of time, and switch every five minutes? Or did we count artillery rounds? If we did count rounds, how close did they have to hit? A hundred yards? Two hundred? In the end, we voted to change at timed intervals. We were real democratic, including our sergeant, who was trying to squeeze under the boards with the rest of us.

As we amused ourselves with these great questions, we could tell by the amount of incoming artillery and small arms fire that the 1st and 2d platoons were having a hard time of it. We expected to get orders at any minute, but instead, we just sat in that nice, deep trench the Germans had left us and listened to the other two platoons having quite a fight. This went on so long that I wondered if our company commander had forgotten us.

Sometime after 3:00 P.M., we received orders to move forward. Our platoon leader gave Sergeant Gore a general location to the left of the company position. We were told very little except that we were being counter-attacked from across the river. It seemed that the 3d Platoon of Company F was going to be the company's left flank.

We dashed from one covered position to the next until we got into town. Arnone was a poor, typical southern Italian village, consisting of one- and two-story buildings, with dwellings attached to barns and animal pens even in the middle of town. We passed through our company CP, a partially open, shed-like building that served as a collection point for the wounded and the dead. We saw their bloodied bodies laying in the wide dirt courtyard as we passed.

We deployed to the left of the company position, where it was reported that the Germans were attempting to counterattack. To do this, the enemy had to recross the Volturno River, and Company F's left flank was exposed.

Sergeant Gore broke down our location into individual areas. We were about to get some on-the-job training in how to fight in a built-up area. None of us, including our sergeant, had any training or practice at this; at most, I'd watched a training film on it. Even when a unit is committed as a full fighting force at the same time—and we had been committed piecemeal—fighting becomes insulated in a town.

I took up a fighting position on the far left flank, on the south slope of the roof of a one-story house. It was made of coarse material, something like straw or thatch, and the ridge ran parallel to the river. This was fast-flowing, but relatively narrow, about fifty to seventy-five yards wide. I couldn't see anyone else from the squad, but I knew there were one or two men to a house, forming an outline of our position.

I had good observation to the far bank. The roof ridge provided a solid rest for my rifle. My position gave me some cover and concealment, but I was still partially silhouetted from across the river. I remember thinking, "I've carried a damn rifle for two and a half years with no real opportunity to use it, and I sure as hell am going to use it now." And use it I did; it was hard to get a good target, but I did a hell of a lot of shooting at suspected positions.

German bullets cracked all around me, showering the house and the roof. My head and shoulders stuck up across the ridge; I kept moving my position left and right, so as not to present a stationary target. I also was afraid my smoke would give me away; our rifle and small-arms munitions were supposed to be smokeless, but compared to the superior German munitions, ours were almost as bad as the old black powder from the Civil War. It was impossible for me to determine the Germans' positions by observing smoke from their small arms. Mine, however, hung over me, like a sign saying, "Here I am."

I had a very difficult time keeping my eye on what was going on in our squad area, let alone on what was happening in the center and right flank of Company F, in the 1st and 2d platoons. The buildings obstructed our vision and made us physically segregated. You never like to break a unit down to more than half a squad, but we were completely fragmented.

I kept on firing for a good while, shooting where I thought the Germans would be if they were in position to give covering fire for the assault on the 1st and 2d platoons. I do not know how long this went on; it could have been about an hour. I had to watch myself so I did not run out of ammunition. I knew we would not be resupplied.

Eventually, I noticed that the fire to our right, in what seemed to be the 2d Platoon's position, was dying down. Orders were still not being passed down. Again, I thought our commander had forgotten us. Finally, we got orders to withdraw, and take roughly the same route back. There was still some daylight as we started moving to the rear.

When we came back through the positions of the other platoons and the CP, the 1st and 2d platoons had already pulled back, leaving two or three people to cover their withdrawal. There were still some dead and wounded to be removed. It took several trips to get them all. I helped several others carry the body of one of our troopers out. We had two to four people carrying that improvised stretcher, and it was still very heavy. I had heard the term "dead weight" before, but that was the day I understood the meaning.

I was greatly relieved to get into our new defense line. This position was strung out along the road that ran parallel to the river, no more than two hundred or three hundred yards south of Arnone. We formed our main line of resistance on the south shoulder of this road. The 3d Platoon was on the left of the company position, with my squad, the 1st, on the left of the platoon.

As the left flank man in the 3d Platoon, I was the furthest out on the left. We were deployed in one-man fighting positions, and because of the distance we had to cover, I was out of contact with everyone else. After a long, hard week—my first week in serious combat—I was a long way out from the nearest man, wondering if anyone except the enemy was on my flank to the left.

It was very dark that night. The road we were along was high-banked, elevated about five or six feet from the terrain to our rear, and thus it provided cover and concealment to the front. I was in a nice, deep, German-dug foxhole.

I don't know how long I'd been in position when I heard movement behind the road and to my left. I waited and got ready. Next I heard very distinct voices moving towards me. It sounded like a number of men were heading my way. I listened with all my might to distinguish words from what seemed to be excited babbling. The voices I heard all were speaking German.

I was more than puzzled—I was almost petrified. I was out there to provide security; if I could not stop the danger, it was my duty to shoot to warn the company. I had my rifle ready to start shooting when the thought went through my mind that there were probably too many of them for me to get at one time. I grabbed a fragmentation grenade and had the pin half pulled when something made me wait.

The sign that night was "Carolina," and the countersign was "tobacco." I challenged and went into a crouch in my hole. The reply "Tobacco" came over loud and clear, quickly followed by the statement that it was Company E coming in on Company F's position. I was very pissed off, and also greatly relieved.

One of the Company E officers advanced to my foxhole, and I proceeded to chew his ass out regardless of the difference in rank. The officer let me go on a few moments, then stopped me to explain. Company E had captured some prisoners, who were being interrogated at the time they approached Company F's position. They had actually been moving into a forward combat position, speaking German, with no point, no scouts, and no security at all out in front of them. The officer agreed it was one of the stupidest things he had ever done in his life. I assured him it came close to being the last.

What happened that night proves my point that Arnone served us as a training ground. That officer must have been very green. Luckily for him, so was the lowly private he encountered. What do you do when some joker comes in on your flank speaking German? Because I was newly committed, I went by the book: "Don't shoot until after you've challenged." They really drilled it into us. Later in the war—in Normandy, for example—I would have opened fire without hesitation.

I didn't get any rest that night outside of Arnone. I spent it in my foxhole, quaking from cold and fever. By daylight I was exhausted, freezing, and almost starving. By then, I had been subsisting on hard biscuits and hot chocolate for more than a week.

Daylight was very welcome. Word came down that another unit was going to relieve us. We had now been on the go for a week or ten days. Things were quiet enough for us to take turns getting out of our holes to go down on the safe side of the road. We could move around, maybe brew some coffee or cocoa, and discuss the previous day's action.

Company F had had a bitter battle, but we had managed to stop the Germans from crossing the river. Some of the shooting we heard was an attack by Company E, led by LtCol Mark Alexander, launched to clear Company F's left flank. They had lost a platoon leader, 1stLt David Packard. I later found out there were sixty or so casualties in the 1st and 2d battalions combined, and the heaviest death rate that the 505 had so far experienced.

While we were moving around early in the morning on October 7, we made contact with the British Army in the form of an officer who was the artillery forward observer for their 46th Division, the unit that was coming to relieve us. The British FO came up to me and we started talking. After a while he said, "You know, soldier, you don't look very well. Your eyes are yellow, and there's a very yellow cast to your skin." He thought I had what he called "yellow jaundice," and he recommended that I see the medics.

When I found our medic, he took my temperature, looked me over, and told our platoon leader he thought I should be evacuated. I managed to get back to the battalion aid station to see Dr. Stein. He and his ambulance driver had miraculously escaped death just a few days previously when a Teller mine had blown up their ambulance on a road outside of Naples. The ambulance itself had been totaled.

Dr. Stein examined me and immediately marked me as a litter case. And so my active combat experience in Italy came to an end with me on a litter waiting evacuation early on the morning of October 7, the day the 505 was relieved from front-line duty. Later that day, I was moved back to the hospital in Naples. The rest of the regiment arrived the following day with the mission to police the city.

Chapter 12

A City Torn by War:
Duty and Bombings in Naples

I was admitted as a patient to the 95th Evacuation Hospital, suffering from malaria and what was then called yellow jaundice, or hepatitis today. It was difficult to get supplies into the port, and the hospital had nothing to eat but the equivalent of C rations. These came in huge cans for mass feeding, but at least they could be heated up, which got rid of the thick layer of grease. Nevertheless, all I could ingest was hot chocolate. The warmth and sweetness continued to be a comfort to me.

The day I arrived, they put me on an IV to feed me intravenously. I had lost a considerable amount of weight. I was eighteen years old, 5 feet 11 inches, and still growing. Even when I was in full health, I weighed no more than a hundred fifty pounds, so I had not an ounce of fat to spare.

The medical authorities at the facility had their hands particularly full because of an atrocity the Germans had perpetrated in Naples. Before withdrawing north, the Germans had loaded the basement of the main post office in downtown Naples with high explosives equipped with a very long time fuse. They had been gone a week when the bomb exploded around noon on October 7, timed to create maximum damage to property and life. On October 11, another delay-fuse bomb or mine went off in the billet of the 307th Parachute Engineer Battalion, the unit to which I had originally been assigned before insisting on a transfer to the parachute infantry. This explosion leveled the building, killed eighteen engineers, and wounded fifty-six.

As wounded and dying people flooded into the evacuation hospital, the staff was ordered to clear out all the patients except for critical cases, so I was transferred to the 3d Convalescence Hospital outside of Naples. The German Army had previously had a very high-level headquarters unit in this facility, which had once been Mussolini's fairgrounds. It was a large, imposing building, constructed of white marble, surrounded by smaller buildings set in an elegantly landscaped garden that included beautiful trees and large reflecting pools forty to sixty feet long, and two and a half to four feet deep. For the first time in a long while, I was under a solid roof.

Although there wasn't any improvement in the rations, I started to gain some strength on the IV. In a matter of a few days, I was able to get out of bed. The hospital staff was literally fresh off the boat, having moved directly to the facility from the United States. Many of the people in my so-called ward, however, had been in combat. These included a number of Rangers, hard-fighting men who had received a lot of tough training with British commando units when they were formed in Scotland prior to the North Africa invasion in November 1942. They were all volunteers, an elite outfit, and were more experienced in combat than I was. I respected the Rangers and became quite friendly with several of them.

After a while, the hospital received a limited supply of other rations. To my joy, we now had cream of wheat for breakfast. It was worth waiting in line for an hour and a half to receive a mess kit full of cream of wheat and powdered milk. We also got a piece of white bread and a cup of coffee. If there were seconds, as soon as we finished our first helping, we got in line and waited for more. If not, we got into another line and waited to wash our mess gear. By the time this was done, it was time to get in line for the noon meal, providing you could stomach it. Everyone who was well enough went over the wall looking for food, especially for sweets, which those of us with yellow jaundice and malaria craved.

With the press of many more casualties than expected, the convalescence hospitals soon filled up with serious and critical cases, and patients like myself were soon displaced again. We went from our rooms in the permanent buildings to temporary wards set up in squad tents about two hundred yards from the center of the grounds. These wards resembled a company street, with six to eight squad tents on either side of a makeshift street running off a hardtop road. The tents held six to eight men each and were equipped with cots and blankets.

One day we got the word there was going to be an outdoor movie—Bob Hope in *Road to Morocco*, with Dorothy Lamour and an all-star cast. As soon as darkness set in, it was going to be shown in the plaza formed by the hospital complex, projected onto one of the white walls. The movie had just started when, without warning, a bomb exploded on the hospital grounds. The Germans' photo-reconnaissance people had evidently discovered military activity on the exposition grounds, then deduced that the Allies, too, were using it as a major headquarters. I recall no Allied anti-aircraft fire, no return of fire at all. The raid was a complete surprise.

Everyone was in a state of panic. It was a clear night, and the white buildings showed up plainly in the moonlight, making excellent aiming points. It is almost unheard of for aircraft to strafe ground targets at night, but the Luftwaffe strafed that hospital. They came in diving, opened up with their multiple machine guns, and, as they started pulling out of their dive, released the bombs. Many of the combat veterans instinctively jumped into the pools and hugged the banks or walls, trying to get some cover. By the time I got to them, they were already thickly crowded. I went for as big a tree as I could find. I actually started to dig a hole with my bare hands—anything to get below the surface. It seemed to me that the raid lasted for an hour, but it was probably only minutes long. Official reports say that eight bombs fell on the grounds. I wasn't counting, but to me it seemed like many more.

After everyone was sure the raid was over, the authorities tried to restore order. Most of the combat veterans reacted more quickly than the hospital personnel, who had never been under fire before. We ran into the wards and attempted to calm the amputees and the critically wounded, who were terrified and unable to take shelter. Then those of us who were able attempted to clear the debris and find bodies or wounded people. After what seemed like hours, a number of us returned to our ward.

Everyone who hadn't gone to the movie had been killed. The squad tents had been surrounded by fairly large trees, and I distinctly remember the absolute mulch of fallen leaves, branches, wood, cots, tents, and body parts that was all that remained of the ward. The situation was so hopeless that we didn't even try to clear the debris. At first light, we went through the piles of rubble looking for bodies or someone who miraculously might still be alive, but we didn't find anyone. This was the first time I saw human brains exposed to daylight.

That morning, once the streets had been cleared of rubble and swept, they started painting huge red crosses on the pavement, roofs, and walls of the buildings. I heard later, but don't know if it's true, that the Germans apologized for bombing the hospital.

After the raid, more tents were put up in other parts of the exposition grounds. The authorities issued shovels, and we all dug elaborate slit trenches alongside the walls so we could roll out of our cots right into a slit trench in the event of any more air raids. A number of us attempted to get discharged from the hospital and return to our units. I stayed about a week longer in the hospital, during which time the Germans visited Naples every night with such regularity that we could almost time their raids. Their main targets now were the harbor and large military installations.

When we didn't go out on the hunt for food, my new friends and I spent our late evenings or early night-time hours in our cots, watching these raids from our hospital vantage point overlooking the harbor. Even though we were located some distance away, the situation instilled us with fear. One day, we debated whether a person who was drunk would feel more or less frightened during an air raid than someone who was sober. We decided to conduct an experiment. We went over the wall, got several bottles of vino, and managed to get to the peak of drunkenness just at the time the raid began. By the time the second or third bomb hit the harbor, all of us were stone sober.

I was finally returned to F Company, 505, in decent health and able to eat normally. I was glad to be back. After the battle in Arnone, our bond was tight, and the more combat I saw with my friends in the unit, the closer I became to them.

About this time, some important changes in leadership took place in the 505. Colonel Gavin was promoted to brigadier general and became our assistant division commander. The new commander of the regiment was Col Herbert F. Batcheller, and our battalion commander, Lieutenant Colonel Alexander, became the regimental executive officer. Luckily for those of us in the 2d Battalion, his replacement was Maj Benjamin H. Vandervoort, one of the finest battalion commanders anywhere in the Army. He would remain our leader for most of the war.

Regimental activities in Naples largely consisted of patrolling the streets, maintaining law and order, doing work details, and carrying out support for the Allied military government. The civilian population of the city was starving. The going price for prostitutes was one K ration or a C ration. Later, as the rear-echelon military personnel increased, the market price doubled to two C rations. Even at this low price, parents were actually selling their daughters into prostitution in order to provide for the rest of the family.

One of our many duties was to enforce discipline along the breadlines at the military government-established ration distribution points. Without strict control over the distribution of food, the situation quickly got out of hand. Life-support facilities were virtually non-existent. Safe drinking water, sanitary sewers, electricity, gas, food supplies, transportation, medical services, refuse collection—in short, everything that makes a metropolitan area function—had been destroyed.

The black marketeers were making a lot of money, but people on the poor end of the scale had a hell of a time staying alive. At the distribution points, we had to fix bayonets and actually prod the people into lines to keep them from going into mob action as we handed out the food. Yet, after duty hours, any soldier who had the money—and most of us did—could walk a block or two, be seated in a black market restaurant complete with linen table cloths and candles, and be served a nice steak dinner with all the trimmings. Returning from the restaurant to our billets, we witnessed adults and children picking through garbage cans outside our mess areas.

There were nightly air raids. The Army had brought in a lot of smoke generator units. If there was any wind at all, they would move these units upwind and turn them on shortly before they expected an air raid to begin, in the hope of hiding targets from the Luftwaffe. The machines would generate gargantuan clouds of smoke that drifted down over the city and the harbor. I carried out my duties in the late afternoon after they had turned the generators on, sometimes working in smoke so thick that it looked like the whole city and surrounding area were bathed in heavy fog.

During this period, rumors about what would happen next were running wild. One day it was said we were going back to the States, the next we heard we might be sent to the Pacific. As far back as Africa, the rumor had been going around that we would eventually wind up in England. We called this type of information a "latrine rumor" because it always ended up being a lot of crap.

Nevertheless, it didn't come as much of a surprise when they finally said we were going to move. They didn't tell us where, they just said, "Get ready." We had to remove our division patches and jump wings, and pull our trousers out of our jump boots to more or less disguise ourselves. The sad part was that General Clark insisted that the division leave one regiment behind for his use in Italy. So, when the 82d sailed out of Naples on November 18, 1943, we left the 504 PIR behind.

Even at that late date—a month and eighteen days after we had taken Naples—the harbor was in such a state that it was still impossible to move in close enough to embark from a pier. We had to take landing barges out to our troopship, the USS *Frederick Funston*.

Chapter 13

Cookstown and Belfast, Northern Ireland

Even as our ship was sailing out of Naples, we heard many competing rumors about our destination and mission. I only knew we were steaming west and conditions were a whole lot more pleasant than those I had endured on the way to Casablanca. The *Funston*, first of all, was specifically designed to carry troops; it was not a converted passenger liner. True, we were still crowded, but there were showers enough, and fresh water, and latrines in functioning order. We were only fed two meals a day, but the food was good, with fresh baked bread and pie or cake for supper.

We passed Thanksgiving Day of 1943 on board in the port of Oran, Algeria. The meal, complete with turkey and pumpkin pie, was one of the very best I had had since joining the service. I spotted soldiers in Oran, fully clothed in our uniforms and armed with our equipment, but sporting beards, mustaches, and long hair that were far from regulation in the U.S. Army. Later I found out they were the Free French Colonial Forces employed in Italy. They were armed with the very same .30-caliber 1903

Springfield rifles that we had meticulously cleaned of cosmoline and carried on the ship to Casablanca.

We left Oran on November 29 accompanied by a huge protective convoy that headed west through the Strait of Gibraltar. At the time, the Spanish still held Spanish Morocco, and General Franco held rule over Spain. Any ship passing through the narrow body of water at the Strait was a prime target for the German U-boats that roamed the area in wolf packs. I spent many hours lying on my bunk, picturing a German torpedo sticking its nose through the bulkhead. If this had actually happened, it would all have been over so fast that I would never have known what hit us. As something to think about, it was down several notches from the magnitude of the day-to-day worry of ground combat.

After safely passing through the Strait of Gibraltar we kept heading west. The rumors that we were going home seemed to be confirmed. I passed some time with a real nice fellow called Dominick DiTullio from the 3d Battalion, 505. I had never met him before, but it turned out he was also from Erie, a local football star at Strong Vincent High School back in the late 'thirties or very early 'forties. We had many long talks about our hometown as we sailed to we-knew-not-where in the middle of the Atlantic. My new friend was killed on June 7, D-Day+1, in Ste. Mère-Eglise. He posthumously received a Distinguished Service Cross for his action on D-Day.

It was rumored that our convoy was at one time closer to the United States than to Europe. That's how big a loop we must have made. After a number of days, we turned north, and on December 9, the 505 found itself on the dock at Belfast, Northern Ireland, at the end of a twenty-one-day voyage. We went by train to Cookstown, where we were billeted in regiment-size encampments that had formerly housed British troops. Our living quarters consisted of long, narrow metal Quonset huts, with one completely inadequate potbelly coal- or wood-burning stove in the middle. Small wooden sawhorses raised about a foot off the concrete floor formed the leg supports for our beds. Between the sawhorses were three planks that supported mattresses filled with straw. At the very most, we had two woolen GI blankets.

There was no running water in the huts, which each housed fourteen to eighteen men. I think we had company-size latrines, located in another Quonset hut with wooden bench-type seats all in a long row, and a 20- or 30-gallon bucket beneath each hole. A trap door opened from the back of the latrine. The Irish farmers came in daily, picked up our waste, threw it in a wagon, and spread it in their fields for fertilizer. It was a convenient arrangement, but the Army warned us against eating too much of the local lettuce.

The Cookstown winter was very damp. We did experience some snow while we were there, which was a first for many of my friends from California and the South. Although they were already seasoned soldiers who had faced the terrors of combat, the memory of those troopers horsing around in the snow for a few, carefree moments always reminds me of our comparative innocence at the time. Those who survived our coming missions in Normandy and Holland would get their fill of snow in the Battle of the Bulge just one year later, where many would die in a desolate, bitter cold landscape.

We had no hard training in Northern Ireland, for there was no terrain to train on. Land was too scarce to take it away from food production and other civilian uses. We did, however, extend our usual cross-training on all individual and crew-served weapons to include the main infantry antitank weapon at the time, the 57mm antitank gun. The PIRs didn't yet have antitank guns, but we hoped to get some in by glider after the initial drop on our next mission. If the crews for the 57mm in the gliders were killed or wounded, the PIR troopers had to be able to load and fire the guns.

While we were billeted in Cookstown, I obtained a pass to visit the regiment to which I'd been assigned for several months back in Georgia and Alabama. The 507 was stationed near Belfast, at Fort Brush. My old company, Company I, was billeted in civilian housing, if I remember correctly, but after the first half dozen drinks with my old friends, I lost track of a lot of details.

I do remember how they all wanted to hear about the use of the parachute troops in combat operations. I got the chance to expound a little on my personal philosophy about staying alive in combat. I had a bunch of very eager listeners. This philosophy boiled down to four main points: Dig in and get below the ground surface; as a private, never volunteer; always stay alert when within enemy mortar and artillery range; and always be security conscious.

We had a very liberal pass policy in Northern Ireland, which was radically different from what we had been used to in Africa, Sicily, and Italy. Belfast was a big town, which for us meant girls, music, and booze.

This latter, like everything else in the United Kingdom, was rationed, so all the bars were open for a limited number of hours each day. One of the most familiar sayings in all the American units was the warning the bar was going to close: "Time, gentlemen, time!" Another was, "The Yanks are over paid, over sexed, and over here." A private's pay in the paratroopers, $50 a month supplemented with $50 jump pay, made us the highest paid military organization in the world.

In Belfast, you could buy a bottle of black market booze—scotch, bourbon, or Irish whisky—for $20, which made it the equivalent of five pounds. This made whiskey expensive even on a paratrooper's salary. On the other hand, we thought that the price of beer and whatever food we could find in the civilian economy was quite reasonable. I was introduced to Guinness, which wasn't too powerful. I discovered that if I drank a lot of it, I still could get drunk. To my sorrow, it gave me a bad case of diarrhea.

We enjoyed the companionship of a good many females, both civilian and military. The female component of the British Army was the ATS, or Auxiliary Territorial Services, also called Terries. After a few dates with some of them, I decided that ATS really stood for Always Thirsty and Starved. They could out-drink, out-eat, and generally out-do a man. The British also had a volunteer women's organization, the Women's Land Army, or the WLA. They replaced farm boys, and wore breeches with knee-length leggings. WLAs were hefty, strong, and physically tough. It was said that a man who made a pass at one of them had better be able to defend himself, whether the response was negative or positive.

On the whole, there were a lot of good people in Northern Ireland, although they could be prejudiced and narrowminded. Many older civilians were quite upset with the Yanks, as they called us. Mothers and fathers were none too happy when we attempted to date their daughters. I guess I can't really blame them. By the time I got there it was late '43, so Northern Ireland had had a steady dose of the American military for a year. Anyone who has lived around war-time U.S. Army soldiers for that long might get a little narrowminded.

Of course, a lot of the Northern Irish were against the Yanks because Americans were often Catholic. Needless to say, Catholics dating their women didn't go over big with the Orangemen, the Church of England people. And I must admit that at times, we Yanks were capable of doing things that only added fuel to the fire. All we had to do was get a few beers under our belts in a pub, and some ignorant so-and-so would suggest we start singing, "They're hanging men and women for the wearing of the green."

Despite the prejudice and tensions, we Yanks had a pretty good time in Northern Ireland. For the first time since we'd left home, we were in a country that had not been too badly disrupted by the war. For the first time, too, we could carry on a conversation with the people who lived where we were stationed. It was our first taste of what seemed like real civilization in nine or ten months, and we were very happy to be there.

I received invitations to the homes of people I barely knew. I particularly remember Christmas Eve, 1943, when I was on a pass to Belfast. I got an early start on the drinking that day and met up with a Northern Irish sailor home on leave. By the time we were both pretty well gone, he invited me to his home. That Christmas Eve, in a strange house and surrounded by a strange family, I got on my first and last crying jag. It wouldn't have happened if I hadn't been drinking, but cry I did. I was ashamed of myself, but the sailor's family graciously overlooked my breach of etiquette. I left as soon as I could after midnight.

On February 13, 1944, our unit left Cookstown and headed for England via Scotland. A rear detachment was left behind to turn in "post camp and station property" to the British Army. I must have been on someone's shit list, because I was selected to stay. In some cases, rear detachment can be a pretty good deal, but conditions always depend on the schedule the receiving agency sets up. We got a British sergeant major too old for line duty. He had a million years in the Army and was an arrogant son of a bitch. He considered it his patriotic duty to account for every bit of equipment owed the British Army down to the last teaspoon.

Two items especially gave us a bad time. One was the shit buckets. We actually had to scrub these by hand with GI soap and water. We also got a hard time about the bed boards. Due to cold weather and coal rationing, we'd chopped some of them up and burned them in the stove. Each cot originally had three bed boards, but by the end some of us were balancing uncomfortably on a single board. He insisted on counting them all, and entered every missing board on his inventory list.

Rear detachment also had a major fringe benefit, especially for the lucky trooper who got the guard post at the main gate to the billeting area. This presented a sterling opportunity to make many new acquaintances when the lonely young women of Cookstown walked out to camp to ask why their boyfriends had abandoned them. Of course, they knew the reason as well as we did, and we also knew this question meant they were looking for new boyfriends. I remember standing guard at the gate and sadly thinking, "So many opportunities, so little time."

Fortunately, discipline in the rear detachments was a lot more relaxed than usual. It was the dead of winter, so it was no longer possible to meet for liaisons outside, and especially in Northern Ireland, the reputation of any girl seen going into a hotel with a soldier would have suffered tremendously. War is hell. Or rather, it would have been—except that there were more warm bodies in the Service Company billets than the number of troopers assigned to the bunks. I'm very glad the officer of the day and the officer of the guard were broad minded, because if they had stuck to regulations some of the rear detachment would still be serving out their court-martials. And so it was that after scrubbing out the shit buckets, counting all the burnt-up bed boards, and closing down our battalion encampment, for a day or two we had some merry times in Northern Ireland.

Chapter 14

Camp Quorn, England

The 505 left Northern Ireland on February 13, 1944. Our destination was Camp Quorn in the hamlet of Quorndon in Leicestershire. Shortly after we arrived, I was promoted back to sergeant and given a rifle squad. I especially appreciated being jumped over the corporal rank. I was assigned the 1st Squad of the 3d Platoon of Company F, 2d Battalion. It was a big job for a nineteen-year-old, and I took it with utmost seriousness. Except for one other, very brief assignment, I kept this position until I was promoted to platoon sergeant in early 1945.

The local population warmly welcomed us. They made us feel as close to home as we could get without actually being there. The entire regiment was billeted in squad tents right in the town of Quorn. If we went over the wall surrounding the camp, we landed on the sidewalk—we were that close. Sometimes we'd be sitting in our tent and decide we wanted something to eat. Off we'd go over the wall, and in twenty minutes we'd be back with fish and chips.

We quickly discovered there were many female military units stationed nearby: the ATS, the WLA, women Air Force members, and female Navy personnel. There was always plenty of fun whenever the ATS girls invited us to one of their company beer parties. They often acted almost as rowdy as we did, which greatly added to our entertainment. We also struck up many friendly acquaintances with civilian women. Most English male adults were stationed away from home in the military, and many had been in the service since 1939. No doubt about it, our troopers were courting a lot of English servicemen's wives. Of course, not all the courting was illicit; about eighty of our troopers married English women they had met while we were there.

Besides going to Leicester and Loughborough, we could set off in any direction and find small crossroad towns. During the war, the English set their clocks *two* hours forward in the spring, so after duty it was still daylight. Many troopers headed across the fields toward their favorite pubs carrying raincoats or ponchos when there wasn't a cloud in the sky. These garments, it was safe to assume, would be used to cover the ground while wooing local women. Coming back across the fields after dark, you had to be careful not to trip over couples lying along the hedgerows. On several occasions, I actually stumbled across two very warm bodies.

Anywhere three or four houses were clustered, the community would have a very friendly, family-type pub, and it seemed to me that each company favored a certain one and adopted it as its own. Company F went to a little pub in Woodhouse Eves, and it was just like coming into Company F's day room—when or if we had ever had one. People gathered to have a beer in the evening, and there was usually a piano in a corner. Someone would sit down, start playing a tune, and maybe sing, and before you knew it, everyone would be singing. It was a good, friendly, relaxed family atmosphere. I always enjoyed walking in the door and seeing my friends and other GIs fraternizing with the locals. Many of the friendships developed in these pubs lasted a lifetime.

We had got in some replacements in Northern Ireland, and at Quorn we got in more. This brought the regiment up to full strength, maybe a little over. We practiced squad and platoon tactics with the men we knew would be in our unit going into the next combat operation. This made a difference in my thinking. To get the most out of our training, I tried to develop teamwork and know every man's true capabilities. The company commander often turned the training over to the platoon leaders and they, in turn, issued the squad leader an order, then left us to decide how we should do it. The type and quality of the training and, I believe, the number of casualties later in combat, depended directly on the squad leader's experience.

Going into Normandy, which would be our next mission, I had the good fortune, reinforced by stiff training, to have a squad that consisted largely of excellent soldiers. Partly because their survivors have requested information about the men who formed my squad, but mainly because I would like to pay them tribute, I here name the men who were with me in Normandy. Of the men who already were in the squad before I entered as a private, four were still with us on D-Day: George Paris and Robert Smith, who both had made the jump in Sicily; Thomas Watro, the squad sniper, and a damn good one at that, and Hubert Pack, a rifleman and fearless combat soldier from Tennessee who joined the squad as a replacement about the same time I did.

Newer members included Harold Post, a good soldier and rifleman, who came in as a replacement in England; Howard Krueger, a close friend and my assistant squad leader; W. A. Jones, a rifleman from Texas and a top-rate soldier; and John Zunda, another good rifleman who later became my assistant squad leader.

Then there were Donald Bohms, Arthur Lemieux, and John Corti, who all were excellent troopers; Lloyd Eisenhart, a good, strong soldier and a married man with children, who later replaced Corti as BAR man; Bill Hodge, an excellent soldier and a close friend to this day; and Andrew Fabis, our first scout and a very good friend, whose knowledge of German certainly spared us from heavier casualties than those we actually endured.

I also have to mention J. E. Jones, another close friend, an excellent NCO, and my assistant squad leader in Quorn, who volunteered for the pathfinders in Normandy. Finally, this list would be incomplete without two other men whom our platoon leader most often assigned to our squad: Lawrence Neipling, an eager-beaver, top-notch machine gunner from El Cajon, California; and Leonard (Tony) DeFoggi, our assistant machine gunner, from Butler, Pennsylvania. I honestly doubt that a better rifle squad can be found in the annals of Company F history.

Having the responsibilities of a squad sergeant was a good thing for me. I was responsible for up to fifteen lives, and I welcomed the duty. I knew I would get along better in combat as a leader than as a private, when I was mostly worried about my own survival and putting up with orders I didn't completely agree with. As a squad sergeant, my mind was on my men. This helped lessen my fear, because I thought much less about the possibilities of being killed or wounded myself. I also no longer had to take orders from a squad leader who wasn't as well trained as I was. I had more confidence in myself than I had in my previous squad leader. My long training and experience as a combat leader taught me many things, but none is more important than this: know your men as well or better than your weapon. Know their strengths and weaknesses, and act upon this knowledge when making assignments and giving awards.

Corporal J. E. Jones and I had to act on this principle when a soldier from another battalion transferred into our squad in Quorn. Jones and I already had a pretty good idea of what had incited the transfer. The man in question was a good peacetime soldier who had joined the Army long before the war; he kept his boots shined, liked joking around, and was good at making friends. But we had observed him under fire in Italy, and when the going got tough, he always disappeared. When the shooting stopped and we looked around, somehow he was there again.

To make matters worse, this combat-shy solder was assigned as our first scout. My corporal and I took action. We paid a visit to our lieutenant, "Little Joe" Holcomb, in his quarters, and asked for the soldier to be reassigned as a rifleman or ammo carrier. At the higher levels of command, our concern could seem like a trifling thing, but Jones and I knew that a mistake on an essential job like first scout could lead to much higher casualties. Our platoon leader asked why we wanted the reassignment, but we wouldn't say. The accusation of being combat-shy was so serious that we would never have made it openly unless we were intent on getting rid of him entirely. We only reiterated that we wanted his assignment changed, and Little Joe complied with our request.

Preparation for our upcoming mission included night jump exercises at Quorn. I think the real purpose was to make sure that *all* of us, new men and old, would jump the next time in combat. The official word, however, was that our commanders wanted to simulate the scatter that actually occurs in a night jump, and practice night assembly procedures. These called for us first to determine the flight direction of the plane directly after our chute opened. After landing, the first half of the stick headed in the direction of the plane, while the last half went in the direction the plane had come from. Theoretically, we would meet in the middle on our designated DZ, where leaders would take over their units.

Two main problems were intrinsic to our night exercises. First, although night jumps did help train us in procedures, every jump produced injuries like broken arms, legs, and ankles. Secondly, the Air Corps typically had a damn hard time dropping us on the right DZs. The Army set about to remedy this by giving troop carrier commanders, pilots and navigators more instruction in night formation flying. New navigational aids and procedures were also instituted in the effort to improve Air Corps efficiency, and the 505 developed Pathfinder teams to use these aids to best advantage. Since each battalion had its own DZ, each one had its own Pathfinder team. The 505 consisted of three battalions, so the regiment had three teams of its own.

To cut out the injuries that had always plagued our practice jumps, we began to practice and train for night assembly operations without actually jumping. Under battalion control, all companies were loaded onto deuce-and-a-half trucks, and scattered on small roads and trails. Units were broken up into individuals or two-man teams that had to make their way back to an assigned assembly point using green flares and lights. These exercises simulated the difficulties we were likely to encounter on a combat drop and provided good training in locating the battalion assembly point.

With D-Day approaching, it became imperative for the Air Corps to conduct a full-fledged dress rehearsal of their part of the invasion. This practice run was all the more necessary since D-Day was planned to be the largest airborne operation that had ever taken place. For some reason, the Air Corps required one or two paratroopers to fly in each plane. I was one of the (not-so) lucky troopers selected. We didn't actually jump; all we did was buckle on a free-fall chute—a chute without a static line—and go along for the ride.

On the day and night of the rehearsal we got fog, rain, and very cloudy skies. As a result, the Air Corps lost control of the exercise and *thousands* of airplanes scattered over England with no strict control. This was in addition to the takeoff of regular bomber flights, fighter sweeps, and so on. Visibility was almost zero, and there were mid-air collisions.

I spent many anxious hours in the plane, looking out the door and checking to make sure my parachute was ready if I needed it. I could see planes going beneath and above us, and passing diagonally. Eventually, our pilot got word to put his plane on the ground as soon as possible. So many of the formations had broken up and scattered that it would have made matters even worse to try to get them back to their home fields. We landed in the south of England, and I was mighty glad to get both feet back on the ground. It was a day or two before we got back to the regiment. This exercise did not inspire us with newborn confidence in the Army Air Corps.

Throughout our time in England, the Army had above-normal AWOL rates. Some of our boys got wandering feet while we were at Quorn, and I got the job of bringing one back. His name was James McCallum. He happened to be a very good combat soldier, but he was also young and from the hills of Virginia, and sometimes he wanted to kick his up heels more than his passes would allow. It was the company's responsibility to pick up its own AWOL soldiers. I went with another sergeant, John Ray, to pick up McCallum and bring him home under armed guard.

Ray and I went up to Glasgow by train, packing our .45s. We reported in to the MP station, signed our trooper's release as the MPs required, and took him into custody. Then we checked into the first overnight accommodations we could find, locked up our .45s, and all three of us went out for a good time. We did get back with the prisoner as ordered, but we managed to squeeze in a night on the town in Glasgow.

Another time, I came close to getting listed as AWOL myself. Word had it that the 4th Infantry Division had moved to England. This was the unit my stepbrother Harry Fitzgerald was in, so I got a three-day pass and set off to visit Harry. Because I had to go through London, I got off the train to look up my old buddy Elmer Carlson, who had ended up stationed in the center of the city. We'd been corporals and sergeants together in the 112th Infantry.

Elmer was one of the special friends who had seen me through the very sad times after my sister's death. It had been a good while since I had met up with him. Instead of being sent to a hot combat zone, he'd been assigned to a transportation company as a motor officer or some other silly thing. He was pretty well teed off about his assignment, but it also meant he could live high off the hog in London as long as his money held out.

By the time I met up with him, Elmer had been in London for quite a while. As an officer, he was able to take advantage of a liquor allowance that granted him the privilege of buying a rationed amount of booze. The city was in complete blackout, but Elmer knew his way around the pitch-black streets like the back of his hand. We really whooped it up. Picadilly Circus was so thick with prostitutes that the standing joke was that they put out heavy trip wire so the soldiers couldn't get past.

Yet the longer Elmer and I were together, and the longer we drank, the more I could see he was champing at the bit to get transferred back to the regular infantry, so he could put his leadership and infantry training to use. I begged him not to rush into anything. "Listen, Elmer," I told him. "Once the war is over, no one will know who's been in combat and who's been sitting on his ass in London. Don't take the risk and get yourself killed." Under the effect of so much alcohol, I became depressed. I was convinced I'd never see Elmer again, and that I'd never make it through the next combat mission.

We were talking about something of the sort, sitting in a pub about midnight, when a large group of MPs from several different nations walked in. I remember seeing American, British, and French MPs, but there were others, too, as well as plain-clothes policemen. They blocked all the exits and conducted a person-by-person search; identification, passes, leave papers, and any and all orders were inspected. They asked not only who we were, but why we were there, and by whose authority.

Now I did have a pass, but it was a pass to my stepbrother's division location, not a pass to London. I had to do a considerable amount of fast talking, but the MPs finally allowed me to remain free, on the condition that I take the next train out of London for my pass designation. Of course I agreed. I then proceeded to complete my pass in London, got on the train and returned to my unit. I never did see Harry.

As I found out later, the MPs were looking for AWOLs and deserters. There was also a counter-intelligence aspect to the sweep as part of a mission to catch spies and espionage agents. It was a well-coordinated effort, conducted throughout all of England at exactly the same time. Back in the units, all the commanders had to account for all their men at a specified time. Naturally, as our billets were right in the center of town, any number of troopers were always over the wall for a while without the benefit of a pass, and many were caught out and tagged with extra duty.

This sweep and subsequent punishment had repercussions for the reputation of our new regimental commander, Col William Ekman, who had taken command of the 505 from Colonel Batcheller in March. The orders came from higher headquarters, but it was mistakenly thought in the ranks that he had personally instigated the check. Right away, he got the reputation as being a very strict, hard-ass SOB. The prejudice against him had a lot to do with the fact that he had taken command without combat experience, and the 505 was a battle-tested unit. It was the same old combat versus non-combat prejudice that got me busted from NCO to private back in Italy. At least Colonel Ekman was given the chance to prove himself. From what I saw, he was a good commander.

As May 1944 came to an end, the 505 felt increasing pressure. Events made it evident that our upcoming mission was at hand. Complete division maneuvers took place in Nottingham Forest. The camp was sealed and restricted, then reopened a couple of times, as a way to confuse enemy intelligence. We had numerous field inspections, repeatedly laying out all our equipment and weapons. In the midst of all this, my friend Russ Brown, who had been injured in a training accident, showed up, his leg still bandaged from a mortar wound. When he had heard that the 82d was getting ready to go, he managed to talk himself out of the hospital. He jumped in Normandy with his leg still bandaged up, and has the honor of being one of the few troopers in Company F who made all four of the combat jumps with the 505 RCT. Elmer also soon got in on the action. Closely following D-Day, when the Army was short of infantry platoon leaders, he was transferred and assigned to the 83d Infantry Division.

I refer to these friends because I think their attitudes were exceptional, yet typical, too, of the sentiments almost all of us were feeling on the eve of D-Day. Many soldiers who could have stayed back for any number of legitimate reasons—illnesses, wounds, assignments behind the lines—did not. They were eager to go into combat, and they made it their business to get there. Many of us suffered nightmares, depression, injuries, and fears during our stay in England, but we overcame them through the incredibly strong solidarity we felt for our friends and fellow troopers. Nothing was more crucial than that bond to our individual will to fight and prevail, nothing more essential to our pride in ourselves as a unit. As we packed our B bags, we still didn't know what our mission would be, but the *esprit de corps* of the 505 had never been stronger.

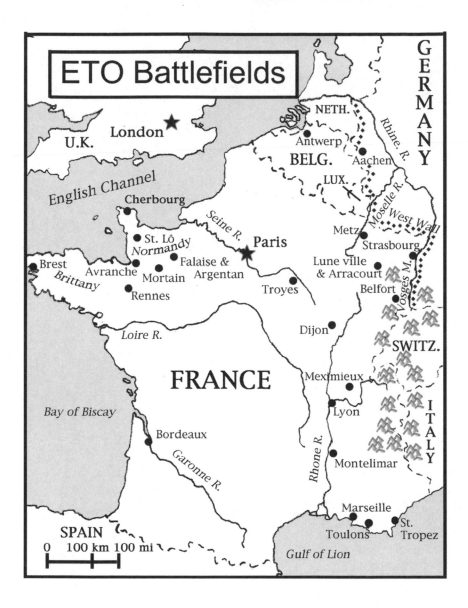

ETO Battlefields

GERMANY

U.K.

London

NETH.

Antwerp

BELG.

Aachen

LUX.

Rhine R.

Moselle R.

West Wall

English Channel

Cherbourg

Seine R.

Paris

Metz

Strasbourg

St. Lô
Normandy

Falaise &
Argentan

Luneville
& Arracourt

Brest

Avranche

Mortain

Vosges M.

Brittany

Rennes

Troyes

Belfort

Loire R.

FRANCE

Dijon

SWITZ.

Meximieux

Bay of Biscay

Lyon

ITALY

Bordeaux

Rhone R.

Montelimar

Garonne R.

Marseille

SPAIN

Toulons

St.
Tropez

0   100 km 100 mi

Gulf of Lion

Chapter 15

D-Day, Normandy:
Preparations for the Big Jump

When you're in the Army, you spend a lot of time in hurry-up-and-wait mode, where you rush everything up only to sit around for an hour, or even a day, waiting to be deployed or find out more about the situation. This is what happened in the Normandy campaign. We were sealed into Cottesmore Airfield on May 29. Barbed wire fences surrounded the airfield, and no one could leave without a guard. Rear echelon units did all our everyday duties, such as K.P. The most important activity was the briefing. For once, everyone got the big and little pictures. Sand tables showed the terrain around Ste. Mère-Eglise, the critical point on the right flank of both invasion beaches.

Our mission was to help hold the town from the outskirts, where we were to go into the defensive position at Neuville-au-Plain, which was key to protecting the right flank of the invasion beaches. My squad was to operate as an outpost, a delaying and reporting unit for the 2d Battalion. We were especially concerned about attacks from German armor barreling down from the north via Highway N–13, a high-speed approach into Ste. Mère-Eglise. As an exception to the usual practice, even platoon leaders had a period at the sand table so they could brief their platoons.

Then the invasion was postponed because of weather conditions. General Eisenhower's decision to change the mission from June 5 to June 6 was undoubtedly the most critical he ever made. A bad weather front was moving down the channel on the fourth, but a break was predicted for a 24- to 48-hour period. Because the Allied plan depended on amphibious landings, we could only launch the invasion during a lunar period producing favorable tides. It was either go on June 6 or wait an entire month.

Normandy was one of the few times before a mission that we received the order to sleep or rest for a specified number of hours. For relaxation, we played some softball and did some calisthenics to keep limbered up. There were also church services conducted right in the field. Otherwise, and this was by far the hardest thing, we spent the time thinking about how to do the job and survive. The extra time in limbo was the worst thing we ever had to endure. It was a terrible letdown after we were all hyped up and ready to go into combat.

It may seem naive now, but at no time did we ever dream that we would not be successful in Normandy. We never even mentioned the possibility of defeat. The commanders may have agreed among themselves that if the beaches were not held successfully, everyone who could get out would head for Ste. Mère-Eglise. But down at my level, absolutely nothing was said about withdrawal or evacuation.

After our briefings and discussion of the mission, they issued our ammunition and grenades, and we packed our bundles using color-coded red, white and blue chutes. The red chute designated mortars and/or ammunition: mortar ammunition, rocket ammunition, and small arms ammunition. The blue chutes, I believe, indicated our machine-gun and its ammunition, and the white were rocket launchers and rockets.

The bundles were about eight feet by ten feet, made of very heavy canvas material similar to a tarp, with a layer of shock-resistant material to take up the jolt when the bundle hit. We spread them out with the insulation face up and folded the edges in to cover our crew-served weapons—machine guns, mortars, and any other gun that required more than one man to operate. Then we rolled them as tightly as we could. Two caps fit over the ends of the bundles, and pieces of harness on either side of the caps extended and snapped them together.

Our orders were to jump, open up any equipment bundle we came across, and carry its contents to the battalion assembly place. Here it would be taken to a supply point, where weapons would be distributed. Of course, we all wanted to find our own particular bundles. We marked the outsides with extra identification and managed to slip in personal items. The crew-served weapons people were familiar with their particular guns, and understandably wanted to use their own weapons.

As a squad leader, I was issued a map of the area. This was a first for me, because they usually stopped issuing maps at the platoon-leader level. From squad leader on up we also had large ID panels to lay out, so our positions could be identified from the air, and orange smoke grenades to indicate friendly forces. We each carried an M1 rifle, with ammunition clips in pouches on our belt, and two bandoleers, each with five eight-round clips. The extra ammunition alone weighed five pounds. Selected people, squad leaders included, also carried a white phosphorus grenade. This could be thrown to set a fire, and once the phosphorus got on the skin it continued burning. It was a very ugly weapon.

The most unpopular piece of our standard issue equipment was the gas mask, which was bulky and came in a canvas case. In contrast to the mask, which mainly everyone threw away, the case was a popular item, convenient for carrying rations, ammunition, cigarettes and personal things. We also had gas indicator paint to dab on our helmets. Under certain types of gas attack, the paint would turn colors. All our clothes were chemically impregnated to protect us against gas attacks. They were very, very uncomfortable because no moisture could evaporate through the cloth. In hot weather they acted like a rubber raincoat.

We didn't have any blankets or sleeping rolls in Normandy. We went eleven days without anything to give us warmth at night, with the exception of parachutes, which were quite effective. If we could find one while we were in the drop area, we could wrap ourselves up in it. We would also have no change of clothing for many days, until our B bags arrived.

We carried our personal items plus extra socks and underwear in our musette bag, hooked and snapped for the jump with very heavy webbing. Most of us strapped our trench knife to our right leg, down at the boot. We also had a "jump knife," a spring-loaded single blade that jumped out with a flick of a button. This was kept in a small "secret pocket" located alongside the zipper on the inside of our jacket, up near the collar. After the first couple paratroopers were captured, the Germans easily found the knife, but it was intriguing to us at the beginning. To the best of my recollection, I only ever used it to cut my way out of suspension lines or open a can of C rations.

Finally, almost everyone had a pistol. This doesn't mean we all were issued a pistol; it means we had acquired one in past campaigns and through other means. At this point, a pistol was not an official item of issue, except for crew-served weapons men and maybe the platoon leaders. Most of our platoon leaders carried an M1 rifle as well as a pistol.

As part of its preparations for D-Day, the Army took special steps so men and equipment would not be misidentified. All the planes participating in the invasion had three huge stripes painted on each wing and on the fuselage, so the Navy or Army antiaircraft gunners had no excuse to mistake Army Air Corps or any other Allied aircraft as those of the enemy. This policy was a direct result of the tragedy in Sicily in July 1943.

Another precaution actually turned out to be dangerous. A white stripe was painted on the back of every officer's and NCO's helmet. A vertical white stripe indicated an officer, while an NCO's helmet sported a horizontal white stripe, about one inch wide and three or four inches long. The idea was that these stripes would allow leaders to be easily located, especially at night. It worked: they made an excellent point for taking aim when snipers zeroed in on us. We called them "aiming stakes," and immediately attempted to get rid of them, darkening them with mud or dirt as quickly as we could after landing.

Judging from the friendly fire we received on the ground, the steps taken to identify us as U.S. paratroopers were less effective than the identification on the planes. The Army then had a solid olive drab combat uniform, whereas we had two-piece khaki jumpsuits. Our regular leg infantry were either inadequately briefed, or they soon forgot what a paratrooper's uniform looked like, judging from the shots they took at us. I guess they thought it was safer to eliminate the unknown.

The Air Corps insisted that airborne commanders make up a list meticulously detailing everything we officially wore or carried. This was an attempt to figure out the total weight on the C-47s. A typewritten sheet was issued to all leaders, listing the items we carried in our jumpsuit pockets, and the different pockets to which they were assigned. It's valid as far as it goes, but it only takes into consideration the first layer of clothing. Our jumpsuit was our outer garment, but we typically bundled up inside, wearing heavy woolen OD trousers and shirts, for we knew we would be without a change of clothes for many days. When it came right down to it, we loaded what we wanted to load, and put it where we wanted to put it. But the "official" sheet was a stickler for details. Under "1 Meal 'K' Ration" and "Pay Card and Immunization Record," it lists "Prophylactics (2)," for a weight of .03 pounds. As the story goes, the first trooper into the battalion aid station at Ste. Mère-Eglise came in to ask for more condoms.

For the first few days of almost any airborne operation, we had very little anti-armor capability, and this posed one of the biggest threats to our success in Normandy. While the infantry had weapons carriers to draw their weapons, and could carry large amounts of ammunition, as paratroopers, we were limited by considerations of weight and numbers. True, all of our .30-caliber rifle and machine gun ammunition was armor-piercing, which could penetrate up to an eighth of an inch of steel plate. But even the lightly armored German vehicles had a minimum of a half-inch of armor plate, at least in the critical areas, and the tanks had a minimum of two to four inches. When we went into Normandy, it was my understanding that the regiment would have at least a dozen 57mm antitank guns arriving by glider at or near dawn. This was the heaviest towed gun we had for antitank protection, but even it was inadequate compared to the German 88mm cannon.

Even if we had had an effective antitank weapon light enough to be dropped, we still would have been limited by the ammunition requirements. Ammunition weighed so much that it was simply impossible to carry a large quantity of shells and mortars. For example, our 60mm mortar was a good little weapon, but we had to carry every round of ammunition on our backs. There were six men in the mortar squad, but it took one and a half to transport the mortar, and the others all carried a limited number of mortar rounds in vests hung over their shoulders. We had to be very careful not to waste ammunition.

We were issued British gammon grenades, a crude weapon only a super hero would want to use. It had a body like a sock that was packed with a pound or pound and a half of plastic explosives. To use it, we had to unscrew the cap very carefully and use our thumb and forefinger to hold down a tape wrapped around the neck of the grenade while we got into position to lob it. One end of the tape had a lead-shot weight, and the other held a safety pin. When we threw the grenade, the tape unwound, pulling the pin and allowing the grenade to detonate when it hit. Not only did we have to get uncomfortably close to the enemy to throw a gammon grenade, but if the safety pin came out accidentally, the thing would explode on the slightest impact.

The bottom line was that it was necessary to let the tank or enemy vehicle get within throwing distance. The worse your arm, the closer you had to let the enemy get. Tanks were almost always accompanied by infantry support, which would be firing away at us as we carefully wrapped a finger around the tape, and stood up to lob our gammon grenade. If we were lucky enough not to get killed throwing the thing, when it did hit the enemy armor, the only effect was a large explosion. This would rattle the people in the tank, but it had no penetration capability. It could only damage the track, or bogie wheels that the tank rode on, turning the tank into a stationary pillbox, manned by irascible crewmen with bad headaches.

As far as antitank mines went, we had both the knowhow and the personnel. The problem was that antitank mines were in very short supply because of their weight and bulk. The American antitank mine weighed from six to eight pounds, and laying a deliberate mine field twenty or thirty yards wide required at least a hundred mines. This meant we were limited to using mines for roadblocks on the main roads to stop high-speed tank approaches to our defensive positions. Sometimes we dug them in and buried them. Other times, we just left them on top of the road with a string attached to them. If a friendly vehicle came along, we could run out and pull the mines off the center of the road, but if the enemy showed up, they had to get someone out there to pull the land mines aside or destroy them, and thus expose themselves to our fire.

We mainly depended on rifle grenades and rocket launchers while waiting for the 57s to arrive. Both the 2.36-inch rocket launcher and the rifle grenade launcher could fire a high explosive (HE) and an antitank (AT) round. But we couldn't really count on either of these weapons. Even if we had a good, brave rocket-launcher man who was able to get within a hundred yards of a tank, a rocket that hit the turret would glance off without exploding one time in three. To be sure of detonation, a rocket had to squarely strike a vertical surface. This left the rifle grenade launcher. The launcher itself was mounted on the muzzle of the rifle, and the tail of the grenade, which had fins on it, fit onto the steel cylinder of the launcher. After the grenade was mounted, the safety pin was removed and the chamber was loaded with one blank round of ammunition. A soldier had better be sure to have a blank in his rifle chamber rather than a live round if he wanted to avoid a catastrophe.

Just before we left for Normandy, the Army got a bright idea to help make up for our weak antiarmor capabilities. At the very last moment, maybe a day before the drop, they decided to issue a second rifle grenade launcher to each squad. There was only one problem: grenade launchers were in short supply for the M1. Then someone came up with grenade launchers that would fit the M1903 .30-06 Springfield bolt-action rifle, so they issued each rifle squad an extra '03 rifle with a grenade launcher on it.

Like the M1, the '03 could be fired using at least three types of grenades. The antitank grenade was a small, shaped charge that was totally ineffective for penetrating the steel on a tank. Again, we aimed at the bogie wheels to disable the vehicle rather than attempt to kill the occupants. We also had fragmentation grenades on frames that we could mount on the launcher. The frame held the arming device safely until we fired, and the grenade went much further than we could throw it. This helped us somewhat in hedgerow country. The third type of grenade was a high explosive.

I had pressing personal reasons for feeling less than enthusiastic regarding the '03 rifle grenade launcher. I was acquainted with the rifle, I was probably the most experienced member of the squad, and I was the leader, so I was more or less volunteered to carry one. This meant that in addition to my personal and squad leader's gear, I had a rifle grenade launcher, a bag of rifle grenades, and a supply of blank ammunition to haul. But these weren't the only reasons I didn't like the '03. The problem was, it could only load five rounds of ammunition, and it took some time to do this. All stocks of clipped ammunition were maintained with a ratio of about twelve or fourteen to one, so if I ran out of clips, I could not replace them as easily as I could for an M1, simply because there were far fewer '03s around.

The '03 rifle also presented me with the very immediate problem of how to get out of the plane. We jumped with our M1s field stripped into three main pieces. We carried the dismounted rifle in a well-padded jump case, worn across our fronts, which permitted us to jump without hampering us. But I had to jump with my '03 in one piece. If I held it cross-wise, I wouldn't be able to get out the door, so I had to mount it intact almost parallel to my body. The mind boggles at what could happen when landing with a rifle sticking up in one long piece.

This detail only goes to show our larger problem in Normandy. The M1 rifle became standard issue in the early 1940s. But here I was, going into combat with a bolt-action '03 rifle left over from World War I. I missed my M1 dearly. And yet, as I said, it never occurred to us that we might not be successful.

Chapter 16

D-Day Jump:
The Defense of Ste. Mère-Eglise

When we finally got the order to go on D-Day, we moved to our planes, loaded our bundles in the belly racks, and saddled up. I taped together all my loose equipment, anything that could flop or swing out from my body, including my holster, by running tape over it and around my leg or thigh. I did have a .45, and I carried it loaded with a seven-round clip. I had a pistol pouch with two extra magazines, and threw twenty to thirty loose rounds of pistol ammo into my musette bag. I also carried a heavy canvas bag of rifle grenades and the blanks to fire them. By the time I was ready to jump, I was loaded down with nearly my own weight in equipment, one hundred fifty pounds, without including the parachute and the reserve.

After I got everything on, I draped my Mae West life jacket over my head and let it dangle. I was so heavily loaded that the life preserver stuck out nearly horizontally. I couldn't even fasten the waist strap. There were many jokes about the likely effectiveness of the Mae West if we were forced to land in the English Channel. We then attempted to get in the plane. One soldier would get in, and another would try to climb up while another guy got behind him. One would pull and the other would push, and together they would finally generate enough momentum for the trooper in the middle to get through the door. Then we waddled down the aisle and found our seats.

There wasn't much joking or fooling around once we got in the plane. We sat down, and everyone was very quiet. When we took off, it was still daylight. We were on English double daylight saving time, so I could see quite a ways from the fenced-in area. A large group of civilians had turned out, some waving wildly, some standing silently watching our departure. Once we got into flight, the rosary beads appeared in the hands of most of our Catholic soldiers. Beads or no beads, I think we all were saying our silent prayers. We had airsickness buckets in case anyone got sick, and some people did.

We did not come in over the invasion beaches. Our flight came from the northwest, taking us in the back door on the northwest side of the peninsula. After the fiasco in Sicily, General Ridgway stuck to his vow never to approve another airborne movement over a naval convoy; when we came in over Normandy, at least we were facing only enemy antiaircraft fire.

The 2d Battalion of the 505 was leading the 82d Airborne formation. Coming in, our lead pilot saw heavy cloud banks at a low altitude ahead. Being a smart commander, he thought he could fly over the clouds and have enough time and distance to be able to get down to the correct drop altitude and speed before we got to the DZ. From what I understand, he misjudged his time and distance. We did go over most of the clouds, but when he started leveling off, he was already over the drop zone.

We were much, much too high, and going much, much too fast. Instead of jumping at 600 feet, we were at 1,800 to 2,000 feet. Normally the pilot would slow down to about 95 miles per hour and lower the nose of the plane when we jumped. This time he simply had to give the green light. Just before I jumped, I glanced at my watch, which was on the inside of my left wrist, like I always wear it. It was an hour and fifty-one minutes after midnight, June 6, 1944.

The opening shock was the hardest I've ever experienced. It ripped my musette bag right off my body, despite the heavy fastenings. I lost that bag and everything in it, including my chewing tobacco. This left me at great disadvantage and put me in a foul mood for at least eleven days. The speed made it impossible for me to get the right position before my chute opened. My body was inverted—head down and feet up.

The first thing I remember seeing as I descended was a large spire in a bunch of buildings that later proved to be Ste. Mère-Eglise. To my surprise, there were fires in the town. Almost immediately after—these things happen in microseconds—I started receiving very heavy light flack and machine gun fire from the ground. This was absolutely terrifying. The tracers looked as if they were going take the top of my head off, but they were actually coming up at an angle. Many rounds tore through my chute only a few feet above my body. The third thing I remember is the explosions on the ground, making me fear the Germans had already zeroed in on our DZ. I later found out that these explosions resulted from our mine bundles. Either the speed of the plane pulled the chutes off, or the bundles dropped faster than expected, and the impact bent the safety clips on the fuses, causing them to explode.

It seemed to me that it took forever to land. A combination of bad body position, heavy load, and that damned '03 rifle added to the jolt I experienced when I hit the ground. But how good it felt to be rid of those damn tracers.

Only many years after the war did I learn what I now consider the true story of what went wrong on the drop. The flights coming in behind the 2d Battalion, 505, went right through the clouds, instead of going over the tops and attempting to drop down through. Many of the pilots broke formation, scattering plane loads of troopers over the whole Cherbourg peninsula. I know for a fact that the pilots who broke formation and had no idea of their location were still under strict orders not to bring any troopers back. So no matter where they were, they gave the green light, and out the troopers went. As it turned out, the 2d Battalion, 505, had the best drop of all six regiments in the American airborne effort. We knew exactly where we were, we knew what we had to do, and we proceeded to do just that.

I landed in a small field with cows over to one side. Because of the bone-rattling opening shock and a very hard landing, my back, hips and joints gave me pain for days. If it had been a training jump, I would have sought medical attention. I didn't have that luxury. Before I even attempted to get out of my chute, I crawled over to the nearest hedgerow to get some cover. I pulled my pistol out, put it beside me, and went to

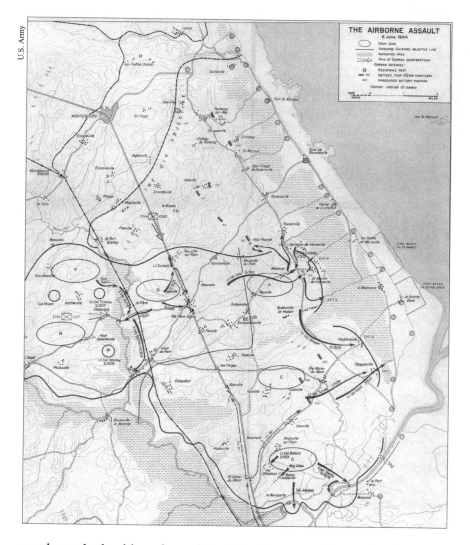

work on the buckles of my chute. I had some trouble getting the snaps undone because everything was pulled so tightly.

I kept looking up, watching the planes. They were taking a lot of ack-ack fire from Ste. Mère-Eglise, and flying off in all directions. This created difficulties in regrouping, because about our only way of finding each other was to orient ourselves by the plane. Soon I caught sight of a green star-cluster flare and started moving in its direction. It shot high into the air and burst in a brilliant cluster. This was the sign that someone in the battalion command group had reached the battalion assembly location.

It was especially tricky to assemble at night, because Normandy was the first experience of combat for many of the men who made the jump. This was the case for two out of three regiments of the 82d, the 507 and the 508, and all the regiments of the 101st. The 504 did not participate, because it had just returned to England from Italy in late April, and was in no shape to get ready for a new campaign in so little time. The 505 RCT was the only veteran American parachute regiment in the invasion.

Luckily, my group and I didn't encounter any enemy troops while we were assembling. We each had been issued a little metal cricket, like the ones that used to come in boxes of cereal or Cracker Jacks, which we used to challenge for the first night only. In times of uncertainty, I would signal with one "click-click" of the cricket, then wait for two in return. Of course, the Germans soon caught on to this, and used the crickets too. We also used sign and countersign, challenging with "flash" and counter-signing with "thunder"—two words the Germans found hard to pronounce. Anyone who hollered "halt" was to be shot, no questions asked. The German command sounded much too much like our own.

I brought in eight to ten men from our own battalion. I was surprised to discover that others I encountered were from the 101st Airborne, which had preceded the 82d into Normandy. They were four or five miles off their DZ. I asked them to stay with me, but they all elected to go on their own. I don't remember anyone in my group bringing in any bundles, and I didn't hunt for them either. Even if we had known where they were, the hedgerow country would have made it difficult to get to them. High banks full of trees and brush had been built up over the centuries, surrounding the fields. They were much more of a hindrance than barbed wire or rail fences. We had to climb up through a tangle of bushes and trees to come out on the far side of a field. Loaded down as we were, this greatly hampered our movement.

One of my problems as a squad leader was to keep the men I gathered spread out. In combat or under any other kind of threat, humans, like all other animals, bunch up together; the herding instinct takes over. We all, myself included, instinctively wanted the safety of numbers, but I managed to keep the men as far away from one another as possible, without losing control. Finally we saw a green glass lantern hung in the tallest tree in the center of the battalion assembly area, a more permanent assembly marker than the flares. Closer in, we encountered troopers who had been spotted around the perimeter to point out the general direction for each company. I was challenged along the way, and at various times I challenged in turn. It all turned out all right; no one shot anyone else.

Signs of daylight were just beginning as we entered the assembly area. One of the first sights I saw was Colonel Vandervoort. He had broken his ankle in the jump and was hopping around on one leg, using a rifle as a crutch. Most of my squad showed up, but I did loose George Paris, whom I never saw again. He was listed as MIA, but I later discovered he had been found with jump injuries.

While the 3d Platoon of Company F was assembling, we spied an individual down at one end of the field standing on the hedgerow trying to observe some gliders coming in. Our platoon leader, Little Joe Holcomb, said, "Go tell that asshole to get down and take cover." We didn't want to give our position away, so I went off in that direction, and hollered at some distance about getting down. I don't know about the politeness of the language I used. As the individual turned toward me, I saw two big stars. It was General Ridgway. I quickly turned and reported to Lieutenant Holcomb. That was the first and last time I tried to chew out the general.

The glider troops that came in that morning took a terrific beating. This is one of the most sickening things I remember. The Germans still controlled the gliders' LZ, and the landing had to be diverted at the last minute. There was a lot of confusion, and some of the pilots were forced to find the nearest available spot to land. They were under a lot of heavy small-arms fire and flak, and I think they misjudged the size of the fields. If we saw them, or heard them coming in at tree-top level, we just crossed our fingers. There was nothing else we could do. Within a few seconds, they slammed into the hedgerow at the other end of the field. In town, others almost hit the aid station and the schoolhouse, and one actually knocked out Company D's CP.

I still can hear those gliders hitting the hedgerows, tearing off wings, smashing equipment, and mangling and killing the crews. We picked up only eight of our sixteen 57s. These were brought in by Capt Alfred Ireland, who had been on detached duty with 82d Airborne Division Headquarters for planning the Normandy invasion. He later told me he would have preferred to jump any day.

I suppose it's miraculous we even got as many guns as we did. But often there was no crew left to operate them, and we now saw the real value of the cross-training we had undertaken back in Northern Ireland because we sometimes had to man the 57s ourselves. We had very few motor vehicles, which meant we pulled them around by hand. Colonel Vandervoort placed one of them near the battalion CP, where a former artilleryman, Pvt John Atchley, single-handedly knocked out a German self-propelled gun only fifty yards from the CP, and disabled the second one behind it.

Shortly after daylight, Colonel Vandervoort decided we had enough of the battalion assembled. We were about 400-strong and close to being completely equipped as we started moving toward our mission area. We went cross-country instead of using the roads. Whenever we saw a farm off to our flank, we sent people to make sure we weren't under observation from enemy soldiers hiding out in the farmhouses. I was selected for one of these trips and took about half a squad with me to investigate. As we got closer, the inhabitants came running out. I didn't have a French-speaking soldier in the squad, but I tried to explain to them that we had to search their house. They were quite put out about it, but I had to do the job. We hollered out in our rendition of German, "Kommst du here," and "Handy hoch, if you're in there!" No one showed.

Once I got into the close confines of the house, my '03 rifle wasn't much use to me. I had to set it down and climb on chairs to get into the crawlspaces. I pushed the trap door up into the second story, thinking to myself, "This is very stupid." As I stuck my head and .45 over the edge, I wondered what my chances would be if there was a German in there who wanted to resist. Luckily, the worst thing we encountered were indignant Frenchmen insulted by our search of their homes.

The 3d Battalion, 505, had entered the town of Ste. Mère-Eglise at daylight or earlier, taking thirty prisoners among the occupying Germans and killing about ten more. One of their first acts was to hoist over the city hall the same battle-worn American flag that had flown over Naples. Once again, I'm sure "Cannonball" Krause, the commander of the 3d Battalion, meant this symbolic act to sound a note for future historians. In any case, the citizens of Ste. Mère-Eglise have always proudly claimed that theirs was the first French city to be liberated.

The 3d Battalion's drop had been more scattered than ours, but they occupied the town with what forces they had and managed to hold it. They were subject to attack at almost any point in a circle, except toward the northeast, where the 2d Battalion had landed near Neuville. And receive attacks they did. Colonel Ekman, the regimental commander, ordered Colonel Vandervoort, our battalion commander, to move the 2d in to strengthen the town's perimeter defense.

Colonel Ekman himself had been dropped in the wrong spot and was unable to radio through to the 3d Battalion in Ste. Mère-Eglise. Our battalion met up with him and his group an hour or so after daylight, very close to our objective near Neuville-au-Plain, and he here decided to reverse our battalion's course of march. At the squad-leader level, all we knew was that now we were going into Ste. Mère-Eglise instead of defending it from Neuville-au-Plain.

As we neared the town, we began to see some of our fellow paratroopers hanging in tree limbs, shot and killed either on the descent or after they had gotten tangled in the branches. This was all the more demoralizing because the majority of a stick from our own company had landed in Ste. Mère-Eglise and most of the men had been lost. For me, the sight of those dead men remains to this day one of the saddest, most vivid, and horrendous scenes of the entire war. As we got into town, one of my most striking memories is of a single dead body. One huge, blond German soldier, a stereotypical superman, lay in the church square. Twenty or thirty yards away, one of our troopers hung shot in a tree.

I had many friends and acquaintances among our own casualties. My friend and a former member of the squad, Blankenship, who had transferred to the 2d Platoon, was found in town, hanging in his chute. Lieutenant Cadish, a platoon leader who joined us just days before the operation, never got out of his chute. According to the regimental history, the trooper in the tree beside the square was Sergeant Ray—Big Ray—with whom I had gone to Glasgow, Scotland. He had landed between the German guard and Privates Steele and Russell, whose parachutes had both become caught up on the church. The dead superman figure we saw had been heading toward them when Big Ray shot him in a last heroic act, saving the lives of Steele and Russell just before he was killed. Like everyone else, I saw John Steele's empty chute hanging from the steeple in Ste. Mère-Eglise as we passed through town.

As we headed toward the cemetery, we started receiving some small arms fire to our right front. We waited a few minutes, and identified it as a German MG42, a very rapid-fire light machine gun. I suggested to the lieutenant that we better try flanking. Soon we discovered that members of Company G had cleaned out some German machine gun crews and were now in the defensive position using the MG42s. This was nice to know, especially as my squad was the right flank squad of Company F in our preliminary defense, tying in with Company G to our right. I told the troopers in Company G that the German machine guns made us jumpy, that we didn't know if the fire was friend or foe. But they kept right on using them.

My squad was positioned to the northeast, just outside the cemetery. We dug in two or three feet from the large stone wall surrounding it, tying in with Company G to our right. For small arms fire, my squad had one of the quietest parts of the front. The situation was quite different for the 3d Platoon of Company D, for example, which was positioned where the entire 2d Battalion had originally planned to take up the defensive, and my own squad had originally been designated to operate as an outpost.

There was firing going on around the cemetery, but we had an outpost in daylight and listening posts at night, located at least one or two hedgerows out in front of our squads and platoon position. But no one in and around Ste. Mère-Eglise was spared intense mortar and artillery fire. The Germans fired everything they had on the town, from corps on down to division artillery. In our position, shells that flew into the cemetery struck monuments, gravestones, and walls. Bits of marble and gravestones were flying all around, in addition to the steel shrapnel. When I went around to inspect the foxholes, I told the men who were digging down deep, "Another six inches and I'll call it desertion."

D-Day duties included patrols. I went out with some men to recover the dead. We went out as far as we could without getting into a fire fight, pulled the bodies out of the trees, then carried them back and lay them out on top of the ground in the cemetery. The best we could do for them was cover their bodies with parachutes. We laid out nine troopers, most of them from Company F, 505.

I also remember Corporal Krueger telling us about his patrol to clear out some houses. The artillery fire was so accurate that we suspected the Germans had left some artillery forward observers in Ste. Mère-Eglise to direct fire on us. Krueger's patrol went into the taller houses and worked up to the roofs. They didn't come across any Germans, but on a couple of occasions Krueger had trouble getting in, so he gave the locks a blast with his tommy gun.

Finally, the patrol walked up to a house whose owner was still around. Krueger was all set to give the lock a burst with his gun when the Frenchman came running up, crying out, "Mais non! Mais non!" Then he reached out, turned the knob, and the door just opened. All Krueger had to do was walk in. When he got back, we all had a good laugh about him shooting his way into the houses like a big-time movie hero.

The artillery fire was heavy throughout the day from very early on. It increased in volume, then died down a little, then continued until well after midnight. That night we were on a high state of alert, expecting attacks at any moment. I was awake around midnight with my head and shoulders out of the foxhole, when I heard one particular artillery round coming in, and misjudged it entirely. It landed a lot closer than I expected, but even then it was quite a ways away. I got hit in the left shoulder, spun around, and dropped in the hole. I felt my shoulder, trying to determine how bad it was. It had gone completely numb. I had visions of the large chunks of shrapnel that I had seen lying around from other artillery shell explosions, pieces as long as eight inches to a foot.

I panicked a little; I thought I might lose my shoulder. This is the type of thing that drives men into shock. Shock is a big killer on the battlefield. It doesn't matter if you're hit hard or lightly, a man who goes into shock is in a dangerous situation. I hollered for a medic and Joe Carnecki, our aidman, also from Erie, came running over. He examined my shoulder and tried to calm me down; he said it wasn't very bad. A small rectangular piece of shrapnel, maybe an inch and a half in size, had lodged in my flesh but hadn't penetrated far. It was pretty well spent when I got hit.

Joe put a field dressing on my wound, gave me a shot of morphine, and asked if I wanted to go to the battalion aid station. I thought I'd be better off right there with the platoon. I was put in a prone position in the interior of the cemetery, just over the wall from my squad position. The one benefit of being wounded was that I didn't have to be on the alert. I let the effects of the morphine take over, and I quickly dropped off to sleep.

Chapter 17

Patrols and Hedgerow Battles: From Neuville-au-Plan and Le Ham to St. Sauveur-le-Vicomte

I awoke before daybreak on June 7, went over the wall, and got back in squad position. I was told that after midnight the enemy had increased the volume of artillery and mortar fire, hitting a lot of headstones and monuments in the cemetery, but I had slept right through it. My shoulder was feeling somewhat better. I thought I could do more good by staying than by being evacuated, so I remained with my unit. I received my first Purple Heart for this wound.

Later on D+1, my squad outpost reported an incoming column of troops identifying themselves with orange panels or smoke. I went to the outpost, stood on a hedgerow one or two out from our position, and welcomed the troops coming in from the beaches. As the first men approached I hollered, "What outfit?" It was my stepbrother's company—Company G, 8th Infantry, 4th Division. As they passed, I kept asking if anyone knew where Harry was. Some of his platoon said he'd been detailed to escort POWs back to the beaches. I stayed a while, thinking he might still come along, but some idiot at the back end of their column took a shot at me. I guess he wasn't familiar with the paratroopers' uniform. He missed me by at least a foot, but I thought, "Harry or no Harry, I'm not about to be shot at by my own troops."

In the early morning of June 8, we received orders to move out in attack formation to the north. On the night of June 7, the 505 had been attached to the 4th Infantry Division, with the objective of liberating Cherbourg, the deep-water port on the northern end of the peninsula. We were attacking toward the Quineville-Montebourg-Le Ham ridge with three other infantry regiments, the 8th, the 12th and the 22d, all newly committed. Our first objective was to clear out Neuville-au-Plain, then to establish a line of departure west to the Merderet River. On our way, we came across one of the worst killing fields I have ever seen.

Two platoons from Company E, 505, headed by Lt Theodore Peterson and Lt James Coyle, with Lt Thomas McClean and his Company D platoon on the right, had successfully counterattacked against a German infantry battalion that had attempted to move into Ste. Mère-Eglise by the main road. The Germans were caught in a sunken lane bordered on each side by a hedgerow. Company E went up the lane with two Sherman tanks from the Howell Force, and the only way the Germans could escape was to run up the path or flee across the open fields.

Company E was working up close in unison with the tanks, and the Germans had run out into the open, exposing themselves to small arms fire by Companies E and D. I later became friends with Lieutenant Coyle, who attempted to stop the massacre and get the Germans to give up. He actually went out into the field and hollered for them to surrender. He got the firing stopped and the Germans moving to the end of the field with their hands up, but a German let loose with a burp gun and hit him in the ass, and so the shooting continued. Coyle made it through in command, and they took more than a hundred fifty prisoners. He got to the battalion aid station lying on his stomach on the deck of a tank.

As we moved up through that lane in the aftermath of the action, we were literally stumbling over the bodies of Germans. It was nightmarish. Many who were not shot and killed had been wounded, or killed by the tanks running over them. The bodies were actually flattened out by the tank tracks. It was pretty dark, and we had a hard time moving, not knowing when we would be stepping on bodies. Some of the wounded were still crying for help.

As we continued on our attack, I was very cold. I was not feeling well because of the wound in my shoulder. At Neuville-au-Plain, we were told that the 8th Infantry Regiment was supposed to come up on our right, but we had gotten ahead of it. The 505 stayed the whole day of June 8 in Neuville-au-Plain, waiting for the 8th Infantry to join up with us. During that time, we went out on patrols, which consisted of at least one rifle squad and sometimes a whole rifle platoon.

We had two scouts in each rifle squad, whom we jokingly called the first and second target. Whenever we were not defending every hedgerow, whether we were attacking as part of a larger unit or on patrol, we sent scouts out ahead to the next hedgerow. They crossed the open field or moved along the hedgerow in the direction of the attack. The remaining squad members would deploy along the hedgerow we occupied, ready to give them fire support. Sometimes this worked, and sometimes it didn't. If the scouts made it to the other side of the field without drawing fire, they looked around as best they could, then the rest moved across. If they got fired on, we knew we had a fight on our hands, and we deployed and fired, or tried to maneuver to the next hedgerow.

I was moving along a hard-top road in a patrol of two rifle squads when we came to a manor. It was part of my job to go into these houses to check if they were occupied by Germans. I went up to the front door and started in, but a Frenchman came out from wherever he had been. I got across to him that I was looking for Germans. "Non, non," he told me, "The Germans, they left long ago."

Just about that time, some of our patrol started around to the left of the manor and courtyard. Lo and behold, around to the right rear they discovered a German machine gun position. Luckily, the gunner was asleep. Maybe he had enjoyed a little too much of the Frenchman's wine the night before. Whatever the case, it was a lucky break for us; we took the gun out and captured the gun crew. I was disillusioned from trusting the French about German positions after that.

As we continued our advance, we began to receive 88mm artillery fire. A round hit in the field about a hundred yards in front of us. But the thing was a dud; instead of exploding, it hit the ground, skipped, leaped, and skipped again right through our formation, passing within maybe twenty feet to my left. There we were, our mouths hanging open, just watching that shell come at us. Whenever we witnessed a German shell like this, we'd holler, "Made in Czechoslovakia!" We thought the slave labor sabotaged the Nazi shells.

The most important event on June 8 occurred when I took a combat patrol out to our front. We were moving cautiously along a hedgerow when I saw some bodies at the far end of the field. As we approached, we saw they were dead Germans. We also found two live friendlies lying close to the bodies, attempting to get some cover and/or concealment on the bank. The friendlies were Lieutenant Colonel Kuhn and his radio operator. The colonel, who commanded a battalion of the 507 Parachute Infantry Regiment, had broken his pelvis when landing on June 6. His radioman had landed close and stayed with him. They had been lying there for at least forty-eight hours, and the colonel was really hurting. He and his radioman were very hungry and thirsty.

Before we found them, a German patrol had come upon Colonel Kuhn and his radioman and captured them. They hadn't resisted, nor would I or most other soldiers in their situation. As the Germans were discussing what to do with them, a high explosive shell landed close enough to kill two or three of the Germans. The remaining patrol members had taken off.

There was a lot of litter laying around—discarded ration boxes, the Americans' possessions, equipment the Germans had left after looting them, and the dead Germans' field equipment. I saw a black shoulder holster among the litter. I had always wanted a shoulder holster, and they were not an item of issue. As this one was black, I knew it was not American, because the official color for all our army's leather items was brown. I picked it up and was starting to strap it on, when the colonel asked, "What are you doing with my holster?" I said, "I'm sorry, sir, I thought it was German," and went to take it off. He then replied, "You can keep it, soldier." I used that holster for the rest of the war, and still keep it in my gun case as a souvenir.

We made some field-expedient stretchers and carried the colonel back to our position, where the medics took over. We then continued on our patrols, meeting with light resistance. We had one platoon on either side of the road. Whenever I heard one of our machine guns, I could almost tell who was on the gun just by the way he fired. Every gunner seemed to develop a rhythm of his own.

The next few experiences I recall are difficult to pinpoint exactly on the map, and I'm uncertain of the dates. This is partly due to faulty memory, as I try to piece together events fifty years after they occurred, and partly to conditions at the time—the difficult, repetitious nature of a terrain full of hedgerows and swamps, and the fatigue and confusion of constant front-line battle waged for many days with little rest or relief from other units. It's also true that our immediate objectives were frequently changed or called off, partly owing to the poor drops of other regiments, and partly to unexpected conditions on the ground. Squad leaders like myself were rarely informed of how our orders fit into the larger picture, and the picture was always shifting. I do know that the following events all took place between the early hours of 9 and 15 June; that is, between the time the 505 began to advance westward from Neuville-au-Plain toward Le Ham and Montebourg Station, and the time we went into a hasty defense just outside St. Sauveur-le-Vicomte.

Around dawn of June 9, the 505 opened a new attack accompanied by the 2d Battalion, 325th Glider Infantry Regiment and a platoon of tanks from the 746th Tank Battalion that had both been attached to the 505 two days earlier. We were advancing towards an area that had a large hangar-type building when we came under self-propelled artillery fire. This was direct, point-blank artillery fire, which is extremely unnerving. The Germans had established a very strong line of defense that forced us to stop to dig in. Our battalion was in an especially bad situation with little cover, under continuous firing with rounds coming in at the rate of one per minute. The gun worked up and down our area, showering us with hundreds of artillery bursts.

I was on my knees, digging in along a hedgerow with my trenching tool. To my right, in an open field, were several cows. One moment I was digging, and the next thing I knew, I was blown out of the slit trench and up against the side of the hedgerow. The explosion knocked me unconscious for maybe fifteen to twenty seconds. Coming to, I looked around and realized the shell had landed between me and the nearest cow. She was lying dead, with all four feet sticking up in the air. At the same time, I realized I could not see normally. The explosion, powder and heat from the shell burst had caused me to lose the sight of my right eye. I was the only one affected by this particular burst, and people started hollering for the medic. All this time, the guns kept right on firing.

Joe Carnecki appeared and treated my burns. He got me to an aid station where the doctor washed my eye out and cleaned my face with solution. He examined me as best as he could, and said my blindness was only temporary. He put a large white compress bandage over my eye and cheek, and I was allowed to rest at the aid station for an hour or so. Then I got up and returned to my squad area. My left eye was still in pretty good shape, but unfortunately, it was not my shooting eye. This incident resulted in my receiving a second Purple Heart.

When I got back to my slit trench, I found my helmet a few feet away, where it had been knocked off in the explosion. A piece of shrapnel had bitten off part of the rim, making a rectangular hole about two and a half inches long along the edge, and maybe one and a half inches wide. Very luckily, we never wore the chins traps of our helmets after the jump. This was precisely to avoid injury in the case of explosions, which could knock the helmet off and injure your chin if you wore the strap.

We held in that area for almost the remainder of the day. The resistance had been building up in front of us, but the self-propelled gun had finally stopped firing. When the warning order was passed to continue the attack, we were still taking a lot of enemy fire from our front and left front. We did move up to the line of departure, which was near where I'd been hit. Then the order was passed down the line to hold the attack.

We took cover as best we could along the hedgerow where we had been going to start the attack. The tempo of artillery fire increased. Suddenly, we heard a shell hit on our left flank, almost at the top of a tree, and the cry "Medic!" went up. Pretty soon people came along to our left rear carrying one of our wounded. It was a fellow by the name of Henry Cloherty, who in addition to being the comedian of the 1st Platoon was one of the oldest men. We called him "the old man" or "grandpa"—he must have been all of thirty. Henry was cursing very soundly, complaining he was afraid of what folks were going to think. This was his third Purple Heart, and he had gotten every single one for being "shot in the ass." He had a nice-sized piece of flesh torn out of his backside.

We continued to wait for word to come down to jump off. By this time it was close to dark, and we were not particularly happy about attacking at night. While it was still dusk, Sergeant Yachechak, a squad leader in the 2d Platoon, walked over to an opening in the hedgerow to the left of my squad and unlatched a gate between the fields. When we got the word to go, at least my squad and the 2d Platoon could dash through the gate, rather than having to climb over the hedgerow. It was a miracle he wasn't shot while standing upright doing this.

We continued to wait, and everyone seemed to have a bad feeling about the attack. We talked amongst ourselves in low tones, and during that short period two or three of the men recounted their life stories. I had begun to remove my bandage from time to time to discover if I could see. Eventually I took it off altogether, for I felt that if we attacked at night the bandage would be an aiming point. I was able to use my shooting eye again twelve or so hours after I had been hit. Finally, just as night fell, the attack was called off, to the great relief of everyone in Company F.

Later during the night of June 9-10, we were given the objective of seizing the Montebourg-Le Ham road. The 1st Battalion was to attack down the railroad line to Montebourg Station, with the 2d behind it. We were then to turn west to take Le Ham. The 2d Battalion, 325, was moved to our southwest flank, and we were given support from glider and parachute artillery battalions. The 3d Platoon of Company F was positioned on the left flank of the company and the battalion. Our left flank was a hundred seventy-five to two hundred fifty yards from the railroad track, which we were supposed to use as a guide on our left flank.

The attack did not get underway until the afternoon of June 10. My squad, the 1st, was in the lead. We came to a hedgerow, glanced across, and discovered the high embankment of the railroad track to our left front. Fabis and Watro, who was acting as second scout, were the first two men across. Krueger, who had taken over from J. E. Jones as assistant squad leader, started across next. About half-way across, he drew some machine gun fire from the direction of the tracks, but he made it safely. We stopped for a few minutes, and tried to pick out the machine gun position. We couldn't locate it, but we fired some rifle rounds in that direction, and it did stop firing. I decided I had to be the next one across. I got about twenty steps out, heading across the field, when I was taken under very heavy machine gun fire.

You really know you're being shot at when the bullets start cracking all around you. I tried to speed up, but I was carrying so much equipment that I tripped and fell. For a split second, I tried to play dead, but I soon changed my mind because the bastard never let up on the gun. The bullets were hitting all around me. I jumped to my feet and started across the field. I vividly remember looking up in the direction I was headed, and there was Krueger. He jumped right out in the open, armed with a tommygun, and sprayed bullets in the direction of the railroad tracks.

Whether he hit anything I do not know, but he sure did make the Germans keep their heads down and stop firing.

I got to the hedgerow without being hit, dove into the mass, and came up and over on the far side. The shooting stopped. There we were, the four of us on one side of the field, and the rest of the platoon on the other side behind us. We could hear German commands, and it sounded like they were moving in on us from the direction of the railroad tracks. I knew Lieutenant Carroll would not try to send any more men across that field. We were cut off.

This is one of the times I unloaded. I threw everything away that was not essential for fighting. I dumped all my souvenirs, any extra stuff, in anticipation of running awfully fast or being taken prisoner. As we listened for the Germans coming down from the tracks, we got into the hedgerow as deeply as we could, and even started digging. We were ready.

Watro was out a little further than the rest of us, having gone across a short field. He motioned to us that he was going to change his position to see if he could locate the machine gun. He disappeared from sight, and then we heard shooting off in his direction. Twenty minutes or a half hour later, he crawled back into view with a big grin on his face. He held up three fingers. He'd gotten a German MG crew with his scoped rifle.

As we waited in position, facing the railroad tracks, we heard firing down to our left front. Then we later heard an attack off to what would have been our front. There was so much noise that it sounded like the 325th was attacking again. I later discovered that Lieutenant Carroll had moved the platoon back to one end of the field we had crossed, where a huge gravel pit was located. He was attempting to cross the field to get to our side, running along the edge of the pit when the Germans opened up on him. This left him only two options: continue running and get hit, or go over the bank and down into the gravel pit. This was almost a sheer drop, about thirty or forty feet deep, but Lieutenant Carroll went right down over the edge. He was pretty badly shaken up, and had numerous cuts and bruises, but he wasn't seriously injured.

Meanwhile, the four of us were sweating it out on the wrong side of the field. We had to remain as quiet as possible. We thought the Germans were moving in on us, and the last thing we wanted was to draw their attention. The same thing could be said for Carroll and the rest of the platoon. If that machine gun had moved one hedgerow south, they could have wiped out our platoon, or at the very least done serious damage. Carroll was doubtless under pressure to keep up the attack; he had no option but to leave us to our fates. After not hearing from us, he assumed we were dead or captured, and reported us missing in action.

We waited until dusk, then we made a break back in the direction we had come from. We finally managed to work our way back to the company position. This episode was fatal to other members of our platoon. After the four of us had gotten across the field, Carroll sent two men down toward the railroad tracks in the attempt to silence the machine gun, but they made the wrong move. Private Eli Potty and Pfc Arthur Lemieux, who was from my own squad, were both killed trying to save our lives.

The company stayed in position as dusk fell, when we got orders to advance under cover of darkness. Any night movement in combat is very tricky. Nevertheless, we followed our SOP and sent our scouts out one hedgerow in advance of the platoon. As we went forward we ran into some small arms and mortar fire, and were given an order to flank the resistance to our front. We crawled for about two hundred yards through a swampy meadow in the attempt to take advantage of all possible cover and concealment. When we completed the flanking movement, the Germans had already withdrawn. We did not take any casualties, but we ended up completely soaked—covered from head to foot with thick, black slime.

Luckily this night we had Fabis as first scout. He and Krueger, who was acting as our second scout, were moving across a field when a German spied Fabis as he approached a hedgerow. The hedgerow obstructed the German's view, so he didn't understand that Fabis was an enemy soldier, and he asked him what he was doing there. Fabis could speak and understand German very well, because he'd been born in Czechoslovakia, where he had spent his early years before emigrating to the United States. In nine out of ten cases, someone who heard German would have started shooting then and there. I know I would have. But Fabis had the good sense to comply with the demand. He calmly turned around and walked back, rather than running—therefore not drawing further suspicion—and reported the incident. This allowed us to get into an excellent position for a later attack on the Germans as a group.

Lieutenant Carroll sent me out to verify the presence of the enemy, so I went across the field to the hedgerow, turned right, and went a few yards until I found a gap. It sloped down quite deeply to the middle before it came up again on the field I was about to enter. I had started down the near slope, which was very short—when I glanced up and discovered a very large German soldier blocking my way at a distance of about fifteen feet. The encounter was especially memorable, because he was in an elevated position on the other side of the bank. As I looked up he was looming over me, silhouetted against the clear night sky.

He saw me and I saw him. I very cautiously moved so my rifle was at the ready—that damned '03 bolt-action rifle with the grenade launcher. I backed up and he backed up. When I got to the corner of the hedgerow and the passageway, I executed a left face and returned back along the hedgerow, which was about four feet high at this particular spot.

Lieutenant Carroll had been bringing up the platoon. I moved quickly down the hedgerow and whispered that the Germans were on the other side. By this time, my squad and most of the rest of the platoon were deployed along the hedgerow. I think Carroll and I stuck our heads through for a look at the same time. And what a sight we saw—a whole line of Germans with their backs to us, resting up against the hedgerow. We, too, had rested this way many times. I got my rifle in position ready to shoot, and Lieutenant Carroll opened up with his .45-caliber tommygun. He had a fifty-round circular magazine on it, the only one I ever saw in the service. When this happened, our whole platoon started shooting.

The muzzle of my rifle was only two feet away from the first man I shot. I continued firing until I emptied the '03. In my haste to reload, I started putting in the blank cartridges that I always carried in my left hand so I could fire a rifle grenade. I realized my mistake, and pulled the .45 from my shoulder holster and emptied one magazine of seven rounds from that.

Fabis was just to my right. He actually reached through the hedgerow and grabbed a German who was crying for help with his wound and wanted to surrender. It was very quick thinking on Fabis's part. In the meantime, the German leader was trying to get his men under control. I could tell he was standing upright from the sound of his voice. Fabis told me later he was cursing his men and ordering them to get their weapons into position and return fire. We shot a whole lot of rounds in his direction. Evidently, we did not hit him, because before too long they got their machine guns into position on either corner of the field and started laying down very effective fire onto our side of the hedgerow.

One of the other platoons was to our right, fifty to a hundred yards away, and the word came down to withdraw. This we did, pulling and dragging our prisoners with us. The wounded man Fabis grabbed was the first man I had shot at close range, and he was hit in the ass. We took two more prisoners, who were not wounded. We moved maybe three fields or hedgerows back and set up a hasty defense.

The Germans kept moving forward just as we had, from hedgerow to hedgerow, taking one field at a time. They had set up their automatic weapons in the corners and blasted away. Luckily, they stopped one field in front of us.

It was very cold that night, and we had not dried off much from the long, muddy crawl we had undertaken. We kept the POWs with us until daylight. The wounded prisoner was hurting, but all we could do was bandage his wound.

I later found out that Captain Barnett, our company commander, had lost contact with the battalion, and was determined to reach Le Ham. In the absence of orders, he had continued the attack that night, and Company F actually got as far as the road on the southeast side of the town. This is why we were sticking out there so far in advance of the rest of the battalion.

Captain Barnett must have sent out a patrol, because we finally made contact with the battalion on June 11, and actually had to move even further back. The 3d Platoon established a hasty defensive position on the left side of Company F, which was on the left flank of the battalion. At about 10:30 A.M., we heard the 325th Glider Infantry Regiment open the attack on our left flank; there was a large volume of return small arms fire, and artillery and mortar fire began to increase not only on our left flank but also in our direction. I believe the enemy thought more units than the 325 were going to attack, and so we got a lot of crap thrown at us. The 325 was some distance away, but even above the sounds of the firing, we could hear the officers and NCOs kicking ass. I wondered about this, because in a similar situation, we would have tried to keep the noise down.

Captain Barnett got a little anxious about the action in front of the company position, so he told me to take a patrol out to the front and find out what was going on. As far as I was concerned, I knew exactly what the hell was happening. I didn't think too much of the order to take a patrol out under those conditions, but I got a couple of my men and we very slowly and cautiously moved out, exposing ourselves to small arms and artillery fire.

We went about two hedgerows further out and got into a pretty well concealed position, from which we could observe to our front. I felt we had gone plenty far enough. We were out an hour or so, then returned to our company's defensive position, which was still taking some fire. I reported to Captain Barnett that I couldn't see anything at least two hedgerows out, and I guess that satisfied him. We went back to our holes.

I can't remember moving back from this particular position. The 325 had a tough time of it, having to advance over swampy ground with little cover for up to six hundred yards through walls of heavy small arms fire. The 2d Battalion, 505, laid down a base of fire for this attack, and the 456th Field Artillery Battalion fired a concentration barrage into the east side of Le Ham, giving the enemy a real pounding. The 325 overran the town at about 6:00 P.M., but by that time most of the Germans had pulled out, leaving their artillery behind.

Division ordered the bridge on the Merderet near Le Ham blown up, and our three battalions made a defensive line from there to north of Montebourg Station, where we linked up with the 8th Infantry Regiment. We stayed in this defensive position until June 13, when the plans for VII Corps were changed. Heavy German resistance in the north made our corps commander, MajGen J. Lawton Collins, decide to cut off the Cotentin peninsula near Barneville-sur-Mer before pushing toward Cherbourg, which now was slated to be taken by the 9th Infantry Division. The new objective for the 82d Airborne was St. Sauveur-le-Vicomte. We were to attack abreast of the 9th, taking the terrain up to and including the part of the city lying northeast of the Douve River. Our mission did not include crossing the bridge into the heart of town; it was to create a defensive line across from it, running along the riverbank.

The 505 was released from control of the 4th Infantry Division and the 2d Battalion, 325 returned to its regiment. We were relieved by elements of the 90th Infantry Division after we had been on the line for eight days. They looked a hell of a lot worse coming up to the front than we did going back. In some cases, it looked like the infantrymen were overweight and hadn't had proper physical training.

On June 13, the 505 moved through Picauville on trucks on the way to our bivouac area, and we also passed through Ste. Mère-Eglise, which now was thronging with rear-echelon troops and other units coming into battle. A bad rain was falling and the night was cold and wet. Our B bags finally arrived on June 14, but we didn't get a chance to use them. That night, the regiment was ordered to prepare for the attack on St. Sauveur-le-Vicomte at 9:00 P.M. We moved to a forward position west of Etienville, but the 505 was not committed to battle until the afternoon of June 15.

The attack began about noon on June 14, with the 325 and the 507 committed side by side on the road between Pont l'Abbé and St. Sauveur-le-Vicomte. The 507 was heavily counterattacked, which slowed the movement down. Rations were not getting down to us. We were so desperate for food that we went out to search the bodies of the 507 dead. This was a dangerous thing to do, as there was still plenty of resistance out in front of us. We waited until after dark, then a couple members of my squad and I carefully crawled out of our hedgerows and went through the troopers' pockets. We did find some K rations the Germans had missed. We crawled back and split them up among the squad.

The one detail that stands out in my mind is that all the 507 paratroopers had sharpened their bayonets to a very keen edge. Some of these were actually fixed on the end of their rifles. I guess sharpening them had been part of the pre-combat thinking of these dead soldiers, more or less to psych themselves up. I remember one in particular that had been ground to an especially fine point.

The 505 jumped off on the afternoon of July 15 and attacked right through the 507. The 1st Battalion was to the right, and our 2d Battalion was to the left, covering some of the 507 territory. The 3d Battalion, 505, was in reserve. It was obvious that the 507 was not in very good shape. To start with, it had had a bad drop. They'd been pretty well scattered, although one large group, the 3d Battalion, I think, had formed the perimeter on the far side of the swamp, where it had held out against repeated German attacks. Now they, like us, were being used as regular leg infantry.

In the 2d Battalion, Company F's right flank was the road. The 1st Squad of the 3d Platoon—my squad—was the right-flank squad, guiding on the road. The 1st Platoon of Company F was on our left, and the 2d was probably in support, but I'm not sure. By this time I'd exchanged my '03 rifle for a good old M1, which made me feel much more secure.

The battle itself was the same old story: the Germans had armor, and we were fighting it out hedgerow by hedgerow, using the main road as a guide. We ran into direct fire by 37mm flak cannons, and there were 75mm antitank guns, and of course, machine guns and mortars. The Headquarters Company mortar platoon sent shells into the German position, but we had no supporting armor. Finally, Colonel Vandervoort borrowed a couple of Sherman tanks from Colonel Alexander and used them to lead an attack with a platoon from Company D that wiped out the German stronghold.

After this, the going was much faster. As it began to get dark, we passed a German self-propelled gun that was blazing furiously. My squad was in front, moving against relatively light resistance. I don't know who or what had knocked it out. We held up at dark or shortly thereafter on June 15, and went into a hasty defense. We were only about two miles outside St. Sauveur-le-Vicomte, but the 60th Infantry Regiment was far behind us, which left our right flank open. The division orders to hold up for the night greatly annoyed General Ridgway. He got permission to go on to St. Sauveur the next morning regardless, and the 3d Battalion moved up from reserve to guard our open flank.

That night was exceptionally cold and miserable. We were on at least fifty percent alert, so only half of us could sleep at any one time. None of us got too much sleep, and all of us were hungry. Little did we know that the next morning, we would not only clear the way to St. Sauveur-le-Vicomte, but actually cross the Douve River.

Chapter 18

Long Days in Normandy:
The Battle of St. Sauveue-le-Vicomte,
the Bois de Limors, and Hill 131

On June 16, we took up the attack toward St. Sauveur-le-Vicomte at 7:00 A.M. As we got closer to town we encountered increased resistance and had to push the Germans back again, hedgerow by hedgerow. We also encountered fields of Rommel's asparagus, poles twenty or thirty feet high, planted in pastures and other open spaces, strung together, and wired with Teller mines rigged to detonate when gliders or parachute troops hit them. The poles would also sheer off a glider's wings.

As we approached the town, the 505 was on the right and the 325 was on the left. The ground dropped off to the Douve, which was more like a good-sized creek in the northeastern United States. In addition to our little 75s, we finally started picking up artillery support from the infantry divisions, including corps artillery. The 505's mission was to hold a defensive line at the Douve on the heights across from St. Sauveur-le-Vicomte, but not to seize the bridge or take the town.

Although there was no way for us to realize it down at my level, Colonel Vandervoort had been surveying the entire scene with a forward artillery observer as we moved into positions overlooking St. Sauveur. From his elevated vantage point on the southeast bluff of the river, the colonel had an excellent view of the major highway—and he discovered it was crammed with withdrawing German troops. He contacted Major Norton, the regimental S-3, who in turn called Colonel Ekman, who communicated this news to General Ridgway. Ridgway came up to Vandervoort's position with the First Army commander, General Omar Bradley, who seized the occasion in the absence of General Collins and gave the 82d permission to cross the Douve.

And so the mission of the 505 changed again: we were now to attack down the slope and across the river, secure the bridge, and clean out St. Sauveur-le-Vicomte. The artillery fire we heard as we moved toward the bridge was a TOT, a huge barrage timed on target and well aimed at the withdrawing Germans, that also blew up half the town. This was a spectacular, devastating, and highly demoralizing attack for the enemy as the shells from every gun in every artillery battalion landed at the same instant.

As the barrage lifted, the 2d Battalion started down the slope in column formation, with Company F leading. The 3d Platoon was in front, and my 1st Squad was in the lead. The 1st Battalion was close behind the 2d. There were houses in the valley two hundred or two hundred fifty yards to our right and left, and brushy terrain to both sides of our front on the opposite side of the river. We moved along the edge of the road, attempting to use a ditch as cover. We were taking considerable small arms fire, which was particularly deadly in our situation. The Germans had us in sight and were firing rifles and machine guns directly on us.

About a hundred fifty yards from the bridge, we were also taken under very heavy direct artillery fire. This was a minimum of 75mm, and probably larger, most likely from self-propelled guns. These were HE—high explosive—shells, not antitank. The weapons were firing at point-blank range or "over the sights"—right over the barrel—and the shells were on us before we heard the report of the guns.

The Germans had taken position on the other side of the river to our left and right front, on slightly higher ground. They let us get almost fully deployed along that open road before they opened up. We hit the dirt as the shells skimmed the top of the roadbed, passing over our heads by two or three feet. The best we could do was get the hell out of there as fast as possible. We had to jump up and run across the bridge. The instant before we made our dash, Corti, a BAR man in my squad, was severely wounded. He had been in a prone position close to a cement power pole, which was hit by one of the shells. As we made our rush, we couldn't stop, but the medic did. If at that instant the Germans had concentrated their fire on the bridge, we would have had very heavy causalities.

As paratroopers, we only carried armor-piercing ammunition in airborne operations. But in some cases, our .30-caliber ammunition could also penetrate the thinly clad German self-propelled guns and armored personnel carriers. At the very least, armor-piercing fire would discourage them. As we crossed the bridge, I tried to find the guns so we could put small arms fire on them. That's how close they were—actually within effective range of small arms fire. But I couldn't pick up their positions, so we got across as best we could and up the other side.

We lost a number of men on the rush across the bridge, but Corti was the only one from my squad who was hit. The shells were coming heavily but still high, skimming the top of the road and hitting trees or the walls of houses scattered on the other side. They exploded far enough away that the shrapnel didn't do much damage, at least to us. I read later that as we forged our way across in the middle of all that artillery, General Bradley, watching from afar with General Ridgway, complemented us on our work. "My God, Matt," he is reputed to have said. "Can't anything stop those men?" Reading this, I felt pretty good even fifty years after the fact.

After we got across the bridge, the 2d Battalion fanned out, with Company F on the right. Our mission was to skirt the town and move ahead until we could cut across and block the road coming in from the west. As we moved off, our own planes took the bridge under very heavy attack. Evidently, the Air Corps had not received the news that we had taken the bridge and were already on the outskirts of town. They actually tried to dive-bomb the bridge.

We released orange smoke. I was far enough away not to throw any out, but I saw it billowing up all around the bridge and the road. This did not deter the planes. I honestly believe the Air Corps used the damn smoke clouds as aiming points. From a distance, I could see Colonel Vandervoort, who had crossed shortly after we did, standing out in an opening with a huge orange blanket or panel. He was waving it like mad, standing there with orange smoke everywhere, trying to deter the planes. The bombs missed the bridge, but the planes also made some strafing runs. My unit did not suffer any casualties from these, but others did. In defense of the Air Corps, I note the bridge and the 505's position on June 16 were beyond that day's bomb line, the line used to control air strikes. The 505 had moved so fast that the rear-area planners couldn't conceive that we had already reached the line.

As we continued to skirt to the right, we shortly came into a built-up area of houses. We got held up by sniper fire and light small arms fire coming from the houses in town. Tommy Watro moved off some distance from our position to stalk some of the enemy snipers and riflemen. He came back a little while later with another one of his big grins on his face and held up a couple fingers to signify he had gotten the Germans who were firing at us. He later swore they were five hundred to six hundred yards out. I didn't dismiss his claim. All men armed with the M1 used to fire courses at two hundred to three hundred yards without a scope and got good scores. Watro, using an M1903 rifle with a scope, could do much better.

We swung a little more to the right to get out of the built-up areas and back into hedgerow country. Bill Hodge was acting as first scout, and I was second scout. We tried to rotate the scout jobs to give the designated men a little relief. We had sustained some small arms fire, so Bill and I worked our way along a hedgerow. I glanced across it, out into the field, and saw three Germans ahead, walking along the inner side of the hedgerow perpendicular to ours. I think Bill and I both spotted them at the same time. They were walking upright, very close together, and they could not see us.

I aimed at one and fired, and then put my sights on a second one. Just as I was about to shoot, Bill opened up with his .45-caliber tommygun. One instant the German was in my sights, and the next he was flat on the ground. He must have been hit by a number of the .45 slugs, because he went down very fast. The other German threw his hands up in surrender, and we approached him after an intense visual search of the surrounding area. Bill and I moved up to where the bodies were lying, and Lieutenant Carroll came up with a few others from the platoon. One of the Germans was dead, and three or four of our men gathered around to watch the other one die.

This is one of the few times I actually saw at close range the result of my own fire, or that of my squad. I thought the German was suffering terribly, and without thinking, I asked the lieutenant whether I should finish him off. Much to his credit, he absolutely refused. The sight of that man lying there slowly dying lingers in my mind to this day. He has been the subject of many nightmares over the years. I hesitate to think what kind of dreams I'd have now, if I'd put the man out of his misery.

We advanced a couple of hedgerows and got into a position where we could see across a depression to higher ground to our front. From there, we caught sight of the road and spied a mixed group of enemy trucks and smaller vehicles heading toward town. Although they were quite a ways out, six hundred to seven hundred yards in front of us, we took them under machine gun and rifle fire. The mortars dropped a few rounds onto the road close to the vehicles. They came to a very sudden stop and the personnel bailed out on the far side of the road.

We had been firing for a few minutes, when someone hollered that he could see some enemy to our right rear. This soldier should have fired first and then warned us, rather than hollering and not doing much about it. I asked where the Germans were, and he pointed to a section of the hedgerow. I was afraid we had gotten caught on the wrong side of it, so we fired for a few minutes in that direction, but we didn't get any return fire. We were lucky.

We continued until we crossed the road and blocked it. Other units of the regiment and battalion had cleared the town. At the roadblock, we heard we were going to be relieved in place. During the night of June 16-17, part of the 47th Infantry Regiment from the 9th Infantry Division passed through our position and took up the attack. By the end of the day, they had cut the peninsula at Canville.

After June 16, we were left in a reserve or supporting position at the St. Sauveur-le-Vicomte bridgehead. Until this time, even when the platoon was in a supporting role for the company, or the company was in reserve for the battalion, we had always been well within German artillery or mortar range. At last we were going to get the chance to relax.

We still weren't getting our rations regularly, and those we did get were K rations. We were bivouacked right along the side of the road, so every time we heard vehicles, we went out, attempted to slow them down, and asked what they had in the way of chow. A lot of the 9th Division soldiers gave us some of their rations. They were riding on vehicles so they were able to carry the larger, bulkier 5&1s or 10&1s, which were much better than our K or C rations. We remained out of contact with the enemy in this area until June 19. Finally we could use our B bags, the first barracks bags that followed us. We had clean clothes, a bedding roll, and for the first time in many, many nights, G.I. blankets to throw over ourselves.

On June 19, the unit was trucked from the St. Sauveur-le-Vicomte bridgehead to the area around Etienville. The 82d Airborne Division had been detached from VII Corps and attached to VIII Corps, with the objective of clearing the Bois de Limors. This, in turn, would serve as a jump-off point for an attack on the Germans at La-Haye-du-Puits. At my level, once again, we were not aware of our objective. All we knew was that whenever there were hot spots at any part of the bridgehead, that's where they sent the 82d.

Our trucks passed some of the areas of the peninsula the Germans had flooded. They had closed the locks at Carentan, a larger town located to our southwest, to dam the Douve. This, in turn, made the Merderet, a tributary of the Douve, overflow its banks, turning the fields into a swamp. The flooding had not shown up in our aerial reconnaissance photographs, and a lot of our troopers came down in these fields, landing in two to six feet of water. Many were drowned before they could get out of their chutes or get their heads above the surface. Even at this late date, the bodies of our troopers were still lying in the water. It was one of the most demoralizing sights I have ever seen. One trooper was lying with his head and left shoulder just out of the water. His bright red 82d Airborne Division patch was sticking out about six inches above the surface. I'll never forget the way that patch stood out.

When we got into the forest, we moved very slowly. The Germans had good observation, and they dropped artillery rounds in around the convoy. The trucks came to a screeching halt. The order was passed to unload and move to the head of the column formation. The drivers started backing the trucks off the road. Every time a shell landed, it speeded up their movement. They were trying to turn those trucks around so fast, they practically ran over us.

We moved in column formation, with squads on either side of the road. The Germans had very good visibility from one of the highest hills on the Normandy peninsula, dubbed Hill 131 on our military maps. As we continued, artillery fire increased, and we began to get a lot of tree bursts. We had experienced these before, and they were nasty. The trees were very tall, so the shell would hit high up, magnifying the effect of the fragments.

We advanced for hours through swampy ground and into regular hedgerow areas. Hill 131 rose up to our front. We were all very tired. We were told to halt and go into a hasty defense. For once the 3d Platoon was in support. We were in a sloping ravine, neither on the main line of resistance nor too far back, which provided a little cover. No sooner had we gotten into place than our platoon was given an attack order. We moved out again.

We started off through some brush, came out of the ravine, and started up a small slope on which the brush was very thick, similar to a field of goldenrod.

The only orders we had received were to attack through two or three more fields, then hold. I had no idea of what we were supposed to do next, and I had a bad feeling about this hasty attack. We started attacking in a column of squads. My squad, the 1st, was following the 2d, with the mortar squad in the rear. Lieutenant Carroll was up front to lead the attack, right behind the first and second scouts. They got to the corner of the first hedgerow to our front. The scouts got through it, and Lieutenant Carroll was just starting through when we were taken under heavy small arms and machine gun fire. This was coming from our left front, so there was a hedgerow between us and the German firing positions. The only thing we could do was go as flat as possible. It was a low hedgerow, and the machine-gun fire was skipping over the bank, clearing our bodies by twelve or eighteen inches. I lay there, prone, as the slugs impacted out in the field to our right rear.

A few minutes after we were taken under fire, some of us tried to move in order to shoot back in the direction of the enemy. Soon the word was passed down from the front to send Minica forward. This was an odd order, for Minica was a mortar man in the squad behind us, and would usually not be called up front. But Minica started moving up, all the while swearing and cursing and desperately trying to time his movements with lulls in the bursts of fire. As he passed me he growled, "What the hell do they want with me?"

As it turned out, the scouts had hollered *medic*, not *Minica*. Lieutenant Carroll had been hit and was one big bloody mess. A slug had penetrated the front of his helmet, bounced off his skull, gone around the inside of his helmet, and then dropped out. Minica made it through. So, eventually, did the medic.

The rest of us tried to stay alive and return fire. The enemy continued to fire, but it was still going high. Finally, the word came from the front to withdraw to our original company support area. I have often wondered how we got it, for we hadn't seen our platoon sergeant going up to the front to take command. I led the platoon back, crawling through the hedgerow to our rear. We made it around the corner, got around the hedgerow bank, set up a hasty defense, and stayed there. I reported to the company commander. I was distressed and depressed, because I thought we had lost Lieutenant Carroll. As it turned out, he returned for our next mission.

Back in our support area, we continued to dig in. We didn't have to be on 50 percent alert, so all of us got a few hours sleep that night. As the sun was coming up, I heard someone singing songs from *Oklahoma*. It was Neipling, belting out "Oh, What a Beautiful Morning" at the top of his lungs! What a cock-eyed optimist. This was the first time I'd ever heard the song, and it remains one of my most distinct memories of the war.

The platoon moved back to the line of departure for our previous day's attack and went into a defensive position. For once, we really had time to dig our foxholes and place our automatic weapons in the best possible positions. Usually, we tried to dig in along a hedgerow and set an outpost a field or two further out. At night, we pushed it out even further and called it a listening post. Now, though, we were in very close contact with the enemy, who occupied the hedgerow to our immediate front. This is where Lieutenant Carroll had been wounded and we had been stopped, so we didn't have the luxury of a listening post.

Our position was at the bottom of Hill 131. We had plenty of time to contemplate that hill; we stayed in position for the longest spell I can remember ever having gone without attacking in Normandy, and we were obsessed with a single thought: "When that hill has to be taken, we'll be the poor bastards who will have to take it."

Because the Germans were very close, we kept on 50 percent alert every night. Just as dusk was falling, we heard the Germans bring up chow by horse-drawn wagons, the creak of the wheels and their voices carrying clearly in the cool evening air. Once in a while, our mortars got antsy and tried to drop some rounds on their chow wagon. In return, they moved either to our right or left flank and fired a couple belts of ammunition into our position. We tried on a number of occasions to eliminate these guns but never succeeded. I often lay or crouched in my foxhole, which was quite elaborate by that time, watching tracers going six to eight feet over my head.

I was mighty glad to have my shoulder holster. Crouching or lying prone in a foxhole, you can get to a pistol at your shoulder a whole lot quicker than one at your waist, although I never actually had to do this. We kept our rifles on the ground at the edge of the foxhole with several hand grenades alongside, ready for use at any moment. But we all had nightmares of looking up and seeing a German staring down into the foxhole, with our rifles up on top. The pistol was like a security blanket that children need to go to sleep.

The weather at the end of June was horrible. On June 19, one of the worst storms of the century hit the beaches, and VIII Corps had to suspend its offensive operation for La-Haye-du-Puits. This left us holding in place in wet, miserable, muddy conditions, constantly barraged with artillery and mortar fire. While we were holed up in the Bois de Limors, a period of about two weeks, tree bursts caused 293 casualties—half the total for the regiment in the entire Normandy campaign.

The storm lasted four days. It damaged the installations on the beaches and supply dumps, which caused items like artillery and mortar rounds to be rationed. This was immediately before one of our major offenses, and the shortage of ammunition called for a new diversionary tactic. The idea was to deceive the Germans about the true location of the attack, in order to make them switch their reserves away from it. First, we made an accurate count of our machine gun and rifle ammunition. Then they ordered us to fire a number of rounds to put on the appearance of an attack. I believe the main attack was to take place on our right, between our position and the beaches. Our orders included the exact time we were to fire on the enemy position, and the exact number of rounds to use. Everything was calculated so each M1 and machine gun raised as much hell as possible without actually moving.

When we got this order, we dug deeper. We knew the Germans would not only be alerted; they would also lay down a final protective fire of heavy artillery and mortar. We dug like crazy and tried to get overhead protection in our foxholes. We designated sectors and fields of fire for each rifle, machine-gun, and BAR. I don't remember if they used a flare for the signal, or if we synchronized our watches, but at an exact moment, all up and down our line, we opened up and fired off the designated number of rounds. The noise was deafening; for every round we fired at them, the Germans must have fired two rounds back. They never did tell us if the attack was successful. We just followed orders, and got a hell of a lot of return fire for our trouble.

Eventually, we got the word that we were going to be relieved in place. The enemy's observation was so good from Hill 131 that instead of withdrawing by platoon and company and marching back, we had to slip to the rear by squads. This way, the enemy would not have large numbers of troops to shoot at, and we would suffer fewer casualties from artillery and mortar fire. It was a good idea, but I initially wondered why we were not relieved at night, for this would have hidden our movements from observation.

We infiltrated back to the rear under squad control to a designated area by following a compass reading. Even in daylight and with a compass bearing, the terrain prohibited us from seeing far, and I think some squads wandered around half the day and night, trying to find the assembly area. I ran into Chappie Wood near a pretty well defined point, as he encouraged the squads infiltrating back from the front. He was a fine chaplain, who made all four of the 505's combat jumps.

My squad's movement didn't go as well as I would have liked, but we managed to find our way back. They put us into an assembly or bivouac area under the cover of some trees. We received periodic rounds of artillery, but we didn't suffer any casualties. There, at long last, we were able to get a few days' rest.

On July 2, our dreaded prediction came true: the 505 was given the mission to take Hill 131. Colonel Vandervoort decided to attack in a column of companies. The whole zone was much too large to clear, and we were never at full strength after the first few days. At the time we got the news, Company F was down to around only fifty-five men.

Securing Hill 131 was the first objective in the plan to rout the Germans from La-Haye-du-Puits. This is one of the few instances we had time to issue a proper field order, and we knew what was really going on. The 2d Battalion was to lead a column of battalions to the first of three phase lines that increasingly narrowed the terrain from our line of departure, encircling the area and Hill 131 and mounting up to the summit. Phase Line A, at the base, ran from the swampy area called the Prairies Marécageuses to the village of Varenquebec to the south. At

Phase Line B, on the crest of a ridge, the 2d Battalion was to turn left and move to take the summit, which was Phase Line C. The 1st Battalion would continue straight ahead to the St. Sauveur-le-Vicomte—La-Haye-du-Puits highway, and the 3d Battalion was to take out the remaining pockets of resistance.

On July 3, Company F was deployed with the 1st Platoon to the left, the 3d Platoon and the remnants of the 2d Platoon to the right. At this point, the 2d Platoon was down to eight or ten men, having lost a stick on the drop into Ste. Mère-Eglise and suffered other causalities. They were to provide security on the right flank of the two attacking platoons.

As we went into the attack formation on the line of departure, Rosen and Brokaw, two of the survivors of the 2d Platoon, moved to the right of my squad. As a flank security patrol, they had a little more freedom of action. I tried to make a joke, saying we sure were glad to have the big 2d Platoon on our right flank. They replied in kind, telling us never to fear about this flank. The fact was, if anyone was to provide flank protection to my right, I would rather have had those two men and the remainder of the 2d Platoon than any other unit.

We moved up well before daylight into terrain that differed from the defensive hedgerow area below Hill 131. As we continued upwards, more brush, cover, and large trees appeared along the side of the hill. The hill was 131 meters above sea level and very wide, so we were only attacking one small portion. To keep us oriented, a .50-caliber heavy machine gun to our distant right rear fired at regular intervals so we could use the tracer streams as our right flank. As we moved up to the line of departure, we saw that Colonel Vandervoort had preceded us. There he was, in a raincoat with his crutch, his leg either still in a cast or heavily bandaged. It was pretty tough going for me and my squad, let alone for someone with a crutch and only one good leg.

We ran into resistance about two hedgerows out in front of our line of departure. The mortar fire was accurate; the small arms resistance was not as bad as we'd expected, but the mortar fire increased to heavy. The 1st Platoon and the rest of the 3d took causalities. I glanced off to my left flank as I approached a hedgerow, and I saw the mortar squad of Sergeant Brown's 1st Platoon just coming up. A mortar round exploded almost between the legs of a mortarman named O'Byrne. He was listed as DOW, but I don't see how he survived an instant.

None of my squad was hit. What really saved us was the weather. It was a rainy day full of mist and low-hanging clouds, which greatly reduced visibility. If it had been clear, they would have been able to drop far more artillery fire right on us. It turned out, too, that some of the Germans didn't like the rain. We actually had to pull some of them out of their foxholes and take them prisoner. They had covered their holes up so they wouldn't get wet, and were either taken by surprise or didn't want to fight.

As we advanced, we came upon a road. The first man in the 1st Platoon got to the hedgerow alongside it and discovered two or three Germans walking along, as if they didn't know an attack was underway. He fired a whole magazine from his tommygun and never touched a hair on their heads! He then hollered for them to give up. Luckily for him, they raised their hands and were taken prisoner, for he had totally emptied his magazine. This incident became a company joke. We kidded the guy about his bark being worse than his bite. He couldn't hit a damned thing with his tommygun, but he sure could scare the Germans into surrendering.

We got up to Phase Line B at about 8:20 A.M. The 1st Battalion went out straight toward the St. Sauveur-le-Vicomte—La-Haye-du-Puits highway, and we went to the left, toward the top of Hill 131. About half way up, we took some prisoners. One of them was a German officer who spoke excellent English. Judging from his accent, I thought he had probably been educated in England. At a lull in our movement I started to question him, not so much about our intelligence needs as about his views on the war. I asked him who he thought was going to win. Of course he said Germany. He teed me off by saying, "Aren't you a bit young to be a sergeant in the parachute troops?" I shut him up and took his watch, which was a good one. I turned him over to a guard to be taken back and interrogated, and we continued forward.

The 81mm Mortar Platoon did some pretty good shooting that day in support of our attack. We came to a German position that had suffered a near direct hit with 81mm mortar fire. One of the dead Germans had had a leg blown off, which was laying some distance from his body. An old song was still popular at the time, "I Ain't Got Nobody." Eisenhart started singing it to the blown-off leg, accentuating the words so it sounded like "no body."

Company F was the first to get to the top of the hill. As we approached the summit, the weather began to clear. We moved over the top and across a short, flat piece of ground that extended to the forward slope. We had very good observation into German-held territory, and the Germans could see us just as clearly.

A column of German infantry was withdrawing on the road, a good thousand to a thousand two hundred yards away. We had some eager beavers in the platoon. My machine gunner, Niepling, was one of them, and he opened fire. The tracers burned out long before they got to the target, but he must have hit close, because the Germans scattered off the road into ditches and hedgerows. Niepling was teed off that he hadn't gotten any good hits. His action did alert a German self-propelled gun that immediately took us under fire. It was eight hundred to nine hundred yards to our direct front, a tank chassis with an open fighting compartment mounting an 88mm. I ordered Niepling to cease firing, and we shifted to get some cover and concealment. There was precious little of either in the area, and the SP rounds hit far too close for comfort.

So there we were, lying out naked on the knob of one of the highest hills in Normandy, allowing a German 88 to fire directly at us. After we had taken a number of close ones, I hollered back for permission to withdraw far enough to get some cover, but close enough to defend the forward slope. The order came forward: no withdrawals. It was German doctrine to counterattack whenever a position was lost, and this is what our officers expected. So we lay there, taking the fire. I sent a runner to find someone with the authority to allow us to withdraw. I suggested we leave one or two men on the forward slope as an outpost and withdraw the rest of the squad back to the military crest of the hill. The answer was still no. The SP was plainly visible to us, but if we took it under fire, we would only draw attention to ourselves. At that range, our fire would have been ineffective, and we had no friendly artillery to call. The only thing to do was stop shooting and start digging in.

Then one of the oddest things I have ever seen happened. Eisenhart rolled over on his back in a very, very shallow slit trench, and immediately went to sleep.

After fifteen minutes or half an hour, I glanced to my rear over the slope and saw the company CP group coming up. I think Lieutenant Case was acting as company commander, because Captain Barnett had been evacuated due to wounds. I am sure they had been warned we were under direct fire, but they came forward enough to be seen from the enemy positions, and bunched up under a few big trees. Within a minute or two, the German gunner put a round right into the trees over their heads. There were five or six in the CP group, and I believe they were all WIA. I don't think any were wounded seriously, but they were all evacuated to the rear. Most, if not all, later returned.

Finally someone got some artillery fire in and around the German self-propelled gun, which stopped firing and moved. An hour or so later, we got orders to move to our right and further down the forward slope, where we could get some cover and concealment. We dug in pretty well in this position.

The day after taking Hill 131, we marked the Fourth of July. Every artillery piece, and I think mortars as well, fired simultaneously in celebration. The 8th Infantry Division took over the mission from the 505, moving through our position on July 8 to continue the attack on La-Haye-du-Puits. For a while, an occasional artillery round still came in, but basically, we were cleaning our weapons, waiting to be moved, and getting some much-needed rest. One of the biggest events was the arrival of some C rations. On July 11, the 82d Airborne Division was designated First Army reserve. Finally, we got the word we were going back to England.

Chapter 19

As Close to Home as It Gets:
Return to Camp Quorn

On D+36, we assembled from our position at Hill 131 and marched down to the road. Just off the road was the body of a very large German soldier, most probably killed in our attack on July 3. He was very ripe and bloated. Some comedian had painted a sign on a piece of cardboard, and hung it over a branch of the tree he was under. It said, "Please bury me, I am dead! Honest!"

We were trucked back to a bivouac area very close to the beaches. The area was entirely littered with a huge amount of government-issue equipment and clothing, all discarded by the follow-up units that had come off the beach and moved inland. Battalion headquarters had acquired several quarter-ton jeeps, which were quickly traded for booze with some of the naval officers from the ship that would take us to England. Within very short time, spray-paint outfits appeared on the beach. Don't ask me where they came from; they must have had their own power sources. The Army vehicles quickly became Navy vehicles, painted Navy gray, complete with fictitious registration numbers, and loaded onto the LSTs that took us back to England.

Our LSTs pulled away from shore late in the afternoon of July 13. We had been in Normandy for thirty-seven days. Company F had gone into combat with about a hundred forty-seven men, and I would guess that we loaded forty to forty-five troopers onto the ship returning to England. Those absent had not all been killed or wounded in action. Some had been evacuated sick, and recurrent malaria had especially been a problem for troops that had come up from the Mediterranean.

We debarked at Southampton amidst bands playing on the docks and crowds of cheering civilians. Back "home" at Quorn, too, we were met by wildly cheering crowds. As we marched along, many young women inquired about their boyfriends. It was hard to shout back the answers as we went by, but I'm sure many of them discovered bad news very shortly. Some people did receive news on the spot that muted the joyful noise of the crowd.

Within a couple days, we were given seven-day furloughs. I returned to Glasgow. Sadly, this time I was not in the company of Sergeant Ray, who had been killed at Ste. Mère-Eglise. It seems to me our whole time in England was quite short. My overriding memory is of how very peaceful it seemed after having been under fire for more than a month in Normandy. It took me a while to get used to the peace and quiet.

There were, however, some significant events. The 82d had the honor of having General Eisenhower troop the line during a division review on August 10, 1944. We were at full strength, having received more than six thousand replacements from parachute and glider schools. This was the only time I saw Eisenhower during World War II. There was also a regimental mourning parade to honor the men killed in action. We marched with our rifles slung upside down, muzzles towards the ground. The names of the dead were read off as the regiment stood at parade rest.

At the end of the parade, General Gavin stood on a jeep with the regiment gathered around him, and gave us a pep talk over the PA system about finishing the war in Europe. "When we get through with these damn Germans, we're going to clean up the Japs!" he finished triumphantly. A mass of groans rose up, as if someone had kicked the entire regiment in the backside. Not even Gavin could get us excited about *that*. We were *sure* that we were in the war until it ended in Europe, but we hoped and prayed we then would be allowed to go home.

Other events in Camp Quorn were significant for me on a personal level. Most importantly, our company commander asked me to take the first sergeant's job. In addition to the prestige, if you want to call it that, this meant a pay jump of three grades. I gave it a lot of thought, and decided to accept with one reservation: if I was not satisfied with the first sergeant's position, I could return to my sergeant's job with the 3d Platoon. This was granted, and I took the post.

Being first sergeant was big trouble. The major problem was that I had no qualified company clerk. This was a key man for the first sergeant, for the company reports could not be submitted in longhand, and it was the clerk's duty to type them. Without a fast typist who knew Army procedures, you soon became hopelessly behind in your work. I also should have had some administrative help from our company officers. In 95 percent of the cases, they were damn good leaders in combat, but a lot of them had no concept of administration. They were in the same boat as me, and thus of little or no help in bailing me out.

It seemed there was no end to the comings and goings that had to be reported, and I was no typist. Men were returning from the hospital daily, and some of our wounded were being sent home. In addition to keeping track of all of these people, reports on men missing in action required taking statements from the soldiers who had last seen the MIAs. On top of it all, we were getting replacements who all had to be accounted for and picked up on the morning report. A special report I remember particularly well asked for the location of each man killed in action, pinpointed by six-number map grid coordinates. It was impossible to locate the place of death for all our KIAs and plot them in such fine detail. In many cases, we were fortunate to have any map at all of the area in which the man was killed.

To add insult to injury, I received thirteen Joneses in a single group of replacements. Someone in charge must have gone down the roster alphabetically and said, "Here are thirteen Joneses! Let's assign them all to Company F!" Believe it or not, four of them had the same first and middle initials. Worse, we already had three or four Joneses in the company already. The only way I could tell one Jones from another was to read their middle names or go by their serial numbers. This is one time I complained loud and hard. I won that battle, for they split up the new batch of Joneses.

I worked many long hours alone at this job, which often extended to midnight. Of course, the first sergeant was also the first man up in the morning to call the company out for reveille, take status reports from the platoons, and perform a dozen other tasks. About the only good thing about it was that I never had to write death letters to the next of kin. I did have to keep after the officers to write them, though, for it was a very hard thing for them to do.

I remember particularly a regrettable incident that occurred one afternoon when I was busy with paperwork. A soldier walked into the orderly tent and asked if he could see a private named Arnold, a very nice kid from the 1st Platoon who had died of wounds in Normandy. Without thinking, I gave him a snotty answer. "The platoon is out for training," I said, "And besides, Arnold's dead." The soldier was Arnold's brother from the 307th Airborne Engineer Battalion, who had made a special day trip for a visit. I quickly apologized and attempted to make amends, but the damage had been done.

Maybe I did a good job as first sergeant, but I didn't think so. I requested to be returned to the 3d Platoon as a squad leader, and the company commander honored our agreement. I'm still very proud that they asked me.

Another important personal event occurred when my good friend Francisco and I were ordered to report to Colonel Vandervoort for an interview. Francisco was a sergeant in the 1st Platoon of Company F, a squad leader who later became a platoon sergeant. I called him the Red-Headed Reign of Terror, because he was always joking and playing tricks on other soldiers. He was a damn good combat sergeant. During our interview, the colonel said he had heard good reports about us, especially in combat situations, and we were candidates for field commissions to 2d lieutenant. The only qualification was that we keep up the good work. I don't know why we were all that crazy about becoming lieutenants. Infantry platoon leaders had the highest casualty rate of anyone in the U.S. Army. But we felt mighty good about it.

At Quorn, I got replacements in my squad, bringing it up to full strength and possibly one or two men over. Many senior commanders at both regimental and battalion level were often away planning new missions which were quickly canceled because the Allied armies moved so rapidly across Europe after they broke out of the Normandy peninsula. One of these, called Operation Linnet, got as far as the airfield. We were briefed on it down to the squad level, sealed in, and ready to be lifted out. The drop was to have been in Tournai, Belgium, and D-Day was set for September 3.

Of all the jumps I prepared for, this gave me the worst case of pre-combat jitters I ever experienced. Those of us who had been in combat the longest felt we had the law of averages working against us. I had such a bad feeling about being killed or seriously wounded that I almost sank into deep depression. I didn't sleep a wink the night before we were to leave. The casualties of "new" to "old" men were at a ratio of about three to one, I thought, but what the hell, the ranks of the older combat soldiers were still dropping. Luckily, the Allied ground armies overran the drop zones on September 2, and the operation was called off. We all breathed a big sigh of relief when they cancelled that one.

According to the regimental history, 186 members of the 505 gave their lives in Normandy. I could very easily have been one of them. After I had been shot at a few times, many things became second nature. Whenever we were moving, whether in an attack or approaching the front lines, whether in artillery, mortar, or small arms range, I kept my eyes open, continuously looking for signs of the enemy. This became automatic, as "natural" as looking both ways before crossing a street. With every step, I asked myself, "If I'm shot at now, where will I go? Where am I going to find cover?" To react quickly, you must prepare where you're going to go, minute by minute, second by second.

I knew a soldier cannot afford to become tired. Get a little wavy, and things catch up with you. Mental alertness and quick reaction time were two essentials that enabled soldiers to come back alive. I had seen its opposite, the thousand-yard stare in the eyes of soldiers—almost a trance. A soldier like this has been too long in combat. He will become one of the next casualties.

I learned the tricks of the trade. When to dig. How deep to dig. Whenever I was placing my BAR and machine guns, I asked myself, "What can the guns cover here that they can't cover over there?" In a defensive position, I always thought, "How the hell am I going to get out of here if I have to? What's the safest and quickest way if I need to withdraw?" I always picked an alternate position from which to cover the same field of fire. I always thought about where I was going to move if I was attacked from the left, the left rear, the front, etc. Much of this is standard procedure, but being shot at really drums it into you. Only after you've been under fire do you *really* understand the importance of your training.

I know for certain that thirteen Company F soldiers were killed in Normandy, and many times more were seriously wounded and never returned to duty. The stick dropped into Ste. Mère-Eglise accounted for many of these men. I have already named some of those we lost, but I shall name them again: Sergeant Ray, my friend, was killed in his parachute; Blankenship, a former member of my squad, was killed in his parachute; Byrant, Tlapa, Van Holsbeck, Lieutenant Cadish—all of these and more—never got out of their parachutes; Paris, a close friend and member of my squad, went missing in action and was later found with jump injuries; Corti, a BAR man in my squad, was wounded in action on the St. Sauveur-le-Vicomte bridge; and Lemieux, a rifleman in my squad, was killed in action trying to save my life. The memory of these men was sharp in my mind as I trained their replacements in my squad at Quorn.

Chapter 20

Market-Garden: The Combat Jump
at Groesbeek and Entry into Nijmegen

After many aborted plans for the 82d Airborne, the Holland mission, Operation Market-Garden, finally took place. The 1st Battalion, 505, and Division Headquarters went to Cottesmore, and the 2d and 3d battalions, 505, and Regimental Headquarters moved to Folkingham Airfield, about twenty-five miles north. We were sealed in according to standard procedure. No one could leave without a personal guard. I don't believe we were there more than a day or so. We were briefed on as much of the mission as was known.

The objective of the airborne invasion was to seize key bridges and the major highway along a 65-mile corridor, to permit the British Army to advance rapidly from the Belgian border through Holland. The plan called for a bold move up through Nijmegen to Arnhem on the northern branch of the Rhine, where the Army was to capture the bridge and make a run into northern Germany. Airborne units were to seize the bridges along the corridor, thus opening the way for Montgomery's ground force, LtGen Brian Horrocks's XXX Corps, to rush 20,000 vehicles up the highway and on into Germany. Moving from the south, there was a gap of seven or so miles between the front lines and the 101st Airborne, which was responsible for keeping open fifteen miles of highway from Eindhoven through Veghel. They were to form a protective corridor, seize the bridges and main highway, keep supplies coming, and permit ground troops to race up and break through the German main line.

The 82d was to drop to the north of the 101st; our division objective was to secure a ten-mile corridor from the Maas River to the Waal (Rhine) River, including the bridge at Grave and the half-mile long highway bridge at Nijmegen. Within the 82d, the 504 was the contact unit with the 505, but a second gap existed between the 504 and the 101st Airborne's area. The final section, from Nijmegen north to the key bridge at Arnhem, where the British 1st Airborne was to drop, was another eleven-mile corridor. General Horrocks was expected to reach Arnhem in sixty hours, and there link up with and reinforce the airborne forces. By this time, the Polish 1st Independent Parachute Brigade under MajGen Stanislaw Sosabowski was also to have jumped into Arnhem, bringing in troops, supplies and ammunition by glider on September 18. The Poles were to drop on the south end of the bridge, and seize it if the British had not already done so.

This was an ambitious plan whose success depended on excellent timing, close coordination, and unabated good weather. I learned during the briefing that in Groesbeek, just outside of Nijmegen, one could look over into the Reichswald, where a German armored unit had been reported. This constituted our main threat, because we were going to drop south of Groesbeek on DZs located within artillery and mortar range of the Reichswald.

We were told there was excellent intelligence in and around Nijmegen and Arnhem. Gavin and his staff expected a large armored counterattack from the part of the Reichswald facing the 505's area. The 2d Battalion, 505, was designated regimental and division reserve, the sole reserve battalion for the entire division. The 505 was to move to what they called the "high ground" north-northwest of Groesbeek and take up a defensive position. The area of operations was so large that there were too few troops to form a solid line around it, so we were to hold selected pieces of terrain and bridges over the Waal–Maas Canal, which ran south of us going into the Waal River. Company A of the 1st Battalion had the mission of taking it. The 504 PIR was to our west, and the 508 PIR was to our east, towards the Waal and the Reichswald.

September 17, 1944, fell on a Sunday. It was the first daylight airborne operation in the history of the European Theater of Operations. The Air Corps was also responsible for "flak suppression," protection against antiaircraft fire on the troop carrier command planes. The troop carriers, C-47s, were good planes, but they were slow and made good targets even for light antiaircraft fire. Because we were going to fly over enemy territory for ninety miles in broad daylight, most of the IX Tactical Air Command, which contained fighters and the fighter-bombers, was designated to support the transport of the troops to the operation area and protect against enemy fighters.

It was the greatest air armada in the history of warfare up to this time. It was said it took one and a half hours for the entire formation to fly past a given point. In all, there were nearly 20,000 troops, and 4,676 aircraft—transports, gliders, fighters, and bombers; 7,250 of these troops belonged to the 82d Airborne, which required 480 paratroop troop carriers and fifty gliders and tugs.[4]

We took off at ten o'clock in the morning. It was such a huge operation that it took some time for the planes to get into the air. We had to form up and get into the right slot in the air stream, so as to arrive at our designated drop zones at the correct time. The planes took off at five- to twenty-five-second intervals, and flew over England in three parallel streams, which taken together measured ten miles wide.

The weather was beautiful; it was a sunny day, observation was good, and it should have gone off without many hitches. To those of us sitting in the plane, everything seemed to be going just fine. Some of us old timers thought the mission couldn't be that bad, because the Air Corps was flying transport planes in formation in broad daylight so many miles behind the lines. At the time, I didn't give this much thought.

I was push-out, or last man in the jump. There were sixteen or more troopers in my plane, a heavy load for a C-47. I was worried that if someone got hung up in the door or jumped late, I would end up in western Germany. I was also apprehensive about the German armor we expected.

We crossed the English Channel quite a bit north of the front lines. From the minute we crossed the coast, heading east, we were under antiaircraft fire. Most of it was 20mm and 37mm antiaircraft weapons and machine gun fire, but as we looked out the windows, we saw our Air Corps fighters swarming all around the C-47s like a bunch of hawks guarding their young. We were flying so low I could see enemy soldiers looking up and firing their individual weapons at the armada.

Usually we had ten to twenty minutes between standing up and the order to jump. On this occasion, our jump master was smart enough to have us stood up, hooked up, and ready to go much earlier than usual because we were taking flak. Whenever we heard the bullets strike the plane, we glanced down the line to see if anyone had been hit. As push man, I had to go into the crew cabin in the front of the plane because there wasn't room enough for all the heavily loaded troopers to stand up in the main part of the troop compartment. I looked out over the pilot's shoulders and head to watch the approach of the drop zones. Planes were getting hit and going down in flames. Most of the pilots kept their formation. Otherwise, there would have been many fatalities as they flew through sticks of paratroopers who had jumped from preceding planes.

General Gavin and part of his division headquarters planned to drop first with the 1st Battalion of the 505 PIR, followed by the 3d and 2d battalions. About twenty-five miles from the DZs, they were surprised to see a serial of C-47s move in under them and drop a battalion of paratroopers from the 1st Battalion, 501, 101st Airborne Division. Gavin knew immediately there had been an error in navigation. As he got nearer to the drop zones, the 3d and 2d battalions were parallel to each other, instead of following in column as planned. The 2d Battalion element from the Troop Carrier Command got a quick change of orders, and we dropped on an improvised DZ to the east of Groesbeek. The two other battalions of the 505 landed on the correct drop zones.

Just before we got the green light to jump, a burst of machine gun fire shot through the plane, and our number-four man slumped. I think he was hit in both legs. I became very apprehensive about having to go out late and ending up as sausage in the Reichswald. But the man went out. I don't know how he did it, but when we got the light, he made it to the door and jumped. I forget that man's name, but I am deeply indebted to him.

Our stick made a good, fast jump and dropped in a nice, tight pattern. It being daylight, I could see the other paratroopers descending, and we all tried to stay away from each other in the air. The Germans were firing at planes and individual troopers as we floated down. Not long after my chute opened, I could see enemy soldiers on a light antiaircraft gun or a machine gun, positioned only four or five hundred yards from where many of us were landing. There was a building nearby, and some of us came down through the roof. Personally, it was the best landing I ever made. I sank up over my ankles into a plowed field, and the earth acted as a cushion.

Our first objective was to silence the antiaircraft guns. I got my weapon ready, got out of my chute, and headed toward the source of enemy machine gun fire. As I approached the gun I had seen from the air, I discovered that someone had already taken it out, or else the gunners had surrendered. From the air, it appeared that the 1st and 3d Battalions of the 505 and one of the battalions of the 508 were almost within sight of where we dropped. You can imagine the effect it made on the Germans' morale to see three or four parachute infantry battalions landing in such a close area. Colonel Vandervoort knew we were dropping on an improvised drop zone. He opened up the radio net and gave a new assembly point: the Molenberg Observatory, a large, German-built tower on the outskirts of Groesbeek.

Our assembly was quick and successful. It was daylight and our leaders had a landmark visible to all the troops on the DZ. It took only thirty to forty minutes to get assembled and ready to move. It turned out very well that we dropped east of Groesbeek, while the 3d Battalion, whose mission it was to take the town, dropped to the south. This permitted both the 2d and 3d battalions to move toward town, killing or capturing all the enemy in a pincer-like, two-battalion movement.

After I assembled my squad and led it into the platoon and company assembly, we moved to the northern edge of Groesbeek, which wasn't far off. We took German prisoners on the way, including some officers who had been driving down a hardtop road in a VW and gave up after a few shots. Along the way, my squad approached a building with a wall around it, and one of us jokingly directed the prisoners toward it. The Germans thought we were going to shoot them. We thought this was pretty funny, but as I look back, I realize it must have been terrifying for the prisoners. I hasten to say we didn't shoot them.

Going through the northern outskirts of Groesbeek, we were ecstatically cheered by the Dutch people. We didn't take many casualties moving from our drop zone to our reserve defensive area. We may have lost one or two men in the entire company. There were no losses in the 3d Platoon.

Our reserve area was on top of what they called Hill 81.8. Back home, Hill 81.8 would be nothing more than a gentle slope; but in Holland an elevation of nearly eighty-two meters is quite a rise. Our area ran northeast to southwest and was parallel to a railroad track, whose bed was a hundred fifty or two hundred yards down the slope. Although the battalion was in reserve, not much over half of Company F was in the reserve defensive position. We dug in and passed the rest of the day uneventfully, awaiting orders. We sent some small patrols out to our front, and some contact patrols with the 1st Platoon roadblock out on one of the hardtop roads, but there were no outstanding events until evening. There were quite a few jokes about having conquered the highest hill in Holland.

Initially the enemy was far more disorganized than we were. We were dropping in the Germans' rear areas and quickly cut them off from communications at higher headquarters. On our first day, a German field artillery unit or logistical support unit drove right into the 1st Platoon's roadblock and was taken prisoner or shot. The Germans had some horse-drawn vehicles that came through first, and the horses got killed in the shooting. It wasn't long before the Dutch came out of their hiding places and asked if they could butcher the horses for food. They received permission, and the 1st Platoon got treated to a horsemeat dinner.

About dusk, we were amazed to hear a locomotive coming from the direction of Nijmegen to our right. There were no other railroad tracks in the area, so we knew the train had to pass directly in front of us. No one, from the company or battalion level right on down to squad level, knew what to do. As a result, we did nothing. I don't know why we didn't shoot. Maybe it was because no one gave the order, or maybe everyone was just caught by surprise. That damn train came within two hundred yards of our position, passed safely right in front of us, wound its way into Groesbeek, and crossed into Germany.

Shortly afterwards we all caught hell. Orders were sent down that no more trains would be allowed through. By this time it was getting dark, so we decided to mine the tracks. But all available mines had been allocated to the 1st and 3d Battalions for roadblocks. Inasmuch as we each carried at least a pound of plastic Composition C explosives in a gammon grenade, we decided to use the grenades. We had no way to detonate these explosives—no blasting caps, no fuses, no primer cord—and we weren't sure we really wanted to destroy the tracks, so we used our Composition C as field-expedient mines, keeping our safety pins to the grenades after we had placed the gammons on the tracks. That way, if a train came, it would set the explosives off, but if none came along, we could reinsert the pins and remove the mines.

By this time it was completely dark, and we were in blackout conditions. Someone remembered I had gone to mines and demolition school, so I was given the dubious honor of supervising the mining of the tracks. It was a delicate job. First, we molded the plastic explosives onto the tops and sides of both tracks. After we thought they were well secured, we unscrewed the caps from the grenades. This allowed us to get to the safety pins, which we very delicately withdrew and saved. If this doesn't sound like much, try doing it under blackout conditions. Once the pin was out, all a grenade had to do was lean over hard from the top of the track, and it would go off.

I don't remember how many gammon grenades we planted, or how long it took us. I tried to tamp the explosive as much as I could. We went back to our foxholes and stayed on high alert for the remainder of the night.

Much to our surprise, we heard another locomotive coming down the track early the next morning. It even blew its whistle. The 2d Battalion unit furthest to the right opened up on it. It got by them, then the 2d Platoon of Company F took up the fire, and it got by them, too. When the train came to the area we had mined, the grenades went off and blew a small section of the track. The locomotive made it just across the break, and came to a screeching halt. We joined in with our small arms fire. Just to make sure, we put a 2.36 inch rocket from our bazooka into the engine.

The shooting died down after a few minutes. We didn't get much return fire. Most of the personnel were rear-echelon German military, and after the shooting started, they all jumped off on the other side of the boxcars. There were some wounded. We had to send out patrols, going under the boxcars and around either end of the train to pick up the prisoners. Most of them were taken within a hundred yards of the tracks and gave us no argument.

We were primarily interested at the battalion level in information that could help us in the next two to three hours. The interrogations were short and snappy. We discovered we had stopped the last train out of

Nijmegen. There was a lot of loot on it, and our company was well supplied with cigars, liquor and other booty for a few days. I heard that the cars near the end were full of radios, furniture, paintings, and other things of great value the Germans had looted from Nijmegen. These cars stretched back outside of my squad's area, so I did not see these things for myself. But I can attest to an even more important cargo. The first or second boxcar behind the locomotive was loaded with German potato masher hand grenades. If our bazooka round had hit that freight car instead of the locomotive, we'd still be flying.

After we had the train secured, some of us took out our ID panels, which were used to identify captured enemy vehicles. They measured about six by eight feet, unfolded. Whenever we captured a vehicle, we tied a panel down on the cab to keep it from being strafed by our own planes or shot up by friendly ground forces. We put two or three panels on the train to protect it from Allied aircraft. But they came down afterwards and strafed it anyway.

After things had quieted down, I climbed up on a boxcar that had some bodies on top of it. There I discovered a man, probably a railroad worker, dressed in a German military uniform. He looked to be in his fifties. I was only nineteen, so he looked to me like an old man. There wasn't a mark on him, and I couldn't determine the cause of death. I concluded the poor guy must have died of a heart attack amidst all the shooting. This dead man on the top of the boxcar is the thing that sticks in my memory. Strangely, it is not the action but its aftermath that I remember best.

These events occurred on September 18. Later in the day, our B-24 heavy bombers came in at very low altitude and dropped large amounts of supplies by parachute. I don't know if we completely recovered them, but we were so hungry by that time that the horse the Dutch cooked up looked good.

On September 19, General Gavin committed his division reserve to capturing the highway bridge and railroad bridge at Nijmegen. Company F, as part of the 2d Battalion, 505, learned we were moving into Nijmegen, a few miles up the line from the outskirts of Groesbeek. Company F was not part of the advance guard, which I think had been assigned to Company E. We also heard that British armor was approaching the division area. As we took up the approach march

Chemistry Class, Millcreek High School, 1940. Spencer Wurst
is sitting in the front row on the far left. *Author*

Members of the First Platoon, Company H, 112th Infantry, of Erie, at Indiantown
Gap Military Reservation, March 1941. Private Spencer Wurst is in the front row,
far right. Spencer's good friend Elmer Carlson is standing on the far left. *Author*

Full field pack inspection, Indiantown Gap Military Reservation, 1941. *Author*

Sergeant Rohaly's extra duty work detail, "port arm" with shovels and picks.
Private Spencer Wurst is holding the sledgehammer on the right. *Author*

Left: Spencer Wurst cleans his canteen cup with steel wool in preparation for a First Army inspection at Wadesboro in 1941. *Author*

Below Left: Corporal Spencer Wurst, Squad Leader, with an M1903 bolt-action Springfield rifle, at the base camp at Wadesboro, First Army maneuvers, 1941. *Author*

Below Right: Captain Gustav Hoffman, 1941. Hoffman was a tough, no-nonsense officer, and one of Spencer's role models. *Author*

Weapons carrier, 1st Squad, 1st Section, 2d Platoon, 1941. Driver: Robert Mesick. In truck bed, from left: Zdzislaw Dabkowski, Walter Zaborowski, Raymond Krupinski *Author*

Spencer Wurst and his brother Vern, reunited in Erie for their sister Vangie's funeral in August 1941. *Author*

Sergeant Spencer Wurst, 513th Parachute Infantry Regiment,
home on furlough in March 1943. *Author*

Sealed in for Normandy on June 5, 1944: members from 505 Parachute
Infantry Regiment, 82d Airborne Division at Cottesmore Airfield. In door of
C-47: Leonard DeFoggi. Back row, from left: unidentified, Richard White,
unidentified (pilot), Clifford Maughn, W. A. Jones, Sgt. Stanley Smith (Co.
G), Ralph Hyler. Front row, from left: unidentified, Lawrence Niepling,
Donald Glovier, unidentified, Dominic Marino (leaning over), Andrew
Kovach. *Leonard DeFoggi*

D+11 after the battle at St. Sauveur-le-Vicomte, Normandy.
Spencer Wurst is standing on the left; Andy Fabis is standing next to
him. Seated, Donald Bohm (left) and Harold Post (far right). *Author*

The squad in battalion reserve area before the battle for Hill 131, Normandy. Front row, from left: Howard Krueger, Lloyd Eisenhart, Harold Post, and John Zunda; Standing, from left: W. A. Jones, Andrew Fabis, Lawrence Neipling, Donald Bohms, and Spencer Wurst. *Author*

Members of the 505 riding on British Tanks during Operation Market Garden. *Daily Herald Collection, Museum of Photography, Bradford, England*

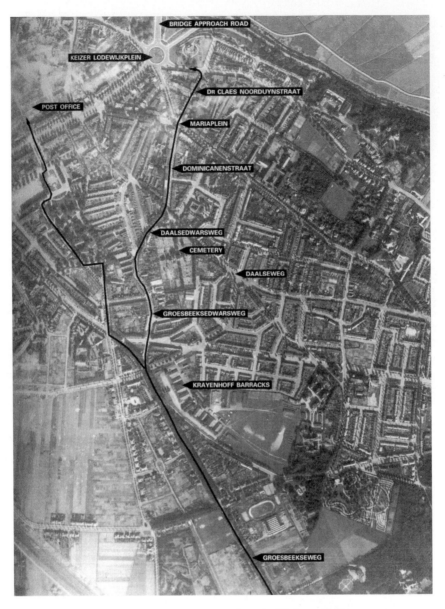

Aerial view of Nijmegen, approach to the Highway Bridge. *RAF*

Above: Aerial view of Nijmegen, Waal (Rhine) River, Highway Bridge, and Railroad Bridge. *RAF*

Left: Andrew Fabis, 1st Scout, 1st Squad, 3d Platoon, Company F, 505 PIR, at Camp Quorn, England, during General Dwight Eisenhower's review of the 82d Division on August 10, 1944. Fabis was killed at Hummer Park, Niemegen, on September 20, 1944. *Author*

Aerial view of Nijmegen, bridge approach, traffic circle, Hunner Park, and the Highway Bridge. *RAF*

A destroyed German machine gun nest in Hunner Park. A dead SS soldier, his head covered with a jacket, lies in the foreground. *Imperial War Museum*

This photo of the 60mm mortar squad, 2nd Platoon, Company F, 505 PIR, was taken at Camp Quorn, England, a few days before the invasion of Normandy. From left to right: John Ray, Philip Lynch, John Steele, and Vernon Francisco. John Steele is the man whose parachute was caught on the steeple at Ste. Mère-Eglise. He survived. The other three men were killed in action. *Jean Francisco Critelli*

Assistant squad leader Corporal Howard Krueger (left) and Private Robert Beckman (right) resting on the high ground west of Trois Ponts on Christmas Day, 1944. Both men were killed outside Arbrefontaine, Belguim, on January 4, 1945. *Don McKeage*

Sergeant Spencer Wurst, shown here in a studio portrait
snapped in Paris in November of 1944. *Author*

Sealed in for Normandy: Members from the 1st Squad, 3d Platoon, Company F, 2d Battalion, 505 PIR, 82d Airborne Division, at Cottesmore Airfield, England, on June 5, 1944. Back row, from left: Harold Post, Victor Sargosa, Howard Krueger, W. A. Jones, John Zunda; 2d row, alone: Donald Bohms; Sitting, from left: Andrew Fabis, George Paris, Thomas Watro, Arthur Lemieux. Reclining: Spencer Wurst. *Author*

Company F members salute a monument to the 505 at Trois Ponts, Belgium, in 1989. Left to right: Robert Reem, John Jacula, George Ziemski, Russel Brown, Chaplain George Wood, Spencer Wurst, Edward Dugan. *Author*

Spencer and Mildred Wurst on their wedding day, January 18, 1946. *Author*

Company F, 505 PIR members at 505 RCT World War II reunion, Columbus Georgia, September 1988. Back row, from left: Ed Slavin, Leonzo "Hoss" Pizarro, Spencer Wurst, unidentified, George Ziemski, Daryle Whitfield, John Jacula, Clafford Maughn; 2d row, standing: Robert Reem, Vincent Wolf, William Borda, Mark Alexander (Colonel, ret.), Donald McKeage; 3d row, kneeling: Roland A. Barone, Leonard DeFoggi, Kenneth Russell, Leonard Rosen, Russell Brown, John Zunda. Front, sitting: Richard "Teddy" Tedeschi. *Author*

Spencer Wurst, with niece Gayle Wurst and good pal Novi in upstate New York, September 2000. *Author*

Spencer Free Wurst, September 2000. *Author*

formation, we did hear tanks, and we were glad to see some armor as we got into the outskirts of Nijmegen.

One of the most incredible things about the battle of Nijmegen is that we went into the city cold. At the squad level, we were absolutely ignorant; we had no information whatsoever on the situation. We were under the command of a new captain who had never been in battle before, Captain Rosen. There was no briefing on the street situation, the boulevards, what to expect at the bridge, or even its exact location. Not only did we not see a map, we were going into urban street fighting at nighttime with no idea as to the size or layout of the streets.

As we moved into Nijmegen, we took advantage of all possible means to help us with our heavy loads. We were a pretty rugged looking outfit. We didn't hesitate to use mules and horses, and I've seen the 60mm mortar squad transport ammunition on bicycles and in baby buggies. We had only been able to find one horse. That poor animal was so heavily loaded down with ammunition packs and carriers it was almost swayback. No one complained about the unmilitary appearance of the various types of transportation.

We started picking up some heavy-caliber artillery fire on the outskirts of town. There was some big stuff coming in, which is especially frightening in a built-up area. We hugged the sidewalks as close to the buildings as possible, ready to dash into a house or take advantage of any cover we could get when we heard the artillery fire coming in. There was also small arms fire—rifles and machine guns—to our front. This caused the leaders to think they needed more automatic weapons, so they passed the word back to send up our BAR men. This order gave me pause, because we had been trained to fight as a rifle squad with all our assigned weapons, and sending our BAR men to the front broke the tactical integrity of the rear squads.

Nevertheless, I sent Eisenhart, my BAR man, to the front. He disappeared up the street, and this was the last I caught sight of him for months. He was seriously wounded in the leg, and I didn't see him until February or March of 1945, when he returned to the unit.

As we were moving into the town, one of our men was killed by artillery fire. I don't know why he was out on the street, but he had a reputation for looting the dead. He went so far as to take rings and very personal items. Each of us had a personal code of conduct that depended on our individual scruples, since senior officers, who were supposed to maintain a higher code of honor than ordinary men, were seldom at the front to supervise and enforce the terms of the Geneva Convention.

My code was never to shoot an unarmed man, but in a fire-fight a wounded man still firing could be shot. Wounded enemy soldiers would not get priority medical treatment, but they did get equal treatment with Americans. I never physically abused prisoners, and never saw any man in Company F do so, either, no matter how critical it was to obtain information that could be of immediate help. As far as looting went, the best trophies were pistols, which we all wanted. Next were military decorations, followed by watches. Almost everyone looted living prisoners of their watches, but most of the men, myself included, would not rob the dead. I positively never saw anyone cut fingers off to take rings.

When our one would-be looter fell on the way into Nijmegen, Dutch civilians ran out and covered his body with a blanket. As strange at it may seem, even though we were taking artillery fire, the Dutch were out on the sidewalks and streets to cheer and applaud as we entered the city. We were very concerned about their safety. Later on, as we got into Nijmegen, we didn't see any Dutch civilians except for members of the Resistance, who were quite numerous and identified by orange armbands. They were extremely helpful to the Allied units; they guarded prisoners, acted as guides, and performed other duties. We attempted to arm them with captured German weapons.

Colonel Vandervoort had given Company D the mission of securing the railroad bridge over the Waal River. Company D split off from the rear of the battalion column and headed toward the railroad bridge. The remainder of the battalion, Companies E and F, continued towards the highway bridge. It was mid-afternoon or earlier. There was quite a bit of shooting up ahead, and as we got deeper into town, British tanks came up on the street behind us.

It seemed the streets were becoming wider as we approached the river. There was at least one broad boulevard. Here the order of march broke up as Company E went to the right on one of the streets going toward the bridge. Company F continued a little further, then made a right turn up another street. This put us in positions that we would hold for the next day or two during heavy fighting, with Company E on the right, and Company F to the left on a two-company front. Within our company formation, the 2d Platoon was on the right, the 3d was in the center, and the 1st was on the left.

Because of the nature of the area in which we were fighting, we could not keep contact between platoons and companies. It wasn't possible to wait for one company or platoon to catch up to the other; each one fought its own little battle in its own street. This left us open to attack on the left and right, but maintaining contact would have slowed us down.

As we moved up toward the river, the streets running to the bridge went from left to right of our direction of march. We didn't know it, but a traffic circle led into the approaches to the bridge just a few blocks down from the boulevard. This was an ideal situation for defense. The enemy probably figured they didn't have enough troops to cover the area, so they pulled their main line of defense in close to the bridge. This, however, didn't keep them from sending out patrols and miscellaneous groups into the houses on the streets that approached the bridge or traffic circle.

As we crossed the streets that ran to our right, we took small arms fire. We double-timed across the boulevard, and continued up the right-hand side of the street for fifty to a hundred feet. There were homes on both sides, and a line of saplings ran between the street and the sidewalk. We flopped down and leaned with our backs to the houses.

At the enemy end of the street, a German antitank weapon was dug in at the traffic circle. A British tank hesitated at the intersection we had just crossed. It was touch and go for the tankers, because they had to dash across the boulevard and hope they wouldn't get hit. The tank turret and main tank weapon were turned to face down the street toward the traffic circle. As the tank crossed, its long axis was exposed, and the turret was at right angles to the direction of movement.

The tank made a dash across the intersection, fired a round down the street, and managed to get across. It headed up our street with its turret still based at a right angle to the direction of movement. As it passed us, the muzzle of the main gun hit one of the saplings along the street and spun around clockwise, almost doing a 360 degree traverse. When the muzzle hit the tree, I think it pushed the gunner forward against the firing mechanism. The last thing I remember, the gun was coming in line with me when the damn thing fired.

Chapter 21

Nijmegen: The Battle for Hunner Park and Control of the South End of the Highway Bridge

When the gun went off, the detonation was close enough to stun me. I was momentarily knocked out or lost my senses. I couldn't hear much for the next few hours, but I recall coming to and immediately remembering what had occurred. Another odd thing happened, too: my watch stopped, and I don't remember now if I ever got it running again. As for the tank, it just kept rolling down the street.

Luckily, the round was armor piercing. If it had been high explosives, it could have been catastrophic, but it was already very bad. The second man to my right was killed instantly. He was such a recent replacement I can't even remember his name. The man next to me was seriously wounded but survived. As soon as I came to I grabbed my first-aid packet and started to bandage him as best I could. We had been taught to use the first-aid packet of the wounded man rather than our own, to insure we still had bandages if we were wounded ourselves. In the confusion I wasn't thinking all that clearly, although my training did click in well enough for me to start working on him.

I was too stunned to have many memories of our actions between the time the tanker hit us and late evening. There was no time for briefing. We immediately went on the move and came under heavy fire. It must have been late afternoon when we reached the vicinity of a traffic circle that led into the bridge. Only later did we discover the tactical importance of the streets we traversed to our front, which ran almost perpendicular to those that led to the approach to the bridge.

We moved across a couple of streets, then made a right turn onto a street that led into Hunner Park. This was situated to the east or, from our point of view, to the left of the traffic circle as we approached the bridge. To the northwest of the large park was a built-up area, the Valkhof, that we called the "medieval castle." The traffic circle to the right of the park controlled all the circulation heading onto the main road that crossed the bridge. The park was at a higher elevation than the bridge and the road that approached it. We made contact with British tanks two or three blocks from the park. Either the 1st Platoon's area included the Valkhof, or this was our left boundary. This was not a single building, but a high bank running parallel to our line of advance once we got into the park. The Germans had fortifications or tunnels in the bank leading to the medieval structure.

What we did on September 19 in Nijmegen flies in the face of all tactical considerations. We were about to fight in the dark with tank support in a built-up area where we didn't know the layout of the streets. That we were ordered to do so is an indication of the crucial importance of the highway bridge over the Waal.

My next memory occurs at dusk. Lieutenant Carroll was back in command of the platoon. He was with a British Army major who was giving us a short briefing. Two squads from the 3d Platoon had been assigned as support for the major's unit. We were to follow close behind two tanks, giving them whatever protection we could. I think the mortar squads had set up to the rear, getting ready to fire into the park.

I led the squad as we set off. We made a right turn and headed up the street. I later learned it led directly to Hunner Park, where SS panzer grenadiers had dug in their defenses. The British tanks were abreast of one another. We followed them as closely as we could, seeking maximum protection as we peered ahead into doors and windows. I don't recall if I fired or saw any enemy soldiers, but they were there. As soon as we turned the corner, the tanks fired rapidly with their two .30-caliber MGs and 75mm cannon. The din was deafening.

We got a lot of return fire from the head of the street, heavy small arms fire. In addition to machine guns, rifles and machine pistols, the Germans had dug in some 20mm antiaircraft weapons. I don't know if they were twins or quads, but when they're shooting at you, it hardly matters. They fired tracer rounds with a ratio of about one to four. It was late enough for the tracers to show up well in the dark.

The fire became so heavy that the tanks momentarily stopped. They weren't damaged by the small arms and the 20mm fire, but it was a dangerous situation for the rifle squads. I got flatter than flat on the street, trying to get below a six-inch curb in a desperate search for cover. The fire immediately over my head cracked the air a foot or two above my body. I lay prone, hugging that curb for dear life, and I wasn't the only one. I don't think it gave us much protection except from our right front. If it hadn't been for the pavement, I'd have started digging.

After a few minutes, the tanks moved forward again. We jumped up and followed as closely as we could while still being able to look left and right for German foot troops with antitank weapons. We suffered some wounded. It's almost impossible to describe the racket of four .30-caliber machine guns and two main tank guns firing rapidly. The British tankers loaded a full 250-round belt and fired non-stop until it was run through. We had been trained to fire bursts no longer than twenty rounds, and I thought they were going to have a lot of burned-out barrels when the shooting was over.

We moved up the street for a block or a block and a half until we came to a burning building to our left front. The flames gave off quite a bit of light. Approximately fifty yards away, the tanks had come across a hasty roadblock made of saplings or the limbs of larger trees. The tankers would not advance or push the brush aside for fear of antitank mines hidden in the branches. Again the British officer appeared. He told us to "pip pip" round the tank and clear the brush and tree limbs.

I was reluctant because of the tank episode earlier in the day. At night, a buttoned up tank is practically blind. To advance around and move in front of those tanks would expose us to friendly fire as well as heavy fire from the enemy. We had almost gone forward enough for the traffic circle to come in view to our right front. It was a large area, and the

Germans had dug it in with at least one 88, as well as other heavy weapons. There were also most definitely mobile 20mm guns.

We nevertheless moved around to the left of the tank to clear away the debris. At that very instant, a German antitank gun let loose. The German gunner was anxious and missed. The fire came from our right front and went across in front of the tanks. The gunner probably couldn't see them, but he had anticipated their movement into his field of fire.

When an 88 fires on you at a distance of a hundred yards or less, you don't get much time to react. The tanks reversed, moving to the rear as quickly as their engines could get them there. One thing, and one thing only, saved us from being crushed—my squad had already started around to the left of the tanks.

Our relief was short-lived. The tanks' surprise withdrawal left us totally without cover. There we were, unprotected in a close group, visible from the burning building to our left front. To make matters worse, we couldn't take cover by running along the front of the buildings. All the houses on the street had a front yard of fifteen or twenty feet surrounded by a tall, spear-headed iron picket fence. There were only two ways to approach the buildings—over a fence, or up the sidewalk and into the house through the front door.

Someone tried the door of the closest house and found it securely locked. The next walk leading to the front of a building was even further forward, in the direction of enemy fire. The thing that saved us was an outside cellar entrance with steps that led down to a locked door. Both squads pancaked into that open cellar way. There wasn't even space for four or five men, but we managed to get twelve or more packed in almost solid, out of the light and dancing shadows cast by the burning building, which now was only a house or two away.

All firing had stopped when the tank withdrew. It was difficult to know what to do next. I moved out nearly to the front of the burning building to assess the situation and try to find more cover. The next day, we discovered the park was loaded with German troops in dug-in trenches and foxholes. There must have been two hundred pairs of eyes on me. Maybe they had orders to cease fire and see what happened, or maybe they didn't want to give away their positions, but why those Germans did not shoot, I will never know.

I went forward but saw nothing to my front except some tall trees. Then someone lobbed a grenade at me. I beat a hasty retreat and got back in the entrance way along with all the other packed-in bodies. We had one or two wounded men in there with us. One was DeFoggi, our assistant machine gunner, who later told me Lieutenant Holcomb had dragged him out from behind a tank back at the roadblock. He must have been wounded when the tanks took off and left us.

As we waited in the deepening silence, a terrible scream came from a house across the street. It lasted for thirty seconds, but seemed like it would never stop. Someone must have been bayoneted or knifed in the lower extremities, because no one could have screamed that long if the wound had been to the chest cavity. The sound cut through the silence, annihilating our morale. We never found out who that man was. He could have been German, English, Dutch, or American. Screams have no nationality.

We had been in the cellar way anywhere from ten minutes to half an hour when we heard German voices, very close and loud. Then the Germans started throwing grenades that landed in the street and sidewalks in front of us. The only thing to do was return the favor. As long as we were stuck in the cellar way, this was our only option. Small arms fire would have given our position away, and I guess the same could be said for the Germans.

A pin-pulled grenade remains safe as long as the safety lever is held against the grenade body. When thrown, the safety lever snaps off, arming the grenade, which explodes five seconds later. We were packed so closely there was only enough room for one man to heave the grenades. So we got one out, pulled the pin, then handed it up to Fabis, who was at the front. As soon as he lobbed it out on the street, we handed up another one. I don't know if he got elected because he was in front or because he had a good pitch.

A brief quiet followed our shower of grenades. We decided to make a break for a house, hoping to get through a doorway and into the back yard, then work our way back to friendly positions to our rear. One or two men went down the street a couple of houses and managed to get through a door. The rest of us followed, passing through the house and out the door to the back. The yards were small and surrounded by fences four to five feet tall. They made hard climbing with our full combat gear. The going was slow as we helped the wounded.

We climbed through several back yards before we stopped for a rest. Here, I discovered to my amazement that a squad member was still holding a pin-pulled grenade! The man had pulled the pin, thrown it away, and was about to hand the grenade up to Fabis when we took off. The whole time we had been going over those fences, he had been holding that grenade in his hand.

I told him to lob it, and pointed to an eight-foot wall separating us from a house facing the other street. But instead of throwing it far over the wall, he just flipped it over the top. Lo and behold, a single strand of wire ran a foot and a half above the solid part of the wall. The damn grenade hit the thing and fell right back into our yard.

When that grenade fell back on top of us, everyone knew what had happened. It was so silent, we heard the safety lever pop the five-second fuse. By the time it exploded, we were huddled in a crouch at the furthest point in the yard. Miraculously, no one was hit. I guess this doesn't speak much for grenades—they usually do a better job than that one did.

We moved back through the yards until we made contact with elements of Company F. We assembled in a house two or three blocks away from the park, close to our starting point. No sooner had we arrived than Lieutenant Carroll ordered us to go right back up the same damn street to establish an outpost at the roadblock we had encountered.

I didn't refuse an order, but we sure discussed it. I replied I doubted I could lead, or that my men would follow me that far. We had been on the go for a good number of hours, under very heavy fire during much of it. We were dead beat, we had taken casualties, and we didn't want to go too far up the street with British tanks still in the vicinity. This led to a compromise that allowed us to move only part way up. We found a building that looked like a school with trenches in the yard, positioned so we could occupy them and still cover most of the street that led up to the park. It was a very tiring time. I never heard anything from Lieutenant Carroll about my reluctance to move back up the street, and the position we occupied allowed us to be just as effective as if we had moved closer to the park.

I don't remember any outstanding events in the early morning of September 20. It seems to me that we moved one street to our right, facing the bridge, went up that street, made a left turn, and went up another street. We were still taking artillery fire. This was larger than 105mm, and could have been 155mm, and it was coming in at a steady pace.

As we searched for a better approach to our main objective, we found ourselves on a street of commercial stores with big plate glass windows on the front and sides. We heard a large-caliber shell come in, and a bunch of us dived for the furthermost recesses of a storefront. The shell exploded too close for comfort, almost in the center of the street. The entrance we were sheltering in was surrounded by plate glass windows, and all of them shattered. Glass went flying everywhere, but again we experienced a miracle. Eight or even more of us had crowded up in that entrance, but only one man was seriously wounded.

This was Lieutenant Carroll, who was hit by a shell fragment; it was a very painful and serious wound. The splinter broke the main bone running from his knee to his ankle. We gave him a shot of morphine from a first aid packet. When the medic came up, the lieutenant asked for another shot, but was told he couldn't have a second right away. The pain was bad, very bad, and the first shot hadn't taken hold, or wasn't going to.

We now had a wounded platoon leader on our hands. We couldn't afford to leave someone with him, and we didn't want to leave him lying where he could be hit again. Yet if we hid him, it was possible no one would find him. Finally we decided to put him in a house with a cellar window facing the sidewalk. We manhandled him down and placed a big white sheet of something on the sidewalk to indicate a wounded man was under cover in the cellar. I had to use some of my persuasive powers to kill the idea of leaving a second man with the lieutenant. If we left someone with everyone who was hurt, we would lose two men for every one wounded. So we left Lieutenant Carroll in the cellar, and moved forward until we again hit the street to our right that led up to the park.

As we tried to organize our approach, we were able to make a little reconnaissance. I put my machine gun crew in the second story of a building that looked almost directly up the street towards the park. They were to cover us as much as possible as we moved up the street. Both rifle squads of the 3d Platoon were on the right side of the street that led towards the park. A lot of heavy small arms fire began to come in again. Worst of all were the 20mm anti-aircraft guns. We worked our way up and through the houses, and sometimes out on the sidewalks, advancing towards the end of the street to get into assault position.

I don't recall who was commanding the platoon. We had gone in with two officers, but I think they both had already been wounded.

We had a hard time moving up the street. We tried to take cover by going through back yards and passing from the windows of one building into another. In this type of fighting, the regular infantry would do what they call "mouse holing," getting into a house and blowing the wall into the next, continuing down the row instead of going out in the streets. We unfortunately lacked the explosives, and the damn picket fences kept us from sneaking along the house fronts. We had to climb over them, and there was just no good way to do it. The spearheads kept catching us and hanging us up. Finally we managed to work our way up to the house on the right-hand corner, overlooking the park, and take cover. This was at the end of the street, directly opposite the house that had burnt the night before. The fire had died out, but the house was in ruins.

We now were very close to the park. We had to exit the house, go past the picket fences, turn right on a wide street, and there we'd be. When we reached the corner, Captain Rosen appeared; he said we were going to assault the park. I'm not sure about the 2d Platoon, but by now the 1st and 3d were on line at the end of their respective streets. We didn't question Captain Rosen's order, but I think we should have. To assault Hunner Park, both we and the 1st Platoon had to come out of our shelter, go fifteen or twenty feet to the sidewalk, move up the street that ran perpendicular to the park, cross the street that ran parallel to the park, and force our way into it.

Captain Rosen led the attack with his tommygun, crying "follow me!" I passed the word that the captain was going to lead, and came out of the house at the head of my squad. Most of the troopers followed me out. We got to the street and started into the park under direct small arms, grenade, and machine gun fire at ranges of fifteen to seventy-five yards. We formed a crude line on the run and assaulted across the street. The enemy was well dug in, fighting from foxholes and trenches located between the sidewalk on back to a hundred yards into the park.

Just as we got into the skirmish line, a crucial thing happened. A very big, scared German soldier—I only saw him flash in my mind—leaped up from a foxhole just inside the park. He lifted his hands up over his head as he ran across the sidewalk toward us. There was absolutely no doubt about his intentions. He had his hands up high over his head, very evidently wanting to surrender. But as he leaped up, many men fired on him. In combat you must react instinctively and quickly. This is what we did, and the man was practically a sieve before he hit the ground.

Years later, I wondered why he had waited so long to give himself up. No doubt, if he had attempted to surrender earlier, he would have been shot by his own men. The park was manned by SS troops, die-hard Nazis, some of the toughest the Germans had. Nevertheless, if that one man had only waited to be dug out of his hole and then surrendered, or if he had jumped up and run toward us before we began the assault, the battle might have been less ferocious.

Because this incident occurred in full view of everyone in the park, I believe it resulted in many needless casualties. We took very few German prisoners. SS troops were very determined fighters in any case. We were facing the 9th SS Panzer Division Reconnaissance Battalion. At least five hundred of them were manning the bridge defenses. Where regular German Army troops might have given up, the SS simply would not. But when they saw us shoot that unarmed man, they thought they didn't have the *option* to surrender. Our casualties were heavy, but the Germans' were worse. At the end of the day, only sixty were still standing to be taken as prisoner. Around a hundred more escaped, but the vast majority had been killed or wounded.

I don't know how many men from either platoon made it across the street on the first assault, but we took many casualties. I got across and into the park. Just before I took cover, I saw Captain Rosen run back down the middle of the street. He passed me going full speed to the rear, holding both his hands over his mouth. He had evidently been shot through the face, and he later died of this wound.

I was just inside the park, near the sidewalk leading around the edge. I dived into a bus stop enclosure with glass on the top half and some other material about halfway up. I took concealment, but there wasn't much cover. I glanced down the street and saw Germans coming into the park a little beyond the 1st Platoon area. As I attempted to take them under fire, my rifle jammed on me. It absolutely froze.

I knew I couldn't stay in the enclosure, which was quickly becoming shredded by small arms fire. I crawled out on the sidewalk. Six or eight feet away I saw a hole, dug very nicely and surrounded with fresh earth that the Germans hadn't had time to carry away. I crawled over to it, dropped down in, and attempted to clear my rifle. No sooner had I got in the hole than a rain of bullets impacted the dirt piled up around it. I looked out and discovered one or two other men from our platoon going back across the street into the houses.

Although the firing never stopped completely, it sometimes slowed down a little. During one of these lulls, I hollered across to the corner house for my squad to cover me, saying I was going to dash across the street. I was closer to a whole lot of Germans than I was to my squad, and if any SS happened to understand English, they would have been alerted to my movements.

I jumped up and ran across the street. Rather than expose myself on the sidewalk, I attempted to vault a picket fence. I didn't do it very gracefully, but I got over and made it into the corner house we had occupied before the assault. There I immediately cleared my rifle. It was filled with plaster dust and other dirt from the houses we had gone through.

Suddenly, a question dawned on me: "Where the hell is my machine gun?" The crew had failed to displace forward from the house we had placed them in an hour or more before. In the excitement and confusion I'd forgotten it! Captain Rosen had been in a big hurry to assault the park, so he hadn't given us much time to follow correct troop-leading procedures. Nevertheless, it was standard operating procedure for the machine gun to displace forward and take up a new position whenever its fire was masked by an advancing squad. I got word back to them to displace forward into our house. I was upset, especially as the machine gun should have been put in position before we assaulted the park.

When I got back from the park, I also discovered we had lost a man by the name of Hall, who had joined us at Quorn. He'd been killed near the entrance of the house, and still lay dead on the sidewalk. Niepling ran out, removed Hall's wristwatch and then dashed back. He assured me he had loaned the watch to Hall the night before, when Hall was next in line for alert status. Niepling considered the watch a valuable personal possession, but I didn't care how valuable it was. I could neither understand nor accept him exposing himself in plain view for the sake of a damn watch.

I moved into a position outside the house, where a vestibule that stuck out offered some protection from the front, then I exited the vestibule and made a sharp left turn behind it. Quite a ways up, a ledge jutted out about a foot from the wall. I climbed up and had a pretty good view all the way to the far end of the park. It was obvious to see the enemy was bringing in reinforcements.

I got into the best firing position I could and took these men under rapid fire. I had to shoot around the corner of the vestibule, thereby exposing my head and upper torso. I also had to lean to the left from the waist up, a very unnatural, cramped position, while I kept my feet in place, planted on the ledge. The enemy was only visible for a short period of time. I fired rapidly, first as they were exposed, and then to cover the area where they might be hidden. The more I shot, the more of them I saw coming up over the bank.

I soon expended all the ammunition in my cartridge belt. I hollered down to the men in the house to throw some more up, and I continued with my rapid fire. My rifle barrel got so hot that it heated up the forearm and front guard over the barrel. It actually boiled the oil residue out of the wood, and probably some of the cosmoline too. I continued to fire, and got a lot of fire in return. All the while, this stuff was bubbling out of the wooden hand guard.

Lieutenant Holcomb came up and gave us a short briefing. "Little Joe," as we liked to call him, had taken command of the company after Captain Rosen was hit. Being a more experienced commander, he didn't try anything spectacular. We were to undertake a new assault of the park as soon as the entire 1st and 2d platoons came on line, and Company E had worked into the near edges of the traffic circle. The assault would be coordinated either by radio or timing. At the very least, we knew that when we went into the park the second time, the coordinated force would be larger than the first assault, in which only the 3d Platoon and elements of the 1st had participated.

As we got ready to go for the second attempt, Lieutenant Holcomb calmly walked out on the street and gave the order to assault. I followed him with the survivors of my squad behind me. We came out of the house on the double and got into a rough skirmish line, formed on the run. I glanced to my right and left, and what a sight I saw! A nearly perfect, coordinated attack by two infantry companies on line. Our companies were probably about 90 to 95 strong at the time, so going in we totaled 180 to 190 men. Our alignment was very good, well formed to my right and left, with everyone going in on the double to get into cover in the park. It was a very grand sight to behold.

The enemy's fire combined with our own was deafening. It was the hottest, heaviest fire I had ever encountered. We took heavy casualties. A 20mm round killed Lieutenant Dodd on this or the first assault. The 1st

Platoon medic went over to him, but he was killed in the attempt. Lieutenant Holcomb was seriously wounded, my close friend Fabis was wounded and later died, and many others were fatally hit or wounded before we reached the middle of the park.

The small arms fire was so overwhelming that it momentarily stopped us. It appeared to me that I could reach out and grab the bullets as they flew. I took cover in the prone position behind a very large tree. I fired as fast as I could, and many rounds of enemy fire burrowed into that tree trunk. They were shooting anywhere from six inches to a foot and a half high. I can't describe the intensity of the fire we were receiving. It's a miracle anyone lived though this short period. A British tank had moved in shortly after the assault, although I don't remember any British tanks in the area before we began. We were firing, the tank was firing, and the enemy was firing. It was one huge, deafening racket.

From behind my tree, I observed Krueger as he crawled fifteen or twenty feet to my right front. He actually reached down into a foxhole, grabbed a German, and pulled him out. He motioned the prisoner to the rear, and both of them crawled back to our skirmish line. The German didn't stop. Instead, he crawled another twenty feet and stopped to help our medic bandage one of our wounded. Very shortly thereafter, he was killed by German fire.

I glanced to my right rear and saw Colonel Vandervoort, our battalion commander, approaching my position. Our dead and wounded were lying all around us, hit only moments earlier. We pleaded with the CO not to expose himself to the heavy fire, but he continued until he reached my position. He looked at me and calmly said, "Sergeant, I think you better go see if you can get that tank moving."

I asked him again to take cover, then I jumped up and ran to the tank. I took off my helmet and beat on the turret. Finally, the hatch cracked open six inches. I hollered to the tank commander, relating the colonel's order to move forward and continue firing. We talked a minute or two, and I pointed out targets. While I was showing him where he should shoot, I had to remain standing. Finally the tank lumbered forward, and I gave arm and hand signals to what was left of my squad to get up and start moving.

We moved forward, still in a rough skirmish line, until we came across barbed wire running mid-width of the park. It wasn't laid heavily, but we wanted the tank to move through to make a path. Instead, it advanced a little to our left front. We went to the right, and had a real time getting through the wire. Niepling, with a shortened belt of ammo, was actually firing his light .30-caliber machine gun from the standing position as he moved through the wire. Then there was a little Greek from the 1st Platoon, George Pagalotis, a bazooka man whose bazooka was almost as long as he was tall. He ran right up to a fortification dug into a bank by the Valkhof and fired a round directly into the opening. I think someone from the 1st Platoon got the tank's attention and moved it over to the bank, where it fired rounds into the fortification from five to six feet away. Talk about direct, point-blank fire!

My squad was the first to break through to the east side of the park. When we got on the east side of the barbed wire, we dropped into a well constructed, World War I-type trench the Germans had dug. From here we had a good view that overlooked the approach road, the entrance to the bridge and the bridge itself. I heard some shouted commands from my distant left rear that I later learned was British infantry moving up by the numbers.

As we dropped into the trench, groups of Germans started to withdraw across the bridge, taking cover behind the girders. This was a bad move. We had seized the high ground overlooking the bridge and had a perfect view. As soon as they dashed to the next girder, we had them. There were thirty or so to start, but I don't believe a single one got across.

Right after, another group of Germans came from our left. This group was pretty smart. They rushed up the left side of the bank all together, went over the top, across the road, and down on the right side of the road that led to the bridge. There was a large drop-off on the east side of the road, and so they gained the cover of the roadbed. They took us by surprise and got away with it.

I took two or three people and scrambled down the bank and onto the road. I thought we could get some good shooting by going over to the berm and looking down, but the Germans had anticipated our movement and barraged us with grenades. Rather than risk death or serious injury, I withdrew to the trench with the men I had taken.

Shortly, off to our far front along the open south bank of the river, we saw a German running through a plowed field with little cover or concealment. He was at great range, eight hundred to a thousand yards away, but our visibility was excellent, so a couple of us fired a shot at him. He continued plowing through the field. Then Niepling got onto him with two or three bursts of his machine gun. The German fell and never moved again.

As I look back on the battle in Nijmegen, for the life of me I cannot remember who was in command of the company after we took the park. To my knowledge, no officer came forward immediately after Lieutenant Holcomb was wounded in the assault. Later that night or early the next morning, a first lieutenant may have come to the company and assumed command. I heard from one of my friends in the 2d Platoon, Corporal Rosen, that a senior officer had approached him after the assault and told him to take command of the remains of the company. When I looked around me at the far end of the park, it appeared to me that I was the senior person. I'm not saying that I took command of the whole company. I'm just saying that after the assault very few authoritative voices were heard on the east side of the park.

The 2d Battalion, 505, received a Presidential Unit Citation for the action in Nijmegen on September 19 and 20, 1944, along with the 3d Battalion, 504. I received the Silver Star for action in the park. All the Company F officers who were anywhere near the heat of the battle became casualties, so I've often wondered who submitted the request for the award. I think it may have been Colonel Vandervoort, but I never did find out.

Chapter 22

Aftermath: Hunner Park and Bridge Security

Our final assault on Hunner Park was over in less than half an hour. Despite disastrous casualties, we took the park and the southern end of the traffic bridge. Meanwhile, the 3d Battalion, 504 PIR, led by Maj Julian Cook, made a river crossing in assault boats about a mile downstream from the Nijmegen railroad bridge in order to seize the railroad and traffic bridges at the northern end. It was an extremely dangerous mission. At that point, the Waal was four hundred yards wide. Crossing in plywood-bottom boats with canvas sides, they actually assaulted in broad daylight against heavy, close-range machine gun and mortar fire—and were successful. They then pushed on for the highway bridge. Major Cook compared his battalion's actions to making an Omaha Beach-type landing all by themselves.[5]

The British were losing their area across the lower Rhine at Arnhem, fighting in circumstances so tough that they were almost decimated. Although we had no idea of any of this down at my level, the 101st Airborne Division, too, was having a very rough time securing the long corridor to our rear, which formed the single axis of advance. Their success was essential to the British Second Army and the British XXX Corps, which planned to sweep up through the corridor to Nijmegen and on to Arnhem with heavy infantry divisions and armored forces. Even after September 17, the Germans successfully pierced the 101st defenses, because they were so spread out. Not for nothing did we call this corridor "Hell's Highway."

This enemy action took its toll on those of us to the north as well, because it stopped the flow of combat units and logistical support needed for the 82d, the British 1st Airborne, and whatever British armor had already preceded north. The Nijmegen highway bridge was absolutely crucial to keeping the corridor open, and everyone knew it was wired for demolition. We all expected to see the bridge go up in pieces. The only question was when.

Following our assault, I heard English accents to our left, and saw people in the area of the British Grenadier Guards on the left flank of our 1st Platoon. Word passed from the British troops that one of their officers was looking for volunteers to go to the bridge, climb the girders, and cut the demolition wires. I don't think any of us volunteered. The request came before we had finished consolidating the park, and we had our hands full. There were still plenty of Germans to our left and left front, between the Valkhof and the underside of the bridge. Very soon thereafter, I heard long, sustained firing. Soon the word came down that the officer and all the volunteers had been killed. There was a lot of area between our left flank and the river. I don't know if they even got as far as the bridge.

Our trench on the park bank gave us a view of the first Allied crossing to the northern side of the bridge. About fifty yards in front of us, parallel to our position, three tanks came down the main entrance road, very close together. The lead tank was about a hundred yards from the bridge when a German antitank gun took it under fire from across the river. The 504 had evidently not yet secured the north end.

The road bank dropped sharply on both sides, so there was nowhere for the tanks to go except backwards or straight ahead. The tanker immediately returned fire, and a second tank fired across the river too. I don't know if they even knew what they were shooting at. The lead commander started popping smoke grenades, and soon had four, or maybe six of them out in front of him. The tanks had to back up, and it was very precarious to get out of the line of fire. Very shortly afterwards, all three made another run and managed to cross, although they may still have been under some fire. This rounded off the success of the battle at Nijmegen, opening up the corridor to reinforce the British 1st Airborne at Arnhem.

We didn't completely consolidate our position until dark. Some classic stories Company F loves to tell occurred about this time. There's one about when little Sergeant Rhea was wounded. He was in the prone position, and Lloyd Ellingson, the 2d Platoon medic, was working on him. Rhea looked up over the medic's shoulder and spied a figure approaching. Lying right there, flat on his back, he challenged the person. It turned out to be a German, who shot and killed Ellingson. The German didn't get far before he, too, was killed. These are more examples of the useless deaths I spoke of earlier. If the German had given up, both he and Ellingson would have survived the battle. As it was, two out of three of our platoon medics were killed in Nijmegen: Ellingson and Vernon D. Carnes, the 1st Platoon medic, who was killed as he helped Lieutenant Dodd.

Another story concerns a soldier called K. B. Hungerford, who had been a sergeant in Company F, but was later transferred to Service Company, a non-combatant assignment. From what I understand, he was quite anxious about his old buddies in Company F, so he came up to the park to see what he could do. It's said he volunteered to go to the bridge when the British officer came looking for help. Completely on his own, he left the safety of his non-combatant unit and was killed in action.

Other stories illustrate how deeply fatigued and worn out most of us were at the end of that battle, like the time I slept through an explosion. Things had quieted down a little, and we had gone on 50 percent alert. My squad was in a trench with a dugout. I was off alert, so I lay down in the dugout and went sound asleep. We hadn't slept much in two or three days, and everyone was beat. I thought we had cleared the park, but while I was sleeping a mortar or grenade exploded almost on top of us. Mike Brilla, a member of the squad, was wounded and ended up losing an eye. This mortar went off just a few feet away from our trench, but I slept straight through it. The squad had to tell me when they woke me up that Mike had been evacuated.

The next morning, after daylight, we were all awake and on alert, taking turns disassembling, stripping, and cleaning our weapons. Up the bank, walking upright, came a German officer with his hands over his head. He wanted to surrender, but only to an officer. I don't remember this story as clearly as Bill Hodge, a platoon member, does, but I know my rifle was in pieces when the German officer showed up. I pulled out my pistol ran down towards him and escorted him to the trench, his hands still over his head. He was wearing an Iron Cross, so I whipped out my trench knife. All I wanted was his decoration, but Hodge says that poor German was sure I was going to slit his throat. I cut the Iron Cross off his blouse and took it as a souvenir, and he seemed greatly relieved. So that's how a lowly sergeant convinced a German officer to surrender by holding a trench knife to his throat. I still have the Iron Cross.

That day, September 21, the Polish 1st Independent Parachute Brigade dropped on the south bank of the lower Rhine as reinforcements for the battle at Arnhem. Their planes flew almost on line over us in the park and continued north. Still well within our sight, they took serious antiaircraft fire. It wasn't as bad as the fire the gliders had encountered on the first evening in Normandy, but it was very heavy. Those paratroopers were obviously headed for extensive casualties.

I later learned that the planes carrying a third of Sosabowski's 1,500 troops had turned back because of bad weather. Those that made it dropped on the south side of the river at Driel on last-minute DZs after the British were overrun at Arnhem. They never managed to get to Arnhem, but they did facilitate withdrawal for the survivors of the British 1st Airborne, which went into Arnhem with 10,005 men and came out with 2,163. Only 160 Poles came back across the Rhine with the survivors. We ourselves were picking up British paratroopers coming back to our lines in and around Nijmegen for weeks after September 20.

September 21 was also the day Company F got a new commander, 1stLt William F. Hayes. We moved to a position south of the park on the east side of Nijmegen for a day or less, then crossed to the north side of the river, where we stayed until September 24. It was a relatively quiet position. We may have gotten a few short artillery rounds aimed at the bridge, but we didn't see much action.

We took over security for the Nijmegen highway bridge on September 24. The 1st Battalion stayed on the south end, and the 2d and 3d battalions moved to the north side. The British had moved forward of our position, and we were more or less covering their right flank. Again, there was little action, but there was a lot of shrapnel from German artillery and a big railroad gun. I saw my first jet aircraft here, a German fighter. It was a sight to behold. We heard a loud noise in the sky, and looked up where we thought it was coming from, but by that time the doggoned plane was almost over the far horizon. We hadn't even *heard* of jet airplanes yet. I don't think the antiaircraft guns came within two miles of the thing, and it was soon out of hearing.

The British took over safeguarding the bridge on September 30. They relieved us at midnight. We were to move back across the river the following day. That night, the Germans sent frogmen down the river to plant explosives around the bridge. Before daylight, they blew a portion of the highway bridge, and dropped a span of the railroad bridge into the river, temporarily putting it out of operation.

This was a pretty close call for us, but we were still on the north side of the river when the explosion took place. Traffic on the highway bridge never stopped altogether, but there were priorities for its use, and troop movement from north to south was not among them. We were moved back across the river in DUKWs, two-and-a-half-ton amphibious trucks primarily used on the beachheads. Coming back across the river, I thought about what a blow it was to come back in DUKWs, after losing so many men and shedding so much blood to take the damn bridges.

Everyone I knew in Company F was proud of the way we had carried out our mission. We had taken our objectives in Nijmegen, and the 82d had elsewhere done everything it was supposed to do. But overall, the mission failed because the British never took the Arnhem bridge—the objective that would have allowed the British Second Army to swing around to the north and enter Germany.

Chapter 23

Defensive Operations: Road Blocks, Dikes, and the End of the Holland Mission

After we recrossed the Waal on September 30, we moved southeast into the flats between Nijmegen and the German border near Horst. In some places, the river formed the border in this area. I understood our defense depended mainly on two large roadblocks between Horst and the German border, where the road branched into a "Y." We were still short of company officers at every level. What had happened to Bonnie Wright, our platoon sergeant, and the platoon sergeant of the 1st Platoon, I don't know. They should have been in charge of the roadblocks, but in their absence, I got the job of commanding one of them, and Sergeant Francisco, my buddy in the 1st Platoon, was in command of the other.

We moved out at night, and put the better part of Company F out on the roadblocks. The ground was flat, and on a clear day we could see a long way to the south, and—even better—to the east, toward the Reichswald along the Dutch-German border. I could just barely make out Francisco's roadblock, and we could hear any shooting from there. Ours was about a thousand yards in front of what should have been the main line of resistance. I don't really know what we had back there. I had twelve to fifteen men with me, probably all that was left of the 3d Platoon.

Once we got our foxholes dug pretty deep, movement in daylight was almost impossible. The Germans were very close, in heavy positions in and around houses off to our left front, with listening outposts uncomfortably nearby. Most days, they got nasty with the sniper fire. We often had to pee in tin cans and throw it out of the foxhole.

We were dug in almost in a circular position. Radios were unreliable and noisy, so we used sound-powered phones and field wire. We had no artillery forward observer officer, but we did have an enlisted man, an 81mm mortar platoon FO, observing mortar fire for both roadblocks. It was a nerve-wracking position. The Germans sent patrols almost every night; they got between us and the company CP and cut our telephone wires. The company commander asked for volunteers to restring the wires and bring us out rations and ammunition at night.

We here were introduced to the *Nebelwerfer*, a multi-barrel, electrically fired, 150mm rocket-launcher mounted on wheels. Its horrifying screeching sound led us to call it the "Screaming Meemie." It sounded like half a dozen steam locomotives all starting up at the same time, with their wheels slipping on the rails. There were six barrels, and the sound when all those 150mm rockets hit anywhere nearby was deafening. There wasn't much shrapnel, but there were a hellava lot of concussions.

I don't know why we were put in this position. Maybe it was an economy-of-force move to try to cover maximum territory with minimum troops. No one ever came out to inspect our positions. We were left to ourselves, and if we were attacked we would be on our own. Our only option would be to stay and fight, because once we got out of our foxholes there was little cover for withdrawal.

I asked for protective artillery fire at and around our roadblock, and finally got someone to listen to me. I was told, "You adjust the fire," so I became the forward observer. This was 105mm howitzer stuff, glider field artillery or British field artillery. We adjusted with one gun, which was normal procedure. After it obtained hits on target, the other howitzers could lay their guns on the same area.

They gave me on-call, close defensive fires and I called the fire in as close as I could without risking casualties. I knew we would have to have a lot of close-in fires if we were to survive a determined enemy attack. Before I adjusted the fire, I hollered: "Everyone deep down in your holes." They fired a round and I adjusted, saying "drop fifty" to pull it back in. I think I got most of the artillery barrages or pre-planned fires within seventy-five yards of our holes, which is very close. The mortar fire was a little bit closer.

I felt a lot better when we had preplanned concentrations. We numbered them, so all we had to do in an attack was call for barrage "one" or "two." We didn't have many fire-fights; it was a "you don't bother me, I won't bother you" situation. That's the way it went for a couple days.

We had a fellow called Hubert Pack in my squad, a very good combat soldier from Tennessee. After a few days in the foxhole, he got bored. In fact, we were all getting a bit bored. Pack had figured out a covered approach to one of the houses that contained a German machine gun, so he approached me with an idea. He wanted to crawl out around four hundred yards to our left front, get within range of the house, and take it under fire with our 2.36 inch rocket launcher. I wouldn't have ordered anyone to do this, but since it was Pack's idea, I approved it.

Pack got together a two-man rocket launcher team, and one other man. The four of them crawled out, finding cover until within good rocket-launcher range of the house. In order to explode, the rockets had to hit their targets at a 0-degree angle, or awfully close to it. I could see Pack and his team very clearly. They fired the first rocket at seventy-five to a hundred yards from the house. It bounced off the wall and never did explode, but the second one went right through a window.

It was like hitting a beehive with a stick. It burst alive instantly, shooting out a great deal of fire from the house and the positions around it. We also received artillery and mortar fire. Luckily, the Germans did not pick up Pack and his group. They started working their way back under fire, and the only way we saved them was by telling the FO from the 81mm mortar platoon to fire smoke rounds. They dropped dozens of smoke rounds between us and the house, as close to the group as possible and in front of the enemy position. The wind was right; Pack and his men made it back without casualties. After that, I don't think we got bored much. I said, "No more of this crap! It's live and let live as long as we're out here in this exposed position."

It seemed like we were on the roadblocks forever, but it probably was only ten days before we were relieved. We got a few days rest in company support or battalion reserve, but we were still well within artillery or mortar range. I learned Francisco had been ordered to lead an attack on the houses near his front. He got close, but was forced to withdraw when the Germans counterattacked and his group suffered casualties. One of these was the rocket-launcher man, a young private named Percy Altman, who was killed.

The reserve area was in a lower position than the surrounding terrain, and had many trees. We received heavy mortar fire, and I'll always remember the incoming sound—*swhoosh*! *swhoosh*! I called this "whispering death." There was very little time to take cover, much less than when an artillery round came in. We dug in deeply, but were still endangered by mortar rounds that hit trees. This produced very effective air bursts that could rain down on us regardless of the depth of our slit trenches. We could not go into the cellars and wait out the attack because they were already packed with headquarters personnel from platoon on up. The only way to protect ourselves against the air bursts was to have a substantial cover over our slit trenches. We stripped the houses in the vicinity of every door, table or other material that could support a layer of dirt and be used for covering.

We next moved into a defensive position on a dike. I believe this was still south or southeast of Nijmegen proper. The left flank was on the river. Another company was defending from the river to the west-southwest, and Company F tied in. The 3d Platoon was the right flank of Company F's defensive position, and our right flank was open. This was a bad position. We had a very large area to cover. Rather than trying to cover it all, we just wrapped the right flank around a little to the right rear and learned to live with it.

Most of our fighting positions were dug in on the dike near the top or the rear, so we could fire over the top of it. We tried to construct two-man foxholes lower down on the friendly side, and dugouts to give us overhead protection. These were just wide enough for two soldiers in the prone or sitting position, and provided overhead cover from the weather and artillery and mortar fragments. They were very primitive, although they were bigger than our two-man foxholes.

From time to time, we rotated for a few days with other 505 units, moving from the dikes to evacuated houses on our left rear. These were closer to Nijmegen and safer than positions on the dike. They were still within mortar and artillery range, but it gave us the opportunity to get out of the weather and let up on the rigid security we had to keep on the dikes.

Generally, we rotated when we had been up on the dike for a week or a little longer. We were always happy to get into a civilian home and out of the weather. Our only duty was to provide local security around the houses we were occupying, so we could relax a little and keep warm and dry after having maintained a twenty-four-hour, seven-day week. We still were never very far from the front: from our comfortable beds, we could look out the window and see German territory across the river.

We observed quite a distance into enemy territory from the dikes. We saw manufacturing complexes with high smoke stacks. We had been taking accurate artillery fire, and someone finally realized the enemy was using the smokestacks for observation posts. Eventually, British artillery got rid of them. Instead of using a forward observer, they moved some guns right up and fired over the barrel; they made a direct lay on the stacks and knocked them down. They tried to start as low on the stack as they could so they wouldn't have to waste shells, but they had to take most of them off in two or three pieces, working their way down. This was quite a sight. After that, enemy artillery fire was much less accurate.

Once we had been on the dikes for some time without much action, we had to be on guard against becoming careless. The more careless we got, the more the NCOs and the officers had to enforce noise and light discipline and make sure people kept awake on watch. We had to keep at least on 50 percent alert at all times. We were short of men, so it became pretty monotonous and tiring, especially at night. We also got orders to provide work details in the rear areas to establish a second line of defense. This is the first time we had ever been in a defensive sector long enough to prepare dug-in positions to our rear. Higher headquarters as well as the front-line units were nervous about the thinness of our front, and decided we needed to prepare fallback positions in case we had to withdraw.

Throughout this entire period, I cannot remember our newly appointed company commander ever inspecting our positions. Some of us lost respect for him. He had a company CP set up behind the front in a nice, warm farmhouse, which I thought was too far back. The platoons were on line in all kinds of weather, and we could have stood some morale-building visits by senior officers.

The Army supplemented our defenses by giving us a water-cooled .30-caliber medium machine gun. This was the gun I grew up with in the

112th, and I thought I knew quite a bit about it. After a few more days on the line, we got a little bored again. They had pounded this indirect-fire business with the .30-caliber into my head during peacetime, so I decided to try it out. We removed the gun from a direct-fire position and placed it in a defilade, or hidden position, behind the dike.

I made some calculations and figured out how to fire on the Germans and fool them about where it was coming from. So we fired off a couple of 250-round belts of ammunition. Things started heating up right away; we instantly got return mortar, artillery, and small arms fire at our front. Then the Germans dropped a few artillery rounds around the company CP. This is what really stopped the thing. In no time at all, someone got on the horn from the company CP, chewed us out for firing, and ordered us to stop. This ended my experiment in indirect fire with the water-cooled .30-caliber machine-gun.

During this period, Colonel Vandervoort had members of the 2d Battalion execute a kind of combat patrol modeled after the raiding party or trench raid of World War I. The objective was to capture enemy soldiers to learn about the enemy's identity and strength. An objective area would be selected and the patrol members would be brought forward to study the enemy terrain from the closest front-line position. Then they planned a route over and back. All the members took part in the planning and knew the terrain, the routes, and the enemy situation. Next, all supporting weapons—artillery, mortars, and in some cases machine guns—were zeroed in on the objective area, but in such a way that the enemy was not alerted to its importance.

At the stipulated time, always after dark, the patrol would slip out and get as close to the objective area as possible without placing itself in danger of supporting weapons. All supporting weapons would then open up, fire for a fixed period, then stop at a precise time. The patrol would rush in right after the fire lifted, grab a couple of the enemy if any were still alive, and hightail it back to the friendly lines.

In a static defensive position, it's unusual to take many prisoners unless the raid or patrol actions on the enemy position are very extensive. The raids were successful, though. The first two or three grabbed their POWs and got back before the Germans knew what hit them. Then the Germans learned the trick and took counteraction. We stopped the raids after the third or fourth one.

After that, the word was passed down that anyone who took a POW would get a three-day pass to Brussels, and we heard some pretty wild stories about people putting themselves in harm's way. In one case, a couple of troopers from the 504 ran out of their position in broad daylight, grabbed a German, and got him back before the enemy reacted. No one in my squad, including myself, was quite that eager for a three-day pass to Brussels.

There was a lot of looting of civilian property in Holland. We heard rumors of grand-scale looting, but not by front-line troops, who were already heavily loaded with equipment. While we were fighting at one end of the town, British officers were busy setting up their Officers' Club on the other end, and they made no bones about collecting expensive furniture and decorations. I actually saw British armor going down the road with overstuffed chairs on them, mounted so they wouldn't get in the way of the turret. Furniture and other civilian items were roped and tied down onto the decks.

Eisenhower issued special orders to both our divisions stating that any officer could require a bill of sale for any civilian item in our possession. If we had no bill of sale, we would be subject to court-martial and severe punishment. Like rape, looting carried a maximum penalty of death in the Articles of War that governed military conduct during World War II and the period immediately following. We used to laugh and make up all kinds of possible offenses mocking the wording of the Articles, such as, "Throwing a cigarette butt on the ground instead of field-stripping it: punishable by death," or "Failure to salute an officer: punishable by death!" The official definition of rape as "any penetration, no matter how small," was the subject of many jokes.

Nevertheless, the warning about looting was repeated so many times that it convinced us Eisenhower was not kidding, and we started throwing away a lot of our civilian souvenirs. Because the higher brass never got down to the front lines, the junior officers enforced the order, but instead of making a big deal of it, they just told us to get rid of the stuff and not collect any more without a bill of sale.

And so we took the order against looting to heart—except when it came to getting something to eat. Mostly we ate British 10&1 rations, but we also always managed to acquire some chickens or rabbits somehow. Then one day, a cow stepped on one of our antitank mines, resulting in instant shredded beef. We soon realized that to have fresh beef legally, all we had to do was challenge a cow after dark as it approached our position. When the cow did not answer, we shot it.

One day Krueger decided to put on a full-fledged, three-course dinner for the squad, having met a cow that couldn't learn the countersign. We got a British halftrack and a rope to drag the carcass to a tree and we had fresh meat for a couple days. Since we had no refrigeration, we distributed it around to make sure it didn't go to waste.

Krueger worked pretty hard at our dinner. He insisted on having fresh baked bread or biscuits to go with the beef. We went into a store near the civilian area, but we couldn't read Dutch. We came across packages of white powder that Krueger figured must be flour, so he baked us up some biscuits to go with his nice dinner. As it turned out, the bags were full of plaster of Paris. Those biscuits were so rock hard we probably could have used them as weapons.

But Krueger tried his best, and we had a real nice dinner that night in spite of the biscuits. We had candles on the table, and somehow we'd gotten a ration of beer. It was drawn out of a huge barrel, and we had to find a container big enough to hold the entire squad's ration. We sent a couple of men off with a washtub, and they came back with it full of beer. The tub was sitting in the kitchen during dinner, and we supplemented the beer with wine and brandy.

We still had W.A. Jones, our Texan, in the squad; and our BAR man, John Corti, a Jewish fellow from New Jersey, had rejoined us after recuperating from the wound he'd gotten at St. Sauveur-le-Vicomte. After those two got to drinking, they got into a knock-down, drag-out fight. One of them stepped into the washtub and knocked the beer over. What a crying shame! A whole tub of beer KIA! But we got Corti and Jones settled down, and there were no hard feelings when everyone sobered up.

During this time they tried to rotate a few men back to Nijmegen, which was nearby, for showers and a change of clothing. The lucky chosen were really clean, and this helped boost morale. On the front line we had a lot of water, but the weather was so brisk it was difficult to wash. In the houses in the so-called rear area, we managed to improvise sponge baths in our helmets or large civilian containers. We had the relative luxury of emptying the water in our helmet whenever it got dirty, and filling it up again as often as we liked.

One of the most miserable nights I ever experienced occurred after we had been off duty for two or three days, and were moving back to the front line on the dike. It was stormy and wet, with freezing rain and winds of around fifty miles per hour. We had to brace ourselves and lean into it; otherwise, it would have blown us over. After marching for three or four miles we were all soaking wet and freezing. Our dugouts were wet, and the foxholes were half filled with water. Before we could use them, we had to empty the damn water out with our helmets.

Sometime after the fight in Hunner Park, the 3d Platoon of Company F got a new platoon leader, Lieutenant John Hamula. He knew his business but lacked combat experience. He was a good platoon leader and a good officer, and was usually willing to listen to his experienced NCOs. After we had been on the dike for a few days, he came to check the machine gun's field of fire and the final protective line. This requires grazing fire, meaning fire not higher than six feet, or the height of a man, out to seven hundred yards.

I said I didn't think we could fire a very good final protective line from up on the dike, where the gun was mounted four or five feet above the field in front of us. Since I had cut my teeth on machine guns, I thought I knew what I was talking about. All he said was, "I don't think the dike is that high. Sight level on it, and we'll check it out." Before I could stop him, he jumped out of the hole and down in front of the dike, and started walking the protective line in plain view of everyone—Americans and Germans alike. He started across the marshy area to our front, hollering back, "Have you got me in your sights yet?" or words to that effect. I quickly said: "Yeah, yeah, yeah. Come back in, Lieutenant. Yeah, you're right." He got back into position without getting shot, but he was very lucky not to get riddled with bullets. I knew we still couldn't shoot grazing fire, but he was bound and determined to prove we could.

While we were manning the dike, the duty of establishing a strong combat outpost was rotated by squads within the company, with each squad taking its turn. The combat outpost force consisted of a reinforced rifle squad of about fifteen men, located about three hundred and fifty yards out from Company F's left-flank dike position. My platoon or squad position was on the right flank. There was a farmhouse with outbuildings, trees, and other concealment in the general area of the outpost. The duties of our outpost force were to move out at first dark, go

into position at 100 percent alert, listen, observe, and repel enemy attacks or patrol operations. We returned to the dike before daylight. The whole operation was tricky. We didn't know the exact enemy position, but we knew the outpost was close to it. We also knew we could be cut off from our dike position if a strong enemy force moved in between the dike and the outpost.

My squad, reinforced by a few other men from the 3d Platoon, finally drew this duty. Lieutenant Hamula was the outpost commander. The best approach to the outpost area was to the left flank of Company F, but we still had to go across a long open area, crawling on our stomachs before we gained concealment. We then went into a low crouch and moved to the objective area. It was very cold that night, and the grass was wet from recent rain. By the time we had crawled to the outpost, we were cold, wet, and miserable. The night was quiet, and we got into position without enemy action. We were too close to the enemy to dig in, because digging noises would have pinpointed our position. Even if we had been allowed to sleep, a single snore would have given our position away—we were that close to the enemy.

We got into a circular, all-around defensive position. I was underneath a small tree, whose lower branches were about four feet from the ground. We were on full alert. After about half an hour, I had to pee badly. I also had an apple in my pocket, and I was hungry. I had to make an important decision: should I pee first, then eat the apple, or eat the apple and then go take a leak? With long, boring hours ahead of us, we often went through this kind of thought process. The first objective was to keep awake, the second to pass the time.

On one hand, I thought I would enjoy the apple better if I emptied my bladder first. On the other, since I could get killed at any minute, I reasoned I should eat it immediately because I otherwise might never get the chance to enjoy it. Why deprive myself of the pleasure of a good apple? Finally, I got up, crouched with my head between the lower branches, peed as fast as I could, then returned to the prone position.

Within minutes, all hell broke loose. At least three enemy machine guns, rifles, and burp guns opened up on us, and there was also incoming mortar fire. The enemy had evidently laid out an excellent ambush position. What saved us was that the fire was going about three or four feet high. I think some of us tried to get lower by digging a slit trench with

our noses. The tree I was under lost all its branches, and the trunk, which was about two inches in diameter, was severed by machine gun fire.

We didn't do anything for the first few minutes, and they couldn't maintain that rapid rate of fire indefinitely. When it slacked off, Lieutenant Hamula passed the word to move back and assemble around a farmhouse fifty yards to the rear. We moved back individually, crawling or sometimes in a crouch, timing our movements with momentary lulls in the fire. The decision to assemble around the farmhouse was a good one. It was a recognizable point and provided some cover from the front. We got into a hasty all-around defense as best as we could and awaited further orders. Either Lieutenant Hamula contacted the company CP or his initial orders gave him the authority to withdraw on his own initiative, for we were allowed to withdraw.

Lieutenant Hamula thought the Germans were starting to move in on us. He decided to give them a hell of a lot of fire from our rifles, machine guns and BARs, firing a fixed number of rounds each before we withdrew. He gave this order to me, the squad leader and second in command. I asked him to reconsider, saying that our muzzle flashes would give us away immediately. I suggested we all lob a couple grenades to the front, and then withdraw. It took a little persuasion, but he finally accepted. Corporal W. A. Jones backed me on how to get the hell out of there.

We got everyone into position so we could all sling grenades as far we could throw them. When they detonated, we got up and ran like hell back to the main line, where we reassembled and got back into our fighting positions on the dike. We escaped without any casualties, but it was pretty rough going.

This episode gave me a lot to think about. The enemy wasn't stupid. We had violated normal tactical principles by going out and coming back from the same outpost area on a regular basis. We should have changed our routine, using different routes and different outposts, as we had been taught. The only thing that saved my life was the decision to pee first and eat my apple second. It was dumb luck and the grace of God.

Finally, after we had spent fifty-some days on or near the front line, the Canadian III Corps relieved us a little after midnight on November 12. We got the company and battalion marching to the rear at approximately 1:00 A.M. It was about a sixteen-hour march to our bivouac area at Oss, where we would stay for several days. It was twenty miles, but it felt like fifty. It took us all day until dark or a little bit after to get there. And of course it rained.

Many trucks passed us by as we marched down that long road in the rain toward the rear. I didn't understand why they hadn't arranged to truck us. We were not in the best physical condition. Being on the line for so many days, we had not exercised much, and poor diet, long hours, and lack of sleep had taken their toll. But as I watched the trucks pass us by as we marched down that long road toward the rear in the rain, there was one happy thought in my mind: For once, we were going in the right direction.

During those long weeks on the dikes and outpost, I had stared into the blackness night after night, knowing nothing was between me and the enemy. The loneliness and vulnerability of a front-line soldier in a defensive position are almost impossible to describe: there is fatigue, physical discomfort, psychological distress—but above all, you are conscious of being the point of the whole U.S. Army in your theater of operations.

You look to your front, and the only thing that may be there is an outpost or a listening post. You look around to your left, to your right. What do you see? If you're lucky enough not to be on an outpost or listening post yourself, you see your fellow soldiers on line with you, and they are part of your unit. But you see only those close enough to be in your range of vision. Yet there were 6,500,000 to 8,000,000 people in the Army during World War II.

As I looked into the night, straining my ears for the slightest noise, my mind racing, I began to formulate what I now call the "Wurst Theorem" of combat and combat support: As the linear distance increases between the front-line combat soldier and the rear, the number of military personnel per mile increases exponentially. A simple way of stating the same thing is, the further back from the front you get, the greater the military strength.

Of course, there is another way of looking at this: this massive military presence is all in *support* of the frontline soldier. But I'm trying to convey the extraordinary psychological state, the point of view of the combat soldier himself, who lives with death, who eats, sleeps, and shits with it for weeks and months at a time. Never knowing if—or when—it will be your turn, you think about what is behind you, and who can come to your aid. There may be a squad or a platoon of your company. If you are lucky, they will be very close behind waiting to help if you need them. But the front is often so wide that the platoon leader has to employ all three squads on the forward lines.

The next people behind you are your 60mm company mortar men. They are your buddies; they are part of your company or your platoon and they are in support of you. Behind them is the company CP group. This is where the groups start enlarging. The company commander is there with a limited number of support people, the supply sergeants, the communications sergeants, and so forth.

Behind them you may have your battalion support weapons. You may have a heavier group of 81mm mortars giving you support. They are good people, willing to help you out, but they are still behind you. Behind the heavier mortars you may have your battalion reserve company. If you are fortunate, you take turns rotating this duty. If not, all the companies of the battalion are on line, and no one is in reserve behind you.

Next may be the battalion command group. The numbers are starting to get bigger now; you have your battalion commander, your executive officer, and your four staff officers responsible for the support of the battalion, broken down into various tasks: S-1 is a personnel officer; S-2 is intelligence; S-3 is operations; S-4 is supply. Each member is needed, and if you are lucky, you will end up in one of those positions. Nevertheless, for now they are behind you.

After you leave the battalion area, you may or may not have the regimental reserve. The Army tries to keep one third of the regiment in reserve, but many times, especially in a parachute infantry unit, this is impossible. In Holland, only one battalion was reserved for the whole division. Further back is the light artillery support, division troops who are very helpful, especially in a regular infantry division. But sometimes a parachute or airborne division does not have them because their weapons were scattered on the drop and only one or two guns are available.

Next is your division headquarters. There are a hell of a lot of people here, which is about as far back as the regular infantry gets. To a front-line infantryman, they are as distant as New York City is from San Francisco. Around and behind the division headquarters are thousands of support troops—supply, maintenance, ammunition, you name it. Maybe you have your medium artillery there. They are good people. They shoot.

They help you out, but not all the time, because other outfits on the line may have priority of fire.

Next we go to corps headquarters. These are not as large as division headquarters, for they are only responsible for operational control. Going back from there to army headquarters, where you encounter a whole logistical command, next is an Army Group that directs a number of field armies. This is getting back to the whole heavy mix: the logistical areas, quartermasters, engineers, military police, military government.

From there, your mind takes it one step further back to SHAEF—thirty, forty, or fifty miles behind the front lines. In addition to Eisenhower's headquarters, logistical support people set up in places like Paris or Brussels. There are good reasons for this: transportation hubs are at these sites. But as a combat solider, when you finally pull a three-day pass to such cities, which are very few and far between, the massive military presence exceeds your wildest expectations. Walking in Paris, you become overwhelmed with the number of Army people in the streets. On the front-line with no one out in front of you, maybe a squad to your left and to your right that you can see, the sights are a hell of lot different from what you see back in Paris.

Going one step further, you hop back to England and then to the United States. Now you are getting into masses of warm bodies. They are doing a lot of jobs that may be necessary for the war effort and probably are, but they do not go understaffed or understrength for days, weeks, or months at a time.

The 505 was supposed to be in combat for less than two weeks in Holland. According to all the guidelines for specialized forces, we should have been relieved, at the latest, after our eleven-day stint in perimeter positions around Nijmegen. But during the entire mission, we were assigned to the British Second Army. From Montgomery on down, commanders were reluctant to give up our services. And so we remained, guarding the dikes and patrolling for a long, miserable month as our casualties mounted.

After finally being relieved, we stayed in the bivouac area for three days. We had minimum security and got the best sleep we could, given the horrible weather. Then we loaded onto trucks. We camped one night in Belgium before we arrived on November 17 at Camp Suippes, France, near Reims. The British had given us a double ration of rum as a parting gift at Oss, but all of us were more than ready for champagne.

Chapter 24

The Ardennes Campaign: From Camp Suippes, France, to Trois Ponts, Belgium

At Camp Suippes we were billeted in French Army barracks dating back to World War I. Other than Quonset huts in Northern Ireland, this was the first time our quarters had had a real roof since we'd left the States in April 1943. The barracks had very high ceilings, which made them hard to heat—for what heat there was, and there wasn't much. The battalion mess section cooked a garrison ration, the first we enjoyed since we had left Camp Quorn. Reims and Soissons had seen terrible trench warfare in W.W.I, and the countryside still bore the scars. It was even possible to pick up relics in the surrounding fields.

As soon as we got some money in our pockets we put in for three-day passes to Paris. I went with J.E. Jones and had a pretty good time, from what I can remember of it. We also went into Reims on afternoon or all-day passes, with a curfew of 10:00 or 11:00 P.M. Here I got my lifetime fill of champagne, which we downed in place of our usual beer.

From mid November to mid December 1944, we didn't do much training. There were no immediate airborne missions in the works and life was pretty routine. We were way back from the front, in theater reserve for the European Theater of Operations. With the exception of England, we were as far back as you could get and still be in a theater of operation. As far as we knew, we were there for the winter.

It was at Reims that I first heard the word "rotation." The big, generous rotation policy the Army started up was no rotation policy at all—it provided thirty days leave or TDY for selected personnel. In the entire 2d Battalion, 505, the quota was only two men. How the hell can you select two people from a battalion of more than five hundred soldiers? Finally, Company F got a quota of one man for the entire company. In the end, two soldiers had to draw straws because the company commander was at a loss to decide between them. The draw of the straw truly could mean whether you lived or died. We had been overseas for nineteen months straight, and there still were only two ways to get out of combat—a million-dollar wound that sent you home an invalid, or the grave.

After fifty-some days on the line, everyone's nerves were on edge, and we sometimes had trouble sleeping because of the schedule we had had to keep for so long on the front. Usually a couple of bottles of champagne would help me sleep better, but like just about everyone else, I was in a nervous, edgy mood. One day I was in the NCO room with my buddy Francisco and a couple other men. I'd piled my clothes on a chair in front of me, and was changing uniforms. My back was to Francisco, who could never resist a joke. I'd just leaned over to slip on a clean pair of shorts, when he reached over and pulled some hairs on my private parts. Just that quick, I grabbed the chair, swung it over my head, and swirled around. It was sheer reflex. That chair was halfway down on Francisco's skull before I caught myself. I stopped just short of clubbing one of my closest friends to death.

During our stay at Camp Suippes, I got detailed on city patrol or CP duty. The better part of the 82d and the 101st Airborne divisions were billeted in the area with numerous black service units—a mixture that always led to problems in a segregated army. It was an absolute necessity for airborne units to have their own soldiers in town to keep a lid on things. Otherwise, fighting, drunkenness, and a whole lot of trouble that combat soldiers get into behind the lines when they've had a lot to drink would get out of hand. We weren't armed; we wore a side arms belt designating we were on duty and an armband with the letters CP on it.

Both airborne divisions also had their own military police companies. We had our hands full, as did the regular MP units. One night, I had to pull a couple officers from the 101st out of a very wild house of prostitution. They were so drunk that they resisted our efforts to get them on a truck and back to their camp, so we were forced to arrest and physically drag them out of the brothel and into our detention center at Reims. We locked them up, waiting for them to sober up so they could report back to their unit.

We couldn't drink on CP duty, a problem we solved by reserving a café or tavern, and going after curfew when we had cleared the town. That night, we got back to the billets from the tavern well after midnight. I had just fallen asleep when I was suddenly awakened by the CQ, or charge of quarters. He and the first sergeant were shaking us out of our bunks, yelling "Everyone up!" I was sure this did not pertain to me, because those of us on CP duty were excused until the next day. So when the CQ grabbed my shoulder, I tried to shake him off, saying I'd been on CP and had just gotten into bed.

This was not a practice alert, but a real one. It was 2:00 A.M. on December 18—and the first time any of us had heard of the Ardennes, later known as the Battle of the Bulge. I started that battle with a very big champagne hangover.

Our unit had a tough time getting ready to go back on the line. When we pulled back to Reims, the Army was in no big hurry to get us refitted to go back into battle or on an airborne mission. We had turned in just about all of our crew-served weapons for ordnance checks and third- or fourth-echelon maintenance, and there were practically no ammunition or rations on hand. Nor did we have any winter clothing to speak of, a problem that would take on terrible proportions once we got to the Ardennes.

The Army had to draw down hard on some of the rear units to provide winter combat gear for the front-line troops. Luckily, after Normandy, the 505 exchanged the old lightweight jumpsuits for heavier M-43 combat suits. Without the newer and warmer suits, we would certainly have frozen to death in the Ardennes. All we had for protection was our field jackets, and we did not even have the liners for these. We also lacked protection for our jump boots, which were some of the coldest footwear you could ever find. The drawing of ammunition and combat rations all had to be accomplished very rapidly. One day's worth of K and

D rations was all we had. We literally went into the Ardennes with nothing much to eat but candy bars.

We also quickly had to get our men out of the hospitals, aid stations, and guardhouse. This may have saved the careers of the two officers from the 101st we had pulled out of the whorehouse that night, provided, that is, they lived through Bastogne. I heard arrest reports were "lost" when the divisions moved to the Bulge. After all this hectic preparation, we were loaded onto vehicles we called "cattle trucks," which offered no protection from the weather. We moved out at 10:00 A.M., December 18, 1944. As usual, we didn't know what we were heading into. If we had had a better idea of the situation, we would have had a lot more security out on the road march. No one was even riding shotgun ahead of the division columns.

We could have been in for a big surprise even before we climbed off the trucks. A lag of two days had occurred between the breakout of the battle on December 16 and the time the 82d and 101st divisions moved out of Theater Reserve. Hitler had launched an unexpected offensive through Belgium to retake Antwerp, using his new Sixth Panzer Army and the reconstituted Fifth Panzer and Seventh and Fifteenth armies. Many gallant actions fought in the Ardennes are now legendary, as are the freezing weather and the rugged terrain that created some of the most horrendous battle conditions in the ETO. The dramatic story of the 101st, the "Battling Bastards of Bastogne," who repulsed German attacks for several days even when completely surrounded, is particularly famous. But it was the immovable defense on the northern shoulder of the Bulge and the decisive stand at St. Vith, where the 2d, 99th, 1st, and 9th infantry divisions held firm, that halted the Germans in their primary objective. It was to this northern arena that the 82d Airborne was sent.

As an immediate result, this defense delayed the timing of the larger German offensive, which depended on a very quick thrust through our lines. Blocking the passage at St. Vith channeled four German divisions and supporting troops into a narrow, ten-mile corridor, which severely limited their maneuvering and resulted in a monumental traffic jam. As most of the German brass realized, their offensive was lost by the first or second day.

Initially, the plan was to attach the 82d and the 101st, the only reserve SHAEF had in continental Europe, to VII Corps and move them to Bastogne. But very early, LtGen Courtney Hodges, the commander of

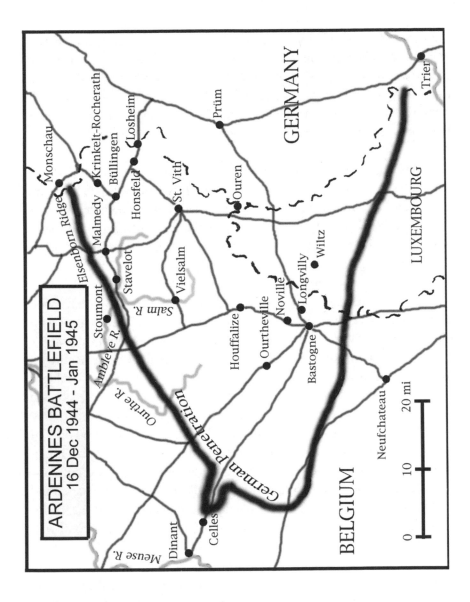

ARDENNES BATTLEFIELD
16 Dec 1944 - Jan 1945

the First Army, decided to send one division further north. As the 82d was ahead of the 101st on the road, we were designated to continue to the crossroads at Werbomont. Our role was to create a forward defensive line, filling a ten-mile gap between Stavelot and St. Vith, where the 7th Armored Division and elements of the 106th Infantry and 9th Armored Division—and others—were under heavy attack by the Fifth Panzer Army.

Once we got within ten or fifteen miles of what had been the rear of the front lines, we started running into the debris of battle. U.S. Army units were withdrawing in panic. We didn't see many combat units ten or fifteen miles back; these were logistical support units normally positioned miles behind the line. Army and Corps headquarters included, they were in a greater panic than those units usually positioned closer to the front. I saw large-caliber artillery pieces traveling very quickly to the rear. I later heard that in order to get our column through the withdrawing mobs, truck drivers in the retreating Army, and even officers in jeeps who did not get their vehicles off the roads, were threatened with shooting.

The closer we got to the front, the worse the panic became. Riding in the open cattle trucks, we saw it all. The sides were three or four feet high, and there was no top or covering. We leaned out and hollered to the retreating men, "Hey, you guys are going in the wrong direction." They would look back at us and earnestly say, "Oh no, *you* guys are going in the wrong direction." Their remarks made us very apprehensive about what we might encounter as we headed toward the splintered front.

We traveled into Belgium, pulled off to the side at dark, and bivouacked right beside the road. We had more than usual local security as we awaited orders. To add to our demoralization, it was a cold, wet, snowy night.

During the night, the new company commander, Lt Harold E. Case, called a meeting of officers and NCOs. He started by saying the Germans had launched a major offensive. He tried to explain what was happening but admitted no one really knew. The words "very fluid" kept recurring. We only knew there had been a major penetration of the front, and contact with friendlies and the enemy both had been lost. He also said that we now had reason to believe the last town we had passed through, just a few miles to our rear, had been occupied by German armor, but this turned out to be incorrect. One thing that did seem certain that night was that a regiment from the 30th Infantry Division was to move from our northern flank into our general area. This never happened. When the 505 did go into a defensive position, the 504 was on our left flank, but much further north, so large gaps in the lines existed on both our flanks.

We didn't get much sleep for the remainder of the night. We had to keep moving just to keep warm. At daylight, the 2d Battalion, 505, moved off, with Company F forming the advance guard. My squad, the 1st, was the point, with the remainder of the 3d Platoon as the forward elements of the advance guard. I was the number-three man on the point.

And so it was that I found myself at dawn on my twentieth birthday, December 19, 1944, at the head of an approach march formation heading towards Trois Ponts, Belgium. *Trois Ponts* means three bridges. I later learned the town was a key road center and communications point at the intersection of two rivers, the Salm and the Amblève. If we could hold it, we would be in a good position to block enemy movements to the west. This was all the information we received. It was thought that a German armored unit of unknown strength was running loose behind the lines, but we had lost contact with this spearhead.

Moreover, we were moving through some awfully damn big hills, following roads that generally conformed to the valleys. The forest

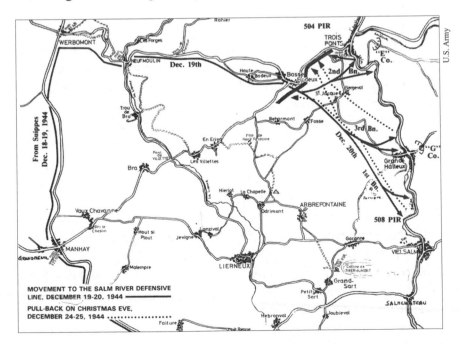

butted both sides of the road, and steep banks ran up into the woods. Those of us at the head of the march were particularly vulnerable because the terrain, bad weather, and necessity to move very quickly made it impossible to put out flank security. We simply marched on down the road, totally exposed to all the ambushes the enemy could easily have set up.

We marched most of the day until we reached the outskirts of Trois Ponts. I halted the column on orders just prior to moving into town, at the hamlet of Basse-Bodeux. The word got down that Trois Ponts was being held by elements of an engineer battalion, which had prepared the bridges for demolition. They had been engaged and had made contact with the German armored column.

On the night of December 19-20, the 2d Battalion was ordered into a hasty defensive position on the first ridge west of the Salm River. After some study, I thought this was much too far back. Once we got to the top of the mountain, our platoon leader, Lieutenant Hamula, was given instructions to take a patrol back down the slope, cross the road in the valley, and proceed through a group of houses where the river ran through the backyards. Here he was supposed to destroy or booby-trap a footbridge.

The lieutenant had a devoted runner with him, Pfc John Stratton, and a close relationship had developed between them. Stratton was going to accompany Hamula as usual, but because the patrol was small and Hamula knew his runner was very tired, he told him to remain in the defensive position instead.

The lieutenant took the patrol down the mountain, and the remainder of the 3d Platoon began to dig in on the ridge. Stratton was within forty feet of where I was digging in along a tree line. He leaned his rifle against one of the trees and started to dig. While we were working, someone on the ridge was trying to range in artillery support, of which we had precious little. I think it was the 456th Parachute Field Artillery Battalion, which had 75mm pack howitzers. It was a quiet night, and after the first shot landed, our ears were attuned for the second one. The damned thing was a short round. It came right into the middle of the company area and hit Stratton's rifle square on.

The hit killed Stratton and shook me up considerably. I had partially dug my slit trench, so I got a little protection. Stratton suffered many wounds, but I particularly remember a terrible sucking wound to his chest. We heard every breath he took because of the holes in his chest and lungs. The sound was very loud in the stillness of the night. Lieutenant Hamula came back from patrol to discover his kindness had led to the death of his runner and close friend. He truly grieved.

The terrain on the ridge was a mixture of open fields with wire fences and tree lines. The heaviest tree line was on the forward eastern slope. The following morning at daylight, a German sniper from way across the valley hit a soldier in the next platoon to ours who was climbing through a fence on the mountainside.

The regiment and battalion were so spread out in their defensive location that there were gaps from half a mile to three miles between units. Our own regiment's defensive line was about eight thousand yards long, and we sent out contact patrols to observe and report on action taking place in the gaps. I patrolled all night. It was bitter, snowy weather. We were exhausted, so we didn't take all the necessary precautions. We used the roads in the valley, periodically patrolling for up to forty-five minutes before making contact with our neighbor's patrols or one of their left-flank units, and then turning back.

We sustained some pretty bad sniper fire from houses in the valley, so I was given the mission of taking out a strong combat patrol. We moved to the north down the ridge and got on the road to the outskirts of Trois Ponts. There, one or two tanks were to be attached to our patrol, coming under my control. We then were to continue down the valley road, where the 2d Battalion occupied the ridge on one side, and the Germans held the ridge on the other. Along the way, we were to clean out houses that were said to contain enemy snipers. Even with a tank or two, this was a tough mission because we could only advance on the road itself, in ditches alongside it, or on the steep banks along its verges. This meant we would be exposed to short- and long-range small arms fire, and the tanks would be exposed to antitank fire the length of our advance.

I had just arrived at the rendezvous point with the tanks and was getting ready to move when up came General Gavin. This was typical of his behavior all during the war. I don't know how he managed to survive. He often went out on patrol by himself. I don't ever remember a bodyguard or aide being with him. But there he was, materialized out of thin air, carrying an M1 rifle with a .45-caliber pistol on his hip and a bandoleer of ammunition on his chest. He asked me my mission, and I relayed my orders. He was smiling while I answered him. He told me to hold up until he spoke with Colonel Vandervoort. The mission was cancelled, and I returned to the company's defensive area.

I believe it was during the night of December 20-21 that other companies of the 2d Battalion set up roadblocks. I heard later this was a very tough assignment, for there were still a lot of U.S. Army stragglers, and men from many different units kept coming through. The situation was fluid, and these people had no idea what the current sign and countersign were. Wheeled vehicles were also coming through with U.S. soldiers hanging on all over them. Some were even holding on and being dragged to reach the rear all the faster.

That night, we heard fighting across the river to the east from our position on the west ridge of the Salm River. By daylight, Company F had received orders to move across the river and up to the top of the mountain. We were to tie in with Company E, which was already engaged in a pretty hot fire-fight. We couldn't use the road up, which led to Company E's area, but had to go cross-country over steep, broken terrain to an area on Company E's right. I don't recall how we crossed the river, but I don't remember getting wet. We may have used a footbridge or the one remaining bridge over the Salm. We climbed the mountain in a column of platoons, with the 3d Platoon in the rear, heading into the unknown. The side and the top of the mountain were heavily wooded. The weather was foggy, with visibility at times down to fifty feet, or even less. I believe this is what saved us when we moved up the face of that mountain.

There was some distance between the platoons as we moved up. My squad was leading the 3d Platoon. Lieutenant Hamula was at the head, and we were all quite close together. The whole time we heard heavy firing up to our left front. The 1st and 2d platoons began to deploy into company defensive positions as soon as they got to the top. As the 3d Platoon came up behind them, Lieutenant Case ran over. He was afraid the Germans would pull a flanking attack on Company E, and then run smack into Company F. He ordered Lieutenant Hamula and the 3d Platoon to move forward of the company's proposed defensive area and to make contact. In other words, we were to delay the Germans long enough for the other platoons to get into position.

This was not a nice order to have to carry out, but we moved out fast with rifle squads in columns abreast. The 1st Squad was to the right, the 2d Squad was to the left, with maybe thirty to fifty feet between the columns. We threw scouts out, but no flankers. I can only guess how far forward we had moved, possibly four hundred yards, when the scouts came across what seemed to be the edge of the woods we were crossing, although this was impossible to determine in the fog.

The scouts held us up at the edge, and then went out a little further into what appeared to be an open field, although we couldn't be sure. Lieutenant Hamula decided to throw a hasty defense, going into skirmishers spread along the wood line. There were some smaller trees along the border, with branches three to five feet above our heads once we were prone. We were pretty well spread out, ten to fifteen yards between individuals. On my left was a rocket man named Beckman, a young replacement.

Very soon we heard armored vehicles to our direct front and left front, moving in our direction. Lieutenant Hamula passed the word there was to be no firing until he ordered it. We couldn't see anything anyway; all we could do was listen. It was very frightening. We never had time to dig in.

It seemed like we waited for five or ten minutes, but it could have been only two or three. The armor got so close we could hear the voices of the infantrymen over the roar of the tank engines as they rode the tanks or walked along beside them. Beckman kept looking over and whispering, "Should I shoot? Should I shoot?" I said, "Shoot what?" We still couldn't see a thing in the fog; he could only have fired in the general direction of the armor.

Finally, Lieutenant Hamula gave the order to fire. When we opened up with our small arms, all we could do was hope the field to our front was level. We were lying prone, and tried to keep our rifles as level as we could. Aiming at nothing in particular, we fired into the fog bank. We had two rifle squads firing rapid-fire with M1 rifles, a machine gun and two to four BARs. We laid down a pretty good curtain of fire, and it was not long before we got return fire in great volume. Of course, the Germans couldn't see what they were shooting at either. Luckily, their fire went high, about six to eight feet off the ground, although they occasionally got a few closer than that. This took a heavy toll on the trees we were under, showering us with shot-up branches, tree leaves, and chunks of bark.

I got the impression that the incoming fire was mostly from the tracked vehicles, but it was impossible to tell whether they were tanks or halftracks. Machine guns mounted on armored vehicles are four to six feet above ground level, so I told myself the Germans were also leveling their guns, which was why they were shooting high. On the other hand, I was surprised not to get cannon fire. Maybe we weren't shooting at tanks or self-propelled guns, but at halftracks used as personnel carriers, which only mounted machine guns. Later I discovered we had encountered the tail end of LtGen Joachim Peiper's column, the 1st SS Panzer Division—and Sixth Panzer Army—spearhead. They were already running especially low on tank ammunition. Cannon fire, and especially high explosive shells, would have been very effective even at that close range. If high explosives had hit the trees we were under, it would have wiped us out.

I cannot say how long the small-arms fire continued. It might have been two minutes or it might have been fifteen, although I think we would have been out of ammunition in fifteen minutes. Someone, either Lieutenant Hamula or myself, thought about using grenades, but it was a very tight spot. We didn't know what they would hit once we threw them. To leave the prone position was to commit suicide, so we had to lob them lying down. To make matters worse, pieces of branches remained overhead. Nevertheless, we attempted to throw grenades to our front, and managed to get some out without much harm to ourselves.

The sounds of the fire-fight to our left, in Company E's area, now became even more intense. Part of an armored battalion had run right into their roadblock with tanks, halftracks and infantry. We also heard some small arms to our right rear, which told us the other two platoons from Company F were having a fire-fight. It looked like the enemy forces to our left and right were cutting us off from Company F's defense position.

I later learned that some of the firing came from a BAR man who had moved forward as part of a two-man outpost covering a small break in the woods. He had just gotten into position when he caught sight of a German column moving along the opening. The Germans appeared to be trying to outflank those of us up front. Evidently, he put his BAR on automatic and fired two or three twenty-round magazines. It was said that none of the group got away.

I don't know how long it was after we opened fire that a runner came up—crawled up, more or less—to say the company commander had ordered our withdrawal. Lieutenant Hamula was very professional and did not rush things. He ordered us to withdraw by squads. We left one squad in position temporarily, while the other withdrew a ways, then the first squad leap-frogged the second squad's position, and so forth. For quite some distance, we had to crawl in order to stay below the line of fire.

Lieutenant Hamula had issued orders that once we got to our feet, there would be no running. The quickest we could move was a fast walk. In a situation like this, it takes only one man to start a panic. I think my squad was the second to withdraw, and as we started out, one of my men began running. I shouted at him to stop. He slowed down to a fast walk, and then after a few steps started running again. I yelled his name and said, "If you don't stop running this minute, I'll be forced to shoot you!" He took me seriously, for he started walking again. We proceeded back to the company defensive area without mishap.

Once we arrived, the company commander put the platoon in position, and we dug in. For the second time during World War II, I fixed my bayonet, mostly for the benefit of the men around me. I honestly thought we were going to make a last stand. Company E was having a tough time, and there was firing from Company F's position as well. The company exec officer, the second in command, had come into my squad's position. As we were digging in, it became evident that Company E was withdrawing, for the sound of their firing was moving off to our left rear. This was a matter of great concern to the exec. "Why are they withdrawing?" he kept asking. "We don't have orders to withdraw."

If communications had been better, we might have learned that Company E had indeed received the order to withdraw, and part of our function was to help get them out by providing supporting fire. Company E was a ways to the rear, but not all the way down, when we finally got the order to withdraw as well. We started back down the mountain late in the afternoon. This was a tricky operation, and it was a good thing that the fog covered our movement. It was quite a distance down, and if the Germans had moved quickly over the top and to our side, we would have been under their direct small arms fire all the way. As it was, we didn't sustain small arms fire from the top and forward western slope until we had reached the bottom.

Once we crossed the river, we came into the backyards of some of the houses on the valley road. The backs of these houses faced east. We should have used them as cover, going in the back door and out through the front. Instead, we walked by one of them outside. Just as I was about to turn left at the right front corner, a German to our rear, up on the side of the mountain, let rip with a long burst of machine gun fire. The bullets almost tore the top off a utility pole eight or ten feet to my right front.

We did lose some men on the mountaintop. One of the KIA was a recent replacement. I'm sorry to say I don't remember his name, he was with us for so little time. Others were killed in Company F, and I later heard the battalion had sent us replacements in the middle of the fight. This was highly unusual, which only indicates just how badly we needed them. Where these replacements went or what happened to them we never learned. They were assigned, sent up, and lost before we ever saw them.

On the evening of December 21, the 307th Airborne Engineers blew up the last remaining bridge over the Salm at Trois Ponts. We holed up for a while along the bottom of the valley in one of the houses with the road in front. The river was forty yards from the back-door, and the mountain rose quite sharply from the riverbank. At least two of our wounded were in the house to our right, which was occupied by friendly civilians and another squad from the 3d Platoon. Together, we formed a strong combat outpost.

We were confined indoors during daylight because the Germans on the mountain slope to the east could look down on these houses very clearly. Every time we tried to step out, we got fired on. We attempted to get the wounded out under a Red Cross flag, but the Germans opened up on us. I had my entire squad in the house, although by then we were at reduced strength. We took turns on watch, leaving two men on alert during daylight from good observation points inside. The previous day, the squad next door had driven off a German patrol, which made us even more alert. We were constantly searching the landscape for any signs of movement and looking at suspected enemy positions.

One of our alert positions was in the second-story bedroom in the back of the house, facing east. We had a very good view of the backyard, the terrain along the riverbank, and the side of the mountain where the enemy was in position. This particular bedroom had double windows that swung out like shutters. I took this position and opened the windows, swinging them out very, very slowly. I then pulled the bed as far from the window as possible, leaving just enough room to get behind it and observe all movements to the east. I now could shoot from deep within the room, and the muzzle flashes would be less visible than if I were leaning over the sill or close to the windows. I piled some extra blankets and pillows on the bed, making myself a shooting rest that was every bit as good as the sandbag rests we had used to zero in on the rifle range.

I sat on the floor and rested my rifle on the support on the bed. It was very early in the morning of December 23. We didn't have any heat, but I draped extra bedding over my shoulders to keep warm. For a combat position, it was very comfortable. At first light I glanced out, and much to my amazement I observed a German two hundred yards up the mountainside. He rose above the ground just like a pop-up and performed one of the longest possible stretches, as if he'd become cramped lying in the hole. This was one of the best open daylight targets I ever had. His whole torso was exposed from the waist up. He was right in line with the open windows, so I could shoot straight through without hitting the glass. Before he completed his stretch, I had him with the first shot. Immediately after he dropped, another man, possibly from a shallower hole, jumped up to help his buddy or to get in his hole. This man went down on my second shot.

I did not see any more Germans there for the reminder of the day. Later on, however, from the same shooting position, I observed a German coming down the mountainside, carrying what appeared to be a large box of our K rations on his shoulder, probably delivering them to his front-line buddies. There was some concealment in his path—bushes, rocks and small trees. The range was about two hundred fifty yards up to my right front. I had to swing my body a little to the left, but I was still shooting through the open window. This man went down on my second shot. To make sure, I emptied my rifle with six more shots. The M1 had an eight-round clip, and we always liked to keep it full. The company saying was, "One round to put him down, and seven to keep him down."

I've spoken of these shootings on very few occasions. They came up only once or twice in all these years, and only after I had been drinking too much. I don't look with respect on men who shoot off their mouths about shooting other men, but I feel I should relate these events to give an accurate account of my experience and describe the horrible duties required of soldiers in infantry combat and all other warfare.

It's also true that before these events, we had been told stories of various massacres the German Army had committed. Malmedy, where one hundred and fifteen American POWs were lined up and shot, had just occurred a few days earlier on December 17. Headquarters made sure the news immediately got down to all U.S. troopers. This was to warn us, first, but also to instill further hatred of the enemy. I can tell you, it worked.

I'm not trying to justify shooting these men or any of my other actions. The things I did were legitimate acts of war. But looking back upon it as an old man, I regret the death of any person. I think to myself, "I killed three men just after my twentieth birthday, December 19, 1944." Happy Birthday and a Merry Christmas.

After dark on December 23, we left the house and put out local security. We had received word that General Gavin had ordered the 2d Battalion, 505, to be relieved by elements of the 504. We had held the defensive perimeter and the Germans had given up on trying to break through the 505's line. But the 508 and 325 were getting a lot of pressure, and Gavin thought our regiment might be needed to bridge a break in the line further south.

A battalion aid station jeep drove directly up to the house next door. The vehicle was equipped with a frame so they could lay at least two wounded men on stretchers and evacuate them. We helped load up the wounded after dark. By the time we were able to get them out they were really hurting. We then withdrew from the houses, moving back to the ridge we had previously occupied. From this point, the 2d Battalion, 505, was trucked back to division reserve. Company F went into a wooded bivouac area with minimum security. This was far enough back to give us relief from the 50 percent alert order and maybe allow for some sleep. If, that is, we could sleep in a snowstorm in temperatures well below freezing.

Chapter 25

From the Battle of the Bulge
to the Hurtgen Forest, Germany

Our relief at Trois Ponts slightly preceded Montgomery's order for a general withdrawal of forward elements, the 7th Armored Division and its attached units, from St. Vith on December 24, as he characteristically "tidied up the lines." Surprisingly, at the same time, Peiper withdrew from Stoumount. Out of gasoline, he abandoned his tanks and other vehicles along the way.

Back in division reserve, Company F tried to rest up and get some sleep. We had our sleeping bags, but they were just GI blankets sewn up with a very light cover over them. They were water-resistant, but not waterproof. It was a hell of a job to get into them and harder still to get out, especially dressed in field jackets and boots. We usually didn't crawl all the way in unless we were in a relatively safe area. And we never, ever fastened them up if we were near the front.

The weather was very cold, and on December 23 it took a turn for the worse, with heavy snowfall and plummeting temperatures. If we did get into our bags, we often had to crawl out again to stomp around and get the blood circulating. I would awake from a few hours of sleep to find a blanket of snow on my bag. After spending a couple nights in an open field with snow blowing in my face, I often prayed for a nice wooded area to break up the wind. We may have gotten some hot coffee and supplements to our K and C rations, but that was about it.

I had been feeling terrible for three or four days just before Christmas week, as though I had recurrent malaria. Lieutenant Hamula sent me to the battalion aid station, where the surgeon diagnosed me as a bad case of bronchitis going into pneumonia. I was confined to a litter and evacuated to a collecting station by a quarter-ton ambulance, a jeep that had litter racks mounted on the sides and back.

It was after dark on Christmas Eve when I arrived at the collecting station, a large, barn-like building housing up to seventy-five litter patients. The whole place looked like a scene from hell. The medical personnel were past the point of exhaustion, working by lanterns amidst terrible moaning and groaning. As we were brought in, the staff checked our emergency medical tags and gave us a quick examination, grouping arriving casualties by the severity of their wounds or illnesses, according to the practice of triage. Those with little or no hope of surviving were low priority, while those who had severe wounds but could be saved by an immediate operation were moved to the top of the list.

Horrific pictures of this collecting station remain in my mind to this day. There was little or no heat. People were dying all around me. There were some very badly wounded, and many burn cases from armored outfits where the tanks had caught fire. All of them had bloody clothes. I felt guilty as I lay there, because so many were much worse off than I was. There were also many cases of trench foot, who were maybe as "well off."

Eventually I was loaded on an ambulance headed for the 102d Evacuation Hospital in Verviers, Belgium. It was a nicely heated building. The care I received all the way back was as good as could possibly be expected under the circumstances.

In Verviers, I was on the receiving end of what the Germans called *Vergeltunswaffen* or "V" weapons, named for Vengeance. We called them "buzz bombs." The Germans never used these in forward combat areas; they always passed right over our positions up on the front. In the fog we couldn't see them, especially if we were in a forest, but we could hear them well enough. They sounded like an old Model A Ford putt-putt-putting along. But Verviers was one of the target areas, a main logistical and supply point for forward troops with large depots of gasoline and quartermaster supplies, as well as hospitals. Even inside the ward, the noise was loud. As long as we could hear the buzz bombs we were relatively safe, but silence meant they were on a downward path. And when they hit, they made quite an explosion.

The Germans sent quite a number of these bombs in the general direction of the hospital. I don't know how effective they were, but I can attest that they were bad on morale. They caused a lot of concern among the seriously wounded, especially amputees who, in the event of evacuation, had to depend on others to save them amidst the explosions.

I now was exposed to another of the wonders of modern science, but luckily, this one was a force for good. If I hadn't already been started on penicillin back in the collecting station, I was started on it in Verviers. The treatment involved massive doses, applied every two or three hours. It seemed they were always waking me up at night to give me a shot. They also started feeding me intravenously. But best of all, I was bathed and dressed in clean pajamas, and put in an actual bed with sheets. It even had a mattress. Buzz bombs or no buzz bombs, with the heat and the sheets and the bed, I thought I was in second heaven.

Since the forward units were completely overloaded, the Army processed the ill and wounded to the rear much more quickly than usual. I was soon put on a hospital train to Paris, a regular old-fashioned coach, gutted out with double bunks built into the sides two or three high. The U.S. Army had taken over the former mental hospital, a very large complex on the outskirts of the city, turning it into the 191st General Hospital. I was hospitalized until January 18, 1945, a total of about three weeks.

The stench from the amputees was almost overwhelming. They attempted to segregate them in a single room, because the odor was so nauseating. The blood would often soak completely through the heavy casts on their amputated limbs, where it couldn't be washed away. We also had many cases of trench foot. These soldiers had gotten their feet wet and couldn't dry or warm them, resulting in frozen or frostbitten feet and toes. Some cases resulted in amputations of toes and even part of the foot.

Trench foot was something the Army hadn't foreseen, and it was a large drain on our manpower. We were simply told to keep our feet warm and dry, which is very difficult in combat. They later issued the forward units extra socks. The 82d Airborne Division combat units were particularly affected, because we were exposed to the cold, wet weather in the Ardennes in our leather jump boots. Later, they issued galoshes to wear over them, which was a big improvement.

Soon I was well enough to become interested in watching the doctors perform diagnostic tests. One method for those with trenchfoot was to uncover the foot of the bed, take out a pin, and stick it in the patient's toes. If the doctors got a reaction, they figured he wasn't too far-gone. If not, they continued to move the pin up toward the ankles, to discover how far he had lost feeling. Pretty crude as a diagnostic tool, I thought, but no one could afford to spend much time on any single patient.

In a few days, I was allowed out of bed and permitted to roam the ward. I slipped out and tried to find people from my unit to catch up on what we called "the news from home." We tried to read *The Stars and Stripes*, but our best source of information was newly arrived patients. Some men from newly committed infantry divisions told me about their first battle experiences, and I walked away shaking my head. They hadn't received the best training for the conditions they had had to face. Again, it seemed their casualty rate was much higher than in the old veteran divisions.

Before long, a couple of us took to bugging the doctor for a pass. We finally bullshitted him enough to get our way, and left the hospital legally. They warned us to stay close by, saying there were several good cafés within a few blocks. Money, however, was a problem. I hadn't been paid since my three-day pass to Paris in November 1944, but I had squirreled away an American gold seal five-dollar bill, the first currency we had received in Africa in 1943 before military scrip came along. In the first bar, I got three or four times the official exchange rate, which amounted to fifteen or twenty dollars in francs. It was enough to get started on.

We proceeded to hoist a few, and the next thing I knew, I found myself in the heart of Paris. Cultural excursions were not on the agenda. Our priorities were booze and women, or vice-versa, and Paris had a lot of both. As a whole, American GIs, myself included, made friends quickly with the French. We wanted to forget the dreadfulness of war and relax to the fullest. The price we paid was often a terrible hangover or a much sadder outlook, or even mental depression. "Eat, drink, and be merry, for tomorrow we may die" sums up our attitude.

I hadn't been out on the streets for long before the MPs picked me up. I was pretty far gone, so I couldn't understand why they were picking on me. They got me on a uniform violation charge because I wasn't in class A uniform. I gave them a pretty hard time, saying they couldn't expect a combat unit soldier with a pass from the hospital to be in a class A uniform, but my argument fell on deaf ears.

Soon I found myself in a cell, a dungeon-like room in an ancient building. By this time, I was sobering up pretty quickly. I would have sworn I was locked up in the Bastille in the days of the French Revolution. After a couple hours in this dreary hole, I was told to appear before an MP first lieutenant, a duty officer. He agreed to let me go on condition that I either report directly back to the hospital, or stay within a very short distance of it. Of course I agreed.

An MP escorted me to the metro system, offering very strong suggestions along the way, and directed me how to get back. By the time I got to the train, I wasn't feeling too bad, so I got off at the third station. Evidently, I still had enough money to start all over again, because I found myself very late at night a long distance from the hospital. How I found my way back again, I do not know. It must have been pure homing instinct.

Luckily, I encountered no more MPs on my travels, because it was past midnight and I was in violation of my pass. But entering the hospital now became a problem. First I tried to go over the wall, but I couldn't quite make it. Then I thought, "What the hell, they can't shoot me for being late," so I went in the main gate. The guard stopped me, and I delayed a minute or two, fumbling for my pass. When he stepped back to look at it under the light, I took off. He challenged me to stop a few times, but I kept going, knowing he couldn't leave his post. But he had my pass, so he knew who I was. In all probability, he also had live ammunition in his pistol.

I had just gotten nicely settled in back at the ward when a big commotion erupted at the front nurse's station. There was loud talking, then shouting. Before long, the nurse, someone from the MP station, and the officer of the day all appeared at the foot of my bed. There the nurse held the others off and was very emphatic about the kind of care I should receive. Sending me to the guardhouse wouldn't improve my condition.

Evidently, she was more persuasive than the MP lieutenant, because they left. I got a good chewing out the next morning by the ward doctor and the nurses. They kept me in bed for the next day or two, but there were no serious aftereffects. I've always been grateful that guard didn't have an itchy trigger finger.

After this adventure I started complaining about wanting to leave the hospital and get back to my unit. Especially in the combat zone, our unit was our home. I learned that Company F and the 505 had taken heavy casualties in the early January offenses that closed the Bulge, and I felt very guilty about sitting back in the hospital while my friends were taking a beating. Finally the doctor signed my form, and I was to be on my way the next day. Meanwhile, someone found a regulation saying no patient would be released unless he had visited the dental clinic, and all corrective measures had been provided. This was a blow, because brushing our teeth in combat had not exactly been a priority. I couldn't remember the last time anyone had looked at my teeth, so I knew I was in for some additional pain. I don't know if it was at my insistence, or if they just wanted to get rid of me, but my dental appointment was set for the following day.

This was a nice facility, but their dental equipment was hardly state of the art. I sat down in the chair, and a very young dentist examined my teeth. He announced I was in the worst possible class as far as dental care was concerned. I asked what had to be done before they would let me go. He proceeded to tell me, and I said, "Let's get at it and get it done." He looked at me in a shocked way and asked, "You want *all* of this done today?" And I said, "Let's get to it."

It ended up that I had to have seventeen fillings and two extractions. The dentist took a break for lunch. It was harder on him than it was on me, initially anyway. They used a painkiller only for extractions, and these he did last. I sat through that full day of dental work while the dentist worked himself up into a very upset, nervous condition. By the time he got through with me, I think he was suffering from combat fatigue.

Meanwhile, the ward had gotten a little concerned, and had been calling down to see what was happening. I finally got back very late in the afternoon. That night and the next day, I was sick. My jaws were so sore I had to go on a liquid diet, and my head throbbed so much I thought it was going to break. So my release from the hospital was delayed one day for dental treatment, and another day to recover from it.

After I was discharged, I had the misfortune to go to a "repo depo" or "repple depple." These had initially been called "replacement depots," which had a sinister sound, as if you were replacing someone who had been killed. (You often were.) So the Army decided to rename them "reinforcement depots" instead, as if to give them some positive spin. Whatever their official name, to us they were the "asshole of the world."

The depot was in or near Verviers. I here received new combat uniforms, a complete reissue of my B bag contents, and a new M1 rifle. The way they handled the rifles was a sore point with all the returning combat people. The Army was still preserving rifles in storage by stacking them in boxes full of cosmoline, which plugged up all the parts and holes. When they reissued the rifles, the whole thing from muzzle to butt, inside as well as out, was completely covered with gunk. So there we were, trying to return to our unit, standing out in the bitter cold in January 1945, and when we got our new weapons, they were coated in an inch of cosmoline and the internal parts were completely filled. Getting them ready for inspection on time was our problem. No cleaning material was provided.

We found the solution in the mess hall, where we used 32-gallon GI cans to wash our mess kits. We either managed to steal boiling water out of the last rinse, or made off with the heater and the can altogether. Then we disassembled the rifles and soaked them. We were careful to get all the parts dried and lightly oiled. The replacement company commander was surprised to see the rifles in such good condition at inspection. To this day, I don't know why they didn't get an extra heater and can and set up a cleaning station.

At the repple depple, we were in a "casual" status, waiting to be assigned. There had been a lot of complaints about this sort of limbo. Finally, someone took heed and sent officers from the Inspector General's office down to talk to us. The IG had a lot of good reasons to perform these visits. At one time, the Army had thought to reassign casuals to whatever outfit needed replacements the most, and the men were ready to commit mutiny in order to be returned to their own units. The plan was quickly abandoned, because they had a mass of AWOLs when the men heard they might not be assigned to their own unit. They just left the depots and returned to their units on their own.

The day the IG came, we were ordered to stand by our bunks. He started a few aisles over from my cot. I could see he wasn't going to get to me, so I jumped over a couple cots and got in front of him. Luckily for me, he had a sense of humor. He asked what I wanted, and I informed him I wasn't happy about my progress in returning to my unit. He asked where I came from and how long I had been at the depot, then said he would look into expediting my movement. That same day or early the next morning, I was on my way back to the 505, which I rejoined on January 25, 1945. I had been away one day short of a month.

The company was in a battalion or regimental reserve area, billeted in the best civilian dwellings I could remember. But we had taken serious losses during the early counter offenses of early January 1945, and many of my friends and platoon mates had been wounded or killed in action. To this day, I feel guilty about this. Maybe it is egotistical, but I always wonder if I could have prevented some of these losses if I had been there. Some of my best friends were among the losses suffered while I was away.

Among the casualties was my close friend Sergeant Francisco. They had run into heavy resistance in a forest, and although a tank had been attached to the company, the tank commander had buttoned up. He couldn't, or wouldn't, open his hatch to man the .50-caliber machine gun

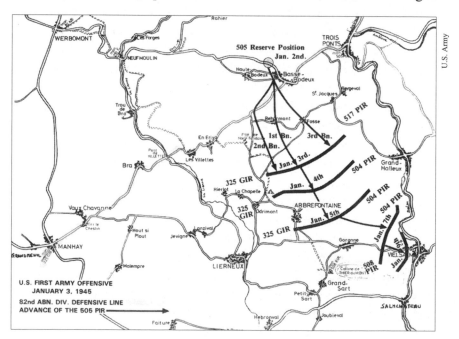

mounted on the outside of his turret. So Francisco jumped up under heavy fire and proceeded to use the .50-caliber machine gun as fire support. He did a lot of good with that machine gun, but it wasn't long before he was badly wounded and knocked off the tank. He died of his wounds on January 3, 1945.

My close friend and assistant squad leader Corporal Krueger died of wounds. My platoon sergeant, Sergeant Wright, died of wounds from artillery fire. My platoon leader, Lieutenant Hamula, died of wounds. Private first class Robert Beckman, our rocket man, was KIA. During the Ardennes, a total of fifteen members of Company F were either killed in action or died of wounds. Five died when hit, and ten survived the hit but later died as a consequence. Add to these losses the critically wounded and lightly wounded, and medical evacuations due to frozen feet or illness.

While I had been hospitalized, the 2d Battalion, 505, had also lost our battalion commander. Major William R. Carpenter took over from Colonel Vandervoort, who was very seriously wounded in the Bulge on January 7, when he lost an eye and part of his face to mortar fire. The colonel was evacuated back to the States, putting an end to the possibility of my getting the direct commission he had spoken about to Francisco and me back at Camp Quorn. Colonel Vandervoort evidently had left no written record of his commitment. I had to start all over again in winning the confidence, respect, and recommendations of another battalion commander.

Upon my return I was promoted to platoon sergeant, replacing Sergeant Wright. At long last, I was platoon sergeant in name as well as fact. The company was little more than platoon size, down to forty or fifty men. This attrition resulted from the relentless offensive operations the 82d Airborne Division had conducted in early January 1945, and the brutal conditions of the weather and terrain. Many times, the fiercest battles were fought over hamlets and even shacks and barns, in the effort to gain protection, no matter how minimal, from the bitter cold.

Toward the end of January, we participated in operations heading for the Siegfried Line. The going was tough and the weather was bad. The incoming artillery was light to medium, sometimes heavy. We didn't suffer many casualties. We always attempted to end up the day where we could get inside a house, a barn, or a chicken coop—any type of cover. We had lost so many officers I can't even remember who was commanding. They came and went so quickly. At one time during early battles in January, Company F had no officers left at all.

We were in reserve for a day or two of rest, then we were alerted for another operation about thirty miles to the north. We were to move in the direction of Schmidt, going through Vossenack in the Hurtgen Forest. I believe the 505 had been made into a special regimental combat team prior to moving the remainder of the division, so we were to be in this area a few days longer than the rest of the 82d. We partly marched, and then were trucked. The date was February 7, 1945. I was heading into my most gruesome experience of the war, to the place we came to call Death Valley.

Our jump-off position in the Hurtgen Forest had been the scene of bitter fighting in the fall of 1944 that had resulted in very heavy casualties for all the participating divisions. We got to Vossenack, our line of departure, a few hours before the appointed time. The place was a sea of mud just emerging from the winter's snow. It was dark, and we had to lie down to try to get some rest in mud an inch to an inch and a half deep. There was very little cover and hardly any bushes as a result of previous heavy fighting. When daylight came, it was a discouraging sight. Only

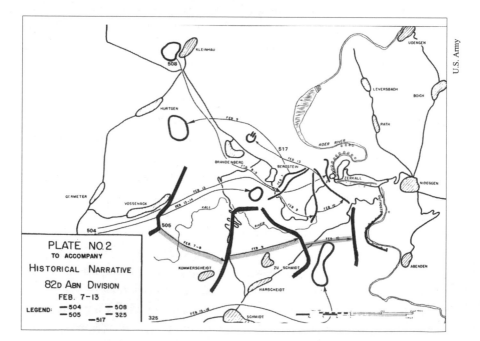

U.S. Army

one house had been left standing, and it was a skeleton. Every other wall in town had been blown down. The tallest structures were a foot or a foot and a half high, and even they were few and far between.

Here and in every other village and town we encountered, the desolation was complete. But the biggest shock of all was the sight of hundreds of dead GIs, whose blackened bodies littered this barren wasteland. Six U.S. Army divisions had been successively committed to the area, the 9th, the 28th, the 4th, the 1st, and the 8th, with the Combat Command Reserve (CCR) of the 5th Armored Division, and all winter long their bodies had remained in the positions in which they had died. Those we passed were from the 28th Infantry Division and the 8th, which had come in to relieve it.

I never got over the initial shock of seeing friends and comrades lying dead. It didn't matter if they were in my company or any other unit. Every time I was withdrawn from the front and then committed again, the first American body I saw always gave me a shock, and it was still a shock to see a dead GI even after I had been hardened by several days of operations. Even now, almost sixty years after the war, the sight of dead American soldiers remains vivid and traumatic in my mind. Never did I encounter more of them amassed in one place than near Vossenack in the Kall River Valley.

Vossenack was on high ground, and we had to go down a long slope to the wooded area of the Kall River valley. By then, February 1945, the German Army had almost shot its wad in the Ardennes offensive. In this we were very lucky. Observation from the east and the northeast of the slope was nearly perfect. In clear weather you could see for thousands of yards.

The Germans were on their own soil, and they had had months to train their fire on different terrain objects. It was said they surveyed them with very accurate instruments, so they were able to get first-round hits with their artillery. The bodies we saw attested to German accuracy.

When we came upon it, the Kall River was only about the width of a large creek. Halfway down the long slope leading to the valley we had to go across open terrain. Here we passed many shot-up vehicles, their drivers still at the wheel. There were dead from two and three divisions, killed before they reached the top of the slope as they tried to escape the valley. We tried to get under cover of the forest. We moved in extended-order formation, taking no small arms fire and very little artillery fire.

As we moved down into the forest, we saw acres and acres of pines whose tops had been knocked off by enemy artillery fire. They were broken off at a height of ten to forty feet, as if a huge lawnmower had gone across the tops. As we got into the tree line, we found a trail leading down to the bottom of the valley. The banks of the valley were extremely steep, with sharp drop-offs on the side of the trail. This was apparently the only way to get supplies into the valley, and of course it had been under very heavy fire.

The bodies had been lying there throughout the winter, and when we arrived the snow was just beginning to melt. We could just about read the battle from the way the vehicles were scattered. A number of tanks had been knocked out from losing the tracks and rolling over the bank, or had been disabled and pushed over the sides. In the valley bottom, between the river and the end of the trail a hundred yards away, was a battalion aid station, full of rows of rotting bodies still lying on their litters. The station had been overrun and the wounded had been killed or left to die. Further on by the river, we discovered the bodies of engineers who had been killed as they tried to repair a small bridge. They still wore their rubber boots.

The valley bottom and the opposite slope appeared to be the most strongly held defensive position, and most of our men had died in place. Tank destroyers and tanks littered the valley bottom. When the artillery reached its peak, the soldiers had evidently crawled under the tanks to escape the fire, and the Germans had moved in very close to their own artillery barrage, caught them lying beneath the tanks, and massacred them. Beneath every vehicle that could have given protection, there were three to half a dozen dead American soldiers.

A sober look at the statistics for the divisions that participated in the Hurtgen Forest reveals the monumental scope of the bloody debacle. The 9th Infantry Division was committed on October 6, 1944, but by October 11, all of the battalions of two of its regiments were down to less than three hundred men each. A single advance of 3,000 yards had cost the lives of 4,500 soldiers. The 28th Infantry Division was committed next. Between November 2 and 19, the 28th and its attachments suffered 6,184 casualties. Within the division, the 112th Infantry was hardest hit. The regiment crossed the Kall with 2,200 soldiers, but was eventually forced to withdraw after its initial success. The official death count was 2,093 lives.

In the 4th Infantry Division, the 12th Regiment, a unit that had come in on Utah Beach, lost 1,600 men. Between November 7 and December 3, the 4th Infantry Division lost 7,000 men. The next division to fight in the Hurtgen Forest was the Big Red One, the 1st Infantry Division, which attacked through the northern fringes on November 15. By November 29, it could go no further. In a four-mile advance that had taken almost two weeks, it had suffered 3,400 casualties. On November 19, two infantry regiments of the 8th Infantry Division, with Combat Command Reserve attached, took over the defensive positions of the 28th Infantry Division. The division's 121st Infantry made very little headway in four days of fighting while suffering 650 battle casualties and about the same number of non-battle casualties.

Units of all six divisions paid a bloody butcher's bill for the errors committed at higher headquarters. In nearly ninety days, the duration of the campaign, 24,000 men were KIA, WIA, captured, or reported MIA. In addition, 9,000 men were victims of trenchfoot, combat exhaustion, and disease. After the war, I spoke with a few of the survivors of my old unit, the 112th Infantry Regiment. A number of them said the remnants of one of their battalions were loaded onto a pair of two-and-a-half ton trucks. From a battalion that had been 750 to 900 strong, only about forty men remained.[6]

Colonel Peterson, the regimental commander and formerly my battalion commander, was relieved of his command. I think he got a very bum deal. He was an excellent officer who was not afforded the consideration he should have been given. I am not alone in thinking the blame for this carnage should be put on higher headquarters, from division to corps, right on up to First Army headquarters. The battle should be ranked as the stupidest, most unprofessional, and callous display of ignorance. They did not even conduct ground reconnaissance before issuing orders, let alone try to adapt our tactics to the terrain. Even MajGen Norman Cota, the heroic commander of the 28th Infantry Division, described the plan as having only a "gambler's chance" to succeed. The lack of intelligence during the campaign borders on criminal neglect.[7]

I'll never forget the moment we started up the opposite bank of the Kall River Valley and discovered the outline of the main American line of defense. Numerous 57mm antitank guns were still in position, and their crews were strewn on the ground, lying around their guns. Almost all of the vehicles, from the top of the slope down the side and right on up to the opposite slope, bore the inscription of the 112th Infantry of the 28th Division. Among them were many men from Company M, the unit I left when I transferred to the Parachute Troops. The sight of Death Valley moves me deeply still, and the memory of this experience was never far from my thoughts in the execution of my duties.

Chapter 26

The End in Sight: Through the Siegfried Line to the Roer River

We were glad to move out of Death Valley to continue our attack toward the Roer River, but my memories only begin a day or two later, as we were going up a steep wooded hill and began to take some pretty hot small arms fire. We threw off our sleeping bags and such to get ready for action, but the Germans must have withdrawn rapidly, because we didn't encounter a lengthy battle.

That night we ended up in some very well-prepared defensive positions, including a pillbox that was completely blown apart. After I got my platoon in position, I decided to sleep in the remains of the pillbox. It was a well-prepared dugout with a big sheet of wood on the ground, so I lay down on it and covered up with my poncho. I detected a strong odor and wondered what it was. I should have known better. At first light I discovered I had slept on top of four dead German soldiers.

We took up the attack again, moving forward rapidly under little or no small arms fire and little artillery fire. We got up to a point on high ground where we could see for quite a distance and observed troops moving to our right. As I looked across that vast expanse of hills and valleys, I saw elements of three American divisions attacking at once. It was an impressive sight: units from the 82d Airborne and 78th and 9th infantry divisions all were on the move toward the Roer.

References say our attack continued for two or three days, but sixty years later it seems to me that it was much longer. I remember one miserable day in the hard rain. We went into a hasty defensive position along a row of trees on a gentle slope with long, open hills on either side of the tree line. At the high end of the trees was a pillbox, a huge concrete bunker that was part of the Siegfried line. It was big enough to have held two platoons. The Company CP might have holed up in it, but my platoon was strung from the pillbox down the hill along the tree line. Sergeant Brown's mortar squad from the 1st Platoon was inside.

During the night, I heard a shot or two up toward the pillbox on my right flank. It wasn't close enough to worry about and no one sounded the alarm, so we let it go. At daylight, I went to check my platoon position and my men. Instead of taking my rifle and putting on all my gear, I just slipped my .45 into my right hip pocket. I was wearing a low-hanging field jacket and a raincoat.

I had just started through the platoon position when an artillery round hit the top of one of the trees about fifty yards away. It must have been a direct-fire round, because I didn't have time to hit the ground before it exploded. I felt the impact of shrapnel on my right hip. It was bad enough to knock me down. I reached back with my right hand to check how badly I was hit, but couldn't find any blood. When I examined my field jacket and raincoat, I found a hole in my pocket. The piece of shrapnel had gone through and hit the receiver of my .45, which saved me from a penetrating wound.

At first I thought I was lucky, but a lot of my men said, "There goes your million-dollar wound." I had thought a lot about that million-dollar wound—the one that's bad enough to get you back to the States, but not bad enough to cripple you for life. The war was drawing to a close. It didn't take a Ph.D. to figure out we were going to win in months or even days, and everyone was hoping that he wouldn't be the last man to die in World War II. In the end, I didn't know how I felt. I was both teed off and elated.

I picked myself up and continued to check the platoon position, working my way from the other end of the tree line up to the pillbox. The body of a huge German soldier lay near the entrance. He was in full combat gear with an impressive radio set strapped to his back. He didn't smell, so I knew it was a recent kill.

I talked to Sergeant Brown, whose squad was responsible for local security at the pillbox. To enter, you had to go down some steps into the ground, where it leveled off. It had been a miserable night, so Brown had positioned one of his newer replacements at the bottom of the steps, rather than put him out in the weather. He had also loaned the soldier his .45, because he could swing it better than a rifle in those close quarters.

During the night, this hulk of a German had started down into the pillbox. The man inside challenged him but got no reply. When he challenged him a second time with no reply, he shot him at a range of ten or twelve feet. Then he panicked, thinking he'd shot one of his own men. He woke Brown, who was sleeping in the pillbox with some of the squad. Brown went to the entrance and identified the body, and they laid the German outside near the entrance. He had intended to slip back into our lines with that powerful radio and direct artillery fire from the pillbox.

Continuing toward the Roer, we first had to make a five-mile march to the rear, and then come up again. The spring thaw was in full progress. The mud was so thick and heavy I almost had to fall out because it was so extremely hard just to pick up my legs. We sank in well over our ankles and sometimes halfway to our knees, then had to pull our legs out again. We kept on like this for five miles. I managed not to fall out, but it used up all my energy.

We finally reached the west bank of the Roer. The Germans had blown up the discharge valves of the dam on February 9, putting the river at flood stage. The west bank was a high slope, a good five hundred yards from the top of the ridge into the valley. When we hit the crest, we were in a big forest of deciduous trees. We sent patrols down to the riverbank, and they reported it would be almost impossible to cross. They didn't run into any resistance on our side, so we were ordered to go into a defensive position on the high ground of the west bank. The trees were so thick from the top to the bottom of the ridge that we actually had to try to clear lanes of fire down to the bottom. We never completely succeeded, but we did manage to clear lanes out to two hundred or three hundred yards. Although we weren't too far downstream, I never did see the damn dams.

We were only there for a week or ten days, but it seemed much longer. We dug in pretty well and got replacements, an unusual occurrence on the front that shows how far understrength we must have been. They had been following us from way back on the other side of Schmidt. They were the sorriest looking group of reinforcements I have ever seen. They had passed through Death Valley in the dark, stumbling over bodies for most of the night, trying to get out of there. Daylight was even worse for their morale. It was very difficult even for some of the most seasoned veterans to go through the remains of that carnage in broad daylight, but this group was fresh off the boat from the States. By the time they got out of Death Valley, they were one subdued bunch. I can say this—we never had any difficulty getting them to obey orders. When we told them to dig in, they dug in. They must have thought the horror they had seen was the norm.

We took artillery and very long-range machine gun fire from the eastern ridge. It didn't cause any casualties, but it let us know the Germans were there. The mess staff tried to get us at least one hot meal a day by means of a Weasel, a full track, open-carriage vehicle used primarily to evacuate the wounded and get food and ammunition to the forward units over tough terrain. They parked some distance away, hidden from the eastern ridge, and a third or so of us would be relieved to go back for a hot meal, and then we'd switch off. We got a little lazy and talked the Weasel driver into coming forward a bit more each day, until he finally came right up onto our position. The visibility was poor that day, we hadn't received any incoming fire, and we were pretty relaxed. Half the company was lined up for the meal, with the vehicle right on the slope of the ridge. Although it was spring and we were in the trees, they weren't in leaf yet.

We no sooner got in the chow line than two or three heavy machine guns opened up on us. We scattered so fast it would have been comical if it hadn't been so dangerous. Fifteen men must have stacked up on the protective side of the Weasel, and the rest of us sprinted for our holes. The Germans were hitting high, but they threw a lot of fire at us. This is what happens in potentially dangerous situations if you relax your guard. As it turned out, we bragged that Company F, 505, was the only outfit that ever got pinned down by machine gun fire in the chow line.

Stories like this that we told about ourselves helped get us through. They relieved the pressure a little, and acted as a psychic survival mechanism. We liked to turn close scrapes into comical exploits. The latrines were prime targets for such jokes, and one of the funniest things in this line happened on the west bank of the Roer. On the front, the procedure was to dig a hole, perform our duty in it, and cover it up. One day a soldier, following regulations, moved away from his fighting position, dug his hole and squatted. A few moments later, he looked up to discover a German ten or fifteen feet away. To make matters worse, the trooper had leaned his weapon against a tree. But the German had a big smile on his face. He very nicely put up his hands and wanted to be taken prisoner. So the trooper caught with his pants down was saved, and the joke went round that he was such a great soldier that he never stopped capturing Germans for a minute, not even to take a shit.

Around February 19, we heard we were going to be relieved by the 9th Infantry Division. We had a very difficult, muddy march back from the front line. We moved to the rear until it was safe to bring up trucks, then we loaded up and moved back to a railhead and onto forty and eights. I remember passing through Aachen, one of the first large German towns for which we had fought, where Hitler had ordered his troops to stand fast and cling to every inch of German soil. They had certainly followed his orders. The town was a complete wreck.

From Aachen we took the train back to Suippes, the camp we had left in December 1944. Instead of occupying the old French Army barracks again, however, we were billeted in squad tents in an area set up for the 505. This was a lot better than being out in the weather, but I can't remember any stoves or heat. We were there throughout late February and early March, but base camp leaves me with few memories. We had a regimental review, and I was awarded the Silver Star for my action in the park in Nijmegen. They may have given me my two Purple Hearts at the same time.

Many men came back to the unit at Suippes from various hospitals, and we received replacements for those who wouldn't be returning. I remember the return of Eisenhart, the BAR man from my squad who had been seriously wounded in Nijmegen. His leg had taken a long time to heal and was still hurting. He should still have been in the hospital, but he insisted on coming back to the unit. I heard that Mike Brilla also came back, even after losing an eye in the explosion in Hunner Park. If this is true, that the Army saw fit to mark him for duty again illustrates how hard up we were for reinforcements.

Sometime in March, we heard a loud noise. We ran out of our tents and looked up to see a huge armada of transport aircraft forming up for the invasion across the Rhine. They were flying at a distance, but we could see them very clearly. For once the 505 was not featured in the main show. We were content to sit back and watch it go by.

About this time I was approached by Lt Joe Holcomb, who had just returned from a lengthy stay in the hospital because of the wound he had sustained in Nijmegen. He asked me if I would be interested in going to a school back in the rear areas. I had some doubts about this, but the war in Europe was drawing to a close, and if I completed this school, I would be commissioned as a second lieutenant. I finally agreed to go, with one qualification: If I were successful, I would be reassigned to the 505. Little Joe assured me it was set in cement that any candidate who finished the course would be reassigned to his parent unit. So off I went to take what I was told would be a "combat platoon leader's course."

As I later learned, this school also had the task of "retreading" Army Air Corps personnel, antiaircraft artillery personnel, and others as infantry replacements for the front line. Even before the German Ardennes offensive in December 1944, frontline units were suffering from a critical shortage of men. The Army had incurred a higher than expected rate of casualties; moreover, higher headquarters, including Eisenhower's own, had been building up their strength to the detriment of frontline units. SHAEF itself was as large as an entire division, with a strength of 16,312 in February 1945. Because senior commanders had been improperly assigning replacements to higher headquarters and rear-echelon units, the front-line infantry was seriously undermanned.

Courses began around April 1, 1945. A regimental personnel sergeant drove me to Fontainebleau, where so many French kings and Napoleon had had their summer palace. First we passed through Paris, where we arrived quite early and spent the rest of the day really hanging one on. Both of us were well into our cups by the time I had to report to school, which was housed in carriage houses, stables, and dwellings that had been part of what you could call the logistical support for the palace and king's court. I was so far gone I could barely walk up to the desk. I think I caused a little trouble there, but luckily not enough to get me kicked out before I started.

I don't remember if Little Joe had mentioned the term "OCS" or not, but I discovered I was enrolled in a very short-term officers' candidate school. It was conducted, of all things, by personnel assigned to a reinforcement battalion, which was actually a school battalion at the

Ground Force Training Center of the ETO. I was the only member of my regiment who was sent to the Ground Forces Training Center at the time. It was there that I received word of President Roosevelt's death, which shocked us all.

The class consisted of 242 officer candidates, organized into a company of five platoons of about fifty members each. About 20 percent would be weeded out for different causes. As far as academics, training, and leadership went, it wasn't much of a challenge for me. I'm not bragging; the fact is, I had served for more than four years. I had been through the mill in basic training, had led a parachute infantry platoon in combat, and had occupied every rank from private on up to platoon sergeant.

Each platoon of candidates was assigned to a tac (tactical) officer, whose sole assignment was to evaluate us. The tac officer was the supreme man. If you got on his bad side, you might as well submit your resignation. Mine, Lieutenant O'Conner, had been a combat platoon leader. Shortly after we started, he called me in for an interview. The school was just as chickenshit as any other in terms of discipline, but I hadn't done anything wrong in my own eyes and couldn't imagine why he scheduled the session.

His first comment took me completely by surprise. He said, "Wurst, what the hell are you doing at this school? Why didn't you receive a direct commission?" I explained the circumstances, and he said that as far as he was concerned, by my grades and my combat record, there was no reason I should have to finish the course, but he didn't have much say in the matter. He couldn't afford to be friendly to anyone in his platoon, but I felt good about having a combat veteran to evaluate me. After our interview, I felt pretty much at ease for the rest of the course.

Twice, we all had to evaluate the other members of our platoon on a scale of one through fifty, and write at least one paragraph describing why we had selected the top five men, and another on the bottom five. The tricky thing was that we all were rated on how we rated each other, so it behooved us to call it how we saw it. It kept us wide awake, continually looking for strengths and weaknesses in all our team members. We called this evaluation "Fuck Your Buddy Week."

We also had physical training run by a lieutenant colonel named Delescue. If someone started lagging behind in a run, Delescue would holler, "You're gonna die! You're a damn combat platoon leader!

Infantry platoon leaders are a dime a dozen! And if you don't get this, you're gonna die sooner than the rest of them!" He harped on this an hour at a time. Statistics show Colonel Delescue wasn't far from wrong. It reminds me of an old combat sergeant major in the British Army who was asked to define the duty of an officer. He replied, "They show us how to die."

To me, the best thing about the school was the instruction in platoon tactics. A school platoon of combat infantry performed a vivid demonstration of the theory of "fire and movement." It was a marvelous sight to behold. Never could more than one or two men have been targeted. They kept making short, quick moves from one piece of cover to the other, taking advantage of folds in the ground, of natural cover and concealment. An "infantry company in the attack" problem was our last tactical exercise. By then, we had been fitted for our Class A uniforms, so all of us thought we had it made, but I think the instructors purposely assigned a marginal candidate as company commander for the exercise. His decisions were faulted and he was washed out within a few days of graduation. Word traveled fast to classes behind us. The purpose of this exercise was probably to keep them on their toes.

We were a couple weeks away from graduation when the end of the war in Europe, VE-Day, arrived. We were reigned in pretty tightly, so our celebration amounted to a few hours' pass on a weekend. VE-Day came to me as a reprieve. I never expected to survive the war. I was like a person on death row who had suddenly been given a pardon. Then again, I worried that, even if I did survive the European war, as a new second lieutenant I would likely be sent to the Pacific. I tried not to give this much thought.

What I did think about was all the good men who had been killed in combat. I strongly believe in God and his miracles, and thank Him for my survival everyday in my prayers. When you've come a fraction of an inch from death many, many times, you never forget it. To be alive yourself seems a miracle, but the deaths of so many of your buddies who have died so brutally, sometimes needlessly, are wounds that time never heals. "Why them and not me?" After almost sixty years, the question still haunts me.

I continued my studies at OCS, and graduated first in my class. We were reassigned to our parent units after graduation, but Army channels were so slow that on the anniversary of D-Day, I still had not rejoined the

505. It was after midnight on June 5 and into the morning of June 6, and I had had a few drinks in a café somewhere in France or Belgium. It was packed with American soldiers, officers and enlisted alike. I hollered and got everyone's attention, and we drank a toast to the men who had carried out D-Day the year before. For a couple of moments in that noisy, crowded café, there was nothing but absolute silence.

Epilogue

Homeward Bound

As it turned out, I didn't get sent to the Pacific. I reported back to the 505 as second lieutenant in June, and became a platoon leader in E Company of the 2d Battalion. We were still at war with Japan, but everyone was clamoring to get the men out of uniform. I was a "high-point man," which meant I was eligible for discharge according to a system that calculated total months of service, overseas duty, combat, decorations, and marital status or dependents. I considered going to Berlin, where the 82d Airborne Division had been selected as the Guard of Honor, but I was tired of moving around. I wanted to go home, marry a suitable girl, have a family, and stay in one spot.

I flew back in mid-August on the Green Project, a program that rotated the highest of the high-point men back to the States by plane. Other than the German jet fighter I'd seen in Holland, planes were all propeller-driven. Our carrier was a C-54, a four-engine cargo plane. There were no seats: we placed blankets and lay down directly on the cargo space.

Crossing the Atlantic was a real adventure: we flew to the Azores and refueled, then went all the way up to Newfoundland. We debarked just long enough to get rip-roaring drunk in the Officers' Club, where I traded a pistol or two for half a case of White Horse scotch. Next we headed for New Castle Air Base in Delaware, where we got sprayed with a bomb against foreign bugs and illnesses. I got off the plane with one big hangover in a cloud of fumigation. When my feet touched the ground, nothing else mattered. Finally, I was home.

But first I had to get through customs. "Do you have anything to declare?" a civilian clerk asked. "Yeah," I answered: "I've got nine pistols and two bottles of White Horse scotch in this bag." This set all his wheels into bureaucratic motion: "It's against customs regulations to allow the flow of fire arms into the United States." I informed him I had a certificate saying they were legitimate war trophies. "I don't think that'll do it," he replied.

The certificate was a mimeographed form with blanks for individual items, written in ink. It was signed by my superiors, and listed my nine pistols with their serial numbers. He looked it over, then replied: "To be legitimate, everything's got to be typed in."

I just knew he was going to take those pistols, and that would be the last I ever saw of them. I said there'd been many times in the war when we hadn't been sitting in our foxholes with typewriters in our laps, busily typing up our trophy certificates. But he repeated, "I can't let you into the United States with these pistols."

Finally, I had had it. "If these pistols stay here, I stay here," I said. "So make up your mind what you're going to do about it." And that was how I passed through customs with nine pistols and two bottles of scotch.

Still smelling of bug spray, I finally ended up right where I began my active military career in 1941, at Indiantown Gap Military Reservation in Pennsylvania. The next day, I set out for the old milk run from Harrisburg to Erie. Several of us were waiting for the train in a bar when a crowd of cheering people burst in. The war was over! VJ-Day totally surprised us——we didn't even know the atomic bomb had been dropped.

Three days later, I hitchhiked back to Erie. There were parties and many visits with family and friends, but most nights I was ill at ease. I was a twenty-year-old combat veteran going on a hundred. Call it wartime experiences, nervous energy, or what you will, but I had a hard time falling asleep if I was cold sober; I often went to sleep in the front room chair, then woke up every hour or two and never went to bed.

I had joined the Army as a high-school sophomore, and now I faced a void. At seventeen, I had my wings, but in civilian life I was suddenly a minor. I had served my country for more than five years, but I still couldn't vote. I had been a platoon sergeant responsible in combat for up to fifty men, but I couldn't get married without my parents' permission. I had made three combat jumps, but I never learned to drive. I could not even legally go to a bar, sit down, and order a beer.

Almost all eligible males were still in the service, including most of my friends and my brother Vern. Nothing between my enlistment and the present had prepared me, or given me any indication of what I wanted to do for a living. I only knew I wanted to settle down to raise a family. I was like the ski trooper who was asked what he wanted to do when he got home. "First, I'm going to climb in bed with my wife and make up for my absence," he said. "Next, I'll take off my skis." First, I wanted to find a wife. Next, I would take off my chutes.

Soon after my return, I bumped into an old friend, Lillian Myers, who gave me the address and telephone number of her friend, Mildred Shugart, written on a little scrap of paper. Millie was twenty and living in an apartment with her aunt Elizabeth. There was only one telephone, and whoever answered it down the hall had to call out to the person who was wanted on the phone. I called Millie for a week or so, but she was always working or out, or no one would call her to the phone. Finally, I decided to try one more time. "If I can't get through now, that's it," I told myself.

Someone, bless him, answered and went and got Millie. We made a date, and within six months we were married. Millie was a beautiful bride, and all I had ever wanted in a wife. We had an evening ceremony followed by, of all things, a tea at the Ladies' Club set up by one of Millie's more uppity aunts. This, of course, meant that alcohol was strictly forbidden. Years later, my friends were still bitching about those little sandwiches. "You didn't even offer us a beer!" they said.

Meanwhile, in late August, I returned to Indiantown Gap Military Reservation for an exit interview from the Army. So it was that one bright morning, I found myself across the desk from an interviewing officer, a captain in his late twenties. He had nothing in the way of decorations except a little "fruit salad"—some ribbons that showed he had never been outside the States, and maybe the Good Conduct Medal.

The interviewing officer was supposed to write my military occupations on some form or other so my prospective employer would know my skills. "So, what did you do during the war?" he asked. I explained I had held the positions of squad leader, platoon sergeant, and platoon leader in combat in the parachute infantry. "Yes, but what did you *really* do in the war?" he replied.

I was getting a little upset. The guy was a captain and I was a second lieutenant. I said, "What do you mean? We fought the war." Then he said, "Yeah, but what skills did you learn?" Now I was really agitated. "You don't have to put *anything* on that form," I said, "because there's not much need in civilian life for how to throw a grenade, push a bayonet into someone, shoot people, tear down a machine gun and reassemble it, or for combat leadership skills. I don't know how you're going to relate these things to civilian experience."

He continued all the same, saying, "Well, then, what did you do after the war?" I said that I had briefly been officer of the day at POW camps. The grand, lump sum total of my war-time occupations on my employment form was "helped guard prisoners of war." I managed not to tear it up in front of him, but if we had continued much longer in this vein, I think I would have reached over the desk and slapped the captain in the face.

All of us on the front lines knew this was what would happen if we managed to survive the war. When it came to civilian jobs, the people who did the hard fighting got the least credit, while those who were fortunate enough to learn a trade taught in the rear echelons benefitted from their occupational training. Combat veterans used to banter about the value of our medals. At the time, coffee cost a dime. One of our standing jokes was that the Silver Star and ten cents would get you a cup of coffee.

And the upshot of my interview? I reverted to inactive duty as a second lieutenant in the AUS, the Army of the United States. So it was that in September 1945 I started looking for my very first civilian job, a period I think of as a comedy of errors. The Army had taught us to trust our unit, and it took me a long time to understand that Millie and I had to take steps to *protect* ourselves. I knew how to defuse a minefield, but throughout my first year back from the war I was often disarmed by civilian life.

I'm happy to say that I'm writing this today, January 18, 2002, on Millie's and my fifty-sixth wedding anniversary. In spite of our early trials, in our case it is really true that "they lived happily ever after." We settled down and established a fine family, two boys and a girl, who now have good careers and grown-up children of their own. I rejoined the 112th Infantry of the 28th Infantry Division and had a successful career in the National Guard as platoon leader, company commander, regimental S-3, and commander of the 112th Infantry, where I first enlisted in 1940 as a lonely, uncertain boy. I ended my military career in 1975 as assistant chief of staff, G-3, and retired as a colonel after thirty-five years of service. Although I never did learn to negotiate the rocky terrain of civilian employment well, I worked at General Electric from 1946 to 1982, with the exception of two years active duty as a tank company commander in one of the first four American divisions of NATO.

Today my wife and I live in upstate New York on a hundred and ten acres of woodland. When I look around at all we have in our retirement, I am constantly amazed. Sometimes I still can see myself as a fifteen-year-old kid, trudging along in an awkward wool uniform, pulling that old water-cooled .30-caliber machine gun on a two-wheeled cart. When I think of the many times I, too, could have become a casualty of war, and realize yet again how dependent we are on chance and the mercy of God, I feel wonder to be alive.

In 2000, I finally got around to framing some of my war photographs, military ribbons, and medals—a project I'd threatened to undertake for years. I've said it before, and I'll say it again: I gave the government all I could, and the government kept its promise to me. And I still have that piece of paper from August 1945 with Millie's name, address, and telephone number on it. It, too, is framed on the wall of my study, one of my most cherished possessions.

Notes

Epigraph

A. H. Smyth (ed.), *The Writings of Benjamin Franklin*, IX (New York: Haskell House, 1970), p. 156.

Preface

1. Epitaph cited in Michael D. Doubler, *Closing with the Enemy: How GIs Fought the War in Europe, 1944-1945* (Lawrence, Kansas: University Press of Kansas, 1994), p. 265.

2. See Doubler, pp. 234, 235, 240, 242; George W. Neil, *Infantry Soldier: Holding the Line at the Bulge* (Norman: University of Oklahoma Press, 2000), Preface, note 4.

Chapter 9

3. For the designated airfields, and in many other instances throughout this memoir, I have relied for details of place, name, and date on Allan Langdon,

Ready: The History of the 505th Parachute Infantry Regiment, 82nd Airborne Division, World War II, Rev. George B. Wood, ed. (Indianapolis: Western Newspaper Publishing Co., Inc., 1986).

Chapter 20

4. Charles McDonald, *The European Theater of Operations, The Seigfried Line Campaign* (Washington: U.S. Army Center of Military History, 1963), pp. 133, 135.

Chapter 22

5. Major Cook, in Cornelius Ryan, *A Bridge Too Far* (New York: Simon and Schuster, 1974), p. 457.

Chapter 25

6. I am indebted to the excellent account of the Hurtgen Forest tragedy in Chapter 7 of Doubler. See especially pages 179-195.

7. Robert A. Miller, *Division Commander: A Biography of Major General Norman D. Cota* (Spartanburg, S.C.: Reprint Company, 1989), p. 117. Cited in Doubler, p. 181.

INDEX

La Donna Detroit

Also by Jon A. Jackson:

The Diehard
The Blind Pig
Grootka
Hit on the House
Deadman
Dead Folks
Man with an Axe

La Donna Detroit

A Detective Sergeant Mulheisen Mystery

Jon A. Jackson

ATLANTIC MONTHLY PRESS
NEW YORK

Published simultaneously in Canada
Printed in the United States of America

FIRST EDITION

Library of Congress Cataloging-in-Publication Data

Jackson, Jon A.
    La donna Detroit : a Detective Sergeant Mulheisen mystery / Jon A. Jackson.
        p. cm.
    ISBN 0-87113-810-7
    1. Mulheisen, Detective Sergeant (Fictitious character)—Fiction.   2.
Police—Michigan—Detroit—Fiction.   3. Detroit (Mich.)—Fiction.   I. Title.
PS3560.A216 D66 2000
813'.54—dc21   99-086204

DESIGN BY LAURA HAMMOND HOUGH

Atlantic Monthly Press
841 Broadway
New York, NY 10003

00 01 02 03   10 9 8 7 6 5 4 3 2 1

To the memory of Henry Wallace Robinson, 1912–1999 . . .
the raconteur supreme, the wit humane . . . *da capo al fine*

Contents

Thanks to the detectives of the Missoula County Sheriff's Department for their suggestions and expert advice.
—Jon A. Jackson, Missoula, November 1999

1

A Bad Beginning

It was as classical as Goldilocks and the three bears, or Hansel and Gretel . . . innocents in the lonely, spooky forest, surprised by experience, and reacting with violence.

This was not the forest primeval, but a pathetic remnant of the great American forest. It was no more than a few dozen doomed elms intermixed with the odd ash or oak, the sparse woods left by a suburban developer who had run out of cash, stalled by a war. It was one of those awkward places, a kind of limbo, where unsettling things can happen. It wasn't really part of suburban development, at least not yet. Maybe it would never be. The developer had put on hold his plans for Crooks Woods—named for the farmer who had owned these acres.

Children had delighted in the abandoned excavations of unsold lots and had roofed over the trench footings and half basements with cast-off pieces of building materials, scrap lumber, and tar paper. The excavations made ideal "bunkers." The kids were crazy about "bunkers," childish imitations of trench warfare, or bomb shelters—the influence of the previous war's stories and the present war's movies. They invented games to employ these bowel-like structures, crawling into them fearfully, stocking them with salvaged and stolen

1

plunder: lanterns, bits of candles, boards hammered into secret altars, stashes for forbidden comic books, condoms from the dressers of lately drafted older brothers, items of daringly pilfered lingerie— including, in this one, an enormous brassiere and an accordionlike corset that could wrap two or three boys.

The bunkers were not for girls. Undoubtedly a few were invited, but they knew better than to crawl into these dens. Goldilocks was a cautionary tale, after all. Still, a few bold girls must have penetrated these caverns, rarely.

Some bunkers were larger, more labyrinthine, but this one was fairly simple, a rectangle twenty-four feet by twenty. The trenches were deep enough that two eight-year-old boys, Carmie and Bertie, could actually walk upright in most places, although they tended to hunch over to avoid striking their heads—there were sometimes nasty nails poking through the rough boards that roofed the trenches.

The bunker was well isolated from the others, almost in the center of the uncleared woods. Carmie and Bertie had known about this bunker for some time but they had never dared approach it until today. They knew it belonged to an older boy named Porky White, who led a gang of teenaged boys who stole cantaloupes from suburban gardens, beer from their parents' refrigerators, candy from stores. All of this exciting loot was stashed in the bunker. The gang, known as the Clawson Commandos—there was an inescapable air of militarism these days—naturally despised little kids like Carmie and Bertie. And they, in turn, naturally writhed in envy of the Commandos, from the helmet liners on their heads to the combat boots on their feet, and wanted to be just like them.

Porky White was a particularly nasty, cruel bully. He ruled this bunker like a Chinese bandit, something they had learned about from movies and magazines. But he lacked the charismatic attraction of their true idol, a Sicilian outlaw recently glamorized in the pages of *Life* magazine, the bold and daring Giuliano. Perhaps the fact that they were themselves of Italian heritage (fairly recent, their parents emigrants) enhanced their idolization of Giuliano. They truly feared, respected, and envied Porky White, but did not idolize him.

They attended a Catholic school. Porky went to public school. On this day, due to the funeral of a priest, the Saint Anthony school was out and public school was not. So they had a perfect opportunity to creep into the citadel of Porky White and see what all was there.

It was a bleak, cool day at the end of winter but before the beginning of spring. The sky was a familiar gray, a featureless overcast, with a feeling that it could rain but probably wouldn't. In this half-begun suburb, if one could climb the water tower and look down, one would see a mildly rolling terrain with woods to the north and east and a city to the south and sprawling to the west. But at one's feet were laid out streets with only scattered houses on each block. Off to the east were farms and the shrunken remnants of farms. There was almost no automobile traffic, because of gas rationing, but there was an interurban trolley zipping along on a distant arterial rail line.

The boys had an old tin flashlight with weak batteries—it was hard to get batteries these days—and it barely lasted long enough for them to get into the sanctum sanctorum, the little eight-by-eight-foot cellar at the heart of the scrappily roofed bunker. This cellar had been meant to house the furnace and water heater of the home that would eventually be built if the war ever ended.

When the light failed the boys were scared. They almost panicked. Carmie, the slighter, more handsome of the two, began to cry, fearing that they were trapped and would never find their way out of this pitch-black labyrinth. He wept, freely lamenting that they had ever crawled in here, evidently giving way to the belief that they had gone down into the earth, that they might be buried in a cave-in and never found.

The chubby boy, Bertie, was scared, too. But he didn't cry. He was almost certain that the bunker was not deep, that they hadn't actually crawled down into the earth, although it had seemed to them on their way into that darkness that they were descending. But he retained a fairly strong impression of the surface of the site, with the scrap-and-tar-paper covering that was itself meagerly covered by raw, clayey dirt—the Commandos had too soon wearied of camouflaging their bunker. Still, as children, the boys did not recognize this excavation for what it was; they didn't see the pattern. To them, it was a subterranean maze, not a simple square footing. But Bertie, at least, clung to the notion that in an emergency they could possibly break out through the roof, as it were, if they couldn't simply crawl back through the passageway to the entrance. He tried to buck up his cousin Carmie. He denied that, for instance, there were snakes in the dark bunker.

And then they saw a light. They almost squealed with relief, but this quickly gave way to a greater terror. The huffing, bobbling figure that lurched toward the inner sanctum, out of the pitch blackness, for a fleeting moment resembled a bear. But a bear with a flashlight? And then Bertie had the weird impression that this was . . . was what? Something familiar, something he had experienced but only obliquely, never face-to-face: his guardian angel, perhaps, or his doppelgänger, another self born at the same time as himself, but already fully formed, or more advanced, anyway, and always lurking on the periphery of his experience.

But in the next instant they both realized with horror that the bear, or weird ogre, could only be Porky White, the awful brute who ruled in this subterranean domain, who must inevitably discover them, and that he would be outraged at their violation of his secret castle. They tried to get away, frantically bolting for escape by another tunnel, like baby rabbits fleeing a badger or a weasel. But it was useless. Porky quickly caught them.

The older boy dragged them back into the pit by their heels. He pummeled them with his fists and shone his powerful flashlight in their eyes. The blows hurt their arms and backs and their heads rung. They cowered in a corner, moaning and sobbing, rubbing their sore arms while Porky lit a candle and placed it on a tin can that sat on a wooden pop carton.

"So, it's you little dago rats," he snarled, looking them over. His big moon face loomed evilly in the flickering candlelight. The little boys blubbered.

"Shut your damn traps, you shitty punks!" he commanded. "So, you snuck into my bunker, hunh? Thought you'd steal my treasure, hunh? Well, now you gotta be punished." He sounded just like a troll from a fairy tale. The little boys quaked in despair.

"You know what I'm gonna do?" the bully said. "I'm gonna beat the hell out of you, that's what! Or maybe I'll burn your fingers. Yah! Teach you a lesson, you little wops!"

The boys wept. They knew there was no escape. They stared aghast at his huge white face with his wet red lips and glowing eyes. He was capable of killing them, they were convinced. He might even eat them.

Porky relished their terror. He tormented them with spectacularly imagined savageries. He would break their bones, poke out their eyes, or even throw them to the snakes. He said he had a snake pit, filled with rattlers and moccasins. The snakes would bite them and they would swell up from the poison, puke, and die. They would never see their families again. Nobody would ever find their wormy corpses. He knew they hadn't told anyone where they were going. No one would look for them down this hole. They were in Hell, that's where they were! They might as well consider themselves dead already. The Devil was coming to get them.

Carmie was convinced that he would be murdered. Bertie wasn't so sure. As the older boy raged on he began to feel less frightened. It was the bit about snakes: Bertie knew from Sister Mary Frances's adamant insistence—"There are no poisonous snakes in Michigan"—that Porky was lying. Porky was just trying to scare them; maybe he would let them go. But when? And after what kind of torment and physical violence? Bertie wasn't so hopeful about that. He didn't know how to deal with this older boy's malevolence. He didn't want to anger him further, stir him up to a fury in which he might do something that they would all regret. He tried to get Carmie to hush, to calm down. Maybe this stupid boy would content himself with just punching them, some painful but not too harmful punishment, and then let them go.

"We just wanted to be in the Commandos," Bertie whispered. "We want to join up, be like you. We'll do anything."

"Anything?" the boy asked. He sat for a while, watching them, his eyes glittering in the candlelight like a goblin's. Then he said, addressing Carmie, "Come over here. You stay there," he said to Bertie. "You don't move, or I'll kill both of you."

Carmie crawled to the other boy. Porky rummaged in a box that seemed to serve as a kind of altar, covered with an old flag and supporting a candelabra and a dented urn of some sort. He pulled out a Boy Scout camping hatchet. He brandished it in the light. Carmie's eyes were like Ping-Pong balls. "Take off your pants," Porky said.

He had to say it again, twice, before Carmie understood. But then the boy unbuckled his belt and unbuttoned his corduroy knickers and let them down. He stood hunched over in the light. He still wore his white underpants. Porky was crouched before him. He reached out and pulled down the boy's cotton briefs, somewhat damp and stained with urine from his fright. Carmie trembled in horror.

"What . . . what are you gonna do?" he asked.

"If you don't shut up and do what I say," Porky said, "I'm gonna chop yer pecker off."

The boy stood still while Porky took hold of his penis and pulled on it, not roughly, but almost tenderly. Porky was breathing heavily. He stroked the child's penis repeatedly, his lips wet and nearly drooling.

"You ever suck a fella?" he asked, suddenly.

Carmie shook his head. "What do you mean?" he stammered.

Porky stood up. He was much taller, and like Carmie, he hunched. He unbuttoned his own trousers and took out his own penis. It was much larger than Carmie's, and it was strangely stiff, sticking straight out.

"Here," he said, his voice rasping, "get down on yer knees and suck it."

Carmie's eyes were locked on the well-sharpened hatchet, but he shook his head. "No."

"Okay, then," Porky said. "I'm gonna whack yer dick off." He grabbed the boy's penis again and held it, stretching it, brandishing the brutal hatchet threateningly.

"Fatty, help me!" Carmie squealed, inadvertantly using a nickname he often applied to his pudgy cousin.

His tormentor seemed to think that the name was applied to him. "I ain't Fatty," he snarled. "Get down, before I chop this weenie off!"

Carmie sank to his knees, moaning. The older boy hunched over him, breathing excitedly. "Open yer mouth," he demanded, hoarsely.

Bertie picked up a bottle that had been used to hold candles, its neck encrusted with wax drippings. He held it by the neck and smashed it into the side of Porky White's head. The big oaf stumbled backward, tripped over his own trousers, then the box altar, and fell on his back.

"Get him!" Bertie cried. The boys leapt on the fallen bully. The candle was knocked away and lay on its side, flickering, but not out. It cast lurid shadows on the walls as the boys screamed and pummeled their tormentor, striking with the bottle until it broke, striking with anything that came to hand—bricks, stones, the fallen hatchet.

Finally, they stopped. Porky was still, crumpled in the corner. In the flickering light they stared at each other, at their grubby hands and faces, smeared with blood and dirt. And then they stared at Porky. He lay with his eyes open, as if in surprise, catching the candlelight, his face gashed and bleeding, his mouth gaping, his front teeth broken. He didn't move.

The boys stood up. Bertie retrieved Porky's flashlight. He picked up the hatchet. It was wet with blood, but whether it had been chopped into the body of Porky he didn't know. Perhaps it had only acquired blood from the wounds. Perhaps it hadn't been used. Bertie looked at Carmie, who was pulling up his pants. He gestured with the hatchet.

"Did you chop him?" he asked.

"No! No, I didn't," Carmie declared. He buckled his belt. "C'mon, let's get going!"

Bertie shone the light around the little dirt room, which now looked like nothing more than a littered garbage hole. The sprawled body inevitably added a suggestion of the grave.

"Maybe we should take some of his stuff," Bertie suggested. The light fell on the stack of precious comic books, a wooden box filled with pop and beer, a deck of cards, some military medals and insignia.

"No! Leave it!" Carmie was possessed with anxious haste now. "Let's go! Let's get out before someone else comes!"

"Maybe we should cover him up," Bertie said.

That idea seemed right. They began to scoop dirt and hurl magazines and scraps of blankets, junk, at the body. They got caught up in this frantic activity.

Finally, Carmie said, "That's enough. Let's go. Let's go, let's go."

So they crawled, or rather scurried in a hunched duckwalk, through the passageway until they burst into the precious but blinding daylight. It was still a dull, overcast day, but it seemed bright to them after the darkness of the tunnel and oh, so blessedly welcome.

They ran from the site almost to the edge of the thinned woodlot before Bertie stopped.

"What?" Carmie said, looking back at him anxiously. "Let's go! Let's run." He was frantic to be away.

"You know what we did?" Bertie said. "We killed him. We murdered him! He's dead." He looked around. It was early afternoon, he thought, almost like coming out of a movie matinee, but earlier.

The world seemed abandoned. There were few houses here. The men of this half-built community were all away, enlisted in the armed services or at work, and many of the wives were at work as well, in factories that made tanks and bombs and airplanes.

It seemed to Bertie that Porky White must have had some unusual reason not to be in school. He must have stayed home, ill perhaps, or, more likely, played hooky. There was no sign of his gang. So there was no great rush. Bertie was not exactly calm—how could he be?—but he was not panicked.

They were in trouble, though. He knew that. And something told him that the biggest part of his trouble was his cousin Carmie. The handsome lad was visibly shaken. They could not go home, not yet. There was no reason for them to go home. They weren't expected. They had been shooed out to play, and normally that meant they would be outside until near dark, when Carmie's mother would stand on the porch and call, over and over again, "Carmie! Bertie!" He talked to Carmie and got him to calm down.

They found a cold puddle of water, where Bertie was able to wash the blood and dirt off Carmie's and his hands and faces and bare legs. The blood on their clothes he rubbed with dirt. Then they went for a walk. It was only a few blocks over to the railroad viaduct; they often played over there, although warned against it. They hung around there until a train came by and flattened some pennies they had put on the tracks. Then they walked to the filling station on Crooks Road and got a couple of Cokes and shared an Oh Henry! candy bar.

Carmie was in pretty good spirits by now. It was as if he had forgotten what had happened in the bunker. But as they walked back toward the neighborhood, Bertie pointed out some important things. When Porky White's buddies got out of school they would go to the bunker and they would find their leader. The cops would be notified. They would question the gang boys, who would deny having killed Porky. Maybe the cops wouldn't believe Porky's friends, but they might also come around and question Carmie and Bertie, and any other kid who lived in the neighborhood. Maybe the cops had some way of knowing that Carmie and Bertie had been in the bunker. Maybe there were fingerprints or something. Bertie didn't know. They had heard about fingerprints and stuff on the radio, in *Gang Busters* and *The Shadow*. Maybe there was something they didn't even know about, that detectives could use to find out who had been in the tunnel. Maybe they would be caught.

Bertie wanted to alarm Carmie, because he was genuinely worried on just these lines, but he didn't want him to be too scared. Still, he had to be scared enough to keep his mouth shut. And so he made him swear that, no matter what, he would say exactly what Bertie said, even if the cops split them up and asked them separately.

And what they would say was that they had gone out playing, had gone to the viaduct, had put pennies on the tracks, and then went to get pop at the filling station. And that was that. They didn't know what time it was because they didn't have watches. One thing they hadn't done, they hadn't gone anywhere near the woods. They had always been told to stay away from old man Crooks's woods, so they never went near. That was their story. Bertie wished he had thought to take the hatchet, to throw it away, down a sewer or something.

It began to rain.

This much of the story Umberto recalled with ease, even after fifty years. Indeed, he *knew* this story, at least to this point. There were other details, he was aware, but he had forgotten them. If he worked at it, however, he could recall—he thought—that nothing ever came of Porky's murder, or death, or whatever you want to call it.

Did they ever find the body? He was not sure. He supposed they must have. Some time after this, it may have been within days or weeks or even months, they had moved away. He remembered his uncle Dom saying Crooks Woods wasn't a good place for them to live and all the other grown-ups laughing. His other uncle was there, he recalled, Uncle Gags. That was his special uncle. Uncle Gags was somehow closer to him than Uncle Dom, Carmie's dad, although he didn't actually live with them. He came around a lot. Bertie didn't know why, then.

The move may have had something to do with Porky. But he was sure that, at the time, he had not connected the events. Still, Uncle Gags had taken him aside at some point and asked some questions about Porky. He couldn't remember what the questions were. It wasn't anything like, Did you do this? Or even, What happened? Or, Were you there? Bertie's answers apparently satisfied Uncle Gags.

Anyway, they moved. Bertie remembered feeling tremendously relieved, happy to move to the city, to the east side. He still lived with Carmie and his family. They were his family. Aunt Sophie was like the mother he'd never had. And then he didn't remember much of anything until Uncle Gags's funeral.

Uncle Gags had been killed, shot by another man. Lots of men came to the funeral, dressed in black suits. Very important men, it seemed. There were a lot of flowers; the body lay in a casket in the front room, dressed in a suit with a flower in the lapel, the hands crossed on the chest. The men drank whiskey and beer and smoked cigars. The women talked. There wasn't much crying. The priest came and they all drove in big cars to the cemetery, where the casket was lowered into the ground. For some reason, Bertie was treated with some solicitude, which he didn't understand at the time. Older women hugged him and said they pitied him. Men shook his hand and patted him on the back and shoulder and said he should be strong.

2

Birds of Prey

Ezio Spinodi was in trouble but he didn't know it. He was like a sparrowhawk who sees a songbird sitting on a barbed-wire fence and makes a casual pass. The songbird turns out to be a shrike that chases him down in a thicket and beats his brains out. He saw Helen Sedlacek, a pretty, diminutive woman sitting in a Colorado ski bar in one of those pricey new concrete hotels in Winter Park. She wasn't dressed like a skier or a local, but he would have noticed her anyway, because he'd seen her earlier, on the Amtrak train from Salt Lake City to Denver, and he'd seen her get off in Granby, just a few miles northwest of here.

It wasn't some huge surprise; Ezio was looking for her. He'd been sent by Humphrey DiEbola, the Detroit mob boss, to find her and Joe Service. When they got to someplace useful, like Denver, he was supposed to call in for further orders.

Ezio, popularly known as Itchy, was a moderately cynical man—he was a Detroiter. *Further orders* would mean only one thing, Ezio felt. But it was significant that he hadn't been given the order from the start. So he was cool. He was not about to drop the hammer until he heard the command.

Only, they hadn't gotten to Denver. Joe Service had been taken off the train in Granby in an ambulance. It looked to Itchy like he'd had a stroke, or a heart attack—some kind of fit. Surprising—such a young man. Maybe it had been dope, cocaine or something. Joe had been accompanied by a cop from Detroit, Itchy knew him—Detective Sergeant Mulheisen. If Joe's fit had incidentally removed "Fang" Mulheisen from the scene, Itchy could not complain, even if it complicated things. But he believed he had obeyed his right instincts in not following Joe and Mulheisen, rather than the babe. He'd definitely gotten the feeling that Humphrey was more interested in the babe than in Joe Service. Not that Itchy believed for a nanosecond that Humphrey had a letch for this babe, no matter how young and good-looking. This babe must have her mitts on some loot. That was his theory. There is a prevailing cynicism among Detroiters. They have an image of themselves as unsentimental, can-do people. They say: Screw *pretty* . . . does it *work*? To hear them talk, the rest of the world is more or less Disneyland. Of course, genuine cynicism gets nothing done; a real cynic doesn't believe in anything, much less that something will "work." So maybe Detroiters are just pseudocynics. Severe skeptics. Beauty is a hard sell, but there are some takers. The point is, practicality is poured on one's morning pancakes.

Helen Sedlacek was no less a Detroit girl than Itchy a Detroit guy. Born and raised on the east side, she had gone to Dominican, a Catholic girls school, graduated from Michigan State University, started her first business in Birmingham (once a suburb, but now the epicenter of the Detroit municipal zone). She had definitely eaten Motor City molasses on her hotcakes. Which is not to say that she hadn't her soft, feminine side.

Helen was about thirty, small, slim, and dark. She had gallons of black hair, with a silver skunk stripe rising from her right temple. She had a boy's physique and she was strong and lean-muscled. Fearless and brave; sweet and demure. Everyone has at least two sides: how they see themselves, versus how others see them. At least two, more like dozens, especially as the years go by.

At one point, when she was about fourteen, Helen had acquired the nickname Sonya. Schoolkids aren't notably discriminatory when it comes to ethnic origins. Or rather, they are very discriminatory, but careless: they don't distinguish between a Yugoslavian and a Russian, especially if both countries are part of what was then called the Iron Curtain, or the Red Menace. No Serbs or Croats in those days, before the walls came tumbling down. She was known as Sonya Bitchacockoff.

She wore nothing but black, and her black hair was long and generally draped over her pale face. She tended toward capes and hoods. She read poetry, especially Anna Akhmatova, and even affected an accent—"Vot do you vant," she would mutter. Or, with a wave of the hand, "Leaf me alone." To her credit, she genuinely liked Akhmatova's verse, although she was more attracted by the legendary image, and she enjoyed correcting the pronunciation of the name by her teenaged friends—"Perhaps you muss be Slaf," she would say, pityingly.

But the "Bitchacockoff" tag was derived from a bizarre incident. It hardly needs to be said that teenagers experiment with sex; it's required. She had a couple of girlfriends with whom she discussed the varieties of sexual experience, a lot. Each pretended to a greater experience than they possessed. They were all virgins, but denied it. One of them, a rapidly developing girl of Italian extraction, even claimed that she had "gone down" on her boyfriend.

"It's not bad," she claimed, "just kind of salty and a little sweetish-sour at the same time. You have to be careful not to gag, when it goes down your throat."

"You mean you let him come?" the others asked.

"Oh, no! Ugh! I could never do that. I mean when it pokes the back of your mouth, you know?"

One night a bunch of them were parked in a van, down by Windmill Point. One of the boys had stolen a bottle of his parents' booze, a fifth of Southern Comfort. It was sweet and palatable to their youthful tastes and soon they were all more or less tipsy, if not drunk. The toughest of the boys, Cazzie, started talking about oral sex. There was a lot of snickering and giggling, boasting, and the conversation evolved to the point where he dared the girls—there were three of them, including Helen—to show their nerve by "going down."

The other girls seemed at least cautiously willing to try, but Helen balked. She wasn't against a lot of kissing and feeling, even a furtive hand job, but she wasn't going to actually allow some boy to penetrate any of her orifices—not in front of other people. The boys, however, were intensely excited by the idea, naturally. The Southern Comfort had emboldened them all, lowered their inhibitions or, at least, had provided them with an excuse if it actually occurred. But not Helen.

"I want to go," she insisted, straightening her clothing.

"Aw, c'mon, Sonya," Cazzie said. He pulled her to him. "A little blow job never hurt anybody." He had actually unzipped and produced a throbbing penis that was about ready to explode. The other kids were thrilled and joined in.

"Do it!" they cried.

Cazzie, encouraged and sexually maddened, grabbed Helen by the head and forced her face to his groin. He was strong and clearly intended to force her to do it, thrusting his rigid organ at her lips.

With a snarl, Helen opened her mouth and then clamped her little, sharp teeth onto the end of his penis, biting down as hard as she could. The boy screamed and cuffed her head away. He howled in agony, then rage. Helen spit blood into the boy's face. That was a brilliant gesture.

Cazzie was so concerned with wiping his face—he wasn't sure that the spittle wasn't semen, an unsettling thought—and tenderly cosseting his penis that he didn't strike her again, or kick her out. The others were scared and the driver quickly started the van and drove to Helen's home. "You bitch!" Cazzie roared when they pushed her out of the van in front of the house.

It was an instant legend. But for Helen, the significant thing was that she had acted spontaneously. She analyzed her behavior incessantly. It was so unlike her, she felt. What was she thinking? She saw herself as poetic, introspective, though daring and unconventional. She entertained the idea that she ought to have made at least a feint at performing the act, and *then* to have recoiled in disgust. That would be the way to do it. Later she might advertise her disgust, so everyone would know she'd had the nerve, but she'd loathed the act.

Or she ought to have become hysterical from the start, perhaps. To have made a scene that would startle the other kids and awaken them to the enormity of what was being proposed. That probably would have worked. Even as far gone as Cazzie was in Southern Comfort and sexual arousal, he should have remembered who her father was. Yes, she could have invoked her father, the gangster. She'd already had some experience with that: often enough, she'd had to endure a definite social coolness, a certain notoriety, from some of the more snobbish kids. What was the good of having a mobster for a father if he couldn't protect her, at least with his reputation?

Her friend Julie, also from a mob family, had shared this semi-ostracization with her. Julie, however, had been in the van. It occurred to Helen that if Julie hadn't been there, the mob threat might have worked. But it was less easy to invoke when Julie was present. Julie, after all, was the one who had confessed that she'd gone down on her boyfriend.

So, faced with the apparent approval of her peers, faced with the penis itself, she had chosen violence. And she had *chosen* it, she had to recognize that. It wasn't just an automatic reaction. She had opted for attack. That surprised her. To say nothing of Cazzie and the others.

Now she was a teenaged legend: Watch out for Sonya, she'll bite your cock off. Before she was thirty she had done a lot more than that. She had killed men and not by accident. Intentionally. Murdered the boss of Detroit's mob, no less. She had all but leaped into the back seat of his Cadillac to blast him with a shotgun. In Montana, where she had gone to lie low with her lover, Joe Service, she had been tracked down and attacked by a hired killer. She had shot him to death in a bloody hot springs. Bitchacockoff, indeed—how about your head?

On the flip side, Helen thought of herself as a good, loving, and dutiful daughter, an ordinary, ambitious, and modern young woman. She'd founded her own consulting firm, she'd been successful in the most mundane of ways. She never thought of herself as a killer. Sure, she had killed, but only once on purpose. The others she dismissed as accidental. She was not sorry for having blasted Carmine Busoni. He deserved killing. He had ordered the death of her father.

In her education she had been told by the nuns and the priest that "Thou shalt not kill" was absolute, it applied across the board. But there were exceptions, obviously. It wasn't ever applied to soldiers in battle. And you couldn't be blamed for killing in self-defense; in fact, not to resist was seen as a kind of betrayal of one's self, one's group. And in her family, the principle of revenge was respected.

She didn't recall ever having a conversation with her father in which he said, "Honey, when someone kills a relative it's your duty to kill him." But there had been many stories recounted by her

father and her mother in which exactly that principle was illustrated and approved. The only thing was, these events had taken place in the Old Country and, romantic posturing aside, Helen wasn't enthusiastic about the Old Country. Her parents' tales of the Old Country bored her—why couldn't they stick to the present? They weren't in the Old Country anymore. So some Bogdanovich, say, angry at a seduction of his wife or daughter or sister, had waylaid and killed a Simonich. Three or four generations of Simoniches and Bogdanoviches have to kill each other? Not in America.

She had pondered this after her father's death. There seemed to be a vague but important reservation that the revenge code applied particularly in the Old Country, not here. She thought it had something to do with the prevalence of family and clan traditions over there, and possibly with the doubtful legitimacy of successive governments. There, governments—the State—were not seen as adequate, reliable, or even just. In America, presumably, it was different. For Helen, there were no family stories about revenge in America *where the initial act of treachery had occurred in America.* Except maybe for hillbillies in Appalachia.

She considered the frequent accounts of gangland slayings where revenge was invoked by the perpetrators. Big Sid and Mrs. Sid would usually shake their heads disapprovingly and say, "Those Sicilians." The Sicilians, then, were to be seen as crude, primitive people—Old World hillbillies, still addicted to a system in which clans and families had reserved the final act of justice to themselves. In the Old Country, sure: revenge was a duty. Here: no. Those Sicilians, they forget that they aren't in the Old Country anymore.

Nonetheless, when her father was slain by Carmine's orders, shot down by a nameless, faceless, hired assassin, Helen Sedlacek clearly saw that justice was left in her hands. The police were helpless, hopeless. She felt that the investigating officer, Detective Sergeant Mulheisen, was unconcerned, possibly incompetent. And

when she encountered the private, independent investigator for the mob, Joe Service, she found a sympathetic and attractive man who would help her obtain justice. She prepared almost religiously for her act of retribution and was thrilled when she was able to carry it out effectively, with Joe's help.

Since then, events had taken unexpected turns. She had soon resigned herself to the fact that her old, straight life was now closed to her. By now, she was caught up in more complex situations, for which she didn't always feel prepared. Joe Service had warned her about this. The mob, he'd said, would feel that they had to respond to her act of simple justice—it was the old code. They would pursue her. And they had. But she had prevailed.

Helen did not have the common attitude toward the mob. It wasn't the stuff of movies and novels for her. It was familiar. She knew the people involved, some of them intimately. She wasn't awed by them, not very impressed, even. She knew many of these people to be stupid and ignorant, incompetent. They had names and faces for her: half-witted James who drooled, incredibly vain Guido who wouldn't dance at parties because he wasn't good at it, neurotic Ari who was sure he was too short, hopelessly fat and blundering Nick who wouldn't go swimming because he was ashamed to be seen in swim trunks. She knew these dorks.

But knowing that her father was a mobster didn't mean that she had any clear idea of what he actually did. He seemed mostly idle, but he was always talking about "business." What kind of business? She didn't know and she understood that it was not to be inquired about too closely. She knew almost nothing about how the organization actually functioned. She was genuinely dismayed when they continued to pursue her after Carmine's slaying. Why hadn't they, of all people, understood that she'd had to revenge her father? Okay, they had to make a show of revenging Carmine, but when she'd survived the attempts to kill her, she felt that should be the end of it.

She had survived, she hadn't tried to retaliate in turn. In a curious way, she believed that her success had crucially altered the equation. It was the *mandate of heaven,* a concept she remembered from a college class in Chinese history, perhaps a little unclearly. Sometimes, it seemed, a perfectly legitimate and long-established dynasty had been overthrown. The new regime justified its usurpation under the handy principle of the mandate of heaven, which turned out to be a form of realpolitik, at least as she understood it. The emperor is defeated, long live the (new) emperor. Of course, she wasn't the new emperor. She was just an agent of change. Humphrey DiEbola was the new don. In fact, in the eyes of the most knowledgeable, he'd been the "real" don for years. So maybe it wasn't a change of regimes. But she had not thought that far.

The first hit attempt had separated Helen from Joe, but they'd finally been reunited, in Salt Lake City. Then they had survived another botched attempt. She'd thought they were through the bad part. Unfortunately, just when she and Joe were on their way to freedom—the vindication of success!—Joe had suffered a serious medical relapse on the train bound for Denver, in the very throes of sexual celebration.

By then, Helen was getting more proficient at thinking on her feet. Mulheisen had actually been on the train, hot on their heels, literally in the next compartment. Under the circumstances, Helen had been compelled to abandon Joe to the detective's mercy, which permitted her to get away.

Not incidentally, she had also managed to throw a couple of duffel bags full of money off the train, intending to salvage them later. This money, amounting to nearly eight million dollars, was the remnant of a larger amount that her father had originally skimmed from an unauthorized mob activity in Detroit. She felt it was her money. Joe Service, who had actually acquired the money, felt it was his, but he was happy to share it with her. Humphrey

DiEbola felt it belonged to the mob, and he wasn't interested in sharing. This complication helped to confuse the issue of revenge: was the mob willing to forget vengeance for money? Humphrey had hinted as much. Vengeance wasn't the primary principle it was construed to be.

Itchy was familiar with an old adage: When a guy says it ain't the money, it's the principle—it's the money. Humphrey's interest wasn't revenge, it wasn't sex. It was money, just as any Detroit kid would know. Itchy was no genius. He was one of those mob figures whom the press like to inflate when they get caught, or take the fall, instead of the real villains. Not that Itchy wasn't a genuine villain, but he was only the visible villain. He was loyal and didn't think too much. Years ago, he had gone to prison for Carmine and the press had described him as a deadly ice-blooded hit man who had taken a softer fall. In the present case, his function was to "bring Helen home."

That's what he told Helen now. Or did he have other instructions? Bring home the money? Cancel her? That's what she wanted to know.

She and Itchy discussed this issue in the hotel bar, in Winter Park. Itchy was a man of fifty years, not much taller than Helen, despite his expensive elevator shoes. He was a careful dresser. He had a very black mustache and was concerned about his thinning hair, which had once been his pride. Now it was streaked with silver, or would have been, if he didn't use dye regularly. He advised Helen that she could get rid of the skunk stripe in her hair with his special preparation.

Itchy was a competent fellow, to a point, and unlike Helen, his ethical concerns stopped with loyalty to the boss. He was willing to use violence, if necessary, usually in the form of a discreet bullet. He didn't like breaking people's limbs, or scarring them. But he would, if so instructed.

He had actually met Helen a couple of times, when she was a child. He had liked her father. Everyone did. And he liked her, as much as you could like a child. Although, it was obvious she wasn't a child anymore. He didn't consider it a factor. To Itchy, Helen was just a songbird sitting on a wire. He called Humphrey as soon as he saw her, sitting at the bar, alone. Humphrey asked about the money. Specifically: "Has she got it with her?"

Itchy: "Not that I can see."

Humphrey: "Well, find out."

Itchy: "And then what? That's why I'm calling. It's cold. I'm standing outside."

Humphrey: "I want to talk to her."

Itchy: "Okay."

Humphrey: "Don't you do a thing. Hear me? I gotta talk to her, first."

Helen didn't want to talk to Humphrey, initially. She felt it was something that she and Ezio—she did not once use that despised nickname, which he'd always resented but had come to accept— could work out. She wanted his help in recovering the money, she said. She brought it right up, without any probing on his part. It was somewhere out in the country, lying near the railroad in two not very conspicuous blue duffel bags. It wasn't very safe there, but it would be safe for a while, she thought.

Helen could see that she was stuck with Itchy, for the time being. He hadn't tried anything heavy, except that he warned her he wouldn't hesitate to gun her down if she tried to run off. She smiled and replied that if he even thought of taking a gun out she would blow his ass to kingdom come with the Smith & Wesson .38 in her coat pocket. Itchy wasn't sure if she was kidding, but anyway, it didn't matter. They were stuck with each other.

"Whether you talk to him or not, I gotta call the man back," Itchy said. "Okay?"

Helen sighed. "Okay, but you don't say a word about the money. I'll take care of that."

Humphrey convinced Helen on the phone that he bore her no ill will. She didn't say anything about the money and he didn't mention it either. But she knew it was her hole card. Humphrey wouldn't do anything until he knew where the money was and how he could get it.

Humphrey was concerned about her, he said. He'd always been like an uncle—Unca Umby. He cared about her and her mother. That was a good touch, just mentioning her mother, in a friendly, non-threatening way. He reminded her again that he had tried to dissuade Carmine from hitting her old man, she must believe that. Here he had precedent on his side. She must know that on an earlier occasion, when Big Sid had dipped a little too deep, it had been Humphrey who convinced Carmine not to whack the likable mobster. It was true. Humphrey had long believed that loyalty was overrated. Crooks will be crooks. You had to convince the underlings that their success was related to your success. You couldn't prosper, no one could prosper, if everyone was going to be ripping off more than was reasonable. A little skim, sure. But nothing messy or pretty soon there's no icing on the cake. That time, Humphrey had gotten Big Sid off with a wrist slap and a season or two of laboring in the latrines of criminal activity—enforcing and discipline.

Once back in good graces, however, Big Sid had gone back to his old sticky-fingered ways. On an earlier occasion Humphrey had told Helen that when the second transgression was discovered, he had felt that a little more severe discipline might be in order, but not a hit. Big Sid was a friendly, likable guy. The business needed these guys, a lot. It made the business a lot easier. But Carmine was pissed, he wouldn't listen. There was no way of proving that this was the truth, but Helen believed it, which, after all, is what mattered.

What was the big problem that was bugging Humphrey? It didn't seem to be the money, or he would have said something. It was something bigger. He couldn't say on the phone. It was too big. He'd tell her all about it when she got home.

Helen, of course, wanted to go home. Especially with Joe in the hospital, soon to be in the penitentiary, she figured. He was no good to her now. Maybe he'd never be anything to her again. She felt drained of whatever little sentimental sweetness her soul had ever possessed. Or maybe only the Detroit molasses remained. Time to cut your losses.

Cutting losses did not mean forgetting about the money. But it was the dead of winter. If the money hadn't been discovered already—and if someone, say a railroad worker or a rancher, had found it lying in the boondocks, next to the railroad, the story would have hit the news with a loud splash—then it could probably lie there till spring. It would take a bit of finding, obviously. She'd simply tossed a couple of duffel bags full of money off the train, somewhere west of Granby. She had a pretty good idea of the location—she'd noticed some signs—but that was not the same as having a dead fix on the site. The idea of it just lying out there, available to any passing hunter or cross-country skier . . . it wasn't a comforting thought. And for all she knew, one or both of the duffels might have broken open on impact and even now the Colorado winds were broadcasting money hither and yon.

She had an image from the old Kubrick movie *The Killing*, where the desperate robber's suitcase of loot breaks open on the airport tarmac and prop wash sends the dollars flying. That vision haunted her.

What the heck. She was here. Might as well go look. Itchy was agreeable. He had a rented car. They took off up Route 40.

The problem was, she knew that the money had to be somewhere west of Granby, not too far, but it was hard to judge distance on the train. It's not like driving your car, where you constantly pass signs, annotated landmarks. On the train you're just riding through the countryside. She thought she had a good idea, though.

Driving westward—that is, in the direction the train had traveled from—she was at first discouraged, because she thought they had been closer to Granby than they had, in fact, been. But when they drove into Byers Canyon, she realized it must be beyond that spectacular red-rock gorge, along which the Colorado River surged. Soon they issued out onto the high plateau, and then she saw, to the south, the mountains she'd noticed when she tossed the bags. Also, she recalled that the tracks had been close to the highway, on the north side. But her hopes fell when they got to Kremmling and the tracks shifted to the south and they couldn't follow them.

She told Itchy to turn around. It had to be on the stretch between Kremmling and the canyon. They were only a few miles east of Kremmling on the return when she saw a railway maintenance shack with the painted inscription H.B.D. 98.9.

"I saw that when I first lugged the bags to the platform," she said. The platform was in the middle of the double-decker car, at the foot of the stairs, with openable upper doors on either side of the passageway. She'd opened the upper half of the northside door and tossed the bags out, on the side away from the highway.

Shortly, the tracks crossed the highway, and now she knew she was close. They slowed and she looked carefully at the mountains to the south. And then another remembered landmark appeared: a large, wooden archway at the gate to a ranch. It was not far. They parked and hiked across the road and began to walk the track.

They walked about a mile and Itchy wanted to quit. He wasn't outfitted for this. He had snow in his fancy shoes; they were ruined. He was cold, and he'd lost confidence in Helen. She wasn't daunted, however. "Just one more curve," she begged.

And then they saw the bags. They were about a hundred yards apart, and no more than a hundred feet from the road. She urged Itchy to go back and get the car. By the time he returned, she was standing by the road with both bags.

Now the big question: How to split?

They discussed it on the drive up over the pass to the highway to Denver. Itchy's initial claim was simple: no split, return the money to Humphrey. But Helen's argument was also attractive: Humphrey had no idea if they actually could recover the money, or how much it was. He hadn't even asked if she'd had it with her. So he didn't know. They could split it, she argued, and he was free to return his share to his boss, if that was what he wanted. Or, he could take his share and go live on a tropical island. She would never rat on him, she couldn't. She was going back to Detroit. She might have to return something to Humphrey, if it came to that, but she'd decide that if and when it came up.

It would come up, Itchy was certain. But he was receptive to her suggestion that even if he returned to Detroit with his share, she would have no reason to tell Humphrey that he had taken a cut.

The first order of the day was to count the money. They drove south of Denver and checked into a new, almost empty hotel off I-25, near Castle Rock. It was an ideal place, comfortable, inexpensive, and isolated by a newly landscaped site that hadn't been completely cleaned up and resodded yet. In the room, they counted up $7,375,223. Fifty-fifty would yield $3,687,611.50 apiece.

Itchy had no visions of palm trees and margaritas. He was going back to Detroit too. And he wasn't going with no three million and change, a hefty chunk of which would have to be turned over to Humphrey. He proposed a 33-33-34 split, with Helen keeping the extra point.

No, no, she argued. Remember that Humphrey doesn't know how big the pie is, or even that they had it. Why not a mil for

Humphrey, maybe a few extra bucks to make it look realistic, and they'd split the remaining six or so? They could figure out a plausible story and Humphrey would have to accept it.

Itchy didn't buy it. They went on in this way for a while, then went for a walk down to the town, for a little air, and Itchy found some cheap cigars in a convenience store. On the way back, nothing resolved, they loitered around yet another construction site, another new roadside motel, while Itchy smoked one of the cigars. He perched on a low concrete wall, recently poured but now cured and waiting for a hotel to be erected on it. He puffed his cigar and examined his ruined shoes.

"Two hunnerd and fifty bucks," he said, disgustedly.

"You can buy yourself a dozen new pairs," Helen observed. "Why do you smoke such bad cigars?"

"That's all they got," Itchy said, poking at his shoes mournfully.

She paced about, gazing at the hazy mountains to the west, beyond which the sun had just set. She heard a cry and wheeled around. Itchy had disappeared. One shoe lay on its side on the earth, next to the wall.

She raced to the wall and looked down into the huge excavated basement. No Itchy. But there was a large circular concrete projection from the earthen floor, perhaps a drain or something. It looked like a concrete tube on end, a vertical culvert. She found a place in the wall where she could clamber down onto the floor, which would soon be poured with concrete, level with the lip of the tube. She could see down into the tube. It was perhaps eighteen inches in diameter, maybe more. She could see Itchy's feet, about three feet down, one of them stockinged.

Somehow, he had tumbled backward and into the tube, no doubt striking his head in the process. He was neatly stuffed in the culvert. She called, but there was no response.

She stood up and took a deep breath. It was horrible, but there it was. The answer to her problems. There was no way Itchy could extricate himself, if he wasn't already dead. He was headfirst down a drain, unable to move his arms. He would soon suffocate, or maybe . . . well, she didn't know just how he would die, but he would by morning, that was obvious.

She could call for help, but that would mean the fire department, the police, and then . . . well, she couldn't call for help. She looked down the drain. There was a muffled groan. She sighed and reached down. By nearly diving into the hole herself, just barely keeping her feet on the ground, she could seize Itchy's ankles. She began to tug.

The next morning, on the way to the airport, she explained the cut to him: with his million he could keep a low profile, and when he eventually retired he'd be in excellent financial shape. She knew of some excellent investments. As for Humphrey, he'd have to be satisfied with the news that they had been unable to locate the money. Hell, he didn't even know it had been on the train.

3

Blackout

It is disarming to find powerful persons engaged in common pursuits—Winston Churchill diverting himself from imminent invasion by laying bricks on his estate, or the archbishop on the first tee at Pebble Beach. Of late, in the middle of the night, the boss of organized crime in Detroit and its surrounding territory was sitting quite bemused at his computer terminal, surfing the Web. Lately, he had established contact with a remote outpost in northern Ontario, an indigenous peoples site. He was wholly engrossed.

It was a bitter-cold night in January. Humphrey DiEbola was finally going to bed. He stubbed out his last cigar, signed off on his machine, and padded across the hall from his study to his bedroom. He disrobed and put on his pajamas, then sat on the edge of the bed and stared across the room at a beady red light glowing at the corner of the ceiling. He was a few years beyond middle age, a man with a large face and a strong nose. His silk pajamas were bottle-green with yellow piping, and the drape suggested not a robust or athletic physique but rather one a little bulky; not obese, but recently reduced, perhaps.

"Bernie?" he said, hardly more than whispering into the gloom.

A crisp, calm voice answered immediately from a speaker mounted in the elaborate headboard of the bed, among the reading lights, the bookshelves, the hidden electronic panel that controlled things like a radio, the stereo, the lighting. "Bernie's gone home, Mr. DiEbola," the crisp voice stated. "This is John."

DiEbola nodded, as if John were in the room. He was aware that John was observing him on a monitor. He glanced at the digital clock nearby: 1:17, in red numbers. "Are the dogs out?"

"No sir. It's a little cold."

"How cold, John?"

"Below zero, sir. It's, ahhh . . ." He sounded as though he were checking his console. "Minus five, sir. I thought it better to keep the dogs in. They don't perform well in low temperatures. And the wind is kicking up. Fifteen knots with gusts to twenty. Sir. But I can put them out, if you—"

"No, that's fine. I just wondered," DiEbola said. He still sat on the edge of his bed. He didn't appear sleepy or confused to John but, rather, pensive, alert. There was a long silence, more than a minute. DiEbola just sat there, his head cocked as if listening.

John was uneasy. He wondered what the boss had heard. The house was very tight, the rooms well insulated; it was impossible to hear any but the loudest noises. One felt more than heard the wind gusts buffeting the house.

It was never quite dark in this house. In the evening, when everyone had gone to bed, or should have been in bed, the captain of the watch, as he was called, would dim the lights in the halls by remote control. At his console in the anteroom off the entry, the watchman had an array of video screens on which he could, by pressing the appropriate buttons, view almost all of the rooms and living spaces on the main floor of this large house: the hallways, the exits, the living room, the dining room, the boss's study, the kitchen, and even the boss's bedroom. He could also view the grounds from several positions. All of these discreetly placed television cameras could be manipulated from the console to scan these areas, to focus very tightly on suspicious shadows. And lights could be intensified to dispel those shadows, if need be.

The watchman must be prudent, of course. The boss liked security, but he didn't like to feel spied upon. If, for instance, he got up in the night to use the toilet, as a man of his age will do, he would expect the watchman to scan the bathroom quickly and briefly, just to make sure that there were no lurkers, but the beady red light on the camera had better wink off by the time the boss unbuttoned his pajamas.

In the same spirit, there were no cameras in the guest rooms, nor upstairs, where the servants and his chef stayed. There were microphones, well hidden, but they were not to be abused. If the boss, entertaining guests in the living room or study, wished his conversation to be quite private, he had a discreet means of silencing the microphones or shutting off the cameras.

And if the boss were to step across the hall from his bedroom to the room occupied by his so-called niece, Helen, the watchman might observe him arise from his bed in his silk pajamas and exit his room, but as soon as his destination was determined, the cameras would go dead, as would the microphone in her room. Presumably.

Outside, day and night, in balmy summer or bitter winter, the twenty acres of the well-fenced and electronically observed estate on the shores of Lake Saint Clair were regularly patrolled by a squad of young, athletic men in constant communication with the captain of the watch and armed with automatic weapons. Dogs were also employed, rangy Doberman pinschers.

From one day to the next, nothing untoward ever happened. But the drill was never relaxed. The captain of the watch served his eight hours, maintained his log of communication, watched his panel to see where his patrollers were, and, if he suspected that any man was goofing off, dawdling, not paying attention, that man would be instantly contacted and warned to "stay on the ball."

Over the years, due to the lack of incident and the perfection of the electronic surveillance, the staff of patrollers had been cut from eight to five, and recently to just three. Reserves of two or three relief men stayed on standby in the little dayroom in the barracks, so-called, over the garage. The security staff were carefully chosen and trained and paid well. Performance was all but impeccable, and morale was high. It was a good job, a piece of cake. Nobody wanted to lose a cushy position like this one.

"The men are on eight-minute patrol," John said. "That's standard for this temperature. Eight minutes out, fifteen minutes in. I thought I'd have them take the dogs out on the hour."

DiEbola seemed to consider this. Finally, he said, "John, let the dogs sleep. And keep the men in the barracks."

Without meaning to be insolent or disrespectful, but in shocked surprise, John said, "All of them? What for?"

"It's cold out, John. Too cold for dogs. You said so. Send the patrol to the barracks. They can catch a nap, if they like."

"Okay, sir." No hint of objection or argument; John had recovered. "What about the gate, sir?"

"What about it?"

"The guy on the gate, maybe he could have a relief, since all the patrol will be in the barracks."

"The gatehouse is heated," DiEbola said. "He'll be all right. But I'll tell you what, John, since you're concerned, why don't you go up and relieve him?"

"But who'll run the console?"

"The console can run itself," DiEbola said. "Anyway, the alarms are all on. If anyone climbs a fence you'll know."

"Well, sure, but. . . . . How long, sir? I mean till the guys should go back on patrol, and . . ." He meant, how long did he have to stay away from his precious console? And there were other concerns that worried him, but he said nothing about them.

"The morning shift comes on at seven?" DiEbola asked.

"Eight," John said.

"Fine. Until eight, then."

"We could run an hourly walk-around," John suggested.

"Just call the men, John. Now. And then go to the gate and send those guys to the barracks. Everybody in the barracks. It's too cold out there. I don't want anybody freezing his butt on my time. Leave the console on and take a headset. I'll call you if I need you."

"Yes, sir. Thanks, sir," John said, dubiously. The fact was, he was scared. Not twenty minutes before, he had observed the chef, Pepe, come out of his room on the second floor, dressed as usual in jeans and a T-shirt with a Dos Equis beer logo, in stocking feet. He had strolled casually along, down the stairs and along the corridor, until he had merely brushed against the door of the room occupied by Helen, the boss's "niece." He had appeared at the door of the control room a few seconds later.

"Hey, Juan," the young man called, his voice lowered in deference to the hour. He was a very pleasant young man; everybody liked him. "I'm going to get a snack from the kitchen. You want anything? I got some good salmon. I could make you a sandwich. Maybe some poppers? Ees very good."

John had been sorely tempted, but he'd decided against a snack, even though Pepe's poppers—jalapeño peppers stuffed with jack cheese, dipped in batter, and deep-fried—were delicious. He was a man of great circumspection: a snack was too irregular. He'd thanked the chef but said no.

He'd watched the young man go on his way, into the kitchen, where he rummaged in the refrigerator, got out various items, and quickly, neatly prepared the poppers, made a sandwich or two, and then prepared a tray, complete with a couple of opened beers. The chef stopped on his way back and offered the tray. It was too good to pass up: John had taken a popper. It was very tasty.

"Ees Miss Helen still up?" Pepe had asked, innocently, glancing at the array of screens.

"I don't know," John had lied. He had, in fact, just monitored her room. She'd been listening to pop music, played quite softly on the radio, and it sounded like she was smoking. He'd heard a match, a puff, a little sigh.

"Maybe I'll check," Pepe had said. "She might want a little snack."

"I wouldn't do that, Pepe," John had advised him. "You know the boss doesn't like her disturbed. You want to be careful about that. The boss . . . it's more than your job is worth." He had decided against telling Pepe that the boss was still in his study, doubtless engrossed in surfing the Web.

"I'll be careful," Pepe had assured him. He'd placed a forefinger on his lips, smiled, and gone on his way. A moment later, the door to her room had opened and he'd disappeared inside. On the monitor John had heard some whispers, giggles, and some muffled sounds.

Jesus, he'd thought, the man is nuts! Screwing around with the boss's girlfriend.

Now, with the boss back in his bedroom, just across the hall from Helen, John was terrified. He was tempted to say something. But it wasn't his business. He wasn't supposed to be listening. He decided to leave it. Let the kid take his chances. The boss had lain down, he'd soon be asleep. He got up, donned his parka, and went outside into the bitter cold.

After a few minutes, DiEbola rose, put on his robe, and left his bedroom. He did not even hesitate at Helen's room but went directly and quietly to the front reception room. John was gone. The console was fully operative. He sat down in John's still warm chair. From here he could monitor the two main corridors in the large house: the one on which his room, Helen's, the study, and so on, were located, and the upstairs corridor, on which the guest rooms and the suite occupied by his personal chef, Pepe Ortega, were. There was nobody afoot.

All these screens, he thought, and nobody to watch them. There was something pathetic, he thought, about an unwatched video screen. On the gate monitor he could see that John had arrived there. John looked a little put out, but he settled into the gate man's chair with a cup of coffee from the automatic maker, and glanced up uneasily at the camera. Then, shaking his head, he fished out a cigarette and lit it. He picked up a magazine from the desk, flipped the pages.

DiEbola watched the screen that displayed an automatic scan of the dayroom of the barracks. The men were all accounted for. They were hanging up parkas, kicking off insulated boots, stacking their gear on tables. "Did you see those northern lights?" one of them said. "Even with the lights from the city, they're pretty bright."

Another answered, "I seen 'em. But that wind's too fucking cold to be standing out there gawking."

"I'll take the first watch," said another man, and the relieved men trooped off to the sleeping bay, where two others were already lying down.

DiEbola was pleased. He dimmed the lights further in the corridors and entry. He flipped a switch and heard Mexican pop music playing in Pepe's room. Another switch: Helen was listening to a late-night disc jockey spinning "easy listening" music. She was moving around. He tried to imagine what she was doing. A clink. Pouring a drink? Then a low vocal sound, "Mmmmm. Yeah." A laugh.

She was talking to somebody. "You're crazy," she whispered. "What if he comes in here?"

A man's low laugh. "I'm just the delivery boy," the voice said, "the pizza man." It was Pepe.

DiEbola sat listening, anger and titillation mingling as the two bantered and played. He heard or imagined he heard cloth sliding on naked skin, the sound of a zipper. "You like that?"—Pepe's voice. "I got something you like better."

"What took you so long?"—Helen. Then they were in bed, judging from the sound of coil springs, rather muffled. In quick order: many oohs and ahs, gasps, moans, grunts. DiEbola listened intently, breathing shallowly. He was mortified to find that he could not suppress his own sexual excitement. But ultimately, he felt a strange, almost despairing sadness.

He shut the sound off. He also shut off the house alarm system and killed the lights in the back of the house, the ones that illuminated the grounds on the lake side. He doused the lights in the corridor and went back to his room, feeling his way and carrying an extra parka, insulated overalls, and boots from the reception closet. He donned these quickly in his own room, then went to the rear stairs and up to Pepe's room.

The Mexican radio station played, some kind of salsa beat. He began to look quickly through the drawers of Pepe's dresser. The room was lived in, but neat. A maid came in every day to change the linen, vacuum the carpet, and dust. There were magazines lying about, the bed mussed. Pepe had sat around, killing time, waiting until it got late enough.

In the closet there were a couple of suitcases, one of them empty, the other containing some summer clothing that Pepe clearly did not need. There was also a nice leather satchel or overnight bag. It contained a couple of towels. Household towels, good big Turkish bath towels. DiEbola couldn't believe that Pepe would steal towels—

anyway, he wasn't going anywhere, as far as he knew. But there was something under the towels, wrapped in a lightweight jacket.

The most important item, at first sight, was a snub-nosed .38-caliber revolver, a Smith & Wesson, Model 58. Under another shirt, however, was a 5.56mm Bushmaster automatic pistol and three fully loaded banana clips—nothing less than a miniature submachine gun. Next to it, however, lay the truly significant find: a leather folder that contained a badge and a laminated plastic ID card, identifying the man in the photograph as Special Agent Pablo Ortega, of the United States Drug Enforcement Agency.

Hastily, DiEbola replaced these items and restored the bag to its proper place in the closet. He took a second or two to see if he had disturbed any telltale devices that would alert Pepe that the trove had been found. But there was no way, he knew, to spot such things; their very essence was to be invisible to the unsuspecting eye. It didn't matter, he decided.

He got out of the room as fast as he could, sweating slightly, just a sheen on his forehead. Perhaps it was the warmth of the parka. He was halfway down the stairs when he encountered Pepe, on his way up, carrying a tray over which a tea towel was spread. In his left hand he carried a bottle of Dos Equis, from which he had apparently been drinking.

"Whatcha got there, Pepe?" DiEbola asked.

Pepe stopped, his eyes narrowed in the dim light. Then he smiled broadly. "A snack, boss. You want some? I got some jalapeño poppers." He gestured at the tea cloth with the brown bottle.

"No thanks. I was looking for you."

"For me, boss? So late?" Pepe stepped back down a couple of steps until he stood at the bottom of the stairs and allowed DiEbola to come to him.

"Yeah. I was restless. I got up. There's northern lights. I thought you'd like to see them. I bet you never saw the northern lights."

"Northern lights, boss? What's that? The aurora? No, I never seen them." He stepped away, putting the tray down carefully on the floor, looking over his shoulder at DiEbola, talking, still holding the beer bottle.

"So you were restless, too," DiEbola said, nodding at the tray. "Those things'll keep you up all night."

"Not me, boss." Pepe glanced at the door that led to the back entry. "Northern lights. It looks cold out there." The light at the back entry shone on snow swirling past the steps. "Too cold for me. I got no boots"—he glanced down at DiEbola's feet, at his parka— "no coat."

"There's some stuff here," DiEbola said. "I'll get you something to throw on." There was a little anteroom where the household staff kept kindling, firewood for the fireplaces, and various household tools, shovels and the like. The staff kept a couple of jackets and slip-on boots handy for fetching firewood. This equipment was normally stored in one of the garages or sheds, but in winter they brought it in here for convenience.

DiEbola rooted around until he found the boots, which he tossed out to Pepe, then a wool coat. "C'mon," he urged, "you gotta see this. We'll just step out for a second. It ain't that cold. Go ahead."

He prodded the young man and followed him out through the entry onto the back porch. It was rather light out, reflections of the snow from the lights on the perimeter and at the front of the house. Deep shadows, but light enough to move about. The wind was huffing, snow hissing across the crusted surface. In the distance it was black. The lake.

Pepe stopped on the porch and shivered, despite the coat and the boots. "I don't see nothing, boss."

"Well, you ain't gonna see nothing from in here. Go on out there. I'm right behind you."

"Ees fucking cold, boss!"

"Just a few steps. Down the path here." DiEbola prodded him with his gloved hand.

"Jesus, boss! Okay, okay, but I'm freezing my ass. This Detroit, ees too fucking cold!"

The man hopped a few steps down the path and stopped, looking up, his arms clutching the coat closed, still carrying the beer bottle. "I don't see nothing, boss."

"You know what, it's too light. Let me turn out these porch lights." DiEbola stepped back onto the porch and flipped off the porch light. He also picked up an axe that the help had left there for splitting wood. He held it behind him and rejoined Pepe. The lights were visible, now, like curtains of pale fire that swept back and forth across the heavens. The rosy lights of the city seemed to tinge them with color.

"Wow!" Pepe said. "I never seen nothing like it."

DiEbola swung the axe. The blade chunked into the man's head. He fell face forward into the snow. DiEbola hurried back to the house and raced upstairs. He stripped a sheet off Pepe's bed and ran as quickly and quietly as he could back down the stairs and outside. With fierce concentration, panting and sweating, he rolled the body into the sheet. There wasn't much blood, less than he'd expected. He kicked snow over it.

A few minutes later he had fetched the toboggan that the maids used to haul firewood from the shed, loaded the body on it, and begun to trudge out toward the frozen lake, dragging the loaded toboggan behind him. Twenty minutes later he was back at the house. He stowed the toboggan and carried the grisly package of blood-soaked sheet into the house. He returned the outdoor gear, carefully wiped clean, back to the reception closet. He turned up the lights in the corridor to their ordinary dimness, then listened to Helen's room. She seemed to be sleeping.

He turned on the alarm system. It was nearly three. He scanned the console. Everything looked in order. John was still poring over the magazine in the gatehouse, the guy on watch in the barracks was talking to another one of the guys who apparently couldn't sleep.

DiEbola sat and stared at the console. He could hear Helen's steady breathing. He imagined her lithe young body, sated with sex, lying warm and moist, curled in her bed. He had a great aching desire to go in to her. He would slip off his silk pajamas and crawl into the warm nest of her bed. Would she reject him? He was not sure. He could practically feel her slim, almost childish arms about his neck, her teasing little hands. Oh, how he wanted to go to her. But he could not.

Now why was that, he wondered. Why exactly? Presumably, he could do anything he wanted in his own house. He had, in fact, just murdered a man. A man he actually liked and considered a kind of protégé. A man, in fact, whom he had until recently considered worthy of his trust to the point that he had been at least tentatively grooming him for succession. But he saw now, of course, that Pepe had not been qualified for that trust, that confidence. Still, from there to the chopping block was a huge step. But he had done it. Only now he couldn't go in and even "check on" Helen.

Why not? Because she would be annoyed. And he would have no credible excuse. He wasn't sure if he could even speak, or if his hands would tremble.

Well, he was a patient man. Also a bold man. This night's work could undo him. But he wasn't worried. He contented himself with the thought that no matter how agonizing his desire, he was strong enough to wait it out. The ability to postpone gratification was, he thought, the very essence of genuine being. It was self-mastery, wisdom, power . . . just about everything.

He forced himself to concentrate on details. He had disposed of everything—body in one hole in the ice, clothes in another, farther out. The rest of it, the sheet, the head, the hands, those were safely tucked away in a bag that, tomorrow, would find its way into the incinerator at the plant. By now, the ice would have closed the holes, the wind would have blown the snow over the tracks of himself and the toboggan.

He went back upstairs and packed Pepe's bags, including the guns and the wallet, all the personal items. That took him a good long while, but no one disturbed him. He wadded up the rest of the bedding and left it on the bed for the maids to take care of. Pepe would probably have done that, he thought. Then he carried the bags downstairs and set them in the anteroom. In the morning, Itchy could take them to the airport. Perhaps it would be a good idea if Itchy took a little vacation, Florida perhaps, or even the islands. He could work out those details on his way to the Krispee Chips factory tomorrow. It would be done, he was confident.

He decided to rely on the alarm system and toddled off to bed without recalling John to the console. They could resume their usual routine when the morning crew arrived.

4

Busy Life

Roman Yakovich had heard a saying in his youth in the Old Country: Even a simple life ends sadly, but a busy life is all pain. Roman had tried to live a simple life, but these were busy times. Still, he had tried. He had devoted himself to a smarter friend, Sid Sedlacek. He thought that if he just did what Big Sid said things would be less complicated. To an extent, it worked: Big Sid's clever maneuverings had brought them through the war and to the United States, to prosperity. In Detroit, however, people didn't seem to agree with the old saying. These were upbeat, can-do kind of people—they loved complications. Life hadn't turned out as simple as Roman had hoped, but it was easier than it might have been.

But now Big Sid was dead, slain by an assassin's bullet. In the nature of things, given that Big Sid was a gangster, this seemed all but inevitable. Still, Roman took it hard, although he didn't show it, of course. The fact was, he felt rather to blame for not protecting Sid, although it was not his fault at all. Roman had not been with Sid at the fatal moment.

And then, besides his normal bereavement, Roman felt a powerful sense of loss of occupation. Fortunately, Roman still had Big

Sid's aged widow, Soke—no older than himself, actually, just sixty-five, but seemingly an ancient woman—to look after. That helped. They lived a quiet life on a quiet street in a huge house, a life that was now as simple as anyone could wish. They went for walks. Not very far. The neighborhood had declined into a drastic poverty, except for this block, which made it dangerous. But Sid was well armed and, anyway, they walked in careless ignorance of danger. The walks were short because Mrs. Sid was a dumpy, gray woman. Her legs weren't good. They walked to the end of the long block on which they lived, near Grosse Pointe, stopping at Kercheval Avenue and walking back. Roman drove her to the Serbian Orthodox church on Eight Mile Road, to the special grocery store in Hamtramck, where she got imported foods. She still cooked for him, heavy Serbian meals of pierogi, *sarma,* dumplings stuffed with liver paste.

The dozens of people who used to come for the Sunday meals—all-day buffet, actually—came no more. And the little angel who had brightened their lives no longer appeared. Little Helen, the only child of Big Sid and Mrs. Sid, was in trouble. She had run away with a dashing young man named Joe Service, who was some kind of trouble-shooter for Big Sid's one-time associates. Little Helen and Joe Service had disappeared after the death of the mob boss, Carmine. Helen had visited at Christmas, but she had stayed at the home of the new boss, Humphrey DiEbola, the one they used to call the Fat Man, although he was no longer fat. This might have seemed a scandal, and it upset Soke, but Roman understood that Helen's stay with Mr. DiEbola was of a business nature, and he calmed her mother with that. And then Helen had gone back out West.

She wasn't gone long. She reappeared in time for the Eastern Orthodox Christmas. Mrs. Sid was very happy and Helen seemed glad to be home, but Roman could see she was in trouble. He didn't ask any questions. He just made sure her room was comfortable and he took both the ladies shopping for Christmas, buying presents and lots of food. And then he called Mr. DiEbola, just in case he wasn't aware of Helen's reappearance.

Mr. DiEbola was very grateful. "The poor kid, she's had a bad time, Roman," he'd said. "Listen, I want to help her. She needs help. Let her settle down, relax. But keep me informed. You did good. If she calls anybody, see if you can find out who she's talking to. Some of these people she's been screwing around with, they aren't good friends. They don't look out for her like we would. She's just a young woman, practically alone in the world, now that her papa's gone. But we can help her. In a few days I'll come by, see what I can do. If she looks like she's running away again, let me know, right away. She's a little confused right now, don't know who her real friends are."

And after a few days, as he'd promised, Mr. DiEbola came around. He was slimmer than Roman had remembered him. He'd lost a lot of weight. Probably, now that he was the big boss, he was worrying too much. It was a difficult thing, running a large and complicated enterprise like the business. But he looked healthy, younger even.

Little Helen didn't seem unhappy to see him, but Roman could see she was anxious. She and Mr. DiEbola went into her papa's study and when they came out, an hour later, she seemed more cheerful. She no longer looked to Roman for support. She even patted his arm and said that everything was all right. So that was good, Roman supposed. He would never allow anything to hurt the little angel.

That same afternoon, Helen moved back to DiEbola's house on the Lake Saint Clair shore. It wasn't far from home, just a few miles, but it was a significant move. She visited her mother at least once a week, and occasionally Roman would drive the old lady to visit at Mr. DiEbola's house, especially when the weather got better. Spring had come early. It was still chilly, except for occasional days when it was nice enough to walk down to the shore across the huge lawn and sit on folding chairs on the deck that had a roof of exposed beams. Helen would bring a cashmere blanket and a shawl for her mother. Servants would bring coffee and even a decanter of slivovitz for Roman. Mr. DiEbola was dashing in a colorful windbreaker. Roman wore, as always, a heavy black wool suit and a white shirt and tie. He also wore the handsome checked wool cap that Helen had given him for Christmas. It sat so well on his large, square head and made him feel good.

He was pleased to see that Helen was happier and that she got along so well with the man she used to call "Unca Umby." There was something about her flirtatious manner with DiEbola, however, and his too eager acceptance of it, that disquieted Roman. But he decided it was just her lighthearted, girlish way and he dismissed it.

Still, all was not gaiety. Earlier, when Helen had first moved to DiEbola's, Roman and Mrs. Sid had visited a couple of times and they had been introduced to an interesting young man from Mexico, a fellow who was apparently Mr. DiEbola's cook. This Pepe had become more than a cook, it seemed. He was doing something at Mr. DiEbola's potato chip factory, but Roman wasn't sure what it was. But he joined them for coffee and drinks, at that time. Now, however, when the winter was ending, Roman never saw him. He didn't ask about Pepe, because he sensed that it was not a topic that would be welcomed. In his idle moments in his room (Roman had moved into the house from his old room over the carriage house, to be handy for Mrs. Sid, in case she felt ill), when he was not watching a hockey game on television, Roman would wonder if there hadn't been some romantic trouble with Pepe. It had been clear that there was some sort of attraction between Pepe and Helen and that Mr. DiEbola wasn't too pleased about it, although nothing was ever said and no incident had occurred in Roman's presence. Now that he thought about it, however, Roman supposed that Mr. DiEbola had sent Pepe packing.

As for Joe Service, his name was never mentioned. Roman had met him only once. That was after the death of Big Sid. Roman had been told to cooperate with Service, who was investigating the death of Big Sid. He seemed like a good fellow to Roman and he had gotten along very well with Helen, to be sure. Too well. When they had disappeared after the assassination of Carmine, Roman felt bad about it. He thought maybe he should have warned Helen about these young guys who come waltzing into town, no attachments, acting like they own the world. But, he had reasoned at the time, she was not a little girl anymore. She had to learn about these heartbreaking Lotharios. And her heart had been broken, he was sure. But she had survived. She seemed very happy now. The thing that bothered him, though, was that she should be so . . . well, flirty with Mr. DiEbola. The man was almost as old as Roman! He was no Joe Service, who, despite the misery he had evidently caused the little angel, was a more appropriate match for her.

Roman wasn't sure how to deal with this development, but it was a complication. He hated complication. He decided to stay out of it. Keep your mouth shut. Drive the old lady around, do the shopping. Play cards when you're asked. Otherwise, watch television, root for the Red Wings, despite their awful dependence on those Russian players.

Roman wasn't worried about little Helen. She might be small, but she was dynamite. He laughed to himself in his room, thinking of the word *dynamite*. He wasn't any genius with words, but he liked the combination of *mite* with the notion of explosiveness. That described little Helen, all right. A dynamic mite. He could pick her up with one hand. When she was a child she would ask him to do just that, delighting to perch on his outstretched hand. She shot around like a little rocket, all over the place, screeching like a devil. She would hide in the shrubbery while he blundered about, searching for her, then suddenly streak away out of the corner of his eye, disappearing around the carriage house, her squeals of laughter hanging in the air.

Now she was a woman, all right, with heavy black hair that incongruously featured a silver streak rising from her pale forehead. She wasn't a lot bigger than a child, however. And Joe Service wasn't a lot bigger than her, so maybe their attachment was natural and reasonable, Roman thought. Two perfectly made small people, very handsome, very well matched. They were grown-ups who still possessed much of the innocence and delight of children. Roman was sorry now that it hadn't worked out.

Unlike Roman Yakovich, Detective Sergeant Mulheisen was very much a Detroiter. Problems were his bread and butter. But lately, however, like Roman he had a desire for a more peaceful existence. In Mulheisen's case, this took the form of burying himself in routine. He'd been running around all over the country, out to Montana, Colorado, and points in between, in pursuit of Joe Service and Helen Sedlacek. He'd finally run Service to ground in Colorado and seen him safely confined to a hospital there, awaiting recovery, questioning, and, he hoped, a trial. Now, he felt, he could turn his attention to precinct work, catch up. This wouldn't last long, he was sure, but while it did, he was happy to immerse himself in local issues.

One major problem was definitely local: according to Chapter 3, Section 48, of the police manual, he was required to reside in the city of Detroit, an issue that he and numerous white officers had dodged for years. His boss (formerly his assistant), Captain Jimmy Marshall, had just informed him that the rule could no longer be ignored.

Earlier, Mulheisen had kept an apartment in the city, but for some time now he had lived in his childhood home, in nearby Saint Clair Flats, with his widowed mother. It was a convenient arrangement for both of them. She was rarely at home, often away for extended bird-watching jaunts or lobbying for some environmental cause. In theory, it was comforting and convenient to have one's policeman son around to mow the lawn, move furniture, and keep the burglars out. For him, it meant free housekeeping and even the occasional meat loaf.

Now the department had cracked down. Once he became resigned to the move, Mulheisen didn't mind. To his surprise neither, apparently, did his mother. High school kids could be hired to mow lawns and shovel snow; machines could answer the phone. Mul had never mowed the lawn once, could not program an answering machine, and often forgot to turn off the coffeemaker. Perhaps burglars had avoided the house—assuming they knew it was a cop's house—but they were welcome to take what they wanted, if they were into monochrome TVs, furniture that was antique but not valuable, old tennis rackets, and boxes of unused housedress fabric.

Mulheisen had looked at an apartment near the Cultural Center. It was small, but it had considerable advantages. It was located in the heart of the city, in an area undergoing extensive renewal and some gentrification. It was the upstairs back in a four-flat brick mansion. All newly remodeled. He could walk to the new ballpark, Comerica Park, or whatever they were calling it, when it opened. It had a tiny bedroom with a closet about the size of a refrigerator, a combination living room–dining room–kitchen, a bath with a new shower and tub combo. Not a lot of room, but maybe he didn't need so much. The rent was reasonable, he thought, at twelve hundred dollars a month.

As for work, there was plenty of it in the Ninth Precinct. For instance, with the breakup of the ice on Lake Saint Clair, some kids throwing rocks at the spectacular ice jam on the Detroit River had discovered a body. Not an ordinary drowning, for sure. This body had no head and no hands. The corpse had been badly mangled by the ice. According to the medical examiner, Doc Brennan, the body had been deposited on the ice several weeks before the breakup.

It was a male, in good physical condition at demise, aged about twenty-five to possibly twenty-nine. Probably about six feet tall, probably weighing about 185 pounds. Mulheisen had absolutely no leads on an identification, but he was a patient man. Something would turn up.

Besides this case, the precinct had a curious one involving a woman who had been shot while ostensibly holding up a supermarket. And then there was the odd incidence of some troubling E-mail messages received by a young boy in the precinct and addressed to Mulheisen himself. Oh, there was plenty to keep him engaged, all right. And all the while he was keeping one ear cocked, as it were, for news about the recovery of Joe Service, out in Colorado. When Service came out of his coma there would be plenty to do.

In the meantime, he was busily packing his books for the move. Or rather, he should have been packing. At the moment, he was engrossed in a history book, one he had purchased months before and had glanced at cursorily, only to set it aside and never open it again. He was leaning against a bookcase reading Richard White's *The Middle Ground*, despite its daunting subtitle: *Indians, Empires, and Republics in the Great Lakes Region, 1650–1815*. He had been in the act of adding the book to a box of other history books marked READ, SOON! when he made the fatal mistake of opening it. He had been standing like this for fifteen minutes, but now he absentmindedly shifted some other books off an easy chair and sat down.

He had innocently looked up what White had to say about Pontiac, one of Mulheisen's abiding interests. White's analysis of that historical figure was somewhat at odds with Mulheisen's own, though by the end of White's comments it appeared that they weren't so far apart. Just out of curiosity, he'd turned to another figure from early Detroit history whose name had also been borrowed by General Motors: Antoine Laumet de La Mothe, Sieur de Cadillac, the founder of Detroit.

The passage that so engrossed him was an account of what appeared to be the first murder in Detroit history. The aboriginal people gathered about Detroit included several tribes. Most, like the Ottawas, were Algonquian people, but some were Iroquoian, such as the Huron-Petuns and the Miamis. In 1706, when this important trading and administrative post was five years old, the Ottawas were warned by a Pottawatomi that when the Ottawa warriors left for a proposed attack on the Sioux, in their absence the Huron-Petuns and Miamis would attack their village. The old Ottawa chief, whom the French called Le Pesant—the Fat One, although he was said to have slimmed down in recent years—counseled a pre-emptive strike on the Huron-Petuns and their allies.

> The Ottawas ambushed a party of Miami chiefs, killed five of them, and then attacked the Miami village, driving the inhabitants into the French fort. The French fired on the attacking Ottawas and killed a young Ottawa who had just been recognized as a war leader. Although the Ottawa leaders tried to prevent any attacks on the French, angry warriors killed a French Recollect priest outside the fort and a soldier who came to rescue him.

This, then, was the murder case.

Mulheisen was puzzled. Which of these killings were actually murders? It was more like war. You didn't prosecute soldiers

for murder. But evidently, the French saw it differently. The priest was clearly an innocent party, although one wondered how the Ottawas were to see it that way—he had intervened in an action, had thrust himself into harm's way. Presumably, his death was a regrettable accident, or at least an incidental consequence of his own foolhardy behavior. Not murder, in the intentional sense.

The soldier, moreover, was one of those who had fired upon the attacking Ottawas; he was a combatant. Nonetheless, the French wanted retribution for both deaths, an eye for an eye, specifically, a trial and execution of the perpetrators.

The Ottawas, like any of the indigenous peoples, made a clear distinction between these deaths. The Huron-Petuns and Miamis, while nominally allies under a treaty worked out by La Mothe, were traditional enemies of the Ottawas and they had instigated this conflict, if they had not initiated it. Blood retribution was the normal expectation of conflicts between enemies. But between friends—i.e, with the French—killings must be dealt with by two means: "covering the dead" (compensation in goods, gifts) and "raising up the dead" (providing a substitute, a slave). The Ottawas were sorry for the death of the priest and the soldier, and they eagerly offered to cover or raise up the victims, but they saw no reason to surrender their warriors to be executed. What purpose could be served by that?

Mulheisen was intrigued. To be sure, in the present day distinctions were made in the nature of killings—first-degree homicide, premeditated murder, manslaughter, negligent homicide, and so on. And, of course, acts of war exempted combatants from even these distinctions. Seen that way, the indigenes' attitudes didn't seem quite so odd.

He reflected that the indigenes' willingness to allow the killing of innocent parties to be compensated by gifts, letting the per-

petrator go free, suggested a deep conservatism: these people were living so close to the bone that a warrior's bloody deeds could be excused, as it were, with ephemeral gifts—perhaps because every warrior was so valuable to the group. Imagine allowing a hit man to buy his way out of a murder conviction! After all, he was not professedly an enemy of the slain victim. (Although, Mulheisen speculated, perhaps the hit man could be seen as an enemy of all private persons, inasmuch as his actions were not undertaken in the service of society—any society—but for mere pay.)

As it happened, negotiations covered the Ottawa dead to that party's satisfaction. But the French were not satisfied with either covering or resurrecting the priest and the soldier. The problem was compounded by political considerations. The French knew very well that they were not powerful enough to continue to operate in the countryside without satisfactory resolution. Governor Vaudreuil, the French authority in Quebec, with whom La Mothe was not on good terms, insisted on French justice—the execution of those responsible. There was also the consideration that these issues must be resolved and seen to be resolved among the various factions of Algonquians and Iroquoians, or there would be widespread war in the frontier, a disastrous consequence.

Le Pesant was the key figure. He took responsibility for the Ottawas' actions. Vaudreuil was actually presented with two slaves to "raise up the gray coat" but rejected them, saying that if Le Pesant was responsible, only his blood would suffice. He ordered La Mothe to arrest him, although he knew very well that any attempt to seize the Ottawa leader would endanger the alliance and that no Ottawa had the authority to deliver Le Pesant to La Mothe. Evidently, Vaudreuil did not expect Le Pesant to be surrendered, which would embarrass La Mothe, Vaudreuil's rival. But it would cut Le Pesant and his band off from the alliance, perhaps punishment enough.

It was clear that neither French nor Algonquian ethics, by themselves, could resolve the issue. A middle ground was required. La Mothe's solution was novel. He let it be known that Le Pesant's death was not his primary aim, but that he wished "that great bear, that malicious bear" to be surrendered to him, after which time he would decide further. The Ottawas agreed. Apparently, they sensed the unique and unprecedented nature of the situation. Le Pesant was delivered as, in effect, a slave—a condition that had never attached to someone of his position. It was a kind of fiction, a staged drama. But it served the needs of the alliance and of both sides.

The drama itself was highly edifying. Le Pesant appeared at the fort with his escort of Ottawas. The Huron-Petuns, Miamis, and French officials (including Vaudreuil) looked on from a distance while La Mothe addressed the trembling Le Pesant imperiously. The Ottawa escort begged for their chief's life, offered another young slave, and asked to be allowed to return to Detroit. But La Mothe was not conceding anything.

That night Le Pesant escaped from his prison, "leaving behind his shoes, his knife, and his shabby hat." La Mothe locked up his escort for a day, in punishment, then released them. He declared that Le Pesant, nearly seventy, nearly naked, and unarmed, would surely perish alone in the woods. Privately, he assured the Ottawas that he had intended to pardon Le Pesant anyway. The matter was closed. Vaudreuil could do nothing and even grudgingly admired his rival's creativity; the Huron-Petuns were evidently satisfied by the humiliation of Le Pesant and the Ottawas, and the alliance was restored. That Le Pesant soon reappeared at his old encampment in Michilimackinac was ignored.

Ah, the beauties of fiction, Mulheisen thought. How gratifying. Le Pesant had yielded to French authority; he was allowed to disappear; a fiction of his death was accepted. Case closed, everybody satisfied. Mulheisen wondered if he had ever done anything like that, himself—accepted a fiction in order to resolve a sticky issue. Perhaps he had, but he couldn't remember it.

Unfortunately, history showed, as White conceded, that the drama was not completely successful: the Miamis were enraged and soon got their own revenge, killing Ottawas and even Frenchmen, kicking off another round of negotiations.

Mulheisen put the book on the top of the READ box.

5

Cigar

Humphrey was regaling Helen with amusing tales of "the guys." They were walking along the Lake Saint Clair shore in front of the house. A blustery onshore wind buffeted them, making their eyes water, yet it wasn't too cold. Spring was in the air. Already, Helen's mother had visited. But today, the lake was dark blue-gray and choppy. The overcast was like an iron lid coming down on their heads, but it didn't oppress them.

Helen was dashing around, playing with a dog, one of the rangy Dobermans from the guard kennel. She called it Fritzy, although that was not its name. Humphrey was smoking a large, torpedo-shaped cigar.

"His real name is Angelo," Humphrey said, continuing a story, "but everybody calls him Mongelo, because he's a biter."

"A biter? Well, he's supposed to be, isn't he?" Helen laughed and capered along the shore like a girl, tussling with the dog, tossing a stick for it to fetch. She looked like a teenager in her woolen cap. "He won't bite me. He likes me."

"Not the dog," Humphrey said, amused. "The guy I'm telling you about. Angelo. Mongelo. You know"—he made eating gestures with his hands—"*mangia, mangia,* like he eats a lot. He's fat. Fatter than me."

"Oh, Unca Umby," she cooed, snuggling him momentarily, caressing his cheeks and attempting a kiss, which he dodged. "You're not fat. Not anymore."

"Well, like I was," Humphrey said. He enjoyed her fooling. He liked her attempted kiss, but felt that for the sake of dignity, decorum, he should pretend not to like it. "Actually, Mongelo's fatter than I ever was. The trouble is, he's a *biter*. He bit a guy's finger off."

"My god!" Helen stopped, appalled. "Why on earth would he do that? Is he crazy?"

"Sure he's crazy, whaddaya think?" Humphrey puffed appreciatively on his cigar. "They're all crazy. Well, not all of them, but some. Yeah." He nodded, thoughtfully, gazing out at the cold lake. "There's some crazy guys we got working for us. That's one of the things, you know, when you're in this business. Some of the guys who work for us aren't wrapped too tight."

"Mongelo works for you?" she asked. She had taken his arm. The dog trailed along as they paced, patiently waiting for the stick in her hand to be thrown again. "What does he do?"

"He bites people," Humphrey said. They both laughed. He shrugged and took his cigar out of his mouth, holding it to the other side of him, away from her. "Well, though, that's really the truth: he's an enforcer for the loans. Guys don't pay their loans, Mongelo bites 'em."

Helen was amused and interested. She wanted to know about the loans. They walked back. They were chilled now. Humphrey tossed his cigar into the chop of the waves. The dog looked puzzled but didn't offer to retrieve it. "Let's get back to the fire," Humphrey said. He made a signal and one of the security men, discreetly standing beyond a fir tree, raised a device to his lips. The silent whistle instantly drew the dog away.

Humphrey explained about the loan business over hot chocolate for Helen, coffee for himself. "There are always guys who need money, need it fast, no questions. Maybe they gambled, maybe they borrowed from where they work . . . and they don't exactly have good credit, but they have access to money. So, you try to figure out if they can handle it. The interest is big, but so is their need. Can they pay it back before it's too big a problem for them? That's the question. It's like all loan business, like a bank . . . with a difference—we collect. We don't write it off. If they pay it back quick, the interest isn't a problem. You're doing them a favor. They're grateful.

"Say an opportunity pops up," Humphrey went on. "The guy finds out he can get his hands on some merchandise that will make him a lot of money, but he doesn't have the large. You want to help a guy, if he's got a chance to do something for himself. And a lot of the time you can get a piece of the action. So you say, Okay, you can have the grand, the five, the ten, whatever he needs. Give him more than he needs, even—Don't leave yourself short, you tell him. And you warn him, the vig can get steep, so pay up. The vigorish, the interest," he explained.

"But he doesn't pay," she prompted. This was not really news to her, but she'd never heard the actual details.

"Yeah, sometimes the deal goes haywire, he screws it up, he lied about it, or he's just stupid. Maybe it wasn't really his deal. Or it was really a gambling debt. He didn't borrow enough. All kinds of reasons." He got out another of his cigars from the humidor cabinet, the big fat ones, torpedo shaped. He waved it. "You mind?"

"Oh no," she assured him, she didn't mind. She liked the smell of cigars, good cigars. Her father had always liked cigars. "Let me try one," she said. "Do you have any little ones?"

Humphrey rummaged in the cabinet and found a small, well-made cigar, a "petit lancero." He clipped it and lit it for her, then lit his own. He had discreetly turned on a device that whisked away the smoke, the aroma.

"The vig can be a problem for the loaner," he said, "for us. It gets to be too much, more than the guy can pay. Sometimes he gets scared, afraid of the collector, and he'll do stuff he shouldn't do, to get the money. It can cause problems. But you gotta enforce it. You send Mongelo around. You can't have these guys thinking they can get away with this irresponsibility."

"And he bites their fingers?" she said. She enjoyed the little cigar, but she was finding the story a little distasteful. She was glad she didn't have to deal with any Mongelo, in any respect.

"That's the problem," Humphrey said. "He didn't used to be so screwy. Used to be, he'd go around, put a little pressure on, twist his arm, maybe even slap the guy around a bit. But then he heard about Action Jackson."

Action Jackson was a legendary collector in Chicago, Humphrey explained. Like Mongelo, he was a big, fat man who bit people. Humphrey told the story, but he didn't think he could tell her about Jackson's worst actions, such as when he'd bit a woman's nipples off. The woman was the mistress of the borrower, not the borrower himself. Jackson had gone to see the man but he wasn't home. Jackson had sat around, waiting, but after a while his attention turned to the woman. He thought he'd rape her. That would send a message. He overpowered the woman, tied her up, stripped her, but then he didn't have the urge—or so it was said. He ended up biting her nipples off. The guy got the message. He paid up. And then he went looking for Jackson.

"Jackson went too far" was all Humphrey would say about it. But Helen wanted to know what had happened to him. She meant, Where is he these days? But Humphrey, still in the train of memory, said, "Oh, they reamed him. The guy he was collecting from, him and some others. You don't want to know. He died from it. The guy was nuts, like I said."

Jackson had died hanging from a barbed plug hammered up his rectum, attached to a wire cable suspended over a girder in a warehouse. Humphrey remembered when he first heard about it, wondering how they had hoisted the man up and how the plug could have held him long enough for him to die of suffocation, his mouth duct-taped. It was a grotesque image: a naked fat man hanging by a wire up his ass. Like a great pig in a slaughterhouse. According to the stories, they'd gone off and left him, and his corpse wasn't found for several days.

Humphrey suddenly didn't like the image and blanked it from his mind.

He wondered how he could get it across to Helen that it wasn't all like this, tawdry and violent and even a little disgusting. It was mainly just business. Business like ordinary business, not a lot different from your friendly bank, say, but with the principles carried a little bit further, carried as far as they could go. It didn't happen that often. Guys needed money but couldn't get it at a bank or any legitimate source. So they had to pay a big price. They almost always paid it back; they were grateful and they knew they could borrow again. That's how it mainly worked. Mongelo was unusual.

What concerned him now, Humphrey said, was that it looked like Mongelo had gone off the deep end. He might try to carry his imitation of Action Jackson to the same extremes, and that would cause problems. He had to do something about Mongelo before he went too far.

"What Mongelo needs," she suggested, "is to diet."

Humphrey laughed. Then he looked thoughtful. "Not a bad idea," he said. "Maybe a forced diet." He abruptly changed the topic. "So, you like the cigar?"

"I like it very much," she said. "Is it Cuban?"

"Naw. You wouldn't like Cuban."

"Papa always smoked Cubans," she said. "Big ones. He used to give me a puff, secretly."

Humphrey remembered. He'd liked Big Sid Sedlacek. A man's man. Full of jokes, smart, a guy who would go out on a limb for a buddy and back him up. He had a lot of stories about Big Sid, though he didn't think his daughter would like all of them. But she was tough. He looked at her, thoughtfully. She'd been through a lot and she'd showed her mettle. She had her wits about her. Maybe she wouldn't be as shocked as he thought.

"Cubans are too strong," he said. "I don't even like them, most of 'em. I like the milder ones." He puffed the torpedo.

"That looks strong."

"But it's not, not really. Here, have a puff." He held it out to her and she bravely took a little puff.

She smiled. "It's pretty mild!"

"I told you. Most people don't know sh—, crap about cigars, even guys who smoke all the time. They hear other guys talking about Cubans, so they all want a Cohiba. Hell, most of the Cohibas they get—if they can get one—aren't even Dominican, much less Cuban. They're Honduran, or Guatemalan, sometimes not even that. Mexican, or Florida. But they got the label."

"How do they get the label?"

"That's our business," he was delighted to tell her. "A label is a hell of a lot easier to make than a cigar. A real cigar, like a Cohiba or an H. Upmann, you got to grow the tobacco right, select it, dry it, age it. You got to have top-notch rollers and makers, and then you got to age them again. There's a lot to it. A good cigar is worth what you pay. But in this country, especially since Kennedy did us all a favor and slapped an embargo on the Cubans, cigar smokers here don't know from Shinola about real cigars."

"What *is* Shinola?" she asked, abruptly. She tapped her little cigar on the crystal ashtray. She let it lie.

"You don't know Shinola?" Humphrey laughed. "It's shoe polish. I think it's still around."

"Shoe polish! I thought it was a cigar. So what is the business, your business?"

"I'll show you. Come on, let's take a ride." This was perfect, he thought. He'd been thinking about having her meet some of the people he worked with and Strom Davidson had come to mind, as a man of some class, not just another hoodlum. Strom would be interesting to her, he thought, but not too interesting.

They drove into the city or, rather, they were driven into the city by a couple of the guys, nice-looking young men who sat silently in the front seat, the glass up between them and the passengers. The Cadillac had dark-tinted windows. It rolled through the rough neighborhoods where every block was missing at least two or three houses that had long ago burned and the lots had been graded and sodded. Many of these empty lots were still weedy, but the general effect seemed to be to let light and air into the old, rundown neighborhoods. That hadn't been the object, presumably, but it was the effect.

Eventually, somewhere west of Saint Aubin, a very old part of town, they entered a kind of warehouse district. The limo pulled up at a door served by a simple concrete stair of six steps. The young man on the passenger side hopped out and opened the car door for Helen. The driver opened the door for Humphrey.

"You want us to go up, boss?" the driver asked.

"No, that's all right," Humphrey said. "You guys wait here. We won't be long."

They went into a little office. A young woman with a fancy hairstyle, all pushed up in back and then artfully messed up to look like a waterfall over her well-cosmetized face, greeted them with obvious interest. She knew who Humphrey was, clearly.

"Mr. Davidson's upstairs, in the shop," she said. "Want me to get him?"

"No, we'll go up. I just wanted to show Miz Sid the operation," Humphrey said.

They pushed through a door and climbed a dimly lit stairs, then passed through another door into a kind of loft. Here there were several rows of waist-high benches, at which more than two dozen women were busily opening plastic-wrapped bundles of cigars and dumping their contents onto trays that traveled along a conveyor belt. At the end of the belt another woman operated a machine that rapidly applied a colorful cigar band to the cigars, which were then carried farther along to be packed into boxes bearing the same "Cuban" label as the newly affixed band. At other tables previously banded cigars were stripped of their bands and new ones were affixed.

All of the women were young, dressed in jeans and shirts, over which they wore a variety of aprons—some of them very kitcheny floral prints, others more standard work aprons supplied by a linen service. Many of the women appeared to be Chicanas. There were no black women.

A tall man in his fifties was pacing about, barking at the girls fiercely. He was berating one young woman in particular, a rather pretty, dark woman of Helen's age who worked swiftly and competently, seemingly ignoring her persecutor.

"You could have done all this hours ago," the man was raging. "I told you to get them out by noon, but no, you hadda take your fuckin' break!"

"We gotta eat," the woman said, calmly, not even looking up. She worked on swiftly. "The girls don't eat, they start screwin' up, they make mistakes, it takes longer. We'll get 'em all out, don't worry."

"Worry! Yeah, it's me 'at's gotta worry! You bitches don't care! Get a fuckin' move on!"

He spun on his heel and strode away. As he came toward them, before he even saw Humphrey and Helen, she could see that he was actually laughing. She was shocked. He'd seemed so furious, so enraged. And yet, she could see the women shrugging, looking at one another, shaking their heads, getting on with their work, brushing back their hair with grimy hands, deftly stacking and sorting, placing bundles out, picking them up from the machine, or loading boxes on pallets.

"Hey!" Davidson cried out when he saw them. "It's the man, himself." He pulled up in front of them, towering. He hoisted his trouser belt unconsciously and looked at Helen. "What'd ya bring me, Hump? More help? I can always use more help." He bellowed the last to carry over the din of the shuffling noise of the women, the clanking and humming of the machines. "I'll fire all a these bimbos, get me some babes who can work!"

Humphrey smiled and introduced Helen. Davidson seemed pleased to meet her. He'd known her father, a good man, he said. Then, "C'mon, let's get outta this racket."

He ushered them through a passageway, toward another room. "It's going good," he told Humphrey. "Great! This fuckin' cigar business is going through the top. You wanta know my biggest problem?" He stopped in the passageway and looked at them. "I can't get enough crappy cigars. No shit. If I could get my mitts on another ten million crappy stogies they'd be outta here in two days, lookin' like Havana Supremos."

Humphrey told him he was showing Helen the business. Davidson was happy to conduct a tour. He had a printing operation in the next room, where elegant labels were being created. He had a couple of artists who designed them, then more who transferred the designs through the processes leading to a beautifully printed label. Helen had never heard of any of these brands, naturally, and neither had anyone else. But they looked good.

"Hell, I'll create one for you," Davidson said, grandly. He bent over a thin, harassed-looking young man at a drafting table, explaining what he wanted. The man quickly sketched a picture of what appeared to be a Greek goddess wearing an Indian headdress, carrying a basket from which flowers, fruit, and cigars tumbled.

Davidson was delighted. "That's it, Ramón," he cried. "And we'll call it . . . " He paused, thinking as he regarded Helen standing there. "I got it! Call it LaDonna Helena. And make her skinnier. She should be sitting on a donkey. You know, some flowers around, a palm tree, maybe some parrots or colorful birds, whaddaya call 'em, macaws. One on her shoulder."

He leaned over the man. "No, skinnier. Not so much tits. She should be more like . . . like her." He pointed to Helen.

The young man tossed his lank black hair back with a habitual gesture and peered at Helen through his glasses. He poked the heavy black frames firmly onto the bridge of his nose with his index finger and smiled shyly. In a moment he had made the changes. "Perfect!" declared Davidson.

They went downstairs then, to his office. He poured a little glass of brandy for Humphrey, one for himself. Helen had declined to join them. "They'll have them labels on a thousand boxes by tomorrow," he boasted. "Our new brand. It'll sell like ice cream in July. You'll see. So, whaddaya think?"

Helen was impressed, even amused. She found herself caught up in the man's enthusiasm. "But why do you have to yell at them?" she asked. "They look like they're going full blast."

"You gotta," Davidson said. "They expect it. If I don't yell they slow down. Pretty soon they're taking coffee breaks, smoking cigarettes . . . as it is, every damn one of 'em has to go to the fuckin' can every ten minutes. This morning three girls didn't show. It's the same old shit. They got their period, their old man's in jail, the kid's got a cold. They come back the next day, but then another three or four don't show. It's a pain in the ass."

He cocked his ear, suddenly, at the ceiling. "See? They're slowin' down. I gotta get back up there. Hey, glad you could stop by."

He started to rush out, but Humphrey caught hold of him, then asked Helen to wait. He went out into the corridor and the two of them talked, the big man hunched over, listening to Humphrey patiently. It wasn't a long conversation. The big man seemed agreeable, slapped Humphrey on the back, and then went bounding up the stairs. Before Humphrey and Helen departed they could hear him screaming, even before he'd reached the top of the stairs.

In the car, Helen asked, "What was all the conversation?"

"Oh, just a little business," Humphrey said. "He's doing me a favor."

Three days later, two boxes of LaDonna Helena Petit Coronas arrived at Humphrey's house. The wooden boxes sported a splendid design. The label assured that the contents were "*Hecho a mano*" and very official looking stamps sealed the box. The principal feature was a picture of a svelte, dark-haired beauty wearing a diadem, with a macaw on her shoulder, strewing flowers and cigars, perched on a white donkey. She looked a lot like Helen, except that instead of her silver skunk stripe, this goddess had two golden stripes rising from her temples. According to the gold medallions surrounding the picture, these cigars had won prizes in 1898, 1910, and 1925, in Havana, Cuba, and Paris, France. Humphrey advised against opening the box. "It's the only good thing about those cigars, the label," he said.

Later that morning, in his office at Krispee Chips, DiEbola received Angelo Badgerri. He was a fat man, about Humphrey's age. They even looked a bit alike, although the resemblance was not so marked as it had once been, when DiEbola was carrying much the same weight. Badgerri's people were reputed to be from the same region in Italy as DiEbola's, though why anyone said that wasn't clear, since Humphrey's heritage was so uncertain. But, until just a year or so earlier, it wasn't uncommon for acquaintances to remark that they looked like brothers, or cousins, at least. After the slaying of Carmine and the accession to power of Humphrey, no one said that.

For all Humphrey knew they could be half brothers. He wasn't sentimental about connections like that. He'd never really known his father, at least not *as* his father. Humphrey had known Angelo all his life and he'd never liked him. As a boy he'd been a nasty little jerk, stupid and venal, and he'd only gotten worse with age. But they got along. Angelo did his job, he was useful. Unfortunately, he was becoming a liability.

Like many of his contemporaries, Angelo seemed unaware that times had changed in the business. Of course, they hadn't changed completely, but the old days of mob arrogance were fading fast. The modern mobster needed a slimmer, less obnoxious profile. That was what Humphrey wanted to talk to Angelo about.

He explained it to him as delicately as possible. "Monge, you're a pig. You gotta get rid of that lard."

Angelo wasn't offended. He grinned. "Like you did, Hump?" Evidently Angelo believed that the length of their relationship entitled him to the "Hump." Humphrey was unperturbed.

"Exactly," he said. "It's gonna kill you. I'm worried about you."

The fat man's padded brow furrowed. Humphrey knew what he was thinking. He was thinking that he was going to get chewed out for biting the finger off the deadbeat. "Boss, I warned that shithead, I—"

Humphrey shook his head. "No, forget that, Monge," he said, in a comfortable manner. "We'll talk about that some other time.

I'm serious. I'm worried about your health. I think you should see a doctor. Get a checkup. Look at you, you're wheezin', your face is red, I bet you don't sleep worth a damn—"

"I sleep fine. I—"

Humphrey cut him off. "I already made an appointment. With my own personal physician. Here." He handed the man a slip of paper with the name and address of a physician in Grosse Pointe. "You go see Dr. Schwartz. Two o'clock. And don't gag down an extra-big lunch."

Angelo squinted at the piece of paper in his hands. "Whatta I gotta see this guy for?" he said. "I got my own doctor."

"Your doctor ain't doing such a good job of looking after you," Humphrey said. He got up and smiled broadly, coming around the desk. He looked almost slim in his elegant blue pinstripe suit, new from his tailor. He patted Angelo on the shoulder and guided him to the door. "You go see Dr. Schwartz. Do it for me, Monge, you fuckin' monkey. And for your family. Don't worry, it's not gonna cost you a fuckin' cent. It's on me. That's how concerned I am."

Angelo was almost out the door before he balked. "I ain't goin' on no fuckin' diet, Hump!"

"All right, all right, I hear you," Humphrey said. "But go see the doctor. A checkup isn't gonna kill you. It might save your life."

That afternoon Humphrey checked to make sure that Mongelo had visited the doctor, that they had done a full workup. "What do you think, Doc?" Humphrey asked.

"Well, I can't discuss a patient's case, Mr. DiEbola," Dr. Schwartz told him, "but since you are a good friend—"

"I've known him since we were both toddlers," Humphrey interjected. "I'm worried about the man, Doc. I don't want to know any secrets and I'm glad you maintain strict confidentiality. I just wondered, how's he look to you? Generally. That's not violating anyone's privacy. I mean, the guy's not dying of some disease we don't know about?"

Dr. Schwartz laughed. "Well, anyone looking at Mr. Badgerri can see what he's dying of. But really, I mean . . . are you sort of in the nature of his employer, Humphrey? Yes? Well, the man's in amazingly good health, when you consider. . . . But if you're really a friend, I'd encourage him to go on the diet I recommended."

"I'll do it. I'm a believer, Doc. You know what it did for me."

Dr. Schwartz did know, although he wasn't as sure of the medical virtues of chili peppers as DiEbola was. That diet was something that Humphrey and his chef had concocted. Still, there was no question that it had gotten splendid results. "Well, I gave Mr. Badgerri a regimen that I believe will work for him," the doctor said. "If you can encourage him, we'd all be grateful, especially Mr. Badgerri."

"I'll do it," Humphrey said. "Thanks, Doc. And, if you don't mind, keep me out of it. You never heard from me."

"You're not in it, Mr. DiEbola. This is not part of Mr. Badgerri's record. But that reminds me, who is his regular physician? It might be helpful to see his medical history."

"Didn't he tell you? No? To tell you the truth, I wouldn't be surprised if the guy never saw a real doctor in his life. These old-fashioned Italians, a lot of them see grandmas . . . you know, some old gal from the Old Country who knows how to cure warts or constipation. But I'll ask him."

"Folk medicine," Dr. Schwartz muttered. "Well, I shouldn't say anything against it. But ask him."

Two days later, Mongelo was picked up by the two men who had driven Helen to the cigar factory and delivered to the back door of that same building. At first, he hadn't wanted to go along. He'd been approached at an awkward moment, when he was going to the bathroom of a restaurant in Harper Woods, not far from his home.

He went there every morning for breakfast, a meal that typically featured veal scallopini, eggs, freshly baked rolls, even tripe soup, and wine. So far, he'd only had a few biscotti and torcetti with his coffee before he'd had to piss. But the boys convinced him that his presence was urgently needed. They'd bundled him out the back door and into the limo, where a couple of other friendly fellas accompanied them downtown.

They entered the building through a disused basement entrance, an old stairwell with concrete steps and a steel door. Humphrey was waiting in the basement of the cigar factory. He was sitting behind a desk, under a hanging light. It was otherwise dark and cool, and an earthy, cellar odor filled the air. On the table before Humphrey lay a brutal-looking object, seemingly of metal, about six inches long and shaped like a large bass plug, except that it wasn't alluringly painted with eyes and scales. At first glance it seemed to be a basically smooth object, but it had many small, flexible steel leaves or scales, rather like a pinecone, and it terminated on one end with a sturdy eye, through which one might, perhaps, thread a wire or a line, except that it was the wrong end: if the object were trolled, or drawn through some medium, the leaves would tend to catch.

Mongelo stared at the object. "What the fuck is this all about?" he said. "You wannida see me, we couldn't meet at the chip fact'ry?"

"This . . . " Humphrey said, poking at the object with his now long and slender finger, then wincing slightly as it almost nicked him, " . . . is the actual dingus that they cut out of Action Jackson's asshole." Humphrey looked up with a smile. When he'd nudged it the device had partially rolled, then resettled itself. It was obviously heavy. "Can you believe it? I got it from the cops in Chicago. It cost me."

Mongelo recoiled. He looked about him. The other men were in the shadows, but they were there. "What the fuck?"

"I can't have no more of this Action Jackson shit, Monge," Humphrey said, quietly.

Mongelo drew himself up, puffed out his cheeks, then sighed. "All right, all right. I get the poi—" He stopped himself.

"Good," the boss said. "But it ain't enough to get the point." He smiled and there were mild, distant titters from the shadows. "All right, that's enough of that," he called to the men. He addressed Angelo again: "You like to play at being Action Jackson, you can get the dingus, like he did. It ain't enough for you to just say *Okay boss*. I want you to go on that diet."

"That diet! What that fuckin' doc you sent me to gimme?"

Now there were guffaws from the back. Humphrey ignored them. "Schwartz gave you a diet and you didn't take it seriously," Humphrey said. "That's your problem, Monge. You don't take what you're told seriously. So now I'm going to see that you do. Come here."

Humphrey stood up and walked toward the back of the basement. Mongelo followed fearfully. Humphrey stopped and flipped a light switch, revealing an open door. Beyond it, lighted, was what appeared to be an apartment. "Come on, come on," Humphrey urged, his hand out. He clapped Mongelo on the shoulder and guided him gently into the room.

Aside from the obvious feature of the steel bars that converted the room into a jail cell, it looked like an ordinary one-room apartment, what was usually described in newspaper ads as a studio apartment. Cozy, they would say. It had an ordinary, department-store couch and easy chair, a couple of lamps on end tables, a small television set, and a tiny little kitchenette, complete with a small refrigerator, a coffeemaker, a radio, some metal cupboards.

"The couch makes into a bed," Humphrey said. "It'll be comfortable enough. And you got your TV, magazines. Back there is a pisser and shitter, a little shower." He thrust the open-mouthed man through the open steel-barred door.

Mongelo caught hold of the bars. They held firmly, Humphrey was glad to see. He'd only had them installed overnight. They were anchored in the joists above. They would be all right if Mongelo didn't make too violent a move on them. They could be beefed up later, if necessary. But there would be someone around to keep an eye on Mongelo. He wouldn't be left alone to work on the cage.

"I ain't going in there," Mongelo declared. He clung to the bars like death, bracing himself against entering.

"Oh yeah, you are," Humphrey said. "And you ain't coming out until . . ." He paused. "How much do you weigh? Three something? Okay. You stay until you lose a hundred."

"A hundred pounds? You're fucking nuts!"

A hand snaked out of the dark and slapped him on the side of the head with a weighted cosh. He reeled and stumbled into the cage. The door clanged shut. It locked by itself.

Mongelo quickly recovered and began to rage, shouting, screaming. But the sound didn't resonate much and Humphrey had turned away, talking to someone in the darkness. "You give him the meals I told you. He can have magazines, videos, get him whatever he wants. He can smoke. Give him some of them cigars, the LaDonnas. He'll like those."

Humphrey turned to go. Mongelo fell silent. "I hope you like peppers, Monge," he said. And then everyone withdrew into the darkness.

6

Dying to Get Out

Every night Joe opened a door and across the room was another door, also opened, and a man leaning into the room between them. The man's head was large, cartoon large. Joe recognized the absurdity of this but also knew that it didn't matter. The man brandished something, a device, a tool. Joe knew what it was though he could not explicitly acknowledge it at first. But the gesture went on and on until Joe granted that it was a gun that the man waved. The gun was aimed directly at Joe and the man almost immediately fired it. It either happened very quickly or agonizingly slowly. Sometimes it never really got to the point of the gun being fired, but sometimes it was as if all this had already happened when the dream started. Usually, however, the bulk of the dream was taken up with the flight of the bullet.

The bullet traveled with enormous, impossible slowness. It hung in space, revolving smoothly, but it moved directly toward Joe with inexorable deliberateness. He always thought, as the bullet was so slow, that he ought to be able simply to duck away from the path of it. But that proved impossible. When he tried to move he found that he could only move rather more slowly than the already impossibly ponderous bullet. He could think quickly, like lightning, it seemed. And he could endure this eternity of waiting, as if he were in a much faster state than the sluggish bullet. He could actually see the bullet rotate, a smooth, machinelike rotation that was fascinating, even beautiful. But horrible.

What agony! He ducked and it took him forever. He could not escape the bullet, even though he had an eternity to observe its passage. He could meticulously examine the interior of the room—which he was not actually in, just thrusting his head within, as the shooter was similarly not in it, the two of them standing outside the room on either side, looking at each other through the doors. Joe peered about, even out the great window, looking out onto grassy slopes, odd-looking funereal trees of a dark color that Joe knew was black-green although there was no actual color in the dream. He also observed the room's curious equipment: wheels, dials, knobs, compartments, benches, handles—all arrayed low on the wall below the great window.

The room was familiar to him and yet not familiar. It belonged to him, but it didn't. And sometimes it changed. Sometimes it was more cavernous, almost a great hall, and the assailant so far away that he was no more than a figure with a pale blob of a face and arms and legs. He never recognized the assailant, but just sort of knew who he was. The assailant, the shooter, was just an agent, one sent to do a job.

And finally, when the bullet was upon him, in his face, as it were, he turned his head, slightly, and took it. And then he woke up.

The dream was unbearable at first. Well, bearable, obviously, since he bore it, but so frightening that he feared he would not be able to bear it next time. Yet as time went on, he bore it more easily and the intensity eased without him noticing. It seems one can get used to being murdered, but it may have been that he was more absorbed with daily events.

The crucial daily event was to determine who would deliver him from captivity. Very early on, within a week or so, he had singled out his man. At first he hadn't even bothered with the various men who came and went in the ward. He had concentrated on the women, as usual. They were the most likely, he felt. Only these women were remarkably invulnerable. As nurses, they had no deficiency of concern and interest in him *as a patient,* but they were remarkable for no interest in him as a man. He wasn't used to this. He was ill, he'd had a serious brain injury. He wasn't sure how long he had been unconscious, but he didn't think it could have been too long. He didn't think he'd been in a coma, although he admitted to himself that it was possible. He could have been "out" for weeks, he supposed. Maybe he looked like hell. He couldn't tell.

When last seen in a mirror, Joe Service had been a slim, fit young man. He was not quite thirty years old, below average height but with a large head that made him seem bigger. He had the sleek, smooth-muscled build of a swimmer. He'd had a beard, but someone had shaved it.

The ladies weren't interested, so he quit thinking about them. The guy he settled on was a cop. Tall, not bad looking, about Joe's age or a little older. Joe didn't say anything for days, just listened. His guy was named Kirk. He was a county cop, a sheriff's deputy, assigned to this boring guard duty at the hospital because he was being disciplined for some mistake. Over a period of days, Joe pieced out from Kirk's intercourse with other officers, nurses, and aides that Kirk had wrecked or damaged some superior's car.

"They told me to take the car," Kirk complained. The others laughed. "They didn't tell you *that* car," they said, and, "They didn't say run a light." Kirk had screwed up before, obviously. He seemed on the verge of something.

Soon, Kirk noticed that Joe was listening. Joe would catch his eye and make a slight movement of his head. It was very subtle, not really a look of commiseration, but at least neutral, willing to listen. Kirk began to air his gripes. It wasn't the screwup, that wasn't the real trouble. It was the lack of promotion, the fiddling with benefits, the lack of camaraderie, and his wife. All that and more, going back to his parents, his teachers, bankers who had turned down loan applications, even grocery-store clerks who refused his checks until the assistant manager came to okay them.

Kirk was one of those people: he didn't trust others and they didn't trust him. He looked more intelligent than he was, and pleasant and amiable, at first. Then you noticed he wasn't so bright, wasn't accommodating or efficient or careful, wasn't genuinely friendly but guarded and suspicious. And he seemed to know something was wrong but riled easily if he wasn't shown respect. In Joe's eyes, Kirk was ideal.

Joe had met people like Kirk. They didn't get along very well. He soon knew with near certainty that Kirk was not going to be a cop for long, that this was probably the fourth or fifth minicareer he had blown, that his wife was leaving him. Joe was happy with him. A guy like this was a cheap guitar: he could be tuned, after a fashion, and a melody or two could be picked out, as long as it was a well-known air that anyone recognized in the first few notes so they mentally helped you out when a fret didn't bite or the tuning slipped.

The problem, Kirk said to Joe one day—by now he was given to spending most of his free time in Joe's corner, sipping coffee and staring blindly out the window with its bars, talking over his shoulder softly, occasionally glancing back to see Joe watching thoughtfully, understandingly—the problem was bosses. All bosses, any boss. A man was never getting anywhere as long as he had a boss. That was obvious.

Joe sometimes wondered if Kirk was putting him on. He didn't think so, but the guy seemed too good to be true, too dumb. Joe couldn't afford to, however. By now, Joe was occasionally replying, tersely. This itself had taken a leap of confidence, for if Kirk were to mention to anyone, a nurse, another guard, that Joe was talking, was alert, he'd be transferred to the security ward. It was very important to Joe that this not happen. As it was, he had his three guards a day who were supposed to sit by the door and check everyone who came in or out. Joe was presumed to be, if not comatose, then barely out of that state and certainly incapable of moving. Definitely not talking. But somehow, Joe had perceived that Kirk wanted to stay, wanted this private audience for his gripes. And maybe something further.

Joe whispered, weakly, "Everybody's got a boss, Kirk."

Kirk shrugged. Well, yeah, he allowed, in a way. Maybe. Somewhere up the line. Even the entrepreneur, he's got backers, shareholders, regulators of one kind or another—too damn many, in fact. But really what Kirk meant was a *boss* boss. Some bastard you had to answer to or he could fire your ass.

Joe managed to look sympathetic, conceding the point. "Marry a rich woman, Kirk," Joe whispered.

"Don't I wish," Kirk said, devoutly. "Me, I got the reverse: Phyl could break Trump. She went out the other day and bought a trash compactor. What the hell we need a trash compactor for? On credit. Now I got to pay for a trash compactor."

"How much is 'pactor?" Joe asked.

"I don't know. Too much. A hunderd'n fifty, or something. Where'm I gonna get that? I need tires on the pickup for Chrissake. She think of that?"

Money is nothing, Joe told him. Kirk didn't agree. Money was everything. With money you were free. Without money you were somebody's slave. And money was hard to come by.

"No," Joe assured him. "Money . . . no prob. Money's free. The prob is . . . be free. Not free . . . do nothing." Or words to that effect.

Kirk was wary. He knew Joe was trying to bribe him. Joe knew he knew. The problem now was to move the dialogue to a point where a bribe could be offered, and accepted, without it being felt to be a bribe. It was an interesting situation, Joe thought, one that could be explored endlessly, right up to the moment when a doctor would say that Joe was physically able to leave the hospital, to be taken to a jail, and tried. Joe didn't have much time, he knew. You could fool the doctors for a while, the nurses for less, but very soon their training and knowledge and their instruments would tell them that Joe was ready to be thrown to the prosecutors.

So every day, every hour, every waking minute, Joe worked Kirk. He had just about got him to the point where he could present the bait when the woman showed up.

Her name was Schwind, which she pronounced *shwin*, like the bicycle. Dinah Schwind, special agent. She strolled in one day, showed her credentials to Kirk, and asked him how the patient was doing. Kirk shrugged, said the patient was in dreamland.

"Still out?" she said. "I thought I heard voices."

Kirk smiled guiltily. "I talk to him. I don't know if he hears anything, but it helps pass the time."

Agent Schwind nodded as if that was a good idea. Then she asked if he could step outside. When he was gone she pulled a chair up next to the bed where Joe lay with his eyes closed, not moving.

"I know you can hear me, Joe," she said. "Don't bother to nod or blink. It's not important. You won't be here much longer, so we have to move fast."

She told him the agency she worked for, but Joe didn't believe her. She described it as a liaison between various other federal agencies, such as Drug Enforcement, Securities Exchange, Immigration, even Central Intelligence. She didn't exactly belong to those agencies, but she worked with them. She was—she smiled self-deprecatingly—a superagent.

Dinah Schwind might smile but she didn't really laugh, ever. She was five feet, six inches tall, weighed about one hundred and thirty pounds, had brown hair cut short enough to show her ears, in the lobes of which she wore little gold studs. She had a square face, a square jaw with a wide mouth. Not very thick lips but a strong, straight nose; didn't wear much makeup; brown eyes and thick, straight dark-brown eyebrows below a high, smooth forehead. She was not pretty, but not homely either. She could doubtless be attractive, if she wished, but clearly she didn't wish. No one would call her nice looking. She didn't look *nice*. She looked determined and serious. She also had a faint suggestion of a mustache. Another woman would easily have effaced that—it wasn't really very visible—but Dinah Schwind couldn't be concerned.

She had a compact build and wore her blue suit well, with low heels. She also packed a gun—the shoulder-harness strap was visible when she reached into her inner coat pocket for a pad and pen—though she wouldn't have brought it onto a security ward for prisoners.

She had been to see Sergeant Mulheisen, a Detroit police detective, who had told her about Joe. Mulheisen had arrested Joe, although the arrest had taken place here in Colorado, which is where Joe was lying in a hospital bed. Mulheisen had obtained a special warrant.

Agent Schwind told Joe she was not concerned about Mulheisen or his interest in him, whatever that was, she explained. She was interested in a man named Echeverria, who was lying in a Salt Lake City hospital, slowly recovering from severe burns. To be exact, she was interested in Echeverria's friends and associates, some of whom were in the international drug trade, others who were in organized crime in Detroit.

Joe didn't know Echeverria, although he soon surmised that Echeverria was one of the men who had tracked him down in Montana, after the initial hit attempt had failed, the one he still dreamed about. Echeverria would have been after the money Joe had lifted in Detroit, the take from a drug scam. Joe wasn't at home when Echeverria got to his country retreat. Joe had thoughtfully booby-trapped that house when he'd left. Echeverria had been one of those caught in the ensuing blast.

Joe didn't say anything about this, or anything else. He was still playing semicomatose. But he didn't want to disappoint the lady. He had a feeling that his long courtship of Deputy Kirk had been blown, so Special Agent Schwind was now his fallback position. It was time to speak.

"Etch," Joe whispered faintly. "Heard of him." Which was true. He'd read about Echeverria's plight in the papers in Salt Lake. A friend in Montana had told him more. He knew where Echeverria was coming from: Humphrey DiEbola. Joe knew plenty about Humphrey. He supposed that was who Agent Schwind was really after. But all he said was that he'd heard of Echeverria.

Special Agent Schwind was not a woman to play games. "They won't stop looking for you, Joe. You've been working for DiEbola for a long time," she said. "Him and several other racketeers, in New York, Miami, Las Vegas. You have a reputation. They haven't forgotten you, either. I don't have anything on you, Service. I can't hurt you, but I can help you."

Joe thought about that one. He thought so long that she stood up and said, "I'll see you later."

"Going?" he asked, surprised.

"You think about it. I'll be back." And she left.

Joe Service pondered. He was an independent investigator who specialized in service to the underworld. He had grown up with close connections to the mob, particularly in the East, and at one point it had seemed that he would make his way in that world. But very early on he had realized that he didn't like the way the mob operated. He had no moral scruples, or not many, about the nature of their business, but there were many things about the way they functioned that he disliked. The mob was very big on loyalty, yet it was based on deception, brutality, and corruption. Inevitably, the mobsters cheated one another, or made serious mistakes in their interface with the general public. Normally, they had no one they could trust who could address these problems. That was where Joe came in.

It was a perfect role for a man like Joe Service. He was *of* the underground culture, familiar with its ways, on good terms with its practitioners, but he wasn't *in* it. For some people this would have been uncomfortable, but for Joe it was ideal. He liked living fast, liked the excitement, and he liked the money. In order to function, however, he had to hold himself apart. He couldn't take sides. He had to assess the situation, see where the virtues lay, such as they were, and implement to a limited degree the sanctions. It wasn't easy, but generally he could stay out of the internecine struggle. He could investigate, report, and recommend. Once in a while, if the price was right, financially and in terms of avoiding compromise of his own status, he could carry out the sanctions.

What was crucial, of course, and this was what was giving him these long thoughts, was that he had to operate in as great confidentiality as was possible. So. How was it that Special Agent Schwind knew who he was and what he did?

If he had never reckoned it before, he now knew just how greatly he had compromised himself when he fell for Helen Sedlacek and agreed to help her assassinate Carmine Busoni, the Detroit don who had ordered the death of her father. Obviously, to the criminal community that he had once served so ably he was now seen as just another rogue mobster. He had sacrificed an extremely valuable thing.

But—he sighed—no doubt it was inevitable. Even his vaunted special status would not have kept him immune forever from their suspicions, their paranoia, their treachery, endless devious plotting, and basic villainy. He reflected that the whole situation had devolved from Carmine's petty cheating on Joe's fees.

That special status, he reckoned, could never be restored. But that didn't mean that some viable similar status couldn't be achieved. He'd have to work on it. Maybe this lady could help.

But what help could she offer? She'd said she couldn't hurt him but she could help. Presumably, that meant help with Mulheisen. Well, no. He felt certain that she couldn't help him with Mulheisen. But maybe she could shield him, at least temporarily, or, at least, spring him. On his own, out of Mulheisen's clutches, he thought he had a better chance.

She returned the next day. He'd hoped it would be sooner; the doctors were starting to look at him speculatively. When no one was around, say on a night shift when one of the other guards was off chatting up the nurses, he could get out of bed, walk around, do squats, even push-ups, but when anyone but Kirk was about he lay as still as a corpse, his breathing as shallow as he could make it, his pulse as erratic as he could try.

Dinah Schwind wore the same blue suit. It looked the same, anyway. Maybe she had a dozen of them. It was well tailored. She wasn't exactly slim, but athletic looking. Good color. He was sure that she didn't smoke. No stained fingers, no dental problems, evidently; clear-eyed as hell.

"Okay, Joe," she said briskly, drawing up her chair when Kirk had discreetly vanished, "drop the possum act. We don't have time for it."

Joe opened his eyes, raised his head, and glanced about. He smiled. "Shoot," he said.

"Imagine," she said, "that you knew a private airstrip in, say, Idaho. Say that you had learned that a private jet would be landing there at a specific time. Say that you had the means to destroy that plane."

Joe imagined. "Just destroy the plane? Not a hit?"

"Just destroy the plane."

"Get a cowboy from a saloon," he said. "Boise's full of cowboys."

She shrugged. "There are usually problems, you know."

"Yeah. But not big problems."

"And then there is the question of deniability," she observed. "A cowboy has to be told something. There has to be a plausible story. And if he's caught, or implicated . . ." She let it hang.

"Whereas," she went on, filling in the blanks unnecessarily for both of them, "Joe Service is on his own. He knows why he's there, more or less, and if caught, well, he's a mobster, anyway."

"Who deals with the people on the plane?"

"That was just a scenario," she said. "A paradigm, if you will. But consider a new scenario. Say you knew when a couple of fellows were going to deliver, oh, fifty grand to another couple of fellows. The money is payment for some heroin, or cocaine, that would be delivered at the same time, somewhere else."

"Say a hundred thou," Joe said, getting into the spirit of this game.

"Why not?" she agreed. "But that's not up to us. It could be more. But say we knew. The way it works, these guys meet in, say, a rest stop on an interstate highway. They have cell phones. Not very secure, but then they aren't communicating anything implicatory. They call a number—the cell phone on the other end could be at a different rest area, or in a warehouse, a thousand miles away—and ask, 'Okay?' The other end says 'Okay,' the money changes hands, the narcotics change hands, everybody goes their own way."

"But I take the money, or the dope. Another agent takes the dope, or the money, depending how it works," Joe said. "Any more scenarios? This is fun."

Dinah Schwind almost smiled. She looked at him with a kind of pleasantness, anyway. She had a couple more scenarios. Like the first two they involved interdicting criminal behavior in what could only be described as extralegal ways.

"Do your bosses know?" Joe asked. That was a very important point, he felt. First of all, because it implied a kind of intervention that he didn't believe could be authorized by any accountable government agency, and if it were, how many people in the agency would know about it, what would be the level of security?

Schwind agreed that he had identified a key factor in the operation, assuming that it could be implemented. So far, she told him, only three people knew about it: herself and two of her colleagues, both of whom she could vouch for. They believed that operations like this could be mounted. They were all for it. They thought that authorization could be restricted to one more individual, but he wouldn't want to know any details. They were planning to suggest it, but they wanted to know they had the right man in the active role. They had the intelligence for several such scenarios, and had every reason to believe that they would continue to obtain further intelligence. Some of the action they would carry out themselves, but most of the scenarios they envisioned required an unofficial agent, an extralegal operative. If he was interested they would move to the next step of authorization. If it turned out that authorization was not forthcoming, or if it required even another step, another level of official involvement, then they would drop the whole proposal as too unwieldy and that would be the end of it.

"Nothing risked," Joe said.

She nodded.

"What's my end?"

"You get out of here," she said. "I can't get Mulheisen off your back, but you'll be outside those bars. And once you got into the prisoner population, of course, you'd be vulnerable to DiEbola and Echeverria." She nodded toward the window.

"How?" he asked. "You got paper? Or do I 'escape'?" He'd
meant it as a joke, but it seemed that her scheme wasn't so different.

"I think you've already got a plan," she said. "We'd just see
that nothing interfered with it. If we can."

"You mean . . . ?"

"Deputy Kirk has financial problems," she said. "I wouldn't
offer him too much. If he gets rich it might attract attention. But if
he's able to pay off some bills, that's not unjust."

This wasn't what Joe had hoped. Now he would be a fugitive. He'd thought that maybe she would at least get bail.

"They'll never give you bail," she said, saving him the trouble
of asking. "There are a lot of charges pending. You're the world's
worst risk for bail. Lee Bailey couldn't get bail for you."

Especially not now, Joe thought. Maybe Schwind couldn't
get him out, legally, but he had a feeling she could sure keep him
in. But he said nothing. Or rather, he said: "I'll talk to Kirk."

"Can you walk?" she asked. "Drive a car?"

"What do you think?"

"Go ahead," she said. "I'll talk to my guys."

After she left, Joe had a great new idea. How about if he just
died? They could fake his death and somewhere between the hospital
and the morgue he could be switched with another body. He was
delighted with this scheme. He'd be free, not have to worry about
Mulheisen, about the mob, about Echeverria and his gang. And he'd
soon shake Agent Schwind. It was perfect. He was dying to get out!

7

Ex-Capo

The secret plan, known only to Humphrey, was to get out. It was the one thing he couldn't talk about. So he talked about everything else. Mainly, he talked about himself.

Helen observed that he was an erudite man (she used the phrase "well read") and yet he pretended to be not too bright. "I don't mean it quite that way," she said. "You don't act stupid, but you have this kind of *dumb* manner, most of the time. But I know it's just a facade."

"Nobody likes a brain," Humphrey said. "People say 'pointy-headed,' or something like that. Crazy, ain't it? Everybody wants to be smart, they don't want to be dumb, theirselves, but they don't like it if you're *too* smart. Sure, I read books. I like to read, always did. But I never went to college, I never even graduated from high school. Nobody ever called me dumb, though. What it is, you gotta act like an ordinary guy, a little dumb, and I guess that reassures people—you ain't *too* smart. But at the same time you gotta make sure that the people who need you, who rely on you, understand that you're not really dumb, that maybe you're pretty sharp.

"Everybody does that, to a degree," he went on. "You're a woman, you know about that—women do it all the time. There's some things you aren't supposed to be a genius about. Guy things. You don't know nothing about football, say. But you probably know quite a bit."

"I don't know nothing about football," Helen said, affecting a dull tone.

"Okay," he said, smiling, "so maybe it's cars, or guns, or something else that you aren't supposed to be interested in—because you're a woman. Me, I'm in the business, as we say. I'm not supposed to know about books. That's for pointy-headed intellectuals. But . . . I read. Machiavelli, for instance."

"Machiavelli," she said, and sighed. "What is it with you and him?"

The Machiavelli thing, he explained at length, came about for two reasons. He had noticed that people frequently invoked Machiavelli's name, generally as a byword for deceit or cunning, but if one inquired more closely, they didn't seem to know much, if anything, about him. He was supposed to be bad, almost the Devil himself, or a close associate. But few even knew when he had lived.

"Oh, they heard of *The Prince*, maybe," Humphrey said, "but that's about it. When I was a kid I heard grown-ups talking about Machiavelli and I thought he was some Italian guy, somebody they knew. And later, I heard him used in that way so much, to me he was like the original Italian. And I had this thing for wanting to be Italian."

"You are Italian," she said.

"You're Italian if your mama is Italian," Humphrey said. "It's like being a Jew. Everybody knows Sammy Davis Jr. is a Jew, but they also know he ain't a real Jew. That's the way it is with me. Everybody knows I'm Italian, but they know it like they know Machiavelli is Italian. Me, I don't know. I never knew my old man . . . well, I knew him, but at the time I didn't know he was my old man. And now I'm not so sure, again.

"My mother, I never knew her or even anything about her. I was raised by my 'aunt' Sophie, Carmine's mother, except she wasn't my real aunt, I think. She tried to be good to me, but she already had a kid—Carmine. I always understood that I was like a charity, or something. And Aunt Sophie would never talk about my mother. Nobody would ever say anything about her when I was a kid. Maybe they thought they were being kind. For a long time I dreamed she was an angel, or a kind of princess, like in a fairy tale.

"When I got older, I was on the street. I was caught up in that. The Life. You know? It's exciting. You learn something new three times a day. By then I didn't want to hear anything about my folks. I didn't want to think about them.

"A little later, now I know a little bit, I'm a little calmer, but still so young. I'm your basic Detroit guy, you know? Tough guy, a cynic. If I thought about my mother at all, I thought she was probably a whore that my old man—by now, at least, I knew who he was, but he's dead—that he knocked up and for some reason he got stuck with the kid and he managed to shuffle me off on Carmine's old lady, Aunt Sophie, who was a sucker for this kind of stuff.

"So I get a little older, not quite so dumb. I even went to Italy by now. Actually, I'd been once before, after the war, with Aunt Sophie and Uncle Dom, but I didn't remember too much about it, I was just a kid. To me they were my real folks. When Uncle Dom died, as a favor to my stepmother, I took the body back to be buried. I also took a little trip to Eboli, to look up some relatives. It's inland a little ways from Salerno, in Campania."

"Eboli?" Helen said. "What's in Eboli?"

"I was born a Gagliano but Aunt Sophie used to say my folks were from Eboli, so when I turned twenty-one I took the name

DiEbola. Anyway, I had some time to kill. I was in no hurry to get back to Detroit."

"You were cooling off?" Helen said. "A little trouble?"

"Well, I escorted Uncle Dom's body, but yeah," Humphrey said. "And I was looking up my roots, you know."

"I thought of going to the Old Country," Helen said, "but I wasn't sure where I would go."

"Well, *your* ma's right here," Humphrey said. "Didn't you ever ask her?"

"Mama likes to talk about *her* home," Helen said. "You've heard her. When she was here the other day, she talked about Belgrade. But whenever I ask her about Papa, she just shrugs."

"Roman would know," Humphrey said. "Ask him."

"Roman!" She laughed. "They don't call him the Yak for nothing. Talk about playing dumb. He's the original dummy."

"Yeah, Roman plays it close to the vest," Humphrey said. "One of these days I'll find out if he's really so dumb. Well, anyway, I went to Eboli after I got Uncle Dom buried, but I didn't find out anything. I don't know what I expected, but over there, you ain't Italian. To them, you're American. I had a few names, people to look up, but they treat you funny. They're suspicious, they don't tell you shit. You sit around in some hotel, you don't know the language, everything's so strange. Finally I went to a church and talked to a priest. He laughed when I said my name was DiEbola. He knew it was made up. So I give him the old man's name, Gagliano, thinking there maybe was a record of the marriage. He rolls his eyes, makes this little hand gesture to ward off the Devil. He said Gagliano was a village way over the mountains, in Lucania. A bad place, he said. 'Don't go there. They eat Christians,' he said. He was half serious. 'Bad people. They won't tell you anything.' Guys leave Gagliano, they take that name, sort of like I did with DiEbola. I gave up on it."

"So you never found your Italian connection," Helen said.

"No, and I never said nothing to Aunt Sophie. I think she meant well. It's like my folks were hillbillies, or something, so it was better to say they were from a nice town like Eboli than from some shithole in the sticks like Gagliano, which I guess is why she'd encouraged me to change my name.

"Anyway, I settled on Machiavelli. He was my Italian connection. Some people, they think Italian, if they don't immediately think of DiMaggio or Sinatra, they think of Dante, or maybe da Vinci, somebody like that. But I started reading Machiavelli, and you know what? He wasn't hard, at all. Right off the bat I understood what he was saying. And he didn't bullshit. It all made sense to me."

Helen supposed a person could make that kind of indentification, but it seemed artificial. Still, if it worked for Humphrey . . . well, she guessed it worked for him.

"Mac—I think of him as Mac, for short," Humphrey said. "Mac talks about things like success, power, glory. Those are the big things. Success is survival, getting power, getting glory. The truth is, I never worried about glory much. Maybe it meant more in Mac's time. To me it's fame and notoriety. Today, everybody and anybody gets famous, at least for a little while. I don't care about that. In the business, which I like to think is a little like Mac's princedom, but after all, ain't exactly like it . . . glory is not in the cards. You get known among the powerful, that's the glory. I think I can claim a little of that."

"So, you are interested in glory after all," Helen said slyly.

"A little. But only a little. Power, though . . . that's the number. I followed Mac as closely as I could in getting to power, but I never lost sight of the fact that I was operating in a different field than Borgia and them guys Mac talked about . . . although, there are plenty of comparisons.

"Mac says that it's better to be feared than loved," he observed, thoughtfully. "People are fickle. When you're good, when you treat everybody good, they love you. They'll do anything for you, praise you, offer their children to you. But you can't always be a sweetheart to everybody. Right? The minute you turn somebody down, you're a bastard. So it's better to be feared than loved, he says. You don't go out of your way to piss people off, you treat 'em right, but when the deal comes down, you can't think about how much they like you."

Helen wondered if it wasn't a bit like being dumb and smart at the same time. Humphrey conceded the point. But he came back with the notion that sometimes, after an act of brutality, even just not being a hard-ass looks like kindness. That was from Mac, he said.

"When I was just the Fat Man, it was no problem," he said. "Carmine was the boss, but he never took the rap for the hard stuff—he said it was *me*." He laughed. "He'd tell 'em, whoever was bitching, that he'd see what he could do, but it was the Fat Man who was grinding them. And when they came to me, I'd say, 'See the man.' And, of course, being a Fat Man . . . everybody likes a fat man, they think you aren't tough. Only now, not only am I not fat, I don't have no Fat Man to lay it off on." He sighed and shook his head.

"The main thing, though," he observed, "is that Mac taught me that a man is what he makes of himself. You got governments, society, religion . . . none of it means shit, if you only got the guts to be your own man. And, of course, if you got the power.

"Everything comes from power," he said, after a moment's thought. "Money, pleasure, and survival. Only, it looks like it's easier to get, maybe, than to keep. Especially when you start getting on. That's why I'm glad you're here. I can use some help. Somebody has to run this business when I'm gone."

"You're not getting on," Helen hastened to assure him. "And I'm no Fat Man. Anyway, I don't know anything about running the business, but if I can help . . . "

"Forget the Fat Man stuff," he said, smiling his amusement. "That was yesterday. Maybe you could be the Bitch. That would help. Then I could be the Fat Man, again. I'll be the kindly old grampa."

"The Bitch!"

"Hey, I'm joking," he said. "But it's a thought. You don't have to *be* a bitch . . . some days I was the Evil Fat Man and the next day the Jolly Fat Man. What have you got goin' for you? You're smart, you're young, educated, you look like a million bucks, and you got connections from your old man—"

"I'm not sure that's a help," she interjected.

"It's a help. It don't matter what he did, how he screwed up. He was in the business. He was well known, and people liked him. The funny thing about something like that is, they don't blame you for his screwups, they just notice that you were born into the business."

"But when it comes to power," Helen observed, "they aren't ever going to give a woman any real power in this business."

"That's the tradition," Humphrey agreed, "and it'll probably go on that way for a long time, but that don't mean there aren't exceptions. You can be an exception. I was reading a while back about this Egyptian queen, Hashaput."

"You've been reading again, you cryptoscholar," she teased. "Who is this? Hasha—?"

"Hashaput, or Hatchep— Oh, I don't know how they pronounce it. Maybe it's Hotchapuss." They both laughed.

"Listen!" he said. "It's you. I saw it right away. In something like three thousand years of pharaohs, there's only one Hotchapuss. But she pulled it off. As far as anyone can tell she was a pretty good pharaoh. It's a long shot, sure, but there oughtta be *one*. Your odds are better today, 'cause we're in America. A woman's got a much better shot today."

"Maybe it's Hatchetpuss," she joked. "She's the Bitch. Hotch-apuss is the Honey."

They bantered this way for a while, but eventually they turned to a serious analysis of the present situation. The way Humphrey saw it, the traditional mob business of the past was in serious decline. The mob had been successful in the U.S., maybe too successful. They had forgotten how they got here. But that was all right. Things inevitably change. The mob had gotten into legitimate business so thoroughly that legitimate business had taken on some of the characteristics of the mob. Maybe it was always so, he wasn't confident of his economic history, no one was, really. There were a lot of theorists out there, but who was right?

This discussion became rather complex and confused, but Helen finally asked: What were the major problems facing them (she was thinking in terms of "us" by now) today?

"A major problem," he said, promptly, "is Mulheisen."

"Sergeant Mulheisen?" she said. "A precinct detective? That's a major problem?"

"Mulheisen is poking around in the Hoffa business," Humphrey said.

Helen was interested. "You were involved with Hoffa? With his disappearance?"

"You don't want to know," Humphrey told her. "It's all history. I knew Hoffa. I know what happened."

"What happened?"

"It's too complicated," Humphrey told her. He'd liked Hoffa, thought he was a good man, but excitable. Not easy to work with. Humphrey was vague. There had been a misunderstanding. An accident. It was nothing, but it wouldn't do for a guy like Mulheisen to dig too deep. It could bring the whole thing down, especially right now, when the FBI had brought a huge case against several guys who used to be major players in the Detroit business. Humphrey didn't think that case could touch him, but the Hoffa case surely could.

"The man's trouble," Humphrey said.

"Hoffa?"

"Mulheisen. He doesn't let go. He's one of those guys," Humphrey said, "they don't seem to be a problem. Like you say, you didn't think he was much help with your old man's case, but then he found out just about everything there was to know. The thing is, he doesn't give up. You think you've put him off the scent, you don't hear anything from him for ages, and then, there he is. He's been picking up a little something here, something there. And then, one day, he's standing at your front door, that weird smile on his face. I hate to see him coming. That face. It's so . . . so flat."

Helen didn't understand what he meant.

"Not physically flat," Humphrey said, "it's that flat, open expression. He seems simple. You think he don't know anything, but maybe he knows almost everything. Believe me, it's a big mistake to underrate Mulheisen."

"So? What are you going to do?"

He outlined a plan. It seemed overly elaborate to Helen. A Rube Goldberg device to catch a mouse. But Humphrey was serious. He wanted to set up a foundation, a phony historical research project. They'd hire a young graduate student, something like that, who would keep tabs on Mulheisen's activities in the guise of doing historical research. Only the kid doing the research wouldn't know what the research was really about, what it would be used for. From time to time they could feed Mulheisen a little info, through the researcher and some other outlets; kind of steer him in the direction they wanted him to go, keep him busy, running down old trails.

Helen thought it sounded dangerous and expensive. Humphrey was excited about the plan, however. He wanted Helen to set it up and run it. She had some expertise in things like that. She agreed to do it. It was something to do. But she couldn't shake her misgivings.

The other thing Humphrey wanted was for her to get acquainted with the business, at least the legitimate side of it. She could do that. If she didn't want to get into the other stuff, well, that was up to her. They'd see about that down the road. But anything she could do with the legitimate stuff would be a big help. Humphrey said he was getting to the retirement stage. He wasn't interested in all the detail work anymore. He didn't have the mind for it, these days, everything was so much more complex, and he had lost the old drive.

At one point, he said, he'd considered bringing Pepe into the business, but then the young man had taken off. Gone back to Mexico, apparently. It was a disappointment. Pepe was a smart young fellow, a lot more to him than he'd looked. But what can you do? Young men, they have other ideas. Well, more power to him.

Helen was sorry he'd gone, too, but she didn't say anything. She kept waiting for Humphrey to say something about the money, about Joe, but he didn't bring it up. Instead, he talked about how she had to start finding herself some allies, people who weren't necessarily *his* guys. "Not just anybody, of course," he said. "I know you're tight with Itchy, he likes you. That's good. But I don't want you getting cozy with guys who might not be friendly toward me, or who'd be thinking they'd be stepping into my shoes—my shoes are going to be empty before you know it. No, don't give me any bullshit about how young and vital I am. I mean it. You gotta be thinking about yourself. About how you would run things. You'll need some strong-arms around you, but guys you can trust. That's my problem now. Thanks to age and the FBI, and Mulheisen, most of my old guys are gone. That's why I'm talking to you."

"The only strong arms I want about me are yours, big boy," she said, playfully. She leaped onto his lap, throwing her arms about him.

Humphrey was delighted. He loved the close feel of her. It aroused him. He made some tentative squeezes. She allowed it, a little. It was amazing, he thought, how she knew just how much intimacy to permit before she stopped him, subtly, with a kind of stiffening or drawing away. Just enough, not too much. In truth, he was grateful. It was the way he saw it. The thought of actually being intimate, really intimate, with her was scary to him. He wanted it, he knew he did, but he couldn't give in to it. He had other plans.

Helen, for her part, was simply doing what came naturally. She loved to tease him, even to the edge of sex. But she was thinking about Joe. She was certain that Humphrey was thinking of Joe, as well, but neither of them could mention his name. "And what are you going to be doing while I'm learning to be HatchetHellion or HotchaHelen?" she asked impertinently.

"Puss. Puss," he urged. "Me? I'll still be running things, don't worry. But I'm gonna step back, as much as I can. I want you out there in the forefront, where the others can see you running the show. I'm like the old spider in the web. I'm thinking what I need is a kind of hidey-hole, a nerve center, where I can keep tabs on what's stepping on the wires, who's rattling the cage."

"You've got that," she said, referring to his security devices.

"That's nothing," he said. "That's sort of what gave me the idea, though. I got thinking, my sensors just go out to the gate. I gotta have real communications that go out to the whole . . ." He paused, searching for the right word.

"The whole kingdom," she said.

He shrugged. "Something like that."

* * *

He started building his web almost immediately. Sending her out to learn about the business, he immersed himself in a building project.

Humphrey wanted to construct the command post right at the house. Why, in this electronic age, was he driving all the way into Detroit, practically downtown, to Krispee Chips? Of course, he'd still go out and check his traps, he said, but in the future he'd keep tabs on things from his new office. It was being built in the basement. A nice little suite, practically an apartment, with the most up-to-date, powerful computers, a place to lie down, take a nap when he got tired. He was amazingly enthusiastic about it. The builders were there for weeks, putting everything in.

Once or twice a week, Humphrey would drive into town to take care of business. Helen usually went with him, but she didn't often stick very closely. She was busy with her projects. Besides the historical foundation she was learning about the potato chip business, reorganizing that office. Another project was the cigar business.

She had done a lot of research. Apparently, Detroit had once been a big cigar-manufacturing center. That had faded after World War Two. The phony cigar business was one thing, but she considered it paltry, more a lark than anything else. She didn't see any reason why they couldn't manufacture real, legitimate cigars in Detroit. They had the facilities. She was looking into that.

Sometimes she and Humphrey would go together to Strom Davidson's operation. She would look at the books, talk to the people, especially the girls working in the loft and the people making the labels. Humphrey would wander off with Strom, for which Helen was grateful. She found him abrasive and difficult. In the new operation, if she got it going, there wouldn't be any room for Strom Davidson.

One of the women, the one Strom had been raging at when Helen first visited the operation, was particularly interesting. Her name was Berta and it was her brother, Ramón, who had designed the LaDonna label. He was not well, and she was concerned about him. He needed to be in a clinic, but they had no health insurance. A business like illegal relabeling did not provide workers with benefits.

Berta was a very capable woman. Besides caring for her brother, she had two children at home, being looked after by her younger sister and her aunt. Berta often worked sixteen-hour days— ten hours packing cigars, then another four to six hours as a waitress at a Mexican restaurant in Dearborn. She herself was Cuban and had left the island with her mother more than ten years ago. The Cuban government had let them emigrate when it was confirmed that Berta's father had died in Miami. He had been a Castro supporter, a revolutionary, but the postrevolutionary executions had soon turned him into a disillusioned expatriate. Berta's uncle Jorge had fled Cuba with her father, but eventually made his way to Detroit, where he landed a fine job on Ford's assembly line. He had brought Berta and her family here. But then he died. Her mother died. Berta's husband ran away.

It was a long sad tale, but Berta wasn't one of those who liked to spin it out in detail. "He died," she said. "She died." No explanation unless asked, and then only if she knew you well. The husband: "Ran away."

Berta didn't seem crushed. While she wasn't delighted with her situation, she was not overwhelmed, not yet. The other women looked up to her, she was their leader. She didn't mind Strom Davidson, she said to Helen. She was being circumspect, of course, but Helen could see she was not intimidated by the boss. She confided that some of the younger, prettier women were the sexual prey of Davidson and he sometimes made a pass at her, but—she made an obscure gesture with her fingers, a scissors movement—"He knows he will not get me."

None of this really shocked Helen, but it disgusted her. She determined to put an end to it. She was also curious how she could go about getting into legitimate cigar making. Her new friend Berta was skeptical. Berta knew something about the business. "In Cuba, it is a matter of pride, of passion!" she declared. "You must grow the tobacco. You must have people who know how to pick it, cure it, age it. And buyers to find the tobacco you don't grow—binder leaf, wrapper leaf. It doesn't all grow in the same place. There is much involved and you must not rush this process. The big tobacco companies came to Cuba before and after the revolution, you know. They would make everyone rich. Lots of employment, big factories. But the Cubans could not see it that way. We preferred the old ways."

It was all very interesting, but not to the point. The problem was that because of the embargo on Cuban goods, the only tobacco that Helen would be able to obtain, if she wanted to seriously go into manufacture, was non-Cuban—Dominican, Mexican, Honduran, whatever. And what could she offer if she were able to get good tobacco? Berta could easily find her some cigar rollers, women who had been expert at this trade in the Caribbean and elsewhere, living right here in Detroit, but so what? There were already too many makers of cigars. Another brand would just be lost in the welter, especially one made in Detroit. Who would buy it? You could not make cigars cheaply enough in Detroit to sell them at a competitive price.

On the other hand . . . Berta had a cousin who rolled for a Canadian maker, in Toronto. That guy put out some very respectable cigars. They were about as Cuban as a cigar could be if it wasn't made in Cuba. The tobacco came from Cuba, the rollers were Cuban expatriates. The Canadian maker, Harold Jespersen, was from a Danish family that had been in the tobacco business in Copenhagen for generations, before relocating to Canada. Berta wondered if it was possible to buy cigars wholesale from Jespersen. The U.S. Customs wouldn't consider those Cuban cigars, would they? They could then be relabeled in Detroit, perhaps sold to a limited clientele. It wasn't what Helen had in mind, she knew, but it might be a start.

Helen would find out. In the meantime, she would do something about Strom Davidson. She went to look for him one afternoon, after a conversation with Berta. She had thought that he was with Humphrey, but he was not. He was perched on the edge of his desk, with his back to the door, when she walked in.

He swiveled his head, and when he saw who it was, he swore. "For godssake, don't you ever fuckin' knock?" He straightened up, adjusted his clothing, and then the secretary stood up, looking rather disheveled. She was beet red as she went by Helen without a word and disappeared into the bathroom.

Helen didn't comment on the scene. "Where's Humphrey?" she asked.

"Don't ask me," Davidson said. "Down in the warehouse, somewhere. What can I do for ya, honey? Or maybe you could do something for me." He glanced down meaningfully at his crotch.

"You can do something for yourself," she said. "Leave these women alone."

Strom's eyebrows shot up. "Leave them alone? Oh, dear! Is some little bitch complaining? She's not getting enough?"

Helen drew a deep breath. She was very conscious of how small she was next to this tall, rangy man. He was old enough to be her father, but he was a bastard. She was not afraid of him. She spoke calmly. "Leave them alone, Strom. I mean it. You've got a nice little racket here. If you want to keep it, concentrate on doing the job right. No more yelling, no more threatening, no more abuse. I don't want to hear one word of complaint or it's gold-watch time."

Strom's face darkened and he leaned over her. "Who in the fuck do you think you are, you dried-up little twat? I've been in this business for fifty fuckin' years. You're gonna come in here and tell me how to run my shop?" He leaned his face down and expelled a cigarish "Hah!" into hers.

Helen could hardly avoid reacting. But she didn't show any anger. Instead, she smiled. "I'm running this show," she said calmly. "I hope you weren't expecting *fair*. *Fair* ain't in it, is it, you stupid prick? No, don't raise your hand, Strom. Think. Think for a minute. How do I come off talking to you like this? Think! I'm not just some little twat. I can talk to you like this." She fixed him with her deep-set eyes, suddenly gleaming like coal about ready to burst into flame.

She could see it was sinking in. He was thinking. This was a woman who had blasted Carmine to shreds with a shotgun. And got away with it. She might not be aiming a Model 70 at him, but she had muscle behind her. She's doing all the talking, but there's heavy muscle here. He wasn't buying it without checking the label, however. He knew better than that. He stalked out, looking for Humphrey. Helen decided not to make the secretary hang out in the john any longer. She went out to the car.

Two of the guys were lounging there, smoking cigarettes. They straightened up when she approached. "Hi, boss lady," they said, almost in unison. They had taken to calling her that lately. She knew Humphrey had put them up to it. They were nice-looking young men, handsome even, in their early twenties. They had the dark looks of Italian men, with beautiful white teeth and flirty manners.

She smiled at the one called Mike. He had a vague European accent, not much. "How's it going, guys?" she said. It was going well, they said, pleased with the attention. "Listen," she said, "if that big old fart comes roaring out here, you know the one I mean?"

"Mr. Davidson?" Mike said, looking concerned. His hand went immediately to his suit jacket, to the bulge. "He bothering you, Miz Helen?"

"Not as much as he thinks," she said, with a smile. "I told him you guys wouldn't stand for it."

"We wouldn't!" Mike declared. They looked eager, staring at the door of the factory. Mike unbuttoned his suit coat and stood with his feet apart, balanced, his arms slightly bent.

She put her hand on Mike's arm. He flexed his bicep underneath it, his teeth gleaming. "I knew I could count on you." She looked him in the eye.

"You can count on us," his friend Alessandro said. "Why don't you sit in the car? We'll be here." He opened the door.

"Thanks," she said, and got in to wait.

But Strom Davidson didn't come out. He was down in the basement. He waited impatiently while Humphrey finished up his conversation with Mongelo.

Mongelo had lost quite a bit of weight. He was wearing some old clothes of Humphrey's, that Humphrey had kept when he was losing the pounds. He had also lost a lot of his anger. The first few times Humphrey had come calling Mongelo had raged. Then Humphrey would haul out the butt plug. He kept it in a leather bag.

"You know what Action looked like when they found him?" he asked. "He was a fucking fat bag of pus. He'd been hanging for a week. His face and arms and legs were swollen up like balloons, filled with old blood and shit. There was a lot of him in a puddle on the floor below him."

Mongelo was frankly scared. He had calmed himself and learned to relax and enjoy his confinement. Humphrey got nicer— or less brutal, which was the same thing. Never a devotee of exercise, Mongelo got out daily for a little workout with a treadmill Humphrey had ordered in for him, while a woman cleaned the cell. He watched a lot of television, especially an enormous supply of erotic videos that the boys replenished regularly. He devoured the food they brought, and although he couldn't say that he loved the peppery cuisine, he was more than a little proud of the way he was looking.

But the main thing that soothed his fury was the way the boss was talking to him, lately. Once Mongelo had adjusted to things, Humphrey had even apologized for the rude way they had kidnapped him and for the confinement. At first, that had made him wary. He still wasn't sure he wasn't going to be whacked. Today, however, the approach was different. The boss was confiding. "Monge," Humphrey said, after he'd sent the boys back out to the car, "I gotta talk to you. We got a huge problem, and only you can help. You heard about the guys," he said, mentioning three or four names of their acquaintance who were undergoing trial for racketeering. "The FBI has got them by the balls," he said.

"Those pricks," Mongelo said.

"Monge, when did you ever know the FBI to get so close? Think about it, Monge. There's no way those dumb fuckers could nail those guys. Unless they had help."

Monge frowned. He caught the drift right away. "Somebody ratted 'em out?"

"Somebody's in deep, Monge."

"Who?"

"We don't know, Monge. But you're gonna find out."

"Me, boss? I don't know nothin'."

"I know you don't, Monge. You're the one guy I can trust. You and me go back a long way. If I can't trust you, I can't trust nobody."

Mongelo nodded, a serious look knotting his face.

"I had to put out the word that you left town, Monge," Humphrey told him. "I even told Ellie," he said, meaning Mongelo's wife of thirty years. Monge shrugged. "And Carla," he added after a moment, referring to Mongelo's frequently battered twenty-eight-year-old girlfriend. He didn't tell him that Carla had said

"Thank God!" "Now sometime soon you'll be moving, Monge," Humphrey said. He could see that made Monge anxious. He was feeling secure here in his comfortable prison apartment. A move might not be a good sign. It might be a long car ride, one way. Humphrey let him feel that anxiety for as long as he could before he reassured him.

"You'll be moving out with me, Monge," he said. "I need you by me. Things are getting a little tight and, like I said, I don't know who's on the team and who ain't. I gotta have someone I can trust. The thing is, you can't breathe a word of this. When I come for you, we gotta be careful. No fooling around. I know it's hard on you, but you gotta keep up the diet, you gotta stay quiet, and no chatting with nobody. I don't want no one to know that you're with me, by my side. If they knew, and I don't know who they are, they'd grab you for sure. Wouldja even make it to prison? I gotta doubt it. They're after me, bad. You're my secret weapon."

Mongelo liked this notion. They talked about it in hushed tones somewhat longer. When Humphrey got up to go, he pointed at a plastic sack by the door and said, "That your trash?"

"Yanh," Mongelo said. "The wetback lady put it there."

"I'll take it," Humphrey said, bending to pick up the bag. He locked the door, smiling apologetically. "It won't be long, Monge. You'll like the house. I fixed it up for you."

Mongelo was grateful.

As he left Humphrey was surprised to find Strom pacing up and down at the other end of the dark cellar. How much had he overheard, Humphrey wondered? From the man's expression, evidently nothing. The man was very hot about something. Helen.

Humphrey listened to his raging as they returned upstairs. But before they got to the office he stopped and said, "So what are you telling me, Strom? You don't like your job?"

Strom looked shocked. Then he recovered. "No, no. I just thought you should know. I mean . . . you know me, boss . . . if that's the way you want it . . . I mean . . . "

"Well, what?" Humphrey said.

"Okay. Nothing."

At the car, Humphrey hefted the plastic bag. Alessandro opened the trunk. Humphrey put the bag in the trunk and then got into the back seat with Helen.

"So, which was it," he asked, "Hatchet or Hotcha?"

"Both, actually."

8

Flight Service

"**D**ead man doesn't walk," Schwind told him, before he'd even finished his pitch. She said it was too complicated, even if they could figure out some way to make him *look* dead initially. Too many complications.

Joe was crushed. Later, thinking about it, he realized that it suited Agent Schwind for him to be a fugitive and not a New Age Lazarus. She'd argued that it was all but impossible to fake a death these days, what with DNA testing and so on. And someone, surely Sergeant Mulheisen, would want to be sure that the corpse in the Denver morgue was really Joe Service. No, no, they would go ahead with the plan as sketched. Poor Kirk would have to take the blame, but then he'd be handsomely compensated. He could find an occupation more to his liking. An airline pilot, perhaps, or marine biologist. He'd have to go to school, but it would be fun. He could afford it.

The way it worked was two days later Kirk was on the night shift. He had to go to the bathroom. When he came back, Joe Service was gone. Kirk looked in the closet and found the money. He counted it. Then he gave the alarm.

Joe found the car, sitting in the parking lot. He shucked off his doctor's smock and emergency room scrubs and pulled on the pants and sweatshirt and shoes that Agent Schwind had left for him.

Joe never noticed any difficulty at all, didn't even see any police cars rushing to the scene. He got downtown and found the main post office, where he dumped the car that Agent Schwind had provided. One thing he had learned from dealing with federal agents was, don't use any car that they've had contact with. It will almost certainly be bugged, with direction finders, transmitters, who knows what.

He traded for an innocuous car belonging to a postal worker who would not get off shift, probably, for another five hours. But if Schwind's provisional transport was bugged, the feds would move in on it within a short time. They would know what he was up to. So he drove to the airport, parked, and rode back into town on the regular bus. He figured that would keep Schwind busy for a while. Even if they figured out he'd stolen a postal worker's car and they tracked it to the airport, they'd be checking to see which flight he had taken.

Despite all the screwing around he had a couple of hours to kill before the banks opened. Agent Schwind had provided him with plenty of money—well, a thousand dollars—but he needed much more and he wanted independence. He had a bank account or two in Denver, he was pretty sure. By the time they opened he had drunk far too much coffee, was a little wiggy, but still functioning better than he had expected. In fact, he felt great. It was great to be out and he'd had a good rest, although he was more tired than he wanted to be.

He'd remembered at least one bank account, from the days when he was flitting about the country unfettered. This one had a deposit box, too. In the box was a brown paper package. He was pretty sure what was in it, but he thought he'd better open it. As he'd thought: a Smith & Wesson .38 automatic, fully loaded with a box of cartridges. Also about $40,000 cash in old bills. He wrapped the package back up and hit the streets, feeling more free.

A good day's sleep in a pleasant suburban motel made him feel even better. Now he could consider his future with confidence. In an earlier day he would have headed immediately for Detroit. He was fairly confident that Helen would be there. She must have the money. If she wasn't there, she was probably dead. At any rate, the Fat Man—Humphrey—would know. But he'd had plenty of time to think about things. No zipping off to Detroit. First, he had to get to the bottom of this business with Agent Schwind.

He kind of liked the idea of being a rogue agent. That might be a good career choice. Just give up this whole idea of working for the mob. The United States government was every bit as powerful a mob. It might be interesting work. But he had a feeling that Agent Schwind's purpose might be allied to his own. She might be after Humphrey. First, though, he had to find out more about her. He went to a pay phone with a pile of change and began to call around.

In his wide-ranging travels, Joe Service had made many invaluable connections. He called five of them now. The usual proceeding went something like, "Oh, hi Joe. What's up?" As if the person had seen him only last week. Nobody asked why he wanted the information or where he was calling from. They just took the request and said they could tell him more in an hour. An hour later, the answer was the same from all five. Dinah Schwind was not known to be an employee of the FBI, the CIA, the NSA, or the INS (Immigration). Joe had not wanted to give too long a list of agencies, so he'd stuck to the federal ones. There were others, of course, but Agent Schwind had mentioned at least two of those. Maybe she was so deeply covered that none of his contacts could find a shadow. Or she might be with a state or municipal law-enforcement agency, he supposed. Detroit? Denver? Colorado? Michigan? He had no doubt that she was some kind of cop. He would find out.

Feeling less secure than an hour earlier, he nonetheless thought that he should contact Schwind now. He called the number she had given him.

She didn't seem upset that he had ditched the car and severed their contact. She had expected him to do that, she said. "Are you ready to go to work?" she asked.

"Sure," Joe said, cheerfully. "What did you have in mind?"

"I'll tell you when I see you," she said. "You're still in the Denver area, I take it."

"Close enough," Joe said.

"We'll have to meet. I want you to meet my partners."

Joe told her to forget that. He had met her, that was enough. It was probably better if he didn't even know their names.

She consented to that. "But I need to see you," she said. "I have to see how you are."

Joe assured her he was feeling fine, not quite up to full speed, but a few days on the outside would cure that. He agreed to meet her, alone. She should drive west on Interstate 70, toward Salt Lake. She might have to drive for a while, he told her, but she would see him. Keep her eyes open.

He passed her in an old pickup truck he'd bought for five hundred dollars, as they were approaching the exit for Route 40. She followed him for several miles, halfway up the mountain road to Berthoud Pass, before he pulled over at a roadside cafe and gas station.

"Sorry to drag you so far," he said. He stood by the car, taking deep breaths and stretching. "Smell that. I love that smell of the firs."

Agent Schwind didn't mind, she said. It was sort of on their way. She was glad to see that he was in good enough shape to go to work. The first job, she said, was in Salt Lake City. Did he want to drive there? They could go back to Denver and fly, or they could take the train from Granby.

"Granby! Hey, that's where they took me off the train," Joe said. "I forgot this road goes through there. I just wanted to get up in the mountains. Smell the firs." Joe was through with trains for a while, he said, with a smile. If she didn't mind, he kind of liked driving. She offered to drive and he could ride, see some scenery. Why not, he said.

They drove right past the spot where Helen and Itchy Spinodi had stopped to look for the money, but, of course, they had no way of knowing that. She drove precisely the speed limit. After they got over the second pass, Rabbit Ears, and were driving through the Yampa River valley, they ran into a cattle drive. Schwind was delighted. She said it was like the real West. Driving cattle right down the highway! Joe pointed out that the cowboys were riding all-terrain vehicles and the cattle were some kind of boutique breed of red Angus, along with a few Charolais. He didn't think that the Goodnight trail was like this.

"Did you raise cattle," she asked, "up in Montana?"

"My neighbor did. They stink too much. Besides, that place is gone."

"Thanks to Victor Echeverria," Schwind said. "You could say he drove you from your home. Well, here's your chance to get back at him." It appeared that "Vetch," as he was known, was well enough to be moved and the Colombian government had issued a request for his repatriation. The United States government had reluctantly consented, although federal officials wanted to question him. But they had no pretext, so they were allowing his transfer.

"A plane will arrive in Salt Lake City in five days," Schwind said. "I'll have everything you'll need to take it out."

"Parked?" Joe said. She nodded. "No one in it?"

She shrugged. "It would be best if Mr. Echeverria was in it."

"But then," Joe said, "there would be an innocent pilot, a co-pilot, maybe some medical people . . ."

"Maybe, maybe not. I'll know more when it leaves Colombia. But we were thinking it might be Echeverria's plane, which is a Gulfstream V. The pilot—we know him—isn't exactly innocent. Medical personnel . . . well, I don't know. You have qualms?"

"Sure I have qualms," Joe said. "The question is, do you?"

"Not many. We want to take out Echeverria, but we'd also like to take out the plane. It would really be better to do this off American soil. We're not real keen on blowing up a plane in the Salt Lake City airport, but we may not have another choice. If we do . . ."

"I like to travel," Joe said. "Let's take a trip to Bermuda. What outfit did you say you worked for?"

"I'm kind of like you, Joe. I don't work for any one outfit, as you put it. But I have worked for just about all the federal enforcement agencies. Do you want to see my I.D.?"

She fished out her card from her coat pocket and handed it to him. Joe peered at it closely. It was her face, her name, her general description. It had a thumbprint. He asked to see her hand. She extended it. He looked at the thumb. He wasn't a fingerprint expert but it looked close enough. He dropped her hand and returned the card. There had been no telltale "void" marks, so it appeared to be a genuine card, issued by the Central Intelligence Agency, signed by the director, George Tenet. Joe didn't know Tenet's signature from Bill Clinton's, but it looked good.

"Could I see your gun?" he asked.

She glanced at him, briefly, eyebrows raised. Then, "Sure, why not?" she said. She unholstered the Browning automatic, deftly ejected the magazine, and checked the chamber to be sure it was empty before handing it over.

Joe handled it lovingly. It had a dull, dark finish. "Model M35," he noted. "A very nice piece. You like 9mm?"

"It works every time," she said. She reinserted the magazine when he returned it. "What are you packing?"

"S&W .38 auto," Joe said. "Want to see it?"

"You show me yours?" she said, one heavy eyebrow arched. "No thanks. You find the .38 more stable, I suppose."

"It's enough gun," Joe said. "What did you have in mind for taking out the plane?"

"Well, not a .38," she said. "Or a 9mm. I was thinking an RPG. I've got a six-pack of them in the trunk."

"Throwaways," Joe noted, nodding. "That'd work. What about an M203 launcher, on an AR-15?"

"I can get it, if you want," she said.

"Trouble is, with the M203 or the RPG, you'd have to be fairly close. Not more than two hundred yards, better closer. I wonder if an incendiary in an AR-15, or some similar target rifle, anything in .225, would touch off the tanks."

Schwind was skeptical. She thought it was too iffy.

"They're very accurate," Joe said. "I could get my hands on one that's as silent as an air gun. I could plink away for an hour till I made the right hit. Nobody would notice."

"They'd notice ricochets," she pointed out.

"Who's your RAC officer?" he asked.

She smiled. "For these purposes, I'm the resident."

When they stopped for coffee and sandwiches at a little restuarant in Craig, Joe said he had to make a phone call. Schwind rattled off the serial number from her handgun.

"You'll find it's registered to me," she said. She didn't smile.

Joe made the call anyway. Before they left he had the confirmation.

"Doesn't prove anything," he said as they got back into the car.

"No, just that I own a gun," she agreed. "Maybe you should have met with my associates."

"What would that prove? Who do they work for?"

She shrugged and they drove on. Later, she said, "Remember, Joe, *you're* the fugitive. I could get in trouble just being seen with you."

"Good thought," he said, and went to sleep. When he awoke she told him they were only an hour or so from Salt Lake.

"I've been thinking about it," she said, when he seemed alert. "You deserve to know what this is all about." She explained that she had been working in various agencies for some years and the most frustrating thing about the work was that oftentimes valuable, hard-won, and dangerously obtained intelligence was tragically wasted because of bureaucratic wrangling and confusion. "We find out a drug deal is going down, or somebody is leaving the country, or expected to slip in, and by the time we get authorization to act, the opportunity has passed. Or a bureau chief refuses to take responsibility, or he's mad at some guy up the line, or in a competing agency. It's a shocking waste. And yet . . . it seemed to a few of us that if we had simply acted, without bothering with authorization, there would have been little or no fallout. You follow me?"

Joe followed her, all right. But he expressed his immediate objection, which anyone would have, that you can't have governmental agencies just charging about, without authorization or accountability. It was too dangerous. Scary, in fact.

Schwind agreed. "But sometimes . . ." she said. "Sometimes . . . take Echeverria, for instance. The man is a known scoundrel, the scum of the earth. He deals drugs on an enormous scale. He practically funds minigovernments. People are killed, others are enslaved, their lives made miserable, because of this, this vermin. Yet he flies in here, no problem. He attempts to kill you—which some would have said would have been no great loss—and we save his life. Now he'll fly out of here, off to do more mischief. No sane and sensible administrator that I know of would authorize any kind of action against him, certainly not what we are thinking of. Yet if he were to be thwarted, harmed, or even killed, none of those same administrators would object or do anything more than cheer."

"Unless you got caught," Joe said.

"Unless we got caught," she agreed. "My friends and I realized that given the intelligence resources we have, we could do a lot. But we have to be very, very careful. And we have to especially be careful that we consider from the outset the value and . . . well, the moral weight of any proposed action."

Good Lord, Joe thought, these people are already out of control. He wasn't so sure he had made a wise choice, getting involved. Still, he'd *had* to get out of the hands of the law. He'd had no choice, really. When a man was hanging on to the edge of a cliff, any bush, no matter how many thorns, was worth grasping.

They talked about it some more and Joe concluded by saying, as cheerfully as he could muster, "I'm with you, Dinah. Sounds to me like you're doing the right thing."

Dinah Schwind shot him a glance that may have been gratitude. But she remarked, "You can call me Dinah, Joe, but don't ever let me hear you refer to me as 'Dinah-mite.'"

Joe smiled and promptly effaced that epithet from his vocabulary.

9

Hell Gate

Schwind was around somewhere, but Joe couldn't see her. Her management style was to let the dog hunt. As long as she didn't get in the way, or complain if he didn't come when she called, he was content.

He was ready. It was getting dark. The mountains to the east reared up huge, their snowcaps red-gold in the last of the sun. Another beautiful day in paradise, here in the Salt Lake valley. No clouds, just sun. But cool, even for March. And a breeze, as always. Joe wondered if airports caused breezes. It wasn't a sea breeze, not a salt breeze, although the lake was just over there to the west. All he could smell was jet fuel.

He watched the Gulfstream V from about three hundred yards. He sat in a used pickup truck, not quite as old and beat-up as the one he'd abandoned in Granby. This one was a GMC. It had a big engine and everything worked. It had cost him fifteen hundred dollars—or rather, it had cost Schwind. Paid in cash to a young fellow who had run an ad in the *Salt Lake Tribune*. This kid would probably be able to identify Joe if anyone asked, providing they showed a picture of a cowboy with a mustache. But it was just a description. It would be a stretch to connect the buyer with Joe Service, an escaped prisoner from Denver. And no reason, for that matter, to connect Joe Service with the kind of activity he was about to initiate in Salt Lake City. And if all those connections were made . . . so what? Just something else to attribute to Joe Service, if you ever saw him again.

When they had finished fueling and the truck had moved away, Joe began to get ready. He'd tried out the RPG in the desert and he felt he had a good chance to make a hit with the second or third shot. Hell, he might even get lucky and score on the first. But he didn't have a lot of time. He figured that from a range of less than two hundred yards, at the fence, he could fire three times for sure, and if nothing interfered, he could fire more if he had to. A week to practice would have been better, but he didn't have it.

What he wanted now was for the attendants and others to leave the scene. But it didn't look like that was going to happen. Regardless of what Schwind wanted, he had no intention of waiting for Echeverria and his friends. He would knock out the plane and that was that. The trouble was, as he'd feared, there was always somebody in the plane, or close by. Obviously, there was a guard— he saw a man in quasi-military fatigues who occasionally left the plane by its open exit ramp, took a little stroll around, and looked like he desperately wanted to smoke a cigarette. This man looked professional, perhaps a former soldier.

This guy appeared to be unarmed, but on one occasion when he had appeared at the door of the plane he'd carried a weapon in a casual way, in one hand, aimed upward. Joe got only a brief glimpse, but it looked like a Heckler & Koch MP5. He wore aviator sunglasses and a beret. It must have taken some kind of clout to be permitted an armed guard on the flight line, although the guy was pretty circumspect—maybe he had orders not to show the gun. It looked like there was only the one guard. Sorry Raul, Joe thought, gazing through the binoculars, you can pack heat, but no smoking on the flight line—that's the American Way.

There were also a couple of women in uniform-type outfits, rather like stewardesses, who came out now and then, presumably to get a little air. There were people who drove up to other nearby aircraft: just people, businessmen, pilots, secretaries, service workers. There were just a heck of a lot of people coming and going. And then there was occasional traffic on the service road, which was why he wasn't parked on the service road. He was parked back off the road, behind some old earthen mounds, grassy piles evidently left over from construction.

The aircraft was larger than he'd envisioned it, having pored over photographs of Gulfstream Vs in aviation magazines at the library. This was a beautiful piece of work, painted fancifully in azure blue with a broad, sweeping swash, a leafy jungle-vine motif in brown and green that started at the base of the low, short nose and ended high on the tail. The aircraft had two big Rolls-Royce jet engines mounted on either side of the rear of the fuselage. The wings were swept and low. He knew from the magazines that the Gulfstream was noted for speed, cruising altitude, and, especially, range. In one of these a drug lord could check on his poppies in Asia or the Mideast, zip to Paris to make a deal, buy the wife a frock, and then head home to Lima, or wherever, with hardly a glance at the fuel gauge.

Obviously, the drug business paid well, but Joe was impressed. The drug dealers he was familiar with drove around in Cadillac splendor, and maybe the odd Rolls. This was spending money on a scale that declared, We gotta get rid of it.

The plane was angled away from the fence, its lofty tail toward him. In this posture it presented just about the smallest target profile it could have. He'd go for a direct hit on the left engine for the first shot. He had just decided that, after watching the scene for forty minutes. It was much as he'd seen three days earlier. Just too many innocent bystanders. The tail assembly was the closest, biggest target available. It was also, he thought, the least likely site for a general explosion, although he wasn't at all sure about that. The magazines he'd looked at had provided very little technical information about the location of fuel tanks. He assumed the main tanks were in the low wings, but then the engines were in the back. If he were designing it, he'd have put as much of the fuel as he could back there, in case of accidents. But he knew there were aero- dynamic reasons for spreading the weight around, and fuel was a big part of the plane's weight.

If he could hit the tail assembly, the explosion of the rocket would frighten the people away from the plane. The exit was right up front, just behind the flight deck, a combination ramp and door. The crew would have maximum access to the exit, and he'd allow them as much time to flee as he dared. But there would be unfore- seen problems, he was sure.

The guard would not run away, or not far. He would locate the source of the attack. He would see Joe, for there was really no place to hide. Standing by the fence would not give him a clear view to the target; he would be a little below grade. Anyway, there wasn't much cover value to standing at a wire-weave cyclone fence. The service road was elevated, however. If he stopped on the road and he stood in the back of the pickup truck, using the cab roof as a rest, he would have a good view, could fire over the fence instead of having to cut a hole to fire through. Of course, the elevated posi- tion, in the pickup bed, would make him very visible to the guard.

Joe accepted the probability that he would have to take some fire, probably automatic fire, probably 9mm, if that was an H&K. And he'd have to wait until he was sure the women had fled the scene, as well as anybody else who might be idly present, before he launched two and three. And, of course, the explosion would bring the cops.

The cops would come from inside the fence, first, rushing to the site, but there would be others who would quickly block the access roads. He had no idea how long it would take them to do this. There was doubtless a way to find out, but he hadn't had the time to do it. Today was moving day; Echeverria was leaving tonight. It was a major hole in the plan, but Joe had weighed the options and decided to go, regardless. There were two alternate exit routes; if either of them had been the primary route he wouldn't have agreed to do it, but as the primary was simplicity itself, he quit fretting.

It was only common sense to make all the preparation you could, but sometimes it was better not to make too fine a plan. Things always went a little wrong. You could never imagine exactly how things would go, so it was better just to have a loose, rather flexible plan—within limits.

He loved the intricate plans he saw in caper movies, usually of bank robberies. He could see the artfulness of the director and the screenwriter: the otherwise uncommitted viewer was drawn into the plot by its seeming explicitness. Everything seemed to be carefully mapped out. One wanted it to succeed, just as one listened in anticipation for the resolving chord of a musical phrase. And then, of course, the enactment was drawn out, heightening the viewer's tension, until some ludicrous little incident cropped up, some dumb little thing that one couldn't have anticipated or predicted, like a kid wandering into the scene, or a car double-parked and blocking the getaway route, whole traffic-stopping parades that materialized out of nowhere. People panic and start screaming, noon whistles blow and startle a gunman, who begins to fire wildly . . . a fire alarm next door, a tiny barking dog that won't go away . . . always a bunch of things. And, of course, it screwed everything up.

Well, it would, wouldn't it? This released tension into action, into another more rapid train of events. Usually it ended in a hail of bullets, sometimes quite satisfyingly in an exhilarated gangster looking back and laughing as he somehow managed to elude pursuit.

And now, Joe realized, at the last moment, something seemed to be happening on the flight line. It was time. It was getting late. Visibility was already reduced. The guard came out and so did the women, not casually but purposefully. They descended the ramp and walked together the few steps to the nose of the plane. Terrific! He couldn't have asked for better. Even the pilots had come out. And the guard didn't seem to be armed.

By god, he saw what it was! A group of vehicles was driving from the air terminal toward the aircraft parking area: a sedan, an ambulance, another car. The reception party was standing by the nose, on parade.

Joe tossed the binoculars onto the seat, started the engine, and drove out to the point he'd selected on the road. He hopped out of the cab and vaulted into the back. With no haste, he hefted an RPG, armed it, and took up his position. He looked up and down the road. No one in sight, which was a great relief. He had a fine view of the target.

He aimed and fired. The rocket whooshed, he tossed the launcher aside and stooped to get another ready. He tried to keep his eye on the rocket while he got the next one ready. It wasn't easy. The rocket took only a few seconds to reach its target. It had a better parabola than he'd anticipated. He'd aimed a little high and to the left, accommodating the breeze. The rocket swerved and smacked into the fuselage, about forty feet aft of the open door. It struck just in front of the left engine pod and exploded. These rockets were supposed to be armor penetrating, but this one exploded externally.

Joe figured the basic weight of the aircraft to be some twenty-four-plus tons. He hadn't expected it to move much, but the explosion kicked the tail of the aircraft sideways, bringing the entire plane now nearly broadside to him. He hadn't reckoned on that, and he was grateful that it worked in his favor. The target was much larger, and everybody was on the other side of it. He could hardly have asked for a better deal.

There was a gaping hole in the side of the plane, and smoke was pouring out of it. People were running, doubtless screaming, but he was not aware of that. Where was the guard? He at least ought not to be running away. He must realize what direction the rocket had come from. Joe couldn't wait to look. He aimed at the spot where the wing joined the fuselage and fired. Whoosh! Toss the launcher. Get another.

Now he heard shots. The guard must have gotten his weapon somehow and unleashed an entire clip. It was 9mm, all right, but Joe couldn't see him, didn't see any bullets kicking up dirt. No impacts on the truck. The second rocket struck the fuselage too high, blew a big chunk off the top of the plane. The approaching cars had turned away, Joe could see them driving away from the plane. But whoever was driving the ambulance was either confused or determined to make delivery. The ambulance swung clear around the nose of the plane and skidded to a halt, nearly crashing into the wing that was extended toward Joe.

The doors of the ambulance flew open, personnel in white uniforms ran wildly, running toward nearby parked planes, frantically seeking cover. Also two men in suits. There would be one person in that ambulance who couldn't run, Joe realized. A man who had intended to kill him. This was an unlooked-for opportunity. If he weighed the ethical factors at all, they didn't compute, didn't even register consciously. This was just too good to pass up. He aimed directly at the ambulance. But then . . . he let the sight drift away, toward the fuselage. The target was the plane, wasn't it? He fired, then tossed the launcher and bailed out of the truck, scrambling into the cab and driving as rapidly as he could down the road toward the terminal parking lot.

He never saw the rocket veer and strike the wing, just above the ambulance. The explosion, the fire on the wing, then another, much larger explosion. But he heard the blast, saw the flashes. It took him less than a minute to reach the spot where he had decided to leave the truck. The service road did not communicate with the passenger parking lot. From where he left the truck it was exactly a minute and forty seconds of walking purposefully, no panic, to reach the lot. That was twenty seconds faster than he had estimated. Must be adrenaline, he thought as he slipped through the hole he had cut in the cyclone fence. He slowed to the halting pace of the man who is pretty sure where he left the car, but not dead sure. He peered about, stopped, and then walked directly to the car he had rented two days ago. It was a white car, like so many rental cars, but also like a huge percentage of cars in the Salt Lake area; for some reason they liked white cars here, he'd noticed. He got in and drove to the exit, where a striped wooden barricade stopped him next to a windowed hut. The attendant had come out and was looking back toward the terminal.

"What's going on?" Joe called, extending his parking ticket.

"I don't know," the man said, coming around. He took Joe's ticket, glanced at it, said, "Be right with you. Some kind of explosion over there. Jeez, I hope it wasn't a crash!"

"My god," Joe said, "I hope not. It didn't sound that loud, did it?"

"No, I guess not," the man said. "It was a couple of bangs. You hear it? That wouldn't be a crash." He took the ticket back into the booth, ran it through a time-stamp device, and said, "That's thirty dollars and seventy-five cents, sir."

Joe paid, got his receipt, and when the barrier went up, drove cautiously out onto the terminal exit road. There was a lot of activity, sirens, flashing lights, that kind of thing, but he just drove onto the freeway and it was soon behind him.

In Salt Lake City he found a parking lot two blocks from where he had earlier left another car that he'd bought with his own money, a very nice four-year-old Ford Taurus, not white but green. He checked the rental car for any evidence that could connect it to Joe Service. There was none, of course. He locked the car and took five blocks to travel two blocks, checking his tail, crossing a hotel lobby, doubling back, entering a large department store, exiting by the parking structure. He was clean. He drove his new car out of yet another lot and back to the freeway. Traffic in the Salt Lake area was nuts. There was still a lot of construction going on because of the bid for the upcoming Olympic Games, but Joe didn't mind. The more confusion, the better. He patiently followed the temporary signs and got onto Interstate 80, then onto I-84, and finally, well north of the valley, onto I-15, headed toward Idaho and Montana.

This was more like it. Even though it was night, he could sense the wide-open spaces. Especially after he got over the ridge, out of the basin. He'd never cared for the basin. The Snake River reminded him of the last time he'd driven up this way. He'd turned around, just north of here, and gone back to Salt Lake City. He wasn't sorry he'd gone back, but thinking about it he was reminded of an odd guy he'd encountered there, a Colonel Tucker. He was pretty sure Tucker had been a federal agent, probably narcotics, but maybe Immigration or Treasury. The guy had staked out Helen's house in Salt Lake City, obviously intent on recovering the money that Helen had boosted from Joe's cabin. Not that Helen would see it that way, Joe thought. It was peculiar, though, that he had not given a thought to this guy before now. He wondered if Schwind knew this guy.

From here it was little more than two hours up over the Monida Pass to the turnoff that led up the road to his now ruined house, near the town of Tinstar. This really was a foolish idea. He'd thought about it as he drove. Almost no traffic at all on that freeway, from north of Idaho Falls, over the Monida Pass, until he turned off at Dillon. A couple of trucks. Then hardly any traffic to here. And all that time he'd known it was not just foolish but stupid.

If anyone was ever going to look any particular place for the fugitive Joe Service, it would be right here. He'd asked himself if this was just a blind, gut thing—a coyote running for his den. But he didn't feel like he was running from anything. He'd soon recovered from whatever adrenaline rush the attack on the plane had given him. Was this some primal thing? He didn't believe it. He decided it was just curiosity, and maybe a little bravado.

Then he laughed out loud. He was not a man to kid himself. There was at least one cardboard liquor box still stashed up there, full of money. Possibly two. As best as he could figure, there was between $500,000 and a cool million up there . . . assuming that the cops or somebody else hadn't found it.

He wanted to see the place, but it was the middle of the night. The house, of course, was just a charred hole in the ground. Too bad—he'd loved that house more than any other place he'd ever lived, but he was a remarkably unsentimental man. He parked and walked up the hill to a secret cache, an old mine shaft that he'd discovered only after he'd been on the property for some months.

Something had happened, he could tell right away. The door to the old mine shaft was pushed closed but not locked. He had no way of knowing the various events that had transpired here, after he had left. It didn't matter. What did matter was that, somehow, there were at least four boxes. And, he was gratified to see, their ghastly guardian, an unknown corpse, now rather mummified.

Joe recognized this corpse, although he hadn't the slightest notion of who this guy might have been. He'd first seen him on the highway, outside of Butte. Hitchhiking with a hired killer, or maybe it was the other way around. He'd stumbled on him months later, when he was trying to provide himself with a little cushion in his flight from Montana. Somebody had transported this corpse some forty miles from the highway and stashed him in Joe's private cache. Who? He assumed it had been Helen, but why? He'd never asked her when they had reunited in Salt Lake City. They'd been too busy with other things. But Joe was glad to see the guy. They were getting to be old pals. The guy didn't look much different, maybe a littler drier and thinner, his beard a little fuller, perhaps—it must be the excellent drainage, the dry air. The guy looked like he could hold out for years, till he resembled the husk of an insect, like a stonefly on a river rock.

More to the point: whoever had been here since Joe left, it hadn't been anyone official. This guy wouldn't still be on watch.

Joe had little curiosity about who the mysterious hitchhiker might be. He wasn't squeamish, but he had no desire to shift the body about. Still, it might be helpful to learn whatever might be readily available, so he took a moment to check the external coat pockets. All he found was a well-thumbed and grimy little spiral notebook and a stub of a pencil. By the light of the flashlight he read some lines of poetry, no name on the book. The last page written on contained a single, apparently uncompleted line: "The hour of transition is".

That was all. An epitaph, perhaps. He stuffed the book in his hip pocket and went directly to the remaining cardboard boxes. On his previous visit he'd been in too much of a hurry. He'd taken a box filled with old bills and records. Obviously, Helen had been more thorough. She had carted off the lion's share of the loot he had lifted in Detroit a lifetime ago, as it seemed. But to his relief, at least one of the boxes was filled with money.

He was tempted to whistle as he carried the box down the hill, but the hoot of an owl startled him and he kept his mouth shut. Also in the old mine were a few of his guns and plenty of ammo for them. He toted off a small arsenal, a couple of favorite pistols, a shotgun, and a special rifle he'd had made for him by a gunsmith over in the Bitterroot Valley. This was the gun he'd mentioned to Schwind, a .225 with a barrel that stifled sound like a vacuum. There was a companion piece, a similarly silenced .225 pistol. He took that as well.

Before he left he carefully closed the door and made sure it was locked. With any luck, the corpse would have eternal peace. Joe was looking for a little peace himself. He was dog tired, he realized, but he couldn't stay here. A freaky thought popped into his head: he knew a nurse in Butte. Nah. That would be too stupid. But where can you go when dawn is in the east? It's too late for a motel, especially in this remote territory. He didn't believe he could drive far. It would be the height of idiocy to pull over on the roadside: roads are empty out here, but eventually the sheriff or the highway patrol comes along. No tremendous danger, maybe, but not one to invite. Maybe the nurse, Cateyo, was not such a bad idea? She was in love with him, he knew, but they might have been watching her since he'd escaped.

He ended up taking a soothing bath and a catnap in the hot springs, just over the hill from the burnt-out house. It was still quite early when he dragged himself out and got on the road. To his surprise, he felt refreshed enough to drive as far as Billings before weariness forced him to stop. He checked into the largest hotel downtown, the Northern, and crashed into sleep.

When he awoke he was starving. It was morning, though. He had slept right through, some fourteen hours. Over breakfast he ransacked the papers, but there was no mention of any bombing or rocket attack at the Salt Lake City airport the day before. Maybe it was just that the *Gazette* was provincial, but he doubted it. Out here, Salt Lake might be a long way off in miles, but there weren't a lot of other large towns providing news. People thought nothing of driving to Cheyenne to shop. He thought it was some very good news management by Agent Schwind. Perhaps she'd convinced everybody that it was just an accident. That didn't make news unless a lot of people were killed. Joe didn't think anyone had been killed. It was possible, he thought, that yesterday's papers had carried a capsule news item, and when nothing further had developed, the story had died.

What next? He knew he should check in with Schwind, but he wasn't ready to yet. When he called her he wanted to be someplace where he couldn't be easily cornered. He hadn't made up his mind what he was going to do now, but he wanted to be free to decide for himself. He needed to be in a larger city. Montana had only a couple of roads out and only a few commercial flights. He needed to be in Denver, maybe. No. Not Denver. He wasn't ready to go back to Denver yet. And not Cheyenne. Nothing for it: he had to drive to Minneapolis. It took him two days and he enjoyed the drive immensely.

It was great to be out here, just driving, alone. He felt free, finally. Driving around America, checking out the scenery. Thinking the long, road thoughts. He thought about Schwind, about Helen, and Humphrey. He thought about his new career, whatever it might turn out to be. He didn't think much about who might have been in the ambulance. If it was Echeverria, so be it. He didn't know the guy, but he knew he'd been targeted by him.

He went to a mall in Minneapolis and bought a tiny tape recorder. Then he drove downtown. He parked and walked. He found a terrific used-clothing store, where he bought an amazing pair of python-skin cowboy boots that fit perfectly and a western-style sport coat that could have been tailored for him. A fellow he'd met in Tucson, many years ago, had shown him the joys of browsing in these kinds of stores. You could buy great clothes for next to nothing. He even found a cowboy hat, a genuine Stetson in dark gray, a modest rancher's hat. The whole shebang cost only fifty dollars.

He found the guy he wanted, on the street. A bearded young man with a backpack and a dog. One of those homeless but not helpless young guys who wandered around the country. This guy was happy to have lunch with Joe at a diner while the dog guarded the pack outside, where they could keep an eye on him. The man ate two big cheeseburgers, his fries and Joe's, and then gladly spoke into the tape recorder. Just a couple of cryptic messages. Joe gave him twenty bucks and left him smiling.

At a phone booth, he called the number Schwind had given him. When he got her voice mail, he played one of the messages. The homeless man's voice merely said, "Call this number," and carefully enunciated a number in Orange County, California. Joe figured Schwind would understand. What he didn't want was his own voice on her tape machine.

It was a beautiful day in Minneapolis, warm and sunny. He found a park near the river and strolled around. When he called the number in Orange County there were no messages. Too bad. Schwind hadn't figured it out yet. He called her number again. This time, she answered. He played the second message on the tape recorder. This one gave a number in Arkansas and asked her to leave a number in Chicago.

"Joe?" Schwind said. "Is that you? Listen, we've got to ta—" He hung up.

By now, he thought, she would know where he was and where he was headed. He could call her in Chicago, make further arrangements, and maybe even meet. That would calm her. Sure enough, when he called his Arkansas answering service, Schwind's voice was more relaxed. And she didn't use his name.

"Hi," she said. "You did a great job. Everybody's pleased. But we need to meet. Call me in Chicago, tomorrow, between noon and four P.M. Have fun."

Joe called the number in Chicago immediately. After four rings a recorded woman's voice, not Schwind's, asked the caller to leave a message, without providing any information. He hung up. That was all right, he thought. Maybe. He wondered where she had been when all the shooting started in Salt Lake. He called one of his old connections and asked for a location on the number Schwind had provided. The guy on the other end didn't take more than a minute. It was a residential number, at an address on the north side. The phone was registered to a D. Schwind.

There was no way he could get to Chicago before her, he knew. Not if he wanted to go armed, and he did. Maybe it was time to trust her. He'd think about it while he drove.

10

Kiddle-Dee-Divey

Helen wondered if Humphrey had ever been in love. They were down by the lake, by the pavilion, which stood next to the little dock. Humphrey's boat, a long low cabin cruiser elegantly crafted in rich, dark woods, had been brought out of storage in the boathouse for the first time this year and moored alongside the wooden catwalk. It was such a nice day, an incredible seventy-five degrees—Detroit got these days in March, sometimes—that they were actually talking about taking the boat out.

Humphrey was not fully convinced that it was a good idea. He kept asking the young fellows whose job it was to take care of and handle the boat if they didn't think it was a little early. Wouldn't there still be ice out there on the lake? No? But what about debris, all that flotsam left over from when the ice went out, some of it pieces of docks from as far away as Lake Huron? No problem, he was assured, they would keep a good lookout, wouldn't be running fast enough to damage anything even if they should encounter a log, to say nothing of a stray shingle or a net float. Heck, they said, it was worse in the summer, all the beer bottles. Clearly, they were eager.

Even Soke, Mrs. Sid, looked anticipatory. She had accepted one of her daughter's windbreakers, a shiny red one with a slick finish and a lightweight lining. Helen found her a pair of white canvas boat shoes and a bright Red Wings baseball cap. She said that she thought the Red Wings played hockey, not baseball, and they all laughed. But when Helen tucked her frizzy mass of iron-gray hair up into the hat, Soke looked ten years younger. Helen was very eager for her to go out on the water in this great boat. Roman was not eager. He was stolid, his dark suit bulging over his shoulder holster. But he said nothing, just watched.

At last, Humphrey agreed. Just for a little run. If it got too cold, if the water was too choppy (it was blessedly still, nothing more than an occasional warm flutter), they could come right back. But there were a few things to be done. Always some fussing by the boatmen, tinkering with the engine, testing the radio, the depth finder, something. And then there was the food and drink to be prepared and brought down. The boating party stood about on the dock, or the lawn, talking and watching.

Helen asked where the name of the boat had come from, *Kiddle-Dee-Divey*. Boat names were often silly, Humphrey told her. But had he named her? Yes, he had. He'd bought the boat a long time ago. He used to keep it down at Bayview, but when he bought this house with its boathouse, he'd moved it up here. He was quite proud of the boat. He said it was the only one of its kind. It had been built by a legendary boatwright from up near Traverse City. This master builder was famous for his many beautiful and fast sailboats, but sometime after the war he'd tried his hand at what he called a motor cruiser. He'd wanted to recapture the classical lines of powerboats from the twenties and thirties, and this was the lovely result. As far as Humphrey knew, he'd never built another. The builder had given the boat to his wife for an anniversary present. When she divorced him, she put it up for sale. Humphrey had bought it from her.

"But how did you come up with that name?" Helen demanded.

He reluctantly confessed that it was a lyric from a goofy song that was popular when he was a child: "Mairzy Doats." As a boy, he had thought at first that it was "Mairzy Boats." He had stubbornly insisted that everybody was mispronouncing the title. The grown-ups were so amused they often asked him to sing it. So when he bought a boat. . . . Helen thought that was funny and she begged him to sing the song. He refused. But he did finally recite some of the lyrics: "Mairzy doats and dozey doats, and little lambsy divey . . . a kiddle-dee-divey too, wouldn't you?" He added, "I still think it should be 'boats,' but that wouldn't work."

"Why not?"

"The words are just a goofy way of saying 'Mares eat oats,' and so on," he explained.

Helen cocked her head, smiling as she digested this example of an earlier generation's idea of comic wordplay. And then, for no reason that she could supply, she asked him if he'd ever been in love.

Humphrey was startled. "Well, I guess so," he said. "Everybody's been in love, once." But when she pressed for details, he would only say, "A long time ago."

"But you never married, or anything, did you?"

No, he'd never been close to marrying.

"It must have been that first love," Helen said. "What was her name?"

"I don't even remember," he said.

At last, the boat was ready. They all went aboard and found places to sit while the young man, Jamie, took the boat slowly out. The boat was surprisingly roomy inside, for all its sleek, low profile. There was a large open area on the back, or aft, with cushioned bench-type seats. But then you stepped down to an enclosed bridge, where the helmsman stood. Another door opened into an amazing saloon, so to speak, complete with a tiny galley, tables, booth seats, and beyond that sleeping compartments. Everything was marvelously worked out in deep, rich hardwoods. There were tiny windows that looked out onto a narrow catwalk on either side of the cabin roof. The builder had obviously not departed much from the design of a sailboat.

At first they all sat in the sunny rear cockpit. But Humphrey went to stand right next to the helmsman, in the cabin, directing him out to the northeast.

It was such a great day that soon they were all sipping drinks and eating grilled sausages, fancy cheeses, and a variety of crackers and tiny sandwiches; there was even a fancy genoise layer cake with caramel-hazelnut icing. Humphrey, true to his peppers despite the loss of Pepe, favored the jalapeño poppers, stuffed with pepper jack cheese.

Soon enough, Helen found an opportunity to bring up Humphrey's lost love. They were sitting side by side on the fantail, as it were. The others had drifted inside. Roman was playing a card game with Soke in the saloon.

Humphrey confided, finally, that the "lost love" had actually been his "first love"—maybe *only* love would have been more accurate. He had last seen her when he was fourteen and she was thirteen.

"My gosh," Helen said, "it's sort of like, what's his name, Dante and Beatrice. Or am I thinking of someone else?"

"It wasn't like that," Humphrey said. "We were just kids. But she was very nice to me."

"Ooh, that sounds a little risqué," Helen kidded.

"It wasn't like that," he insisted. "She was just nice. We didn't do anything. We traded books—I forget what. King Arthur, or something. Maybe it was Robert Louis Stevenson. Something like that. Poetry, maybe."

Helen was intrigued. She could see that it had meant a lot to him. It was sweet, she thought. A childhood romance, and then . . . "Well, what happened?" she asked.

He shrugged. "We moved away," he said. "Carmine's folks moved into the city. We grew up on the east side. Things got a little crazy. You know? Growing up, gangs, I had a little trouble. That kind of thing."

"Whatever happened to her? Didn't you ever call, or write?"

"I don't know why I never called," he said. "Maybe it was . . . well, I just don't know. She was too far away. She was history. I was into other stuff, like I said. She wouldn't have liked what I was doing."

"But you never forgot her," Helen said. It was sad, but cute. Still, he had never gotten married. She asked him why not.

"You know," he said, in a hopeless tone, gesturing at his torso. "I was a fatso. I had a few times with the bimbos, but it wasn't my thing. I wasn't into it."

Helen didn't understand. She knew Humphrey had been terribly obese; that was how she remembered him from her own youth—nice, fat, jolly Unca Umby. It was hard to believe, in fact, that this rather handsome, distinguished-looking man had once been a sweating, panting mess. But lots of heavy men, she thought, managed to get married, have children. Why not Humphrey?

He explained. Lots of men just gave up on sex and love, all of that. They channeled their energies in other directions. In his case, he got interested in the business. Carmine was enough of a playboy for all of them, him and her father. He apologized if it sounded disrespectful, but her dad was a lover. Humphrey wasn't. He realized in his early twenties that he had a lot of catching up to do, having dropped out of high school. He studied, he watched and listened and learned. He saw that he was going to have to be the brains behind Carmine, who was being groomed to take over. He had accepted this. He thought that his chance might come someday, and it had.

"But maybe too late," he added. "The business is all changed."

But Helen wasn't having another business pep talk. They were on an outing. She wanted to know how a man just "gives up" romance.

"You mean sex," he said. He was uneasy, but also excited. He had expected to have this conversation with her, as they had gotten closer these last few weeks. He hadn't dared to hope that anything could actually come of it, but it was hard for a man not to dream. He hadn't imagined that the conversation would come up just like this, on the back of a boat with her mother and Roman and the crew not far off. But they were effectively alone. Maybe it was the right time.

He gave it some thought, then said, "It's hard, at first. A man has natural feelings, of course, and you see these babes hanging around . . . I mean, they're there for the taking. Good-looking, too, a lot of them. I had a couple . . . well, I was coming up in the world, I had power, already. They *had* to go to bed with me. That's the way it was. I'm not gonna 'pologize. They were looking out for themselves, too. But it was no good. I could see why they were doing it. Eh? I couldn't do that, after a while. Besides, it was getting in my way.

"So . . . I just made up my mind: to hell with it. Forget about it. And it went away. I don't know just how it came about, but pretty soon I could see it was an accepted thing: the Fat Man ain't into broads. Something like that. And then, it's funny, the babes started coming around."

Helen didn't get it. "Coming around? You fell in love?"

"No, no," he said, with a snort of laughter. "Get over this falling in love thing. No, they saw . . . I guess . . . that I was safe. It was okay to horse around and be a little flirty, because it wouldn't come to anything. I was the Fat Man, right? I didn't like babes, not that way. I liked to kid around, but nothing funny. Right?"

She saw it, all right. It sounded awful, but she didn't say anything.

"And it was all right," he went on. "It didn't bother me. I forgot about it. But now . . ." He looked at her in a strange way.

Oh dear, she thought. This is it. She'd been afraid of this. But if he'd gotten over sex, a long time ago. . . . Maybe he was thinking of something else.

He was. Nonetheless, he took a breath and launched into a little speech. He had deep feelings for her, he said. Yes, very deep feelings. It went beyond their former relationship. He wanted her to forget about that. This was different. He wasn't her Unca Umby, see? But before she got any ideas. . . . He raised his hand, to stop her from replying. Just let him finish. He wasn't some dirty old man.

He actually used those words. "I'm not some dirty old man," he said. "I'm not interested in that kind of stuff. Oh, maybe a little kiss, a little squeeze." He laughed uncomfortably.

She sat there, gazing at him, wondering. Was she supposed to jump up and kiss him, hug him? She liked him. She thought he was smart, a strong, deep, mysterious man. She thought that, if it came to that, she would go to bed with him. She had long ago decided that sex didn't commit you to anything. But what did he want?

What he wanted, it seemed, was an intimacy. He felt they were practically there already. He wanted, he said, someone he could level with.

Well. That wasn't much, she thought, at first. But then she began to see what he meant. He hadn't had anybody for some time with whom he could talk unguardedly, someone he could trust and believe in. He was willing to eschew certain physical liberties to have this. He wouldn't be pawing her, wouldn't expect. . . . He left it unsaid.

Maybe he'd never had this intimacy, she thought. He'd had some kind of rapport with Carmine, his lifelong pal, almost a brother. That wasn't the same, at all, couldn't have been. He needed this intimacy with a woman, but a special kind of woman. Someone like her. Perhaps there wasn't any other such woman on the planet, she thought. She felt strangely proud to be that one person, that woman. Her heart filled with empathy toward him.

He had stopped talking. The boat rumbled along, its powerful engine nearly silent, but felt. The water was blue and the waves were light. The sun danced on occasional sprays. It was warm on their backs. They had turned and were angling toward the distant shore, toward home. He must have given some kind of signal to the helmsman. She hadn't caught it.

"So, whaddaya think?" he said, comically. He smiled sadly at her. He had brown eyes, she noticed. Well, she'd always known they were brown, but now she saw that they were. So this man wants me, she thought, gazing at him. She felt fond. He wants a—what was the word? morganatic? no—wife who can be intimate in a wifely way, but with a difference. An intimate. But not ultimately intimate. An arms-length romance.

"I could do that," she said.

They both laughed. He gave her hand a squeeze and she kissed his cheek. "You're sweet," she said. And suddenly, she was filled with affection for him. She wanted to say, "You know what? I love you, you big lug," or something coolly, movieish. But she didn't.

"You're great," he said.

"I think we can be great together," she replied. "But one thing. What about this what's-her-name? Are you still pining for her? You know, I can't have that."

"Oh, no way," he assured her, solemnly, shaking his head. "I've never even seen her again, I swear."

"Well, you don't have to swear," Helen told him. "Anyway, for all we know she might be dead."

He didn't like that thought, she saw instantly. That had been a mistake. But then he seemed to brush the thought aside.

"What about Joe?" he said abruptly. "You still carrying a torch for him?"

She almost gulped. She'd forgotten about Joe. Just thinking of him now made her feel like a fool. What had she been thinking of? Romancing Humphrey, imagining some kind of weird affair, and all the time. . . . What about Joe? Her foolish heart was wrenched.

"Joe?" she said, faintly. "Ah, well, Joe . . . I haven't seen Joe. I don't even know where he is, what he's doing." Firmly, she declared, "I haven't given a thought to Joe in weeks. That's over. That's past."

Humphrey looked at her closely, then nodded. He seemed satisfied. "Okay," he said. "Good. I like Joe. I always liked Joe. Me and him, we got along. The best I ever saw at what he does. So it wouldn't bother you to see him?"

"You've seen him!" She throttled back her sudden enthusiasm, tried to sound indifferent: "You heard from him?"

Humphrey elected to ignore her sudden excitement, she was relieved to see. "No," he said, offhandedly, "but I got a feeling."

"What kind of feeling?"

"A feeling like we haven't seen the last of Joe Service," he said. He wouldn't say any more. He had a feeling.

They soon docked. It had been a fine day. Her mother stayed for supper. Roman stayed too, of course, but he acted kind of funny around Helen. He looked at her almost reproachfully, she thought, but he didn't say anything. The new chef had prepared grilled salmon with two sauces, one of them a peppery one for Humphrey. Soke talked recipes. She sampled the peppery one. She used to cook with peppers, she said, Hungarian and Italian ones, but not this hot. This was too hot, she said. It was too much for the salmon. Humphrey disagreed, but politely. He had a theory that peppers never really masked other flavors but actually brought them out. Now, heavy cream sauces, he said, that could mask flavor.

After that day, things changed. There was a new intimacy. Not only did Humphrey begin to tell her inside things about the business, sometimes shocking her, but he began to act more possessive, in public. They would be talking to other men, his underlings, men with position, and he would insist that Helen be included in the talk. He'd ask her opinion, or voice "their" opinion—"*We* think . . ." or "In *our* opinion. . . ." And he'd sometimes rest his hand on her shoulder, or her waist.

She liked it. She was beginning to know her way around. She would talk about business practices, informatively, authoritatively, and Humphrey would beam at her, agreeing with her. Telling the other men, "You see? She's a bright one. That's the ticket. That's what we gotta do."

The one area where they didn't agree was the cigar business. He couldn't see her scheme. He listened to her spiel, discussed it with her and Berta. Unfortunately, Berta wasn't her best ally. She claimed that the problems were too intractable. Sure, Humphrey still knew people in Cuba, he could get tobacco, it could be smuggled in. But what was the point? They couldn't make as good a product as the Cubans, or even the Dominicans. And where was the market? Guys weren't going to pay the kind of prices they'd have to ask to make it worthwhile, not while they could get Dominicans and, even, smuggled Cubans. At best, over a period of time, they might build up a small, loyal customer base, but they could never be big while they couldn't go public.

The problem was, their major market consisted of guys who liked Cuban cigars, and even liked the added sense of adventure and danger that went with smuggling them in from trips to Canada or overseas. They couldn't compete with that. And these guys tended to know their cigars. They wouldn't accept a homemade version, even if somehow you could convince them that this cigar was what it was: a cigar hand-rolled by rollers from Cuba, using Cuban tobacco. It was not going to be a top-of-the-line Cuban cigar, not for a long time, anyway. But with the cost of production, her cigar—he called it "LaDonna Detroit"—would have to be priced up there with the real goods. It couldn't compete. And once the embargo was lifted, as it had to be, someday, the whole game was up. Who could compete then?

He finally conceded that maybe, what the hell, if she really wanted it, they could make a cigar and sell it at a loss. He figured the quality of the tobacco would guarantee at least a five-dollar price, maybe a little more. The cigar business was booming, after all, crazier things were happening. They'd lose money on every cigar they sold, but he could afford it. If that's what she wanted.

No, she didn't want that. She was too good a businesswoman. She believed that with Berta's help she could get her girls to turn out a quality cigar. They could go two ways: her girls would slap labels on them, any label she wanted, and they could be peddled as "illegal" Cuban "seconds"; and they'd also work on a public, over-the-counter cigar, the LaDonna series. Five bucks. Basically the same cigar, quality tobacco from the Dominican

Republic, Honduras, and so on; they'd be good cigars; they might lose money for a while, but they would slowly build a clientele. You could consider it a form of advertising, buying a market. Then, who knows, a year or two down the road . . . they could maybe jack up the price, get in the black.

She was satisfied, for now.

And then, Joe called.

11

Joe's Nature

Dinah Schwind watched Joe from her apartment. He had been by the building at least twice, but she had a feeling that he had been by more than that. She stood at the fourth-floor window, gazing through the muslin curtains. She had to smile. He looked goofy as hell, she thought. Where did he get that outfit? He was in jeans, very fancy cowboy boots, and even a hat. His mustache was full, already, she saw, and it had a western look, too—kind of droopy at the corners. Goofy but also, she had to admit, attractive. She couldn't imagine many men capable of carrying off this absurd drugstore cowboy look.

She had not liked very many men in her thirty-four years. She liked her dad. He was not what some would call a successful man—a finish carpenter. He didn't make a lot of money. He took too long. He was not a union carpenter. He worked in upstate New York. A nice guy. A family man. Her mother was nice, but she seemed to favor Dinah's older sister, who was pretty. Her sister had married a doctor, had babies, and that was her mother's interest: Jennifer and the kids, and Dr. Swanson. Her mother almost never called Jennifer's husband Glen, but Dr. Swanson. She was appalled that Dinah had become a federal agent. They sent her to law school for this? She'd done so well at the state university in Rochester. She had offers from many fine law firms but went into enforcement. What a waste.

Joe had disappeared. She moved the curtain aside, looked up and down the street. It was not a busy street, one of those north side Chicago streets with a store on the corner, a tavern, cars parked. Where had he gone? She let the curtain drop. Damn! Well, he'd no doubt come knocking when he was ready. But he must be pretty strung out, nervous as a cat. Although he hadn't looked nervous down there.

Some people, she thought, seemed to have a kind of unself-consciousness. Certain athletes, for instance. They moved about with remarkable grace but didn't seem aware of it. Joe had that. He'd looked natural as hell down there, a cowboy in a ridiculous outfit, perfectly at home on a residential street in Chicago. But he must be running scared.

She hoped he wouldn't be long. She was cooking something that she hoped he would like, braised lamb shanks. It had to be something of that sort, something that could be kept warm, because she hadn't been sure when he would show. It was a very tasty recipe; she'd picked it up in the Mideast.

She wasn't sure why she'd bothered. Maybe she felt that she owed him something. She had tossed him into a losing situation, as she saw it, and he had come out smelling like a rose and making her look like a genius. From Joe's point of view, of course, it was an opportunity. It had gotten him out of the hospital, headed off an indictment, almost certainly a long stretch in prison. But he'd hardly blinked. And now that she thought about it, she wasn't so sure that she had actually saved him from anything. His budding deal with the deputy sheriff had looked lame, grasping at straws, but now she thought he might have made that work. He might have been better off.

The problem was the colonel. He had absolutely insisted on Joe. You'd have thought he would be pissed, the way Joe had snookered him. Joe had, in fact, left the colonel handcuffed to a pipe in a house the colonel himself had staked out. The hunter wasn't supposed to be caught in his own trap. But the colonel was like that: extremely practical. No, the colonel just shrugged it off.

"Sometimes it's not the horse," the colonel said, "it's the jockey. That doesn't mean you want to trade horses, of course."

She looked at the lamb shanks. They were getting pretty tender, but the onions and raisins and cinnamon . . .

"Smells good," Joe said.

She somehow prevented herself from whirling about. She looked over her shoulder and raised an eyebrow. "It's an old recipe," she said. "Want some?"

"I'm starving," he said. He smiled.

White teeth. Some people were born with even, white teeth. That would be Joe. She was willing to bet that he'd never been to a dentist in his life, that he did not floss regularly.

He was leaning against the doorjamb, facing into the kitchen, his hands in his jeans pockets. He seemed totally at ease. For a man who had spent weeks in the hospital, he looked as fit as a gymnast. Good color. He appeared taller than five-whatever. Maybe it was the high heels of the cowboy boots. But he had such an elegant shape; even in the floppy ER greens he'd escaped in, he'd looked taller. He had a swimmer's build: wide shoulders, slim hips.

Dinah Schwind was suddenly shocked. For the first time in her life she had looked at a man and wondered what his belly was like, what his thighs were like, his penis. She had never had such a reaction in her life.

"Something wrong?" Joe said.

"I have to put on the rice," she said.

"I should have called to set a time," Joe said. "Put it on! I'm starving. Do you need some help?"

"No, no, I'll get it. I already made the salad, and I bought some flat bread. I saw you hanging around on the corner." She turned to her tasks, eager to be busy.

"Not too cool, eh?" Joe said. "Well, I came by earlier, but I guess you weren't here."

"Came by?" She looked at him. She was stirring the rice in the oil, before adding the stock. "You mean, you came in?"

"I didn't think you'd mind," he said. "We're partners, eh? I thought it was better than getting a place."

"You're not thinking of staying here?" She poured the hot stock over the rice and set it on a low burner.

"Whatever you say," Joe said indifferently. He pulled out a kitchen chair and sat on it, casually. "We going to eat in here? Or do you want me to set the dining table?" He nodded toward the nearby dining room.

"Open the wine," she said. "Will this Oregon pinot do? It's kind of full-bodied, but it has a dryness that should go with the lamb and the sauce."

He thought it sounded fine and he opened the bottle and poured for both of them. They tasted it. She was right. It was good, a solid wine, but a little young.

She didn't ask him how he'd gotten in. She might later. It was worth knowing. In the event, he volunteered the information: he'd told the super that he was her brother. Just back from Paris. Very friendly guy, the super. Thought Joe and Dinah were very much alike, not in looks, so much, although the nose. . . . She laughed. Later, she considered that he obviously had conned the super, but there were still a couple of details, field craft . . . that hadn't been the whole story.

The lamb was very good and they ate it all, and all of the rice and the salad. They drank two bottles of the wine. She couldn't wait to tell him how pleased they were with his work.

"It was surgical," she declared. She said it several times, with an enthusiastic emphasis on the first syllable, *surgical*.

"Just luck," Joe said. "Five minutes before the bell, I was ready to bolt. But then . . . everything worked out."

"You're kidding," she said. "You seemed cool."

"Where were you?" he asked.

"Inside the fence," she said.

Joe doubted that, but he didn't say anything. There was nothing she could do inside the fence. Unless . . . "You were set to pop Echeverria when I didn't?" he said.

She shrugged. "We considered it. If the operation didn't go well."

But then, he thought, you would be inside the fence. Maybe that would be all right, but he was skeptical. "Well, luckily, everything went well." He raised his brows. "How is Mr. E?"

She shook her head. "He didn't make it," she said. "You didn't know?"

"You did a good job of press management," Joe said. "Anyway, I did what I could. If I didn't succeed, well, that's life. Have to wait for another chance."

She was amazed. She thought she'd seen just about all there was on offer, killers, robbers, con men, revolutionaries, high-rolling mobsters, hardened janissaries . . . but she had never seen anyone so cool. "Do you enjoy this . . . work?" she asked.

Joe looked puzzled. "It's fun," he said. "It's exciting. Besides . . . well, what are we talking about this for? You know what I can do." He leaned forward, suddenly. They were sitting not across from each other but across a corner. "You know what I'd like to do?"

She shook her head, flustered. "What?"

"I'd like to go to bed with you."

That's what she heard—at first. But then she realized he'd said, "Do you have a bed I can use?"

She had a bed, in a guest room, for when her parents visited. But Joe told her he preferred her bed. "Don't get excited," he said, "I don't have any amatory plans. I just think I'd like you close by. Anyway, the last time I got amorous I ended up in the hospital. I think I'm going to have to ease into that."

When they were lying chastely, side by side but not touching, he said, "What happened with Echeverria?"

She explained that the fire had quickly engulfed the ambulance. Echeverria hadn't had a chance. It was a fluke. The driver of the ambulance had thought he was protecting the patient by driving around the plane. He'd thought the danger was from the guard shooting. But then, seeing the plane on fire, he'd panicked and fled. Nobody blamed him. Perhaps the attendants could have dragged Echeverria out, but. . . . Nobody was blamed.

"How about me?" Joe said. "Do they connect me with it?"

"Not so far," she said. "The cops might have, if they'd gotten hold of the truck you abandoned. But one of our guys spotted it and just hopped in and drove it away. Good thing you left the keys."

Joe didn't comment. He was asleep, but with his arm flung over her body. Presumably, he just wanted to make sure she didn't get up without him knowing, but she couldn't help hoping there was more to it. She lay there for a long time, willing him to wake up. They could talk, maybe make love. Then she drifted off.

In the morning, she woke to the sound of the shower. Joe came out shortly. He was naked, toweling himself dry. She looked up at him and tossed the covers back, frankly invitational. She was naked, too. Joe looked down at her and smiled. She looked a lot better naked. He admired that kind of lean, hard fitness. He sat down on the bed and laid his hand on her hip. She was very warm. She shifted lazily, her thighs opening. She laid her hand on his penis. It grew.

Joe was tempted. He had the desire, he was sure it would be satisfying, maybe even thrilling, and he didn't want to disappoint her . . . but he wasn't ready to trust her. He didn't want her to see that, however, so he opted for lameness. He leaned over the bed and kissed her cheek.

"Not today," he said.

"Scared?" she teased.

"You bet." He stood up and took his stiff cock in his left hand. "When this gets like this"—he shook his cock, while tapping his head with the forefinger of his right hand—"it's like the circuits get overloaded. Sometimes, fuses blow."

"It looks like it's functioning all right," she said. "Maybe a little exercise would be good for it."

"Maybe," he said. "Maybe later."

He dressed and went to make coffee for them. "Now tell me again," he said, as they sat at the kitchen table, "how you're going to pay me."

"Pay you?" She shook her head. "You got paid, for this one. We got you out. Maybe another time, another scenario, there'll be some money. You can keep what you find."

"You mean the scenario where I knock off some dope dealers?"

"Something like that," she said.

"Well, how about that," Joe said, disgustedly. "I bust my buns for you, I'm on the run, and you guys say 'Thanks, your country is grateful, but . . .' You are grateful, aren't you?"

"I said we were grateful, last night. And we've got more plans. Don't get so uptight. Of course, we can provide you with some money, a little, if you need it. But it's not like you're making a big score, you know. I explained all this from the start."

"You painted a rosier picture in the hospital," Joe said. He considered the situation briefly, then decided. "All right, this one's gratis. I'd have gotten out anyway, but you helped, you made it easier. So what's next? Do we fry another dope dealer?"

"First, the others have to meet you. It's absolutely essential," she said.

"What if I don't want to meet them?"

"Joe." She sighed. "Don't be this way. Don't force me to use pressure."

"You mean blow my cover?" He laughed. "And then I'd blow your operation. But you figure that A, I wouldn't do that, and B, who would believe me?"

"Something like that," she said. "But it's more, 'Why should you do that?' Your old role with the mob is blown, pretty much. You need something to do. This is a good job for you."

"You mean lots of kicks, fighting the war against drugs, Our Nation's enemies, that sort of thing?" he said. He paused and eyed her thoughtfully. "You said, 'pretty much.' What does that mean?"

"You caught that, did you? It means that we don't think you're *completely* blown with the mob. You've still got friends there."

Joe nodded slowly. He saw it. They figured he still had a connection. With Helen. So she must have been taken back under Humphrey's wing. And maybe they thought that Joe could still approach Humphrey himself. He wasn't so sure. But if it were so, what would be the point? Then he got it.

"You want me to hit Humphrey," he said.

"Gosh, what an idea! It's so crazy, it just might work!"

Joe was surprised. It wasn't like Schwind to joke. His amazement sobered her.

"Sorry," she said. "I didn't mean to make light of it. Actually, we weren't thinking of that, particularly."

"Any more than you were thinking Echeverria should get toasted," he said.

"No, really. It's just. . . . Here's the situation." She explained that recently they had become aware of a change in activity in Detroit. Humphrey seemed to be pulling back, or at least realigning his enterprises, changing his focus. People were being shuffled around, Humphrey wasn't making his normal appearances, money was being shifted. These phenomena were more felt than strictly observed. But the overall picture was getting distorted, hard to see.

"Something is happening," Joe prompted, with a musical lilt in his voice, "but you don't know what it is."

"Yes," she said. "We had an agent in there, a very good man. But he disappeared. A little while back, his body floated up, without a head. We think Humphrey tumbled to him and had him killed. We want to know what happened, and what's happening now. We think you could find out."

"And what's my end?"

"Your end?" She sighed. "You know, over the years I've had my hands on . . . oh, I'd guess about ten or twenty million bucks. Contraband, confiscated loot. I never took a penny, although in many cases there was not another person who could have said that I had, or even noticed, really. I was never even tempted, Joe. It wasn't my money. I couldn't have said, in most cases, whose money it was. Maybe it was no one's. But it wasn't mine. If you want money, Joe, I'm sure we can supply you with money, from those sources. It wouldn't bother me. Just because I don't take it, that doesn't mean that you can't . . . assuming, of course, that it isn't otherwise accounted for."

"That's nice to hear," Joe said, "but it's kind of iffy. I don't work on those terms. I like to know what I'm putting my ass on the line for. And," he continued, carefully emphasizing each word, "*I want to collect*. You see, that's what started all this: Carmine hired me to do a job, but then he didn't want to pay off."

"Okay, we'll pay you," she said.

"Pay me what? You keep saying that, but you don't mention figures. I'm just a simple guy, Dinah. I don't go in for philosophy. What's the payoff?"

"What do you want?"

"I want immunity. Freedom. Money. A new car. Time to myself. Better movies. Let's see . . ."

"I see," she said. "Immunity is the problem. You're in the system now, Joe. You have a number of charges pending against you. In order to get any of them dropped, to obtain official protection, we'd have to employ you. We'd have to be able to say what you were going to do for us. And we can't do that. But . . ." She pondered for a minute. "There may be something. I'll have to confer with the others. Possibly . . . I'm just thinking out loud, now . . . we could get you some kind of protection, get your name removed from the wanted computers, give you some kind of cover. But I think you'd still be vulnerable to arrest and detention, and prosecution, if some obstinate cop or prosecutor or judge insisted. I'll try, if you're content with that."

"It'll do for now," Joe said. "It just means being careful. But then, I'm always careful. The guy I have to watch out for is Mulheisen."

"The Detroit cop?" Schwind was surprised.

"I guess you don't know Mulheisen," Joe said.

"I've met him. He wasn't impressive. Seemed a little dense, even, a time server. I mean, the guy is a little long in the tooth to still be a sergeant of detectives, isn't he?"

"What is that, a joke? Look, I don't care what his rank is. The guy is a force of nature, or something. Water flows downhill, at thirty-two degrees it turns to ice, at two twelve it turns to steam. Mulheisen keeps looking. He probably doesn't even know why he does it. You've heard the story of the fox and the goose?"

"The fox wants a ride across the river?" Schwind said. "Is it like the scorpion and the frog?"

"I think so," Joe said. "The fox pleads mutual self-interest, but then he bites the goose's neck in midstream—"

"They're both going down and the goose cries out, 'Why?'"

"And the fox says, 'It's my nature.' Well, enough of fables, go ahead, find out from your pals." Joe gestured at the telephone. She seemed reluctant. He said, "I'll leave."

The next time she heard from him he was in Detroit and he wanted a boat.

12

Kiss and Make Up

Humphrey seemed a little uneasy. Helen hardly noticed, she was so excited about seeing Joe again. But she did notice, finally, when they were motoring out of the slip onto the lake, aboard *Kiddle-Dee-Divey*. Humphrey was running the boat, only the two of them aboard. Joe was supposed to meet them at Peach Island, in the Detroit River. Once again, it was pleasant weather, though not as sunny as on their last boating jaunt. It was the familiar high, thin overcast, quite bright out—they both wore sunglasses—but a little breezy. The lake was gray and choppy.

"What are you worried about?" Helen asked.

Humphrey shrugged. He looked very fit and nautical today, wearing a navy blue cashmere turtleneck under a windbreaker but, as always, no hat. If Humphrey had any vanity, it was about his hair, which was still dark and thick. He didn't like hats. He ran the boat with confidence, no fussing.

"I'm not sure about Joe," Humphrey confessed. Helen looked surprised, and he went on: "Joe can be difficult. Hell, he usually is difficult. But usually it's a put-on. Lotta swagger, the perennial wise guy. Most a the time, he had a legitimate beef—about Carmine. You know," he said, thoughtfully, "I ain't seen the guy in—what?

A year? Not since before he split for Montana with you. I talked to him, a couple times, but we didn't meet. I'm not sure of him, and I know he ain't sure of me. I'm countin' on you to make it good between us."

"Well, of course," she said, as if it were all agreed. "Can't we go a little faster?"

Humphrey looked at his watch. "We got plenty of time. I don't wanta get there before Joe. I don't want him thinkin' we're settin' something up."

A downbound freighter was looming in the eastern approach to the Fleming Channel. There was little other traffic out today, a few sailboats, a handful of motorcraft. Humphrey took the sleek cabin cruiser across the channel well ahead of the freighter and throttled back as they approached the upbound channel along the Canadian shore. They were still well east of Peach Island.

"Setting something up?" Helen said. "Why should he think that? He called us. I thought this was all for his security. I mean, he's the fugitive. He must feel pretty secure or he wouldn't have agreed to this boat business."

"Oh, I don't think Joe's too worried about being spotted by anyone," Humphrey said. "It's just . . . well, there's something a little funny here. You remember that plane that got blown up in Salt Lake City last week?"

Helen didn't. She hadn't noticed.

"You remember that guy, Echeverria?"

Helen remembered him all right. She had almost taken a plane ride with him, up in Montana.

"That was his plane," Humphrey said. "And Joe walked out of that hospital in Denver just a few days before. There was something about that, made me think of Joe. Vetch got torched in that plane hit. Now, I know it ain't like Joe to go around torchin' guys just 'cause they caused him a little trouble, but . . . I don't know, there was something about it. And now, a few days later, Joe calls. So, I set this up. This way, Joe can see it's just me and you, and we can see it's just Joe."

"So what do we do? Pull alongside? There could be people below. Or do we stand off, like in *Moby-Dick*, and shout at each other through megaphones?"

"We both pull up and anchor off the island. Actually, it's very shallow there, a couple feet. We can run right in and wade ashore, maybe even jump ashore. These boats don't have much draft. We'll probably get a little wet, but it ain't that cold."

They ran down toward the island. Helen pursued the question of Joe's activities. "You think he's working for someone?" she asked. "Like Mitch? The eastern organization?"

"I doubt he's workin' for Mitch," Humphrey said. "Those guys are still pissed he's out walkin' around. No, I don't know what the deal is. Joe don't like to work with other people, much, but he likes money. It took a little help to get out of that hospital, but maybe he just charmed his way out. Maybe he just misses us—you, anyways. Then again, maybe he's wacko. Maybe he's flipped out. I don't know. Do you?"

Helen had to admit that she'd had some thoughts along those lines herself. A man who has been shot in the head, seemingly recovered, but then had some kind of relapse. . . . Who could say?

"Could be he's on some psycho vendetta," Humphrey said. "But he's always been a kind of bold guy who did things different, so maybe this is just normal—for Joe." He tapped his forehead with a finger. "Could be, he's got some new clients. Well, we'll see. There he is."

They had swung around the head of the island, on the Canadian side, and there was the little sixteen-foot powerboat with an open cockpit, with Joe Service sitting jauntily on the gunwale. He was not in cowboy gear, but more like an outdoor-catalog version of what the sporty yachtsman wears: colorful windbreaker, light sweater, rainproof pants, bare feet in deck shoes. No hat, of course. But wraparound shades. Helen thought he looked terrific, but she didn't care for the closely clipped beard and mustache. She felt it hid his finely chiseled chin and emphasized his sensual lips too much. But she soon forgot that.

There was no uneasiness now. They pulled alongside and she leaped onto the deck, embracing Joe. They laughed and hugged, even kissed. Humphrey beamed and stepped across, a little more carefully than Helen, but still quite agilely. He too embraced Joe. Helen stood back for a moment, grinning at them. They were all clearly delighted to be reunited, though Helen noticed that Humphrey, for all his jovial exuberance, made sure to hug Joe thoroughly and practically pat him down.

Joe noticed it too, but he joked: "Hey, Slim, take it easy! I'm not wired. I'm not packing." It was clear, though, that he had made sure of Humphrey's lack of weaponry in their embrace. But now that formality was over. They were just glad.

"My god," Joe said, stepping back to look Humphrey over, "they said you were slimmed down, but this is amazing. You look like a fashion model." He laughed, and Humphrey laughed too.

"Actually, I gained back a few pounds, lately," Humphrey said. "Gee, it's good to see ya, Joe."

They all agreed, it was great to see each other. They quickly moved to the more comfortable boat, the *Kiddle-Dee-Divey*. They were standing in the well of the open rear cockpit, still delightedly patting each other's backs, when Humphrey looked over at Joe's speedboat and said, "Helluva nice little rig, Joe. How'd you get hold of her?"

"Ah, the Feds got it for me," Joe tossed off.

Humphrey and Helen both turned to stare at him, not quite with open mouths but clearly waiting for the punch line. "The Feds?" Helen said, after a while.

"Yeah, I'm working for the government these days," Joe answered innocently. "Hey, don't look at me! A guy's gotta make his car payments."

"You're working for the Feds?" Humphrey sounded disbelieving.

"Sorta," Joe said. "I get the feeling I'm still kind of on probation. But they like my work, so far."

"So far," Humphrey said. "You mean the Salt Lake City job."

Joe nodded. "They helped me walk, in Denver. I felt I had to return the favor. I got a new assignment, now." He waited. They waited. Finally, he said, looking at Humphrey: "You."

There was a silence in which the gentle slapping of wavelets against the boat's hull could be heard. It seemed longer than it was. Then Humphrey smiled. "How can I help?" he said.

They all laughed.

The ensuing discussion lasted for at least a couple hours. Fortunately, Humphrey had arranged for a lunch to be put aboard, of cold roast beef, fresh sourdough bread, three excellent cheeses, and a hot chili stew. He explained that this wasn't chili, per se, but a pork stew with root vegetables and chilis. They ate it all.

They ate and laughed and kidded each other, and Helen was pleased to see that Humphrey didn't seem at all disturbed by her obvious physical closeness to Joe. The two of them sat side by side on the banquette in the cabin and she stroked his hands, or his cheek, even kissed him a couple of times. Humphrey seemed easy with this. He smiled and nodded, almost like a real uncle.

Joe told them about Agent Schwind and her friends. He hadn't met the friends yet, but he was pretty sure he knew who was the chief, a guy who went by the name of Colonel Vernon Tucker, presumably a retired Air Force officer, now a federal agent of some kind. Helen was mildly amazed. She remembered the colonel from the incident at her rented house in Salt Lake City. She was curious about the colonel's attitude toward her, naturally. He had actually witnessed the attack by the hit woman Heather, in which Helen had managed to blast the killer.

Joe explained that it was her smurfing of money that had initially caught the attention of the Colonel and his team. They had staked the house out, hoping to rope in a few more confederates in what they saw as a scheme to launder dope proceeds. The intervention of Heather was inexplicable to everyone there, although Joe had encountered her earlier, up in Montana.

It was Humphrey's turn to explain. He swore he'd had nothing to do with Heather. He had explained it all to Helen, much earlier. It had been a faction of the mob that was working against him. This problem had been resolved, more or less, although there were some aspects of it he wanted to discuss further with both of them. The main item for discussion, though, was Joe's relationship with the Colonel and Schwind.

"Basically," Joe said, "they want me to take you out. But they don't put it that way. Not yet. They're a careful bunch. They want me to re-establish myself within your organization. I'm supposed to be some kind of spy. Now, I can tell you I'm not a spy and you can believe me or not, it's up to you. I come to you as a friend. You were always straight with me, F—, er . . . " Joe hesitated.

"You can call me Fat, Joe," Humphrey said amiably. "But only you."

"I'll call you Slim," Joe said. "That's what popped out before, without thinking. Anyway, you and I never had any problems. It was always Carmine. I understood that. But Schwind and the colonel don't know that. They think I've got a real beef with you, but it's something we can work out. Plus they think they have a hold on me, because I'm a fugitive, or maybe they think they can hang the Salt Lake City thing on me. Who knows, if we're talking about convincing a jury, they probably could. They'll have fingerprints on rocket launchers, cars, that sort of thing. They could make a case that I was seeking revenge against Echeverria. The point is: they think they've got leverage here, that I'm their man. They seem to be able to delude themselves, about that and a lot of things. They think they're lonely crusaders against crime, something like that. Me, I don't have any illusions. I'm just Joe Service, at yo' service."

He paused, looking from one to the other of them. When they didn't say anything, he went on: "See, their theory is that beef or no beef, I can get back in with you. I figure they're not so far out in that."

Helen and Humphrey both signaled their acceptance of this assessment.

Joe went on: "Once I'm inside, I'm supposed to feed them info and maybe, ultimately, I take you down." He pointed to Humphrey. "They didn't say anything about you, honey," he told Helen, with a smile. "They're very vague about this. But that's their style. On the one hand they're running this rogue-agent show, but then they're like any bureaucratic operation—it's in their genes, or something. Sometimes, I wonder if they even know what they want. It looks to me like they're trying to be the cowboys *and* the Indians. But here I am. So, what's the situation? How do we get out of this one?"

"It's amazing," Humphrey said, shaking his head. "I couldn't have asked for better."

"Really?" Joe said.

"These people are a gift from the gods," Humphrey said. "Let me explain. I already told Helen a lot a this, but not all of it." He told them he had concluded that the day of the old mob was over. He found it ironic, that he had worked to achieve something, to become someone, only to find upon attaining his goal that the game had irrevocably changed. It was a natural progression of events, he had decided. Times had changed. New people come in, new opportunities arise. New problems arise. If the old organization doesn't address these problems, these opportunities, it gets pushed aside.

"I got nobody to blame but myself," he said. "Well, maybe Carmine, too." He had not been shrewd enough, and Carmine had refused to change. Nowadays, most of the organization's income was derived from essentially legitimate enterprises—with a little of the old scamming and chiseling and muscle applied as part of the new business technique. Nowadays, he claimed, the regular business world had absorbed the mob's techniques, their hard policies. Whatever, he'd had enough of it.

"I'm too old to start over," he said. "But I ain't exactly old. I'm glad I'm still able to enjoy life. What I want is to step out, to pursue my own private interests. I'm outta here, as the kids say. But you guys, you're young, full of drive. You can take this show in any direction you want. Now, I've made some plans, and you can help . . . if you wanta."

Joe didn't seem very comfortable with this. He'd never envisioned himself as a mobster. He wasn't interested in running rackets. Helen wasn't either, not in that sense. She was interested in business, however. They wanted to hear more.

Humphrey looked at them, as if sizing them up, then plunged right in: "First, some old business. I ain't interested in that money Big Sid took. I don't wanta hear no more about it. I got plenty of my own. I made my arrangements. That's all I can say about that, for now. I could use your help, both a you, on a couple details. But you can tell your new friends, Joe, that you seen me and I said we could let bygones be bygones. Maybe that'll satisfy them for now. I think I got it set up, pretty much, so that Helen can step in and run things. It won't be much trouble, for a little while, and then you can figure out whether you wanta go on with it."

Their noncommittal stance didn't seem to bother him. He shrugged and continued. "The thing is, when I say I'm outta here, I mean outta here. There ain't no quiet retirements in this game. I been working out a way so it looks like I copped it. This business with the feds could be a big help. You guys could make it work, if you're willing."

Joe smiled. "Like you say, Slim: 'How can I help?'"

The three men arrived at Humphrey's compound separately, a few minutes apart. The first man was Kenny Malateste. He was thirty years old, a nice-looking fellow with a heavy beard that reappeared within an hour of shaving. He was smiling and flirtatious with Helen, familiar even, although they had met only a couple of times. Already he was holding her arm, talking her ear off. She got him a shot of Humphrey's favorite single malt, from a bottle that had a brown paper label that was hand-lettered—only a few hundred gallons of this whiskey were made in a year, and then put to age for twenty years or more. Helen couldn't pronounce the name. She told Kenny not to tell anyone: Humphrey would kill her if he knew it wasn't Glenfiddich in that glass.

The second man was older, a stocky middle-aged man who looked like a pile of rocks in a blue suit. The broad collar of his yellow sport shirt was spread on his suit-coat lapels, and he wore dully brushed brogans. He had a belligerent face and the manner to match. His name was Leonardo, but he was called Nardo. He stood by himself, rubbing his hands, not nervously but in a habitual manner, flexing his hand, forearm, and upper-arm muscles. He watched everybody, his eyes glittering. He refused whiskey, but asked for a Stroh's. "Bottle," he stipulated.

The third man was also middle-aged, but looked more youthful. He was a smooth, friendly man, well-dressed in a quiet way—a good suit, well cut, and deeply burnished cordovan shoes that could have been made for him. He was called Aldo Soteri. He happily settled for a Scotch and soda.

They stood around chatting for fifteen minutes with Helen and Humphrey and one another, although Nardo barely nodded to the other two guests. The talk was about the Red Wings, the Tigers, the weather, the traffic. Soteri and Helen talked about golf. But soon enough a young male servant, a Filipino, came to the living room and announced that dinner was served.

Dinner was prime rib, a crown roast. The guests looked relieved. They had fearfully anticipated another of Humphrey's peppery preferences. Nothing to fear with prime rib. It was delicious. The Yorkshire pudding was superb, the roast potatoes beautifully caramelized, the carrots done to the very edge of softness, but not quite. The wines were robust, not pretentious, very drinkable. For dessert, there was a delicious puff pastry filled with custard and drenched in chocolate syrup, but Helen and Humphrey did not eat theirs, so neither did the three guests. They all drank the good black coffee, however.

Afterward, back in the living room, they tasted Humphrey's excellent cognac and they seemed delighted with the LaDonna cigars that Helen offered around. She explained that they were, in fact, Cuban in everything but place of manufacture. Nardo, in fact, asked for and promptly received a box to take home. He liked a good Cuban cigar, he said. He was almost amiable.

Business. Humphrey said it was a shame, after a fine evening with friends, but, without business, what did you have? The news was generally good, except for this trouble with the sanitation contracts. Nardo was the garbage man, he should know who was behind these lost contracts. No? Well, Humphrey knew. It was an Armenian bandit named Pelodian, moving in from Cleveland, of all places. This could not stand: Pelodian had to go. If Nardo saw it Humphrey's way, he would take care of it. Nardo saw it just that way. He would take care of it.

"Good man," Humphrey said. "I gotta tell you, it was Helen who figured out who was behind this. The guy's been underbidding our contracts under a dozen names. Here's where you can find him." Humphrey gave Nardo a piece of paper with a couple of addresses on it, one of them circled. Helen said that if those didn't find Pelodian, give her a call, she had a couple of other leads, maybe she could even pinpoint when he would be at one of them.

"Don't worry, lady," Nardo rasped, "I can find the bastard." But then he remembered his manners and said, "Thanks anyway."

On to what Humphrey called "auto reclamation." That after-hours enterprise was booming, they should all emulate Aldo. His new acid technique was amazing. It took a number off the block like Ajax, and the new number was on in a matter of minutes. No muss, no fuss. A little hand for Aldo. They knew it was in fun, so only Humphrey, Helen, and Aldo applauded. Humphrey wanted a word with Aldo, later, so stick around, he said—and to Helen, "Remind me, in case I forget."

Kenny's security service was very productive. Humphrey and Helen wanted to take this opportunity to thank him for increasing his numbers. Just a super piece of work. Only, they'd heard vague reports of problems in the Eight Mile area. What about that? Kenny said, offhandedly, that they'd run into a thing with some Arabs, can you believe it?

Humphrey noted that the world was changing. These Arabs—he'd heard they were Palestinians—they don't got enough trouble in their own country, they gotta come over here and raise hell. Did Kenny know the outfit? Kenny didn't, but he was working on it, don't worry, it'll be taken care of.

So, that was that. Business was good. Humphrey and Helen thanked the guys for coming. The guys thanked them for dinner. Helen reminded Humphrey that he needed to talk to Aldo. The other two left and Aldo joined them in the study. Over a glass of the unpronounceable single malt (could it really be "Choigaloigach"?), Humphrey confided to Aldo that he was not as happy about Kenny's work as he'd let on.

"These Arabs are tougher than he thinks," Humphrey said.

"And they've got a lot of money behind them," Helen added. "This could just be the spearhead of a new invasion. The guy to watch is Hassan. He lives in Dearborn."

"Does Kenny know that?" Aldo asked.

She shrugged. "You know Kenny, if he knew he'd have said so. But he's not like Nardo—you don't hand him a piece of paper. He'll figure it out."

Aldo was clearly pleased to be let in on this inner-circle discussion. But he had little to contribute. He didn't know much about Kenny's field of expertise. It sounded serious. Did Kenny have any input on Humphrey's—and Helen's, he added, with a graceful gesture—personal security?

No, Humphrey assured him. Kenny wasn't really into "security," as such. His work was protection, which you could say was "security"—you had to protect the guys you collected from, but in the way of things, the problem almost never arose. Mainly, Kenny protected his clients from Kenny.

Anyway, that wasn't what they wanted to talk to Aldo about. Did he know there was a chop shop down on—Humphrey turned to Helen—"Where is it? Shoemaker?"

Yes, she confirmed. She gave an address on Shoemaker. Aldo was surprised. He hadn't known. But he'd check on it. Did they know who was running it?

They didn't. They were sure he'd take care of it. Just another encroachment. They were getting a lot of encroachment, these days. They hadn't mentioned it in front of the other guys, because they hadn't been able to check it out, and anyway, they didn't want to interfere. They knew Aldo would want to handle this his way. Maybe it was nothing.

Aldo appreciated their confidentiality. He hated being shown up in front of the guys. A guy like Nardo, his skin was so thick, nothing bothered him. While a Kenny, you couldn't tell him anything.

"Well, just between us," Humphrey confided, "I'm not so sure Nardo isn't slipping. This Armenian, he never coulda made any inroads in the old days. He's smart, too, which you can't exactly say about Nardo. Nardo's a tough cookie, but so is the Armenian. They eat rocks, you know. An Armenian told me that. They can live on rocks! I hope Nardo don't have no trouble."

Aldo was sure he wouldn't. And he'd be on this outlaw chop shop like . . . well, like frosting on a cake.

When he left, Humphrey shrugged. "Well, we warned them. I hope all that wasn't too much of a bringdown, baby," he said to Helen. "I know you're not into all this racket stuff."

No, she'd rather enjoyed it. It was amusing, all the posturing and grandstanding. She found Soteri a pain in the butt, but she thought Kenny was a kick, for all his strutting. She sat on the arm of Humphrey's chair and stroked his hair. She told him he was masterful, very suave. But she wondered if it was wise to take Soteri into their confidence?

"Oh, he might let it get around that we aren't so happy with Kenny and Nardo," Humphrey said, "but that's the point—he'll pass on the information. They need to know, and they ain't exactly the kind of guys you can tell to their face. They get all puffed up and belligerent. Plus, the rest of the guys need to know that we ain't sittin' on our hands, we're a little annoyed. This will put them on edge. Maybe they'll sharpen up."

Helen didn't comment, but she wasn't so sure of the strategy. "Where's Joe?" she asked. She'd held off asking all night.

"I can't have Joe coming here," Humphrey reminded her. "It don't look good. When I'm outta the picture, you can bring in Joe. That's your business. But that's how it's gotta be. I thought you understood that. Say, they liked your cigars."

Helen was pleased. "They're good cigars," she said. "You'll see, this thing will work out."

"Maybe you're right," he conceded. "The operation going all right?"

"Except for Strom," she said. "We should do something about him."

"Okay," Humphrey said. "We'll find something for Strom." He got up. "I'm headin' down to the bunker, play around on the Net."

"The bunker? Where did you get that?" Helen asked.

"I don't know," Humphrey said, thinking. "Well, you know what it is, that's what we called those underground hideouts we had when we were kids: bunkers. Sometimes, we called 'em forts. Pleasant dreams."

Humphrey's bunker was not as modern as one might expect, given the electronic gear installed there. It really was much like a bunker. The house had a perfectly modern full basement, providing more than enough room for the so-called command post. Presently, it housed a small gym, complete with a weight room, a sauna, and another exercise room, where Helen often worked out. There were the usual furnace, laundry, and storage rooms, but they were discreetly partitioned off, along with a temperature- and humidity-controlled wine cellar. Space was given over to a pool table, a Ping-Pong table, and a recreation room for servants, with a large television. And still there would have been room.

For reasons of his own, Humphrey had decided that additional excavation was needed. At the far end of the basement, toward the lake, he'd had a tunnel dug, slanting deeper into the earth. The tunnel was secured by a heavy steel door, practically a vault door, with a locking system to match. The tunnel itself was not the standard eight feet in height but, rather, a mere six feet, which induced at least a slight stooping by most persons who used it. Few did use it. It was also merely thirty inches across, not really wide enough for two people abreast, and it wasn't well lit.

The walls of the tunnel were roughly finished reinforced concrete. The room at the end of this ten-foot-long tunnel, beyond yet another steel door with a heavy lock, was again no more than six feet high, a twenty-by-twenty chamber, a concrete box complete with air-conditioning and venting and fully plumbed with a neatly partitioned shower and bathroom. The walls were concrete sheathed with painted Sheetrock on studs. The floor was covered with an industrial-type indoor/outdoor carpet. The computer equipment was housed in steel racks. There was a queen-sized bed in a partitioned alcove, a refrigerator, a microwave oven, a table and a couple of chairs, a number of television monitors, plus a large TV for recreational viewing. It gave an impression of functionality. The lighting was more than adequate, but was usually kept fairly dim. The whole effect was definitely that of a bunker.

Yet another steel door provided an emergency exit, served by a roughly finished tunnel, less cramped than the house entry—this was how the various appliances and equipment were brought in—leading to a set of steps and another locked steel door that opened on the lawn, discreetly shielded by shrubbery. From this exit to the dock was only a hundred feet.

Humphrey punched in the combination to the lock and let himself in. He went immediately to the long metal desk-counter and dialed a telephone. "That you?" he said. "It's me, yeah. All right, I told him. He'll be coming your way. It's up to you. Okay, I can do the job, but if I do it, you don't get the franchise. We talked about this. You want me to do it, I got no trouble with that. All right, then. What are you bitching about? You do it."

Jon A. Jackson

He hung up and made two more calls, with much the same results. "Okay," he said to himself, when he was finished, "that's that." He grabbed a jacket out of an old wooden wardrobe he'd dragged in, and went out. He took a dark Ford out of the garage and drove out the gate. Fifteen minutes later, he picked up Joe Service. Humphrey went over the plan again, while he drove to the medical offices.

"Leave the computers to me. Like most of these guys, he's got two sets of files, some of it on the computers and some of it still in the usual paper-folder files. You take care of the folders."

"Couldn't you just crack into the computers? What do they call it, 'hack' in?" Joe said. "Why do you have to be along at all?"

"I awreddy did," Humphrey said, "but they got some crypto code, which I didn't know about. The key will be in the office. Anyway, I thought you'd like company."

Joe Service smiled. He felt quite easy, if not exactly relaxed, but he could see that Humphrey was tense and excited. "Been a long time, eh Slim?" he teased.

Humphrey scowled, but then he laughed. "Yah, like the old days. If bein' the boss was more like this, I wouldn't be quittin'. Instead, it's all meetin's, that kinda crap. Guy needs to get out once in a while, get his hands dirty."

Joe wanted to warn him that it wasn't just a lark. That kind of thinking almost always led to trouble. It would be stupid to get caught doing a simple break-in: the consequences could be out of all proportion to the act. Nixon's guys had learned that the hard way. But what could he say?

Dr. Schwartz's offices were typical, in a low brick building with its own parking lot. Humphrey did not park there, but in the much larger lot at Bon Secours hospital, a block away. They casually strolled across the way to Schwartz's offices. The entry was lit, in a kind of sheltered walkway. There was no guard, but there would be an alarm system. There was no money on the premises, not much to attract burglars, and there were frequent patrols.

Humphrey had taken sensible precautions: he knew how the system worked. Doctors often worked late, or had to return to meet a patient, look something up. And Humphrey had a key. He didn't say how he'd gotten it and Joe didn't ask. They simply strolled up, unlocked, and entered. Humphrey punched the requisite numbers into the alarm system, and they went to work.

It was time-consuming, but they did not hurry. Joe found Angelo's records and then Humphrey's. He went to the secretary's desk, located the appropriate forms, where possible, and retyped them. They made little sense to him, mostly numbers, so he made sure that he got them exactly right. The various signatures—there were only a couple—were a little tricky, but he thought that because they were largely hasty scribbles, his duplications would stand up. Where the forms were not available, as with lab reports, he made do with carefully replacing the name tags with labels that were in the secretary's desk and typing in the new name.

While Joe did this, Humphrey attacked the computer files. He soon located the access codes and he knew the technique, but it was more time-consuming than he had reckoned. They were both deeply engaged in the process when the phone rang.

Joe looked across at Humphrey. "The alarm company?" he asked. The phone rang again.

Humphrey considered. "It must be," he said. "Answer it."

"You," Joe said.

The phone rang a third time.

"No, you," Humphrey said.

Joe picked up the phone. "Hi," he said. "Who? Yes, this is Dr. Schwartz. No, I'm not on call. I'm just doing a little work. What is it? Who? Are you a patient? The who? No, you'll have to call Dr. . . . Well, who's on call? Me? You're sure? Well, wait a minute. Give me your number. Where are you? I'll call you right back."

He hung up and looked at Humphrey, a look somewhere between disbelief and bafflement. "Can you believe it? Schwartz is on call. He's got a patient on his way to Bon Secours with a heart attack. They tried his home, but no answer." He glanced at the wall clock: it was after midnight.

"Find his pager number," Humphrey snapped.

"Right."

They both hunted around frantically, looking at rosters, Rolodexes, until Joe found it on a list taped to the side of the secretary's phone. He dialed the number. It was not a pager, but a cellular phone. "Dr. Schwartz!" he said. "You've got an emergency. Heart attack—Mr. Cowan. He's on his way to Bon Secours." He slammed down the phone.

"Let's git," Joe said. "I'm done. If he sees the lights when he drives by . . ."

"I'm almost done," Humphrey said. He stared at the screen before him, pecking out numbers while Joe restored the files to the cabinets. "That'll do it, I just gotta log off."

A minute later they were outside. An ambulance whizzed by as they strolled to the car.

"You know what I forgot?" Joe asked as they got in. "I didn't call that number back, to tell them I was on my way."

"It won't matter," Humphrey said. He started the car. "It's an emergency. He'll be there. Somebody called, he came. Nobody'll even remember."

"The alarm company will have an entry on their log," Joe said. "The alarm was logged off and back on, such and such a date."

"Nobody'll notice. Why should they?"

"I hope you're right," Joe said. He relaxed, then added, almost to himself, "There's always some little thing. Well, what's next, the dentist?"

Humphrey pulled an envelope out of the glove compartment. He tossed it on Joe's lap. "X-rays," he said. "Full set. Just pop 'em in my file and take the others. I already took care of Angelo's."

13

Lucani

Dinah Schwind was wishing that while they had Joe Service in the hospital, they had thought to implant a locator beacon in his ass. She hadn't seen him in days, nor heard from him. She was kicking around in Detroit, visiting various federal agencies, police, just killing time and trying to convince the Colonel, who was in Washington and calling every day, that everything was fine. She had no such confidence. Beyond that, she missed Joe.

Two events tightened her tension. The first was a slaying in Pontiac, a city north of Detroit that doesn't like to think of itself as a suburb, because it had a fairly long separate history. The deceased was a well-known Detroit hood named Kenneth Malateste. He'd been shot in the head in a municipal parking garage. The woman who ran the booth at the entrance told the police that there had been two other men in the car with Malateste, but she hadn't paid much attention to them.

The car had been left, with Malateste lying on the front seat, slumped over. It had been there for several hours before someone noticed that there was blood on the windshield. Obviously, he'd been shot by someone in the back seat. No robbery; his identification and money were left on him. The doors were locked. Of no particular interest to Schwind, when she read the report, was that Malateste had a couple of cigars in his suit-coat pocket, in a plastic bag of the pressure-fastener sort. She was interested, however, in the fact that the victim was considered to be a key enforcer for Humphrey DiEbola, in recent times the administrator of the mob's protection racket.

Two days later, another body was found, another known associate of DiEbola's. This was Wallace Leonardo, a tough waste-removal contractor, popularly called Nardo. He'd been found by some kids playing around a flooded quarry in Lapeer County, north of Detroit. He had been pretty badly battered. The coroner thought his fatal wounds had been inflicted either in falling or by the skull being crushed with rocks. In addition, his abdominal cavity had been cut open and filled with rocks, presumably an attempt to keep the body submerged, but that hadn't sufficed. He had not been robbed. His personal effects were still in his pockets, including a couple of cigars.

Schwind could no longer ignore Joe's failure to report. Colonel Tucker flew into Detroit to confer, along with two other agents from other federal agencies. Counting Schwind and one other man, they constituted the ad hoc group that Schwind had described to Joe. Besides the Colonel and Schwind, the members were Bernie Acker, Dexter Collins, and Edna Swarthout. They had all worked with the colonel in one group or another. They were united in their impatience with bureaucratic bungling and corruption, coupled with a bold willingness to take direct action. Edna Swarthout, who had been with the colonel in his encounter with Joe and Helen in Salt Lake City, had not been able to make the meeting.

They were staying at a hotel in Southfield, in the northwest Detroit metropolitan zone. They conferred in the colonel's room. "Do you think this is Joe's work?" the colonel asked.

Dinah did not think so. She was emphatic. "If you're suggesting that Joe is initiating a campaign, no way," she said. "I never mentioned these men to him, and he's not an enthusiastic killer. I've talked to the police investigators in both cases. These appear to be unrelated killings, by different assailants. The techniques are different. What links them is the relationship to DiEbola and the closeness of events in time. This is either more evidence of the diffusion of criminal hegemony in the Detroit area—a natural consequence of the decline of mob power—or it may be a kind of weeding-out process instigated by DiEbola himself. Neither of these men were considered very staunch allies of DiEbola's, but neither were particular enemies, as far as anyone knows."

"What does Joe say about it?" the colonel wanted to know. Schwind was unable to say. She hadn't heard from Joe. "Well, we better find him," the colonel said.

"Any ideas?" she asked.

"I'd keep an eye on the woman," the colonel said. "He came looking for her in Salt Lake. He must be in communication with her here."

Schwind saw his point. She had been observing local events, but that had not extended to physical surveillance; she was contacting police and other investigative organizations, trying to get a clearer picture of general activity.

They were only a small group, and their activities had to be carried out while ostensibly on other missions. Schwind's presence in Detroit, for instance, was being attributed to a larger investigation of organized crime.

The colonel saw the problem even as he spoke of it. "I'll get you some help," he said. "I'm supposed to be liaising with the INS here. I'll clear it with the director."

Two days later, after tailing Helen to the cigar factory, Schwind was sitting in a surveillance van with a couple of INS agents, parked down the block, when she saw Joe Service enter the building. She wondered what Joe saw in this skinny little woman with too much hair, with that ridiculous silver streak. Some men might find Helen attractive, she supposed, but in her eyes the woman was superficial, affected, pretty but insignificant.

Joe and Helen came out together and took her car to the Renaissance Center hotel. They went up the elevator together. Presumably, one of them had booked a room. They stayed there for more than an hour, then returned to the cigar factory, where Joe got into his car. They followed him in the van to Saint Clair Shores—at first Schwind thought he was going to DiEbola's, but he didn't stop in Grosse Pointe—where he pulled into a parking lot at a marina and entered a restaurant. Schwind went inside.

Joe was waiting for her. He had reserved a table. They sat, looking out over the boats at the lake. He was pleasant and friendly, apologetic for not calling her. "I kinda figured you'd be around," he offered. He had noticed the van when they were coming out Jefferson Avenue. Schwind found it difficult to be annoyed.

When she asked him about the killings he readily volunteered the information they sought. "Humphrey's up to something," he said. "Malateste and Nardo were hit by rivals. I think Humphrey tipped the killers. I don't know what he had against the two. Maybe incompetence, but now he's got a couple of new allies, only they aren't traditional mob guys. Maybe that's his plan, to broaden his base. The thing is, you'd think that it would weaken his support among the traditional guys, but the feeling seems to be that it was another guy, Soteri, who screwed up. Soteri talks a lot. He was telling everybody in town that Kenny and Nardo were screwups, that they couldn't run their own show. I don't know where he got his poop. Maybe Humphrey put him up to it."

Schwind knew who Soteri was, a dealer in stolen cars. She wondered what advantage DiEbola could get from this.

"Malateste was a protégé of Rossamani's, who was one of Carmine's boys," Joe said. "Rossamani was involved in some kind of action behind Humphrey's back, with your buddy Echeverria. He got his when my cabin blew up. Maybe Malateste was thinking of making a move on Humphrey, I don't know. Nardo? He was an all right guy, maybe a little old-fashioned. I heard that his operation was under pressure from outsiders. Maybe they bumped him. Maybe Humphrey sold the franchise. Who knows? Humphrey is very deep."

Schwind digested this. She was very pleased with Joe. He was giving them great stuff, she felt. "What's next?" she asked.

Joe had a theory. "I think Soteri's in trouble. The mob guys don't like him. Things are changing around here. A lot of incompetent people are getting weeded out. It looks like Humphrey is building a leaner, more effective mob."

"Who else?"

Joe told her about Mongelo's disappearance. "Word is, he was run off," Joe said, "several weeks ago. He hasn't been seen. But they say that he was an old friend of Humphrey's, they were kids together. The word is, he got paid off and told to retire. Rumor says he went to the Bahamas, or maybe even farther."

"Another step toward the New Look?" Schwind offered.

"Trimming the fat," Joe said. "I guess Humphrey is remaking his organization in his own image. You might want to keep an eye on Soteri. They say he's making a move on some rivals." He gave her an address on Shoemaker.

Schwind, grateful as she was, still naturally wanted to know his sources. Joe said he'd gotten some of it from just talking to Humphrey; other pieces had come from conversations with a variety of old Detroit hands. None of it was ironclad, just speculation, but it sounded plausible. When you saw Arab gangs operating Malateste's business without retaliation by DiEbola, or the Armenian prospering in the suburbs, you had to conclude that the rumors were valid. But who knows? Maybe Humphrey was biding his time. Maybe he'd crack down.

"How are you getting along with Helen?" Schwind asked.

"All right," Joe said. She couldn't tell if he had been aware that he'd been followed to the Renaissance. "Helen's okay."

"What's her role in all this?"

"She's Humphrey's new pal," he said. "Well, he's known her since she was a kid. He relies on her to take care of the legitimate side. She's pretty capable, you know."

"Just the legitimate side?" Schwind said.

"Yeah," Joe said. "What are you doing for dinner?"

"What did you have in mind?"

"Do you like Arab food?" he asked. "I heard about a place in Dearborn."

"I'd be delighted. I'm sure the colonel would like to join us, and a couple of other guys. It'd be a good opportunity for you to meet the Lucani."

Joe raised an eyebrow.

"That's what we call ourselves," Schwind explained. "It's from Lucania, a province in Italy. DiEbola is supposedly from there."

"It's a date," Joe said.

Dinner was great, if you like tabbouleh and that sort of thing. The colonel was very affable, as were Acker and Collins. The colonel was congratulatory about Joe's progress. He made no direct reference to their encounter in Salt Lake City, when Joe had thwarted an operation aimed at breaking up Helen's attempts to smurf the cash that she and Joe had taken, but he asked after "the lovely Miss Sedlacek."

Joe took this opportunity to say that he would have no part in any operation that targeted Helen. The colonel was quick to allay his fears. "We have no interest in Helen Sedlacek," he said. "You have my word on that."

Joe noticed that Schwind looked steadfastly at her plate.

They were eating some kind of spicy goat stew when the colonel got a call on his cell phone. There had been a shoot-out on Shoemaker. Aldo Soteri was dead. There were some federal agents on the scene. The colonel suggested they all take a run across town. Joe didn't think that was such a good idea. It wouldn't be good for him to be seen in their company. The Lucani conceded the point.

Sometime earlier, at about the moment the Lucani were sampling the tabbouleh, Humphrey was at the cigar factory. He'd asked Strom to meet him there.

They met at the loading dock. Strom was alone, as was Humphrey.

"Where's your boys?" Strom asked.

"They had work to do," Humphrey said. It was dark, just a few minimal lights. The parking lot and loading area were empty. "Don't you have a watchman?" Humphrey asked.

"Don't need one," Strom said. "This ain't a great neighborhood to be out in at night, and the guys who make it not such a great neighborhood know who runs this biz. They don't fuck with us. Besides, you got your boy downstairs, watching Mongelo. If anybody tries to break in, he can tend to it."

"That's not why he's here," Humphrey pointed out, "but never mind. Let's go see Monge. You got a piece?"

"Sure," Strom said. He patted his breast.

They went down to the basement. The guard was a young fellow from the potato chip factory. He didn't speak English. He was sitting outside the cage, watching a porno movie through the bars, with Mongelo. He jumped up when they approached. Humphrey's Italian was poor, but he managed to convey to the young man that he was relieved, he could go.

After he left, Humphrey told Strom to leave him and Mongelo alone, but not to go too far. He was unarmed, he said, and while he didn't expect Mongelo to make any trouble, it wouldn't do to give him too much slack.

"Why'dja let the kid go?" Strom said.

"None a your business," Humphrey said. "I gotta talk to Monge. Just back off, but stay handy. Capisce?"

When they were alone, Humphrey unlocked the cage and went in. He could see Mongelo was edgy. "Relax," he said. "Listen, this is it. You're gettin' outta here." That didn't seem to relax Mongelo. Obviously, he was thinking that "gettin' outta here" might mean something final. Humphrey tried to calm him.

"You're lookin' good, Monge. I'm proud a ya." It was true. Mongelo looked ten years younger. He had lost over a hundred pounds. He looked better than he'd looked in . . . well, ever.

But he was a chronic complainer. Tonight, it was the fillings that Humphrey's dentist had put in. They had gone to the dentist a few days earlier. The dentist hadn't been a very fancy one. Mongelo had been surprised that Humphrey would go to such a sleazebag dentist, but Humphrey had assured him that he'd been going to this guy forever. And the guy had found some cavities that Mongelo didn't know were there. His teeth were fine, he'd thought, but the dentist said no. All those X-rays, before and after! Who takes X-rays after? But that was what made this guy so good, he was told: he X-rayed after to be sure the fillings were right and all the decay removed. Mongelo was still sore, though.

"Monge, forget the dentist," Humphrey said. "I told you I was having trouble, remember? Well, now I need you with me. I want you to come to my place. I got a 'partment all fixed up for you. Together, we'll fix these bastards that are ratting us out."

"Who is it? D'you find out?"

"I got a line on them. Malateste was one. I took care a him," Humphrey said. "But there's others. We'll discuss it. So, you ready to go?"

Mongelo was ready.

"Can I count on you?" Humphrey asked, fixing him with a sharp look. Mongelo said he was ready. He was Humphrey's man.

Humphrey called out to Strom. When he loomed up in the light, Humphrey beckoned him in. "Give me your piece," he said. Strom looked surprised, but readily pulled out his gun. It was an automatic, a nice, flat, compact .38. He handed it to Humphrey, who held it on the flat palm of his gloved hand. Then he turned to Mongelo.

Mongelo's eyes grew round. His mouth fell open. But then Humphrey handed the gun to him. He nodded toward Strom. "Do him," Humphrey said.

Strom whirled and started away, but Mongelo did not hesitate. He blasted Strom down with three quick shots. Strom's body sprawled on the concrete, in the semidarkness. The shots had reverberated in the chamber, but there was no response in the silence that followed. No one had heard a thing.

Mongelo stood outside the cage, staring down at the body. Humphrey took the gun from his hand and dropped it into a plastic bag. "We'll get rid of this," he said. "C'mon, let's get outta here. Leave him."

In the parking lot, Humphrey explained that Mongelo would have to ride in the trunk. "Boss, I don't wanta," Mongelo said.

Humphrey produced a revolver from his pocket. "Get in the trunk, Monge," he said. "Trust me. I ain't gonna hurt you. It's only, you can't be seen."

Mongelo got in the trunk. Humphrey drove home. When they passed through the gate, Humphrey stopped to tell the gate man that he was home for the night. He drove around to the other side of the house, toward the boat slip, and parked. He went into the house. The watch commander was at the console. "Go relieve the gate," Humphrey said. "Tell him to go to the relief room. I might have a visitor tonight and I don't want nobody around. I'll give you a call."

When the man left—it wasn't John, tonight—Humphrey switched off the monitors. He went down to the bunker, let himself in, then went out through the emergency exit. He got Mongelo out of the trunk. "See?" he told him. "It's all right. I told you."

When they were in the bunker, Humphrey showed him around and explained a few things. He had to understand that he was there in secret. It was crucial. The rats in the organization couldn't know he was on watch. Nobody would know. Together they'd root those bastards out. Mongelo seemed ready. The bunker was not luxurious, but it was better than the cage. There was plenty of movies, plenty of food.

14

Mouse Hole

Much to his surprise, Humphrey found Mongelo to be an amiable companion. They had known each other all their lives and had more in common than Humphrey cared to admit. Considering the bums they'd hung out with, the fiascoes they'd endured in common, this wasn't necessarily a happy congruence. But they had an enormous fund of mutual experience. Down in the bunker, they worked out together on the fancy machines that Humphrey had installed: StairMaster, treadmill, weight machines. It was good that the ventilation system was so effective, but it was certainly being fully tested. Even the copious numbers of LaDonna cigars that they smoked could not daunt this system.

Humphrey appreciated a situation in which he was free of just about any social constraints. They swore, farted, belched, made scurrilous comments about everybody, speculated on who was on his last legs and who was still getting it up. They bragged about monstrous acts and indulged each other's exaggerations and bullshit. It was all quite harmless and foolish, and after a while it palled on them both, although both continued to make tired gestures at it, to keep up the pretense of youthful exuberance.

But soon enough, Humphrey remembered why he had always disliked Mongelo: the man had an appallingly narrow focus. You could start him on a track and he was like the bunny in the television ad: he just kept banging away until he was redirected.

In the evening, after Mongelo had finally sunk into a snoring sleep, Humphrey would take care of his electronic business. He did some of it during the day, but it wasn't easy, with Mongelo hanging around, yapping and watching amazingly sordid pornography all day on the VCR. Humphrey had not bargained for this. He was glad it wasn't going to last long.

One thing he needed was for Mongelo to wear his clothes, all of them, and to take showers, to leave his hair and sloughed skin everywhere. Humphrey had some of it cleaned up and bagged, as he'd been doing from the start, when Mongelo was in the cage at the cigar factory. He washed this crud down his own drains upstairs, sprinkled hair on his old hairbrushes, and kept the sheets Mongelo slept on. It was all part of the big plan.

He was happy to see Helen and Joe getting along so well and taking more interest in the operations, although Joe kept pretty clear of that end. Joe had a profound distaste for the prosaic drudgery of business. He could work pretty hard at something that directly concerned his own well-being, but he wasn't much for financial intricacies. They did get into a conversation once about the possibility of setting up what Joe called "hospices" for AIDS victims, ones in the terminal phase. But here again, Joe seemed to think there were great possibilities in it, for himself. Humphrey couldn't see it: it was too much trouble for the prospective value of having a ready supply of dead folks who could inherit and leave money—an overelaborate money-washing scam.

Humphrey was busily collecting money and transferring it to offshore accounts, much of it from new franchisees for old mob operations—Russians, Arabs, various South Americans. He was also putting the finishing touches to his grand exit strategy. One of these touches, perhaps the most crucial, was selecting Mongelo's executioner. For this, in a step that he found wonderfully appropriate, he drew in Mongelo himself.

Mongelo was eager to help, idle as he was, and unaware as he necessarily was of the true end of the process. Together they pored over information that Humphrey had carefully compiled on personnel in the organization. The ostensible purpose was to determine who were the traitors, the rats, and who were their allies and fellow conspirators. Mongelo was very useful here, doggedly sifting through lists, relating anecdotes, remembering who had done what. He knew everybody, knew their backgrounds, and by now was thoroughly into a paranoiac frame of mind.

Mongelo agreed that Nardo was a traitor. "I was allus 'spicious of da bastid," he said. "He was such a fuckin' hard-ass. He never had much to say f'hisself, an' nothin' good about nobody else." He approved of the way that Humphrey had set it up, having him beaten to death with rocks and thrown into a stone quarry. That would point the finger at the Armenian, all right.

As for Kenny Malateste, he'd never liked the punk. "What a fuckin' wiseass," he said, "thought he could screw any bimbo walkin'. You ast me, these guys, some a them, all they think about is gittin' their ashes hauled, they don't take care a bidniss. Well, he's gittin' his ashes hauled now." Mongelo was a little curious if Kenny had actually been popped by the Arabs; Humphrey just winked, and Mongelo nodded with a little smile.

Soteri? What a bum! Always talkin' down the next guy. Mongelo was surprised the jerk had lived as long as he had. As for the late Strom Davidson, well, Mongelo could see it had to be done and he was glad to have been of assistance.

Mongelo spotted, without much prompting, what all these guys had in common. They were all allies of the late "Rossie"

Rossamani, one of Carmine's old buddies. Who else was in that circle? Mongelo named a dozen guys. They went over them, one by one. By and large, they were okay fellas, capable enough, seemingly loyal to Humphrey, not too upset with Carmine's demise, and none of them in a position to do any harm. Who could the rat be? Who to pin the tail on?

At last they came to two figures, John Nicolette and Matty Cassidy. Nicolette was particularly interesting because he was married to Rossamani's widow's sister. Humphrey hadn't known that. In fact, the only reason he was on the list (although he hadn't told Mongelo this) was because he was the crew chief of the security group that had been working the night Pepe had disappeared. He now became the number one candidate.

Humphrey shook his head, marveling. "Imagine that," he said, "the devious bastards! The guy who is actually supposed to be watching my back turns out to be one of the traitors. It's a wonder he didn't cut my throat while I was sleepin'."

They had to do something about Nicolette, that was for sure. And Matty Cassidy. Matty was the guy who had brought the killer Heather to Rossamani, who'd suggested her to Humphrey as someone who could take care of Joe Service. She had come close to succeeding, and she'd almost taken down Helen, as well. Humphrey didn't mention any of this to Mongelo. But it was clear that Matty was another old Rossie buddy and he'd have to go.

"How do you want to handle it, boss?" Mongelo asked.

Humphrey had a plan, but he pretended to think. Finally, he said, "We'll have 'em down here. I don't want to take them out unless I'm sure they're guilty. They oughta have a chance to tell us their side, anyway. With these other guys, Nardo and them, I had them in before you came in on this, and I kinda felt them out. And you know from your own experience, I like to give a guy a chance to do what's right."

Mongelo thought that was pretty white of Humphrey. "You just ask 'em right out, eh? An' then, if they 'fess up, you . . . ah, what do you do then?"

Humphrey had to laugh. "It don't work that way, Monge. You ask 'em about somethin' else, some kinda innocent questions, then, when they're kinda relaxed, you lay it on 'em. See how they react. That's where it all comes down. A guy can kinda show his hand, sometimes. Sometimes, you don't learn nothin'. But, you at least gave 'im a chance. So then you gotta fall back on what you learned. You make your decision. That's about it."

Mongelo was impressed. This was a valuable management tip. He was pleased to have a suggestion when Humphrey asked what he thought would be a good excuse to ask the guys in. "A card game," he said.

"A card game?" Humphrey suppressed a smile. But then he saw that Mongelo wasn't so stupid. Matty was a gambler. He'd had to cough it up for Mongelo at least once, for getting in too deep. They'd invite Matty and then, just to fill out the table, they'd get Nicolette down from his post. It was ideal. An evening of poker, a lot of talk, plenty of beer, maybe even a little pizza—he could see Mongelo salivating. Small talk that turns a little serious, maybe revealing.

"An' we could prob'ly win a coupla bucks, too," Mongelo suggested. Humphrey laughed.

Things were getting close. Humphrey had a world of details to take care of. He was sending men out left and right, all hours of the day and night. On one occasion, just to get away from the fug in the bunker and Mongelo's monomaniacal drivel, he and Helen took a moonlight jaunt out on the lake to meet Joe.

This time they met in midlake and tied up together out of the shipping lanes. It was a great place to meet, a beautiful warm night. Humphrey told them over coffee that he was getting a little frazzled, but things were going well. The thing that worried him, though, was that Mulheisen seemed to be getting somewhere on the Hoffa case. If he could just hold him off for a day or two.

Joe didn't see much of a problem. "Just put him off, give him a little something, send him on a wild-goose chase. What do you care what he finds out? You'll be gone."

"I sure hope so," he said.

Helen watched him. Suddenly, she said, "This whole thing is about Hoffa, isn't it?"

Humphrey equivocated. "Not exactly. Well, maybe. I always knew it would blow up one day. It was a mistake, a big mistake. You can't . . . well, let me put it this way: you can maybe cover something like this up, but there's gotta be a payback, somewhere down the line. So, yeah, it's Hoffa, but it's all the other crap I been telling you about. So, I'm doing what Mac kinda showed me, when he was talking about Borgia and them. You gotta know when to fold your tent. I'm folding. But I'll be damned if I'm gonna leave the business in the hands of these pricks we got around us nowadays. I'm gonna clean up some a this trash."

More than that Humphrey would not say. He firmed up his plans with them, to the extent that he wanted them to know them, anyway. On the big night, Joe would wait for Humphrey pretty much where they were right now. Helen did not like this plan, Humphrey knew, but she kept her peace. She would not be involved. That was crucial. She would stay to deal with the aftermath, and when that was accomplished . . . well, it was up to her and Joe.

"I give you kids my blessing," Humphrey said. "Whatever you decide, I'm sure it'll be for the best."

The next day, in an amusing little performance at the Krispee Chips offices, Humphrey and Helen met with Mulheisen and gave him the very strong impression that they were lovers. It was a bittersweet act for Humphrey, one of the few occasions when he'd actually had his hand up Helen's skirt. He'd miss that, he thought, an intriguing possibility there. But he knew he didn't stand a chance as long as Joe Service was around.

Still, Mulheisen had jarred him. The detective was much closer than he'd realized. Humphrey had left things dangerously tight. It was time to set it all in motion.

The day before, he had invited Matty Cassidy for poker, tonight. When the gambler appeared, Humphrey talked to him in his study, prior to joining Mongelo downstairs. They were alone. He needed Matty's help, he explained. He had Mongelo downstairs, he said. The guy had been ill, he was a little crazy. Well, everyone knew Mongelo was nuts. He'd taken the guy in, nursed him. Now, whaddaya think? He had discovered that Mongelo was out to whack him.

"Jeeziss," Matty said, "and you got him right here, in the house?" He looked around nervously.

"I'm not worried," Humphrey said, "just careful. I got my eye on him. Only, I can't have no guns in the room. You understand."

Matty understood, but he said, "What if Mongelo's got a gun hidden somewheres? Wouldn't it be better if I could back you up?"

Humphrey nodded. "Good thinking. I tell you what, give me your piece. I'm not really worried about Monge, you know, but if he gets a little squirrelly, like if you're winning too much—which you prob'ly will be, if I know you . . ." He smiled at Matty.

"Monge never could play cards worth a shit," Matty said, chuckling.

"Yeah," Humphrey agreed. "But if he gets actin' crazy, I'll slip the iron to you. Maybe we could pull that old gag, stashin' it in the john. We'll see. If I get up and go to the john, you go in next. The gun'll be in the drawer of the washstand. Anyways, I'll have Johnny Nicolette down to play. He's the night man here. You know him?" Matty had met him, but they weren't well acquainted. "John won't be armed either, but between the three of us, we won't have any problems. The guy is actually a lamb, I really don't expect no trouble, Matty. But I figured, better safe than sorry. If he gets excited . . . you just don't know with psychos." Humphrey patted Cassidy on the shoulder.

"The guy is sick," Humphrey explained. "He's a little pissed at me because I did what hadda be done, I locked him up, kept him under wraps. It was for his own good, but he can't see that. The guy was a walkin' time bomb. But he needs a little break. I want the guy to have a little fun, he's been cooped up so long with this . . ." He whirled his finger around his ear. "Just keep your eyes open and we'll have a good time."

Matty handed over his gun, a 9mm Glock. Humphrey stuffed it into his belt and pulled his bulky cable-knit sweater over it. "Make yourself a drink," he told Matty. "I gotta talk to John, he's working the console. We'll go down in a few minutes."

Humphrey went directly to the control room, carrying a box of cigars. "John, we're gettin' up a poker game, downstairs. We need another hand." He glanced at the monitors. "Things are quiet, why don't you come on down?"

Nicolette looked pained. "Gee, Mr. DiEbola, I'd love to, but I'm kinda light just now."

"No problem," Humphrey assured him. "I didn't expect you to spend your own money. Here." He got out his wallet and thumbed off five hundred dollars in fifties. "Play with this. If you lose it, forget it. If you win, you can pay me back and keep the winnings. If you need more, just give me the nod. No, no. You're doing me a favor."

"Great! But what about the—" He gestured at the monitors.

"I'll tell you what," Humphrey said. "You go around, check everything out, and . . . oh yeah, be sure the dogs are in. It could get kinda stuffy down there, if we're all puffing away on cigars, and I wanta leave the passageway open to the yard, get a little fresh air.

I'll open up the yard door and you can come down that way. And don't say nothing to the other guys, eh? I don't want anybody thinking I'm favoring one guy over another, you see what I mean? The patrol guys can hang in the relief room, maybe they'll get up their own game. Who knows? The gate man can handle things. Anyways, you can keep an eye on the monitors down there. Oh, and one more thing—I told these guys no guns down there, so don't bring your piece."

"Won't that look kind of odd?" Nicolette said. "I mean, I'd have to leave it in the safe, in the relief room."

Humphrey thought for a moment, as if stumped, then said, "Tell you what. I'm glad you're careful. I'm careful, too. Maybe it would be better if your gun was handy. Let me have it. I'll stash it in this cigar box." He opened the box and scooped out the cigars, tossing them onto the desk. "I'll carry this box down there. You'll see it on the counter. Anything crazy happens, you can grab it. Okay?"

"What if someone wants a cigar, opens the box?"

"There's a couple boxes down there already. I'll make sure they're open. They'll be handy. Nobody'll bother this one. They won't even notice. It'll be where you can see it."

So that was settled. The gun fit nicely into the box. John said he'd start his rounds right away and he should be able to join them in fifteen minutes or so, when he got the dogs and the patrols settled in the security quarters. Humphrey told him to take his time. He went to collect Matty and they went downstairs in the conventional way. Matty was very impressed with the security arrangements.

Mongelo greeted Matty like a long-lost friend. He was clearly pleased to see a fresh face. He gave him an embrace that clearly included a weapons check.

Matty smiled, confidently. "I can't believe how skinny you are, Monge," he said. Then, remembering that the man had been ill, he said, "You feelin' all right?"

Mongelo frowned. "I feel great. How 'bout you?"

They popped open a couple of Stroh's and sat talking while Humphrey went to the desk to call for refreshments. "Guys," he called over his shoulder, "I gotta go up to get the pizza. The help has already gone home. Help yourselves to more beer, or whatever. I'll be back in a minute."

He went upstairs quickly. John was out. He could see him on the various monitors, making his rounds, getting the dogs in. He went to Helen's room. "You all set?" he asked her.

"I'm staying," she said.

Humphrey shook his head.

"I can do it," she said. "You know I can do it."

Humphrey looked at her. "Got your Hatchet Puss on," he said. But it was too late. He hadn't told her all his plans; they didn't include her. Still, he owed her something. "I know you jumped in the car and blasted Carmine," he said. "You can do it. But you don't want to. You don't want this racket."

"Maybe I changed my mind," she said.

"Too late, babe. Get outta here."

She saw how it was. "I'll be at Mama's, if anything goes wrong."

He nodded. "Go to Soke. You gotta be away from here. You gotta establish that. Make sure somebody else is there, as a witness."

She kissed him. "You're something else, Unca Umby."

"Yeah, yeah." He was embarrassed now. "I'll miss you baby. But . . . what the hell. This is the way to go. You take care of yourself."

"Say hi to Joe," she said.

"You say hi yourself," he replied. "You'll see him soon enough. Listen, I gotta go. I'm choking up, here." He kissed her again and they went out together.

The last she saw of him, before she went out the door, he was picking up a huge tray filled with pizzas. He had tucked a box of LaDonnas under his arm, saying, "The guys'll like these."

* * *

Roman Yakovich had made up his mind. Mrs. Sid had told him that Helen was coming over. She had invited some of her lady friends. They were going to have a good, old-fashioned hen party. She had cooked innumerable little goodies, *flancate*, walnut *povitica*, *priganica*. She prepared a selection on a plate for Roman and told him to get lost. "Go watch your hockey game," she said.

From his upstairs window, Roman watched Helen and the women arrive. When they were starting to laugh and gabble downstairs, he crept out the back way and drove to DiEbola's house. What he had seen in recent weeks had troubled him greatly. DiEbola was making a fool of himself over Helen. Roman had seen this sort of thing before. A rich and powerful older man can have his way with many a young woman, but not with the Little Angel. He would be polite; he would be respectful; but Mr. DiEbola must know that Little Helen was not one of these silly girls that he could tamper with.

At the gate the guard would not let Roman in. He recognized him, all right, and he knew that Roman was an old friend of Mr. DiEbola's, but the boss was entertaining guests. No, he would not call the house. Mr. DiEbola had personally given him strict orders: no one was to be let in. No one. Sorry.

The guard stood within the ornamented steel gates, wisely out of arm's reach. Roman stalled, a hulking bundle of a man with long arms stuffed into the sleeves of his suit coat like sausages. He stared around the area, looking toward the distant house, which was not visible from here. He seemed lost. Finally, the older man said, "He got women in there?"

The young guard sneered. "Sure, he's got women. Miz Helen went out for the night, so he ordered in a buncha whores. He's having a fuckin' orgy. Now get lost, old-timer." He stood and watched until Roman got back in his car and drove away. Then he went back into the guard booth, to his girlie magazine.

Roman drove several blocks away, then stopped when he came to a small stone bridge over a canal. He parked the car and walked back to the canal, then followed a path alongside it toward the lake. Several large estates had boathouses on the canal, he saw. These estates, like DiEbola's, were well fenced, and the boathouses effectively blocked anyone from walking farther. But a lovely little skiff was tied up to the piling of one of the houses. He would have to wade in the dark water to get to it, and he had no idea how deep it was, but he was determined.

The water was well over his waist. And it was cold. But Roman was not daunted. He waded to the boat and nearly swamped it crawling in, his gun in his hand, to keep it dry. It was a huge cannon, a .44 magnum revolver. He set it on the thwart before him and began to row out toward the lake.

It took him the better part of an hour to find the slip at DiEbola's. He had noticed that the dogs were not out, so he didn't worry about them, and he had no notion of patrols anyway, so that didn't concern him. Nonetheless, he was quiet about rowing up to DiEbola's sleek, low-slung cruiser and tying up. He clambered onto the dock and then walked across the lawn.

What luck! Some kind of cellar door was open, light spilling out and illuminating a faint haze that rose from the opening. It was cigar smoke; Roman smelled it. The opening was not attached to the big house, but from the voices—among them DiEbola's—he realized that he had found his man.

Humphrey glanced at the clock on the desk. It was a glowing red digital-readout device. It was 9:48, time to start the ball rolling. In fact, the ball had been rolling for some time. He had initiated a series of sly digs at Matty, mentioning the late Rossamani, and as he had expected, Mongelo had taken it up. Unlike Humphrey, Mongelo was wont to be less than subtle.

"That fuckin' Rossie, what a prick," Mongelo said, "and he was fuckin' queer, too. Gimme two fuckin' cards, you little chiseler."

Matty was dealing. He looked at Humphrey nervously. Humphrey smiled and nodded. Matty dealt. "Rossie wasn't queer," Matty muttered.

Mongelo looked at his cards and threw them down with disgust. "Jeeziss, what a shit hand. You deal like you fuck, you little prick. Sure, Rossie was queer. Maybe you are too. You deal like a fuckin' pansy." He sat back and stared, daring Matty to respond.

Before Matty could say anything, Humphrey showed three jacks, whereupon John triumphantly slapped down a full house, aces and eights. It was a big pot and John crowed, "Come to me you sweet things" as he raked it in.

"Whatta you so happy about?" Mongelo demanded of him.

John shrugged, unfazed, and nodded toward his full house. "If you can't beat it, you gotta eat it," he said with a laugh.

"Now you're callin' me a fuckin' pansy," Mongelo challenged him.

Humphrey put a hand on his shoulder, rising. "Take it easy, Monge. It's just cards. I gotta piss. You keep an eye on these crooks, make sure they don't steal anything." Behind Mongelo's back, when John was stacking his chips, he made a curt gesture with his head toward the bathroom, to Matty. When he returned a moment later, he nodded again and was pleased to see Matty got the message.

"My turn," Matty said, getting up to go to the bathroom. He would find the Glock there. Humphrey was all but certain that he would not check the magazine; that would make too much noise.

"Don't be playing with your dick in there," Mongelo bellowed after him. "You'll get the cards all sticky."

"Up yours," Matty retorted and shut the door.

John laughed and picked up the cards to shuffle. Humphrey nudged Mongelo's leg under the table. That was the first sign. Mongelo let his hand drop to his knee and then advanced it slightly under the hanging edge of the green felt table cover. He would be able to grasp the grip of the .38 taped there.

There were two bullets in this gun. Humphrey had given this number a good deal of thought. Would two be enough? Or too many? He figured that Mongelo would shoot Matty first. Then he'd try to shoot Nicolette, assuming that he actually hit Matty with his first shot. If he didn't hit him, he would surely fire again. Then he'd try to shoot Nicolette.

Or, Humphrey thought, he'll try to shoot me. Not likely. Mongelo trusted him, he was into the game.

What would happen next, however, couldn't really be predicted. Humphrey had read somewhere, maybe in Machiavelli, that after the first shot all battle plans change. But they wouldn't change much, of that he was confident. Nicolette had only one bullet.

Matty came out of the bathroom. He looked more assured. He had found the Glock. Humphrey didn't need to look at his face: he could see the bulge in his pocket. The idiot had put the gun in his pocket! Of course; he had removed his suit jacket. He had no other good place to put it, except in his waistband, under his shirt, and then he wouldn't be able to get at it easily. So he had his hand in his pocket, as if to mask the presence of the gun.

Nicolette didn't notice. He was shuffling cards. But Mongelo noticed. His eyes flickered toward Humphrey, who smiled. So this was it. The curtain was going up. Humphrey rose immediately and went around Mongelo toward the desk-counter, where the clock and the monitors were, the cigar box—and the Bushmaster he'd stashed last night. He didn't even look at the monitor, which would have shown him Roman Yakovich, stealthily descending the steps from the lawn.

"You son of a bitch!" Mongelo roared. He jumped up, knocking the table away, holding the .38.

Matty yanked the Glock out of his pocket, but he never got a chance to fire. Mongelo's bullet hit him in the chest, knocking him backward. The din of the shot was shocking to the ears, but Humphrey didn't notice. He scrambled for the Bushmaster, ready to hand in a desk drawer. In the same moment he slid the cigar box down the counter, toward Nicolette, who was reaching for it when Mongelo's second shot struck him in the back.

Nicolette fell to the floor but managed to carry the cigar box down with him. He fished out the pistol. He almost pulled the trigger on Mongelo, but he heard the click of Mongelo's empty gun just in time. Mongelo stared down at the gun in disbelief, then at Nicolette.

Nicolette said, "Drop it."

Humphrey said, "Shoot!" He pointed at Mongelo.

Both men turned to look at Humphrey. Then Roman's arm came through the door and he shot Mongelo. The .44 made a much bigger racket than the .38 had. Mongelo was flung backward, crashing into the treadmill.

Nicolette fired at Roman, but he had a very poor angle and Roman was all but hidden in the door opening. The bullet ricocheted off the concrete wall and zinged around the room like an atomic wasp. Roman pumped two shots into the security man. The blasts tossed the body back under the counter.

The smoke lay in dense reefs—cigars and gunfire. Roman was only dimly visible to Humphrey, who considered blowing him away with the Bushmaster. Instead, he suddenly realized he'd been hit himself. He didn't feel any pain, not exactly, but a shock. It must have been the ricochet. The bullet would have been badly deformed, doubtless fragmented. It had hit him in the right side, in the ribs, about three inches below his right breast. He wasn't sure if it had penetrated deeply, but there was blood.

"Jesus!" he cried, "I'm fuckin' hit!"

Roman lumbered forward hesitantly, still holding the .44 before him.

"Watch whatcher doin' with that thing," Humphrey barked. "Here, help me. I feel a little woozy." He had his right arm clamped against his side. He slid down to the floor, sitting in a puddle of spilled beer. "This ain't workin'," he said.

Roman peered through the smoke, waving the gun as if to clear the haze.

Humphrey was having trouble staying conscious. "What the fuck are you doing here?" he said.

Roman spoke, almost casually: "I come to talk to you."

"What about?"

"Liddle Helen. You gotta leave her alone." Roman was stern, reproving.

"I am leaving her alone," Humphrey said. "I'm leaving every-body alone. What do you think all this is about?" He gestured weakly with his left hand, at the bodies. "I'm leaving town. But I need a little help."

Roman couldn't take it in. Who could? "Leaving?" he said. "For good?"

"For good or bad," Humphrey said. "Give me a hand, here."

Roman jammed the .44 into his holster and stooped to hoist Humphrey to his feet. He helped him to the door, practically carrying him. But Humphrey stopped at the passageway.

"No," he said, "we gotta make it look right." He leaned against the doorjamb and directed Roman to drag Nicolette's body up the passageway and outside. Humphrey followed. He felt better in the fresh air. He looked around. Nothing. No sounds. No lights. No sign that anyone had heard a thing. He had been certain that they wouldn't.

"Can you get him to the boat?" Humphrey asked. Roman nodded and hoisted the body onto his shoulder. Humphrey waited. He tried to examine the wound, but it was too awkward, too dark. Nonetheless, he felt reassured. He could breathe all right. He was afraid of shock, but he wasn't bleeding too badly. He told himself he'd be all right.

When Roman returned they went back downstairs. Humphrey ignored the sprawled bodies, for the moment. He scanned the monitors. There was no activity. The man on the gate was reading a magazine. Nothing was stirring.

Not even a mouse, he thought, or a rat.

He had a few tasks for Roman, such as smashing quart canning jars filled with gasoline on the floor, especially around Mongelo. He had a nice little bomb, packed into a cigar box. He managed to kneel and clasp Mongelo's hands around it.

What next? He glanced around, picked up Nicolette's service revolver, and stuck it in his pocket. He wiped the Bushmaster and put it into Matty's right hand and closed the fingers, then tugged his left hand over to grasp the receiver, then let the gun fall away.

A few other touches . . . time to go. Roman helped him up the passageway, up the steps to the lawn, and let him sit. Then at Humphrey's direction he went back down the passageway with a Molotov cocktail. A moment later, there was a muffled *whump!*

A moment after that, smoke roared out of the passageway, followed by a coughing Roman. The bomb had gone off quicker than he'd expected. Roman was almost clear of the passageway, but the blast actually knocked him down. He got up and scrambled out onto the lawn. Together they hobbled to the slip.

Humphrey struggled aboard while Roman cast off the lines to the cruiser, then jumped down into the cockpit, treading on the body of Nicolette. Humphrey had started the engine and they pulled away. Flames billowed out of the hole in the ground, lighting up the night. Humphrey heard a splintering and a crushing noise.

"What the fuck is that?" he yelled.

"The liddle boat," Roman said.

They left the wreckage sinking at the end of its painter at the slip and roared out into the lake. Fifteen minutes later, they idled up next to Joe's boat.

"What happened?" Joe called out. He jumped into their boat to help. He and Roman got Humphrey into the other boat.

"I fucked up," Humphrey said. "Get my bag. Here." He handed Joe another jar of gasoline. "Break that in the boat."

Joe did as instructed and, at the last moment, noticed another box of LaDonnas. He tossed it to Humphrey. "Souvenir," he called. Then he came aboard. From ten feet away, he tossed another bomb into the cockpit of the *Kiddle-Dee-Divey*. This bomb took longer to react to the heat. The burning boat was visible for half a mile, then came the explosion, and shortly the flame snuffed out.

Humphrey thanked Roman for his help. "I couldn't have done it without you," he said. "I don't know what I was thinking about. I should've known something would go haywire. That goddamn ricochet! But you came along and saved my ass."

Joe examined the wound. "Well, it's in you," he said. "I can't tell how deep, or how much bullet is left. But that's a nasty situation. You have to have a doctor."

They argued about this. Humphrey was sure he'd be all right, and finally he said, "That's where we're going, anyway. Let's just go with the plan."

"It's a long ride, Slim," Joe said. "But if you've got someone at the other end. . . . Let Roman go with you, to help. I don't want to just drop you off."

Humphrey consented to that. Roman helped him down into the bunks and Joe set their course. After a while, Roman came back to the wheel with a cup of coffee. He sat in the seat across the companionway and watched through the night, occasionally going below to check on Humphrey. When Joe would ask how Humphrey was doing, he would just shrug. But he seemed content.

15

Moving Day

Mulheisen was moving. Or rather, he wasn't moving but he should have been. Instead, he sat in an old easy chair in his bedroom, gazing out at the shipping in the channel, across the field behind his mother's house. It was very quiet, very peaceful. He wondered if he was making a mistake. He glanced at the clock radio next to his bed. It was nearly three in the afternoon on a Sunday. He was all packed. Becky would be here soon with the truck. He looked around him, relishing the quiet familiarity of this room, his boyhood bedroom. When would he sit in this room again?

Becky was a small, fast-mouthed woman in her late thirties. Mulheisen wasn't sure of her last name. She'd lived with a man named Marvin Berg for years, until he died. Had she taken Berg's name? Had they ever married? He was shocked at his lapse, as a detective, in not knowing this. She had helped Mulheisen on a case not long before, and given him some nice, vintage H. Upmann cigars left over from the days when Marvin had owned a great little cigar store down on Fort Street. Becky's help had consisted in providing Mulheisen with some notebooks, left in Marvin's care by the late and not much lamented detective Grootka, that had proved useful in the never-solved disappearance of Jimmy Hoffa. It had been nice to see her again. Mulheisen thought she was . . . attractive. Not beautiful or cute, but nice looking. And she had been only halfheartedly insulting.

The house she had inherited from Berg was much too large for Becky. Mulheisen had mentioned that he was looking for an apartment and they had kidded about him moving in, but he had told her that it was pointless. The house was in Pleasant Ridge, one of the numerous little suburbs that ringed the city. It wouldn't qualify as a Detroit residence.

Then, soon after he'd found the apartment downtown, Becky had called. She had discovered something interesting: the village of Pleasant Ridge had only a single police patrol, so they had contracted with the city for additional services. Could it not be construed that Pleasant Ridge was, in effect, part of the Detroit Police Department responsibility and, hence, its employees could legally reside there? It was worth an inquiry. He had pitched it to his boss, Captain Jimmy Marshall, and he'd approved.

Still, Mulheisen hadn't been sure. What would sharing a house with Becky entail? He had decided to take a run out there and investigate.

Becky looked better than on the previous visit. She was not so pale; maybe it was makeup. Also, she was dressed better: instead of dungarees and garden boots, she wore shorts and a tank top. She was lean and muscled; evidently she worked out. Her body might be hard, but her new life since Marvin had died seemed to have softened her. She wasn't so caustic as before, though given to occasional sarcasms.

She said he ought to pitch his beloved H. Upmann cigars—not the vintage ones she'd given him, but the new ones. They were overrated, she said, living on their past glory. Before Mulheisen could voice misgivings, however, she was quick to add, "Don't look like that. I didn't mean you should quit. I like a good cigar as much as the next guy. You know me, Mul. I'm just saying, as an old cigar seller, Upmanns are what we'd call a parlor pitch. You can price 'em like a virgin, but they're more like an old slag. Here, try some of these."

She gave him a box of LaDonna Detroit figurados. They came in a fancy wooden humidor-style box with a clasp, and the picture inside was a splendid painting of a woman on a milk-white mare, strewing flowers and cigars on the world. They claimed to be hand-made in the U.S.A., in Detroit, of "highest Cubano-quality to-bacco." That was a nice touch, he thought. It didn't actually say Cuban. He raised an eyebrow at Becky.

"Try 'em," she said. "You'll see. It's as good a cigar as you can get, and only five dollars per. No, no charge for this box. I got 'em as a promotion."

"I didn't know you were still in the business," he said.

"I do a little wholesale," she said. "Why waste experience and connections? It keeps the money tap open. Try one."

He took one out and sniffed. It wasn't cellophaned, which he liked. They seemed handmade, all right, and well made. Tight, no large stems obtruding. The shape was terrific, a true torpedo with a double taper, thicker on the smoking end. He clipped and lit it. She was right. It drew very well, though a little tight at first. It was mild in the mouth, but had a full body. There was no disagreeable aftertaste. Kind of earthy. He liked it.

"Five bucks," he said. "How do they do it?"

"Somebody's underwriting it," Becky said. "You can't sell that for five bucks, not made in the U.S. Or anywhere else, probably. Maybe they figure on building a clientele, then raising it to ten. But you oughta take advantage of the introductory offer, as they say. I get 'em at wholesale, of course. That'd be one of the advantages of living here."

"What are the others?" He looked at her through the smoke.

"Low rent," she said. "No upkeep. Of the house and grounds, I mean. I'm not washing your clothes or sheets. Maybe you can run them out to your ma's." She laughed then, evidently envisioning him lugging an armful of sheets out to his car, stepping on the trailing edges. "Maybe I could do the sheets," she said, grudgingly. "Throw 'em in with mine. And you could help me put up the screens and take 'em down. But no leaf raking, lawn mowing, painting, or. . . I don't suppose you know anything about plumbing? Good. I do. I hate a man screwing up the plumbing with his ignorance. Rent's five bills. That'll pay my utilities and help with the taxes."

He decided to look at the room. It turned out to be most of the second floor. He'd have a large bedroom that overlooked the parklike street. A private bath that she had totally remodeled, much more splendid than the one in the flat he'd looked at: this had an enormous walk-in shower with a built-in bench, plus a huge, jetted tub. Heated towel racks, infrared heat lamps in the ceiling, full-length mirrors.

He could also have a large, shelf-lined study that adjoined the bedroom. She had repaneled it herself with old cherrywood she'd found up north and had remilled. Everything was rewired, new lighting that could be adjusted with a rheostat. There was room for his stereo equipment, and she said that she'd insulated when she'd repaneled the rooms. With the insulation he could play music fairly loudly without disturbing her, in her downstairs domain.

She showed him her fabulous kitchen. All new appliances, beautiful maple countertops with inlaid marble and lovely Mexican tiles where one would need that kind of surface. Professional- quality ovens and cooking surfaces, and hearty exhaust venting. A couple of huge refrigerators. "You could have a designated reefer," she said, "if you think you'd need it. Otherwise, help yourself from these. I don't eat much, but I like to cook. Kind of hard to cook for one, though."

The whole tour took quite a while. It was a huge house. They could stay out of each other's way. He'd noticed that it was a nice place when he'd visited before, but he hadn't seen much, just the basement, where the cigars were kept and she'd put in a lot of exercise equipment. He was glad to see that she was not a neatness freak, but liked things pretty much picked up and stowed in the obvious places. And she didn't mind cigar smoke.

"Be pretty weird if I did," she said. "I kinda got this joint jerked back into shape after the slob kicked. Oh, Marv was a good man. I miss him. Once or twice a month. But he was hell to pick up after. You don't look like a slob."

Mulheisen said he didn't think he was. An early stint in the armed forces had left its impact. He made his bed tight every morning. Clothes up off the floor, that kind of thing. His desk might get a little messy.

"How come you didn't sell those vintage Upmanns?" he asked her. She had twenty boxes, stored in a walk-in humidor that was bigger than the apartment downtown—another enticing feature (or was that two?). She had offered them to him at the time and he'd had the impression that she wanted to get rid of them. Now it seemed she was still in the cigar business.

"Marvin said he kept 'em for you," she said. "Don't you want 'em?"

"For me? Well, sure. How much?"

"I figured it was a bequest. From Marvin."

Mulheisen was not sure how to take this. Could it be true? Marvin had retired at least a few years before he'd died. He'd never called, never mentioned any such thing. But who could object? As far as he knew, the cigars—vintage Cuban—were perfectly legal pre-embargo goods. Perhaps Marvin had forgotten, or was just too ill to pursue it, had put it off until the right moment—which never came. Mulheisen certainly didn't care to debate the issue, in case the offer was withdrawn.

"One big thing," she said, when they were back in the downstairs living room. She stood there with her hands on her slim hips, engaging his eyes frankly. She looked younger than her mid-thirties. Maybe it was the sandals or the short hair. "Fucking."

Mulheisen laughed quietly and glanced about, embarrassed. "Hey, I'm only renting a room. Rooms. Thinking about it," he amended.

She nodded briskly. "I know. But a man and woman live in a house and fucking inevitably pops up, causes a lot of tension. I'm not agin it."

There was a silence of perhaps ten seconds, although it seemed much longer. Mulheisen looked at her.

"I hate tension," she said. She smiled. She had wicked little teeth. Like a baby panther. "How do you feel about it?"

Mulheisen didn't know what to say. "It's . . . ah . . ." He watched her for a clue, thought he had one, and finished, "It's bad. Oh, you mean the other? I thought you meant tension. The other is good. I like it. I wasn't thinking about it, just now."

"You got a girlfriend?" she asked. "I didn't think so. Me neither. I'm not a lez, I mean. No boyfriend, either, although I don't mind going out once in a while, maybe getting laid. Used to, anyway. That's over. AIDS and stuff. Bad times for fucking. It was fun while it lasted, though. I had the tests. I'm clean. You?"

"Oh, yeah. Well, we have to get regular checkups."

"So that's all right," she said.

"Ah, well," Mulheisen said, hoping this discussion was concluded, "that's good." He nodded and glanced around the room.

He was about to make a comment about the nice fireplace when she sighed.

"Shit," she said. "I guess I could have put it better. Let's see." She furrowed her brow in thought. She looked up. "I'm not saying we should . . . no, that's not it. How about this? If you wanta fuck, we could try it. We might like it. Maybe we'd hate it. But I hate the tension, waiting for it to happen. You dig?"

"You mean . . . now?"

She shrugged. "If you wanta. *I* don't, particularly, right at the moment. But it's there if you wanta give it a whirl. I just don't want it hanging in the air, screwing everything up. So to speak." She laughed, a throaty chuckle.

"Okay," he said, relieved. "That's good to know. Thank you. Uh, I wouldn't, you know, dream of bringing a woman in if that's . . ."

"Well, I don't think I'd care for that," she said, "but it'd be none of my business, I guess. Those things happen, sometimes. I'm not likely to be partying down here, either. The thing is, two people live in a house, they want to keep their own lives, you know? Their own space, as the kids say. That's important."

He agreed. "But the thing is," he said, "I've found an apartment, downtown."

"Oh." She lifted her eyebrows. "Nice place?"

"Yeah. It's all new. Not as big as this, but . . . I already made a deposit, first month's rent, that kind of stuff."

"How much?" she asked. When he told her twelve hundred dollars, her face registered shock, then relief. "Well, hell," she said, "I can get your deposit back for you. No big deal."

So that was settled. They proceeded on to other things, like when he wanted to move, whether there was room in the garage for his Checker. He wondered what his mother would make of her. Fortunately, Cora Mulheisen was in Galápagos, or was it Ulan Bator?

Someplace where they had cranes. She knew he was moving, of course, but she'd have to be told about Becky, some time.

Becky arrived with her pickup truck, right on time. Mulheisen's gear would take at least two trips. When they had taken one load across town and returned for another, she came up to his room and suggested he might like to take his chair. She was pretty strong for as slim as she was; she hauled as many boxes as he did and didn't get winded, either. And she didn't even comment when he did.

Mulheisen was exhausted. He offered to take her to dinner, but Becky insisted on cooking a tremendous grilled flank steak with a special barbecue rub. Becky had some good wines. A rather boisterous cabernet seemed appropriate. It revived and yet relaxed them.

After that, they went to bed. It was . . . energetic. Becky was as lively as a trout and as hard to hold. Sometime during the night she eluded his embrace.

In the morning, he found her in the kitchen, where he'd gone in pursuit of a delicious aroma of freshly ground and brewed coffee. Becky thanked him for his efforts of the previous night in a friendly, matter-of-fact way and accepted his compliments.

"You were better than I'd hoped," she said. "That doesn't mean you get breakfast. I mean, you were excellent. Really. It's just, I've got stuff to do. We'll have to do it again. I'm glad we got that out of the way, though. No tension, see?" And she disappeared into the basement to work out.

Mulheisen went to work. It was a long drive to the Ninth Precinct, but he had a LaDonna figurado and thought about that slim body as he waited for lights. He felt great. He wondered what she had hoped. But she was right. No tension.

* * *

"**Y**ou look like
the shark that ate a whale," Jimmy Marshall said. "You get laid, or
something?"

"What do you mean? What makes you say that?" Mulheisen
came back at him. But Jimmy wasn't listening.

"We've got a guy here, wants to talk to you, about the Fat
Man," Jimmy said.

"Why me?" Mulheisen said. "That's a Grosse Pointe case. Or
the FBI. Why didn't you send him to them?"

"He's been to them," Jimmy said. "They brushed him off. He
asked to see you. Said he'd heard about you. I'll send him in."

A stocky, muscular man about fifty appeared in the door.
He was blond, with thick blond eyebrows and pale eyelashes, an
old-fashioned G.I. haircut. A tough guy, it seemed. He was Jimmy
Go, he said. "Golsen, but they call me Jimmy Go." He seemed to think
that Mulheisen would know him, or know of him, but Mulheisen
didn't. Mulheisen got him to sit down. They were in the cluttered
cubicle that Mulheisen called an office. He wondered, as he cleared
some files off a chair for Jimmy Go, what Becky would think of
the mess.

"What was the name again? Golson, with an *o*, like the tenor
man?" he asked, scribbling in a notebook.

"E," the man said. "I thought Golysczywzki was bad. I had to
change it. Nobody could pronounce it, or spell it. 'Specially at the
motor vehicle department. Now I gotta spell Golsen. I'm a trucker.
Gravel, stuff like that. Got a fleet of trucks. Yeah, it's about the Fat
Man. Diablo, or whatever they call him."

He sat foursquare, hands on his powerful thighs, looking directly at Mulheisen. The detective waited.

"He ain't dead," Jimmy Go said.

"FBI says he is," Mulheisen said. "They did an autopsy, fo-
rensics identified him. They seem satisfied, from what I've heard."

"That's what they say," Jimmy conceded. "But it ain't him. It's somebody else. It's bullshit."

"What do you know, Jimmy?"

"The Fat Man ain't gonna get whacked by some security guard, a guy he hired, like the papers said. It's a put-up job. I know the guy. I had dealings with him, for years, the prick."

"What kind of dealings?"

Jimmy explained that for years the mob had tried to muscle in on his business, had harassed him, harassed his drivers, had tried to push him off jobs, sabotaged his trucks, and so on. It was a familiar story. Jimmy had fought back. He was tough. And finally, he made a deal with Wally Leonardo. Nardo was running that end of things in those days, when Carmine was boss.

It turned out that Nardo and Jimmy Go's sister had been acquainted. His sister had been a whore. He said it as if she had been a waitress. She had been Nardo's mistress for a while. And later, when his sister had fallen ill, Nardo had paid for an operation, even though they were no longer lovers. Jimmy Go's sister had died anyway, despite the operation. But Jimmy Go had found that Nardo played pretty straight with him.

Jimmy Go had been protected, for a not unreasonable price. It was the cost of doing business, he said. And Nardo had kept up his end. They got along. They were cut from the same stone, Nardo had told him. And now DiEbola had whacked Nardo. They had tried to lay it off on Pelodian, but Jimmy Go wasn't fooled. He'd talked to Nardo the night before he died. Nardo had told Jimmy Go he'd been to dinner at DiEbola's. Nardo knew it was coming. He knew what that dinner was all about. He'd said that the other two guys who were there, Malateste and Soteri, were gonna get it too. And they had.

Mulheisen didn't think that was much. What else was there?

Jimmy Go said Nardo had shown him a piece of paper. He'd given it to him. It was an address, where he could find Pelodian. It was way the hell out in the country, not far from the stone quarry where Nardo's body had been found. It was written in DiEbola's hand. Jimmy Go didn't know DiEbola's writing, but Nardo did. He knew it was a setup.

"Why did he go, then?" Mulheisen asked.

"I think he figured he could handle it, and if he couldn't, then it was his time," Jimmy Go said. "He wasn't scared. He said he'd gotten away with a lot of shit in his time, but maybe this was the payback. He never expected an angel chorus. But, what the hell, he might win! Only he couldn't. They must have jumped him."

"Maybe it happened that way," Mulheisen said, "but so what? DiEbola's dead. Well, maybe we could get the guys who did the deed. Did you show the paper to the FBI?"

Jimmy Go had. They didn't think it was much. They had taken the paper. They said they'd get back to him if something came of it. But they hadn't. Jimmy Go didn't think they were going to do anything. Trouble was, DiEbola wasn't dead. He was sure of it. Nardo had told him that he believed something funny was going down. The Fat Man was getting ready to cut. He was settling old scores, clearing the decks. He'd been knifing guys right and left, selling his operations to the highest bidders. That's what Nardo said and it looked like it was true. And if the Fat Man sold the biz out, could he stay on? No. He had to bolt.

"What do you care?" Mulheisen said. "He killed an old buddy of yours. Leonardo told you . . . what was it Nardo said?"

"He said he never expected to die in bed, flights of angels singing him home." Jimmy Go almost smiled, but he was a pretty mirthless sort of guy—his thin lips writhed for a second. "He was a pretty good guy, for a crook. He wasn't no Holy Joe, but he treated me good. Most of 'em out there"—he waved a thick, callused hand at the dirty window with its protective bars—"you reach out for a hand up and they'd as soon shit in your palm. Nardo was all right.

I gotta do something for him. He did something for Nita. He didn't haveta do nothing, but he did."

Mulheisen sat and stared at this knotty-looking man. He was impressed. The guy rambled on about his sister, Nita. She was never a nun, he said. They'd been orphans, stuck in a succession of foster homes, where they'd been kicked around. His sister had been raped when she was ten by one of the foster fathers. Jimmy had been younger by a couple years. He had tried to protect her, but it was she who had protected him from the beatings, she who had insisted that they couldn't be separated and had pitched such a bitch that the social workers had capitulated and found them homes together.

"She always thought she was so smart, but she wasn't that smart," he said. "She was good to me, though. I tried to look out for her when I got big. But you couldn't help Nita. She was into drugs, that kinda shit. But I ain't gonna let DiEbola get away with this."

He was raging inside, Mulheisen could see. But he kept it well muffled, choked off.

"I'll find the bastard, somehow," Jimmy Go said, getting up. "I'll find him and pound his fucking head in like he did old Nardo."

He was through talking to Mulheisen. He could see that Mulheisen couldn't help him.

"Well, wait a minute," Mulheisen said. "Where would I start?"

"Hell, I don't know," Jimmy Go said. "You're the fucking detective. There must be something that would tell you, some way to figure it out."

"I'll look into it," Mulheisen said. But Jimmy Go was gone, out the door.

An hour later, Mulheisen was talking to Brennan, the medical examiner. He had done the autopsy. Was there any way that the body was not DiEbola? No, Brennan said. It was DiEbola. The body was pretty destroyed, but they had plenty of identification, blood, tissue, teeth. They had ransacked the house upstairs, which hadn't been damaged. They were able to match hair and sloughed skin from the bedsheets. Good matches.

Good matches? Not perfect matches? Mulheisen asked. Well, there were some anomalies, sure, Brennan conceded, but there always were, and they were heavily outweighed. The medical files were the clincher. Nothing ever matched up one hundred percent. But the evidence was there. That was DiEbola.

What anomalies?

Well, there was some blood they couldn't account for, some fingerprints, some hair, some tissue. The investigators thought there may have been another man there, possibly he had perished in the boat that blew up and sunk in the lake. Probably one of the assailants. They hadn't been able to make a match on him. No body. Probably never find it.

Mulheisen drove to the Federal Building offices, to visit the FBI. He was surprised to find a federal agent he had met before there, Dinah Schwind. She was kind of cute, he thought. He looked at her differently today, perhaps because of his experience with Becky. Women looked more attractive today.

The last time he'd seen her she'd been looking for a missing agent, evidently investigating Humphrey DiEbola. She was like a lot of federal agents in Mulheisen's experience: they asked the questions, but they didn't provide many answers to your questions. She had pumped him for details of his investigations of DiEbola and was particularly interested in his comments about Joe Service and Helen Sedlacek. As for the missing agent, she hadn't been able to provide him with much information; in fact, she'd said that he was more on the order of an informer, or a source, than an actual agent. He'd been working at Krispee Chips. His name was Pablo Ortega.

At the time, the name meant nothing to Mulheisen, but not long after he'd received a visit from Ortega's brother, from Mexico.

The family had heard from Ortega, months earlier, in a letter that suggested he was doing very well at Krispee Chips. But when Mulheisen and the brother had gone there to inquire about the missing man, they were told that Ortega had left the company and there was no information on his whereabouts.

Mulheisen mentioned this to Dinah Schwind now. "I'd have passed this on before now," he told her, "but you never said what office you worked out of. You're not FBI?"

"Oh, no," she said. "Right now I'm in and out of the country so much, *I* don't even know who I work for. My mother can't even get hold of me. But you did find Ortega?"

"No," Mulheisen said, "just his brother. But, you know, I've been thinking about it . . . you must have blood tests, that sort of thing, on your agents, eh? I've been talking to the medical examiner about the bodies they found at the DiEbola crime scene and they're still up in the air on some of the identifications. Maybe you should see if your guy wasn't one of the sources of some of the tissue and blood they found there."

Schwind was skeptical. The guy wasn't really an "agent," after all, but she was grateful for the suggestion. She'd get back to him on it. And before he knew it, she had run off. Oh well, it wasn't as if he didn't have other work to occupy him.

The FBI had a big file on DiEbola, but it didn't tell him much. They were totally convinced that DiEbola was a closed case. They weren't looking any further. They had listened to Mr. Golsen, but his information wasn't helpful about the actual perpetrators of the Leonardo murder. One of the other agents had the note. They could send him a copy if he needed it. They left Mulheisen to examine the file. He took some notes.

According to the records, Humphrey DiEbola had been born in Detroit, in 1935, and christened Umberto Gagliano. His mother had died soon after, his father in 1947. Custody of the youth had been awarded to Dominic and Sophia Busoni, of suburban Royal Oak, maternal relatives. He first attracted police attention in 1944, an Oakland County juvenile matter, no record. Later, the family moved into Detroit, and Umberto began to rack up a long series of police attentions, but no arrests and no fingerprints. At age twenty-one he had legally changed his name to Humphrey DiEbola, a simple matter of requesting the change through probate court.

Over the years, DiEbola was often suspected of violent crimes, often questioned, but never formally arrested. And again, no fingerprints. It was an amazing feat for a man so active in crime.

Mulheisen was strangely at peace as he left the federal offices. He stood on the sidewalk, among the tall buildings. It was a cool day in late spring, a milky sky. A good day for something. He felt good. Maybe it was Becky, he thought. But it had a old, familiar feel to it. He'd felt this way before, though not lately. He felt like doing something, but he wasn't in any hurry. He was in a zone, as the kids said.

He went to juvenile court and was denied access to ancient records. He didn't blink. He called an old Royal Oak detective, a man named Hearn. They had met years ago. Hearn was in his eighties now, but he remembered Mulheisen. Did he remember any significant juvenile cases in 1944, involving a kid named Umberto Gagliano? No. But he remembered the Busonis.

"They were real gangsters," Hearn said. "They had a half dozen kids. The wife was something, a real beauty. She was Sophia before Sophia Loren. Nice gal, too. Busoni was always into something. We were glad when he split to Detroit."

"Why did he leave?"

"I don't know. Moving up in the world, I guess."

Mulheisen called a friend at the *Detroit News* archives. She said she would put together a little file of DiEbola stories. They flirted a little. She hadn't seen him in a long time, she said. They should get together for a drink, or something. Mulheisen said he'd like to, but he was seeing somebody. It probably wasn't wise. His friend picked up on that. "Sounds serious," she said.

Hearn called back. He'd thought of something. "Busoni got run out of Royal Oak," he said. "It was funny, because it wasn't his fault."

"What do you mean, 'run out'?"

"The neighbors got after him. Him and his gang. They wanted him out. They even had a scene, what we'd later call a demonstration, in front of his house. We had to go out and break it up, protect him." Hearn laughed. "I mean, the guy was into a lot a stuff, but we had to protect him for something that didn't have anything to do with him."

"He had a gang? In Royal Oak? This was during the war?"

"Well, not a real gang, as such. But he always had guys, foreigners, coming around. Yeah, it was the war. People were wary of foreigners, you know. We had another deal out there, same neighborhood, where a baby-sitter saw a copy of *Mein Kampf*, Hitler's book. She told her folks, they told somebody else, next thing you know, a mob is shouting 'Nazi' outside the guy's door."

"I heard about that," Mulheisen said. "That was in Royal Oak? I thought it was Harper Woods. What happened?"

"Aw, nothing," the old policeman said. "The guy came out and said it was a free country, he could read any damn thing he wanted to, told 'em he wasn't a Nazi, just wanted to know what this Hitler guy was up to. That's all. We broke it up."

"Was the Busoni thing like that?"

"No, no, I don't even know if Busoni could read. Not English, anyway. It was . . . let's see . . . yeah, a kid had disappeared in the neighborhood. Didn't have anything to do with Busoni, though. He'd been out of town at the time. But maybe they were used to getting up mobs by then. Anyway, after that, Busoni and his family moved to the city."

"What about the kid?"

"The one who disappeared? They never found him. Oh, I take that back. They dug up his body, excavating. It was quite a while later, maybe ten years. Just bones. The guy on the cat, he didn't see it, at first. Bones were scattered all over, all crushed up. They figured the kid had crawled into an old abandoned excavation, got caved on. There were a lot of those old excavations, housing project that got started but then the war came along and there were no building supplies, no customers. After the war, though, they started to build like mad. By the late forties, they were . . ."

Hearn went on for a good long while about the postwar building boom. Mulheisen made some notes, hung up, and began to look at some of the other available records on DiEbola's career. Late in the day, his friend Sheila from the *Detroit News* called. She had a nice collection of stuff, if he wanted to come out and look at it. It was all in Sterling Township, at the *News* offices. Mulheisen felt a little odd about going there. He supported the *News* staff that had gone on strike some time back and hadn't been recalled. In the end, he figured that the archives belonged to an earlier, prestrike era. His union sympathies didn't apply. He said he'd come out.

He called Becky to say he wouldn't be home until late. "For godssake," she said, "let's don't start this crap. You're a big boy. Just because we had a little fun doesn't mean you have to call every time you're gonna be out. What, did you expect supper or something?"

She didn't sound cross, so he was relieved. "Oh, okay," he said. "I wasn't sure."

"So now you know. Jeez, no tension, remember?"

"Okay, okay," he said, "no tension." He almost made a crack about not feeling any tension all day, but decided against it.

When you look at old files a certain weariness sets in quickly. Especially if you don't know what you're looking for. Soon enough, he was grateful for the bad coffee that Sheila brought to the viewer.

Here was a depressing and seemingly endless parade of articles, many with pictures, of a younger, fatter Humphrey being questioned about and denying murder, theft, arson, you name it. In no case was he arrested or charged. It was an amazing performance. And at about age thirty, the pictures ceased. He was no longer even brought in, or if he was, it was handled more discreetly. That meant powerful lawyers.

Mulheisen knew, of course, who the lawyers were, but there was no point in approaching them. He wondered, however, if there weren't some documents that must now be made public, given the official demise of DiEbola. He would have to check.

He sat back and sipped the coffee. A thought struck him. He explained to Sheila about the disappearance of the schoolboy, in Royal Oak. About 1944. She soon found it. The boy was named Arthur Cameron White Jr. He had been fifteen. A large, heavy boy, certain to have been called "Tubby," though probably not to his face, not by his classmates. He was only in the eighth grade, so he'd been held back at least one year.

The original article described him as missing. The article hinted that he might have run away. He had run away before, it said. He had left the school that day for disciplinary reasons—sent home. But there was no one at home. Things were a little looser in those days, it seems. It appeared that for the first few days the police looked for him in bus stations, hobo jungles, highway stops, that sort of thing.

Mulheisen was entertained by the "hobo jungles." He remembered scouting them, in his uniform days. He supposed they still existed, in some form. Nowadays, they would look among the haunts of the homeless.

After a few days a more general search was made of the neighborhood. But it was too late. Evidently there had been "torrential" rains. He supposed that meant several days of pretty heavy, more or less constant rainfall. Not much chance. He'd participated in a search like that, once, as a young cop. There was nothing drearier than walking through parks and neighborhoods, looking but not knowing what to look for. Sort of like what he was doing right now. You soon fell prey to the conviction that nothing would be found. Nothing was found. It was rare to find anything that way. Just a bunch of men, stumbling around, wishing they were somewhere else, watching the leaders for the first sign that it was time to call it a day.

He didn't feel that way now, though. He felt interested. The story had moved to page 2, dropped to page 5, and then disappeared. It was revived by the mob that had besieged a neighbor's house. The reports didn't identify the neighbor. It was an unfounded rumor. Where the rumor had originated was unknown and not pursued. The story disappeared.

In 1950, Crooks Woods was finally sold and chopped down and the abandoned sites were bulldozed for a new subdivision. That's when the body was discovered—six years later, not ten. Much too late. The White family had moved away, to Ontario. They were from Ontario originally. An ambitious young reporter had evidently talked her editor into letting her do a lengthy Sunday feature piece on the sad tale. It wasn't much of a story. The family had believed that "Porky" (Aha! Mulheisen thought) had run away. They had never believed that anything bad had happened to him.

Porky was a bad boy, Mulheisen concluded from the article. They were secretly relieved at his disappearance. Anyway, he was the kind of kid who hurts others. Not a victim. The principal had expelled him that day for twisting a smaller kid's arm so violently that the child had to be taken to the hospital by the school nurse. (They had a school nurse!)

The main interviewee in the feature article was a teenage girl, Ivy, the younger sister, one of three girls. The youngest girl had died of diphtheria not long before Porky vanished. The parents were despondent and went back to a small town near Midland, Ontario. But the teenaged girl remembered that Porky "had a kind of hideout somewhere, he never would say where." She thought he must have gone there, but they had no way to find it, no clue.

Oh, this is a waste of time, Mulheisen thought. He gathered up his stuff and thanked Sheila. She asked him what his new girlfriend was like. He said she wasn't his girlfriend, just a woman he was living with. "That's cute," Sheila said. He didn't feel like explaining. He promised to take her to lunch, soon, and drove home. He was tired. Becky had gone to bed. He didn't know whether to be pleased or disappointed. He just tiptoed upstairs and got in bed himself.

The sheets were clean. They smelled nice. He thought she must have washed them. This might work out, he thought. He fell asleep wondering if she was his girlfriend.

16

Netherworld

Helen was gracious. She looked tired, though. Mulheisen thought she must be finding the life of a don hectic. A donna? She did not look like a crime boss, none he'd ever seen, anyway.

"I thought you'd be around long before this," she said. "Mr. DiEbola has been dead for weeks."

"It wasn't my case."

She just looked at him, disbelieving. "What do you want, then?"

"I'm trying to close out another case," he said. "When did you last see Pablo Ortega, also known as Pepe Ortega?" He was pleased to see a flicker of alarm cross her face. Before she could answer, he hastily rattled off the standard Miranda warning.

"What's that all about?" she asked, carefully.

"We've identified Ortega's body. He was murdered. Do you want an attorney?"

"Am I a suspect?"

"Not the primary suspect," Mulheisen said. "But you could be an accessory." They were sitting in the living room of her mother's home. Helen had left DiEbola's estate, although she was the heir in his will.

"What happened to Pepe?" she asked.

"For one thing, someone chopped off his head."

"My god!" Her emotion was genuine.

"He was dead before that happened, according to the medical examiner," Mulheisen said. "His hands were chopped off as well. It was an attempt to conceal the identity. Effective, as long as we had no clue to his identity, but ultimately the DNA matchup was definitive." He had delivered this information in a calm, almost casual way. It allowed her time to recover her poise.

"I'm very sorry," she said. "Pepe was a nice man, very talented. Do you have any idea why he was"—she hesitated—"killed?"

"Yes. He was an undercover agent for a federal agency. Presumably, DiEbola discovered this and either ordered him murdered or did it himself. But you haven't answered my question: When did you last see him?"

She thought for a minute, then gave up. "Sometime in January," she said, "I'm not sure of the date."

"Think about it," Mulheisen prompted her. "It could be helpful." When, after a moment, she shook her head, he went on: "What was your relationship with Ortega?"

"What do you mean?"

"Were you friends? Lovers? Did you have any extended conversations?"

"We were friends," she said. "He was Humphrey's chef. So we talked, occasionally. Not anything extensive. He was funny, fun to be around."

"Not lovers?" When she shook her head, he saw that she was lying. "I'm going to tell you something," he said. "The M.E. thinks he made love just before his death. The FBI is pulling his room apart, right now. They may find evidence that will link him to a lover. A hair, fluids, maybe a note. I'll be surprised if they don't want to talk to you."

She denied again any intimacy, more firmly this time.

"DiEbola's the main suspect, of course," he said. "And he's dead. Did he say anything odd about Ortega's disappearance to you, or in your presence?"

She said that Humphrey had shrugged off Pepe's absence, he didn't seem to regard it as anything significant. She wasn't sure, but she thought that he may have said that Pepe had simply decided to leave. Her impression was that Humphrey and Pepe had discussed this, prior to his leaving. She wasn't sure, now, but that was always the impression she'd had.

Mulheisen asked if DiEbola had seemed excited, or disturbed, acting unusually during this period. She said he'd talked a lot about his life, his youth, but that she hadn't paid much attention.

"About his childhood? That's interesting," Mulheisen said. "Did he by any chance ever mention a boy, Porky White? From his youth?"

"I can't think of any names at the moment," she said, "but he talked a lot about some childhood experiences." When Mulheisen pressed her on this, she went on: "He told me about a boy who had been killed, a neighbor."

"Killed? When did this happen?" Mulheisen asked.

"When he—Humphrey—was about, oh, eight or nine. Maybe older. I didn't try to calculate it."

"What did he know about this killing? Was he involved?"

"I didn't think he was involved, but the incident seemed to have had a strong impact on him," she said. At Mulheisen's urging she described DiEbola's account of the incident: a neighbor child had wandered off into the woods, where he encountered some kind of pervert who murdered him and buried his body in a cave. The murderer was never caught.

Mulheisen was jarred. He didn't know what he'd expected, but it wasn't this. There were serious problems with this story, even if one hadn't any awareness of the events. He enumerated them for Helen: Arthur White had disappeared in 1944, his body found in 1950. Nobody knew how he had died. So: How did DiEbola know what had happened to the child? If the killer was never caught, how did he know he was a pervert?

"I thought it was a dream," Helen said. "The way he talked about it, and . . . come to think of it, he said he'd had trouble sleeping, nightmares. And then he told this story. I guess I just thought it was his dream, or something like that had actually happened, but this was his dream version. I got the impression that he'd been troubled by this dream before, a lot, since childhood. He must have talked about it a half dozen times."

"Tell me about it," Mulheisen said. "Was there any particular time, say the first time, that he told you more?"

Helen considered this. The first time was fairly early, not long after she had moved in, say early January. Humphrey had complained of a sleepless night, of nightmares. He didn't tell her about the dream right away, but later that afternoon, in the study. It was awful weather, they hadn't gone out. He'd been reading, then more or less spontaneously he had told her this story, which, at first, she'd thought was a variation on a fairy tale. But then, from something he said, which she couldn't remember now, she realized this was the nightmare. She really couldn't say if he'd told her all the details at that time, or if she was just conflating various versions that he mentioned, piecemeal, over the ensuing weeks.

"He started out talking about being buried alive," she said. "I think that was it. Or maybe he asked if I'd ever had that nightmare. That's pretty common, isn't it?"

Mulheisen supposed it was, but he was curious about the further details. What was that about a fairy tale?

"At first it sounded like Hansel and Gretel, or even Goldi-locks," she said, "you know, babes in the woods. Lost children, ogres, giants. I didn't take it seriously, of course."

"But later?" he prompted.

Later, the dream and the fairy-tale element seemed to have faded away, somehow, she said. She was trying to reconstruct the sequence, but not having much luck. She really hadn't given it much attention at the time, although she could see that it was bothering him. At some point, she said, he began to talk about it as a real incident, something that had actually happened.

"I know what it was," she said. "There was another child in-volved. Humphrey had heard about it from him. It had always both-ered him, it seems, because he had felt protective toward this second child, a cousin or something. This child had barely escaped, but was scared witless and had made him promise never to tell anyone, and he hadn't, not until he told me. Well, that's what he said, anyway."

The full story went like this, as best as she could remember: the neighbor child and his cousin—he had never named him—had wandered off one day, playing. They had gone to a woods, forbid-den to them. There they had found a cave, which they crawled into, knowing it was wrong. In the cave they had found stuff.

"Stuff?" Mulheisen said.

"Grown-up things, maybe dirty pictures or something," Helen said. "He didn't describe what they found, but from his tone or manner I got the impression it was something like that. The whole story was very dark, very scary. Anyway, they found the stuff. Then, just when they decided they better get out, the Boogey Man came home. That's what he called him!" she said, pleased to have re-covered this tidbit. "Or, another time, he referred to him as the Ogre. The Boogey Man punished them for messing with his stuff. That's how he put it. Then he tried to force them to do bad things.

It sounded sexual to me. The Boogey Man grabbed the neighbor boy, who was the smallest, and while he was fooling around with him, the cousin escaped. The neighbor boy never came out of the cave, and the Boogey Man, or Ogre, must have gotten away. The cousin was afraid to say anything, because he knew the Boogey Man was still out there, would get him. So they never told anybody anything. Let's see." She stopped to think, then went on after a minute. "I think that's all the details, all I remember, anyway."

"He never mentioned the name Porky? Porky White? Or Arthur?"

She was sure he hadn't. He'd also told her several stories about scrapes he'd gotten into with other kids, later, and she did remember some of those names: Carmine, Angelo, Howard, Denny. She couldn't remember all the names. But no Porky, or Arthur.

They went on to talk of Humphrey's surprising interest in books, particularly Machiavelli, his theories about power, influence, and so on. Mulheisen was intrigued. He asked about other people in DiEbola's life. She told him what she knew, but guardedly. It wasn't of much interest. He asked if she thought DiEbola was homosexual. She said she didn't think so. He seemed interested in women, although he didn't have any attachments. She told him about Humphrey's idealized love for the little girl. If he was gay, he was well closeted. The culture in which he operated was male, exclusively, but she knew of no associates of his who were even rumored to be gay. And no, she stated firmly, before he could ask, she had not been his lover. But she knew men. Humphrey had been a man. They'd been close, and, if he wanted to know, she'd considered it. The notion had been entertained, in a civilized way, by both of them. They had decided against it.

Mulheisen listened to all of this attentively, and not just because it reminded him of Becky's voiced dread of tension. Never once did Helen betray even a hint that she thought Humphrey DiEbola was still alive. That was convincing, to Mulheisen. He began to think that he'd been unduly influenced by Jimmy Go's stolid certainty. After all, he considered, Jimmy Go had strong feelings about the man and probably just wanted him to still be alive so that he could wreak personal vengeance.

Just to satisfy himself, he asked her, point-blank, if she thought there was any chance that the body found in the ruins of the basement was not DiEbola. To his surprise, although she claimed she had no doubts, he detected a measure of uncertainty. What was this? He pursued the question.

"He was talking about retiring," she said, finally, yielding to his pressure.

"But how could he retire?" Mulheisen asked. "Did he have somebody in mind to succeed him? Was he ill?"

She didn't know. She denied any knowledge of his plans, but she was unconvincing. At long last, she conceded that she'd had some doubts about the explosion and the fire. He had insisted that she not be present in the house that night. She had come home, to her mother's.

"Then, maybe it wasn't his body," Mulheisen said. "Maybe he ran away, like the Boogey Man."

"If he ran away," she said, "he ran away on the boat, the *Kiddle-Dee-Divey*. And that blew up. So he's dead, anyway."

"They didn't find a body," Mulheisen pointed out.

"You mean, he could have destroyed the *Kiddle-Dee-Divey*, to make it look like he was dead, just in case someone doubted the basement scene? Humphrey was a plotter," she conceded, "but that's too elaborate. If he'd gone to all the trouble to fake his death in the basement, he wouldn't want to do something like the boat. That would make the basement deal look fishy. No, no way. He was crazy about that boat."

"If he escaped on the boat," Mulheisen pointed out, "it would have been a dead giveaway."

"So maybe he wasn't on the boat," she said. "I don't know. But he wouldn't have purposely destroyed it."

"Why not?" he persisted. "He apparently abandoned everything else personal—assuming he escaped. Didn't he? Surely he had some other objects, books or pictures or whatever, that were dear to him. Is anything important to him missing?"

"Nothing that I know of," she admitted. "But he would never have destroyed the boat."

She was convinced, and Mulheisen could see she was convinced. "That's a funny name for a boat," he said. "It sounds like the old song 'Mairzy Doats.'"

"That's what it was," Helen said. "You know the song! He told me that was what he named the boat after."

Mulheisen reverted to DiEbola's health. Helen saw through that one. Humphrey had been in better physical shape than he'd been in in years, perhaps since his youth. Of course, losing a lot of weight could bring its own problems, she conceded, but he seemed fine. Still, you could never tell. It was possible that he'd had a terminal illness and had decided to go out in a grand blast, but the idea was too iffy. She suggested he consult DiEbola's regular physician, Dr. Schwartz. She thought he'd been to see him not too long before his death.

Mulheisen got up to go. He told her again that she could expect to see the FBI, about Ortega. Then he asked about Roman Yakovich. He wanted to talk to him. Here was another surprise: she seemed uncomfortable, said she hadn't seen Roman lately.

"When was the last time you saw him?" Mulheisen asked. She was evasive. She didn't know. Maybe a week. He kept to himself, she said. Mulheisen asked to see her mother. Her mother was ill, she said, under a doctor's care. She couldn't see anyone. Mulheisen insisted.

Mrs. Sedlacek didn't seem ill, but she was withdrawn and uncommunicative. She acted as if she couldn't understand English, or speak it. She spoke Serbian to her daughter, who translated.

"She hasn't seen Roman lately," Helen said. "She thinks he went on vacation, maybe he went to Florida."

Mulheisen hadn't heard anything in the conversation that sounded like "Florida." He persisted: How long had he been gone? Maybe a week, he was told. Had he ever gone away like this before? Oh, sometimes. He was a grown man, he didn't have to tell them where he went. That was the story. Mulheisen gave up.

"So what are you doing these days?" he asked Helen, as he was leaving.

"What's that supposed to mean?"

He didn't want to say, How do you support yourself now that your sugar daddy is gone? But that's what he meant, and she knew it. He tried to cover up the gaffe with a jest, but as usual he went too far. Mindful of the joke around the precinct that Helen Sid was now the don, he quipped, "Just as long as you don't start thinking you're La Donna."

"But I am," she said. She said it with pride.

"You're what?"

"That's me," she said, picking up a box of cigars and thrusting them at him. "La Donna Detroit. Take them. On the house. Or do you consider this a bribe?"

"These are you?" he said stupidly.

"All legit," she said. "I own the company. Hell, I invented the cigar. I know you'll like them."

"I do," he confessed. "They're very good. Thanks."

"I'll tell you a little secret," she said, leaning close. He was reminded of Becky. It was the feral mouth, perhaps, or the catlike litheness. "They really are Cuban."

"How can that be?"

"Trade secret."

He smoked one on his way to Dr. Schwartz's offices. Schwartz was not happy to see him. He'd been through all this with the Grosse Pointe police, the FBI, several times. He had verified the findings of the Wayne County medical examiner from his records of Humphrey DiEbola. He was frankly hostile, wanting to know why the Detroit police were involved. Mulheisen managed to present a vague justification that Schwartz could have refuted if he'd cared to take the time. But gradually, after Mulheisen allowed him to pontificate about medical expertise and the infallibility of his record keeping for a while, he grew more friendly.

"I know DiEbola was supposed to be this monster," Schwartz said, "but really, Sergeant, I can't say I found him to be so. The man was a pussycat, as they say. It's odd, isn't it? You read these newspaper articles, you'd think he was a cold-blooded killer, but he wasn't."

"No? Well, he was never indicted, anyway," Mulheisen said, "or even charged. An amazing record."

"Maybe he never did what they say," Schwartz suggested. "If you ask me, he was a businessman. A little shady, maybe, but basically just hard-nosed and pretty astute. He talked like a truck driver, but he knew how to run a business. And he could be generous, too."

"How is that?"

"Well, he sometimes sent friends or employees to me for medical care, and then he took care of the bills, out of his own pocket. That's pretty decent."

Mulheisen agreed. He recalled that Leonardo had acted similarly. He wondered if Humphrey had paid for medical care for a mistress. That would be worth finding out. He'd dearly love to locate a mistress of Humphrey DiEbola's, it could be a valuable link. But Schwartz said he'd seen no female referrals. All males. He didn't care to speculate, at Mulheisen's quick follow-up suggestion, on the possibility that DiEbola was homosexual. He doubted it. He'd seen no such signs.

"Who did he send, for instance?" Mulheisen asked.

Schwartz said he didn't mind discussing with the police a client who was deceased and under investigation, but he didn't think he should discuss or even identify other patients, even if they had been referred to him by the deceased. Of course, if Mulheisen could obtain a warrant, or a court-ordered deposition, that was another matter.

Mulheisen nodded agreeably. He could see the point. But had DiEbola sent him many clients? It turned out that he'd sent in only one, in the last year. That was about three months ago. The man was in poor physical shape, grossly overweight, but as far as he knew—he hadn't seen the patient recently—he had benefited from DiEbola's interest. He'd lost weight, gotten into shape. Schwartz supposed that it had interested DiEbola because he'd turned his health problems around in a similar way.

Mulheisen thought about this on his way back to the office. He hadn't pursued it with Schwartz, although normally the doctor's stiffness would have provoked him, but the idea nagged at him. He called Andy Deane at Rackets and Conspiracy and asked who in the mob was a fatso, someone DiEbola might have thought he could reform. Andy laughed. They were all pretty tubby, these days, he said. He named half a dozen notorious thugs who were seriously obese. Angelo Badgerri was probably the worst. A vicious swine, a collector. But he'd disappeared a few months ago. He was said to have retired, to have left the country.

"Who says?" Mulheisen wanted to know.

It was mostly rumor. Deane said that people were so relieved not to have Mongelo around that they soon put him out of their minds. He was an old buddy of Humphrey's, though, from the early days. They called him Mongelo, he said, because he bit people. But a lot of mobsters were disappearing, he said. He described it as a shake-up, the changing times. Besides the killings of Soteri, Malateste, and Leonardo, there was the murder or disappearance of minor hoods like Strom Davidson and Matty Cassidy. Davidson had been found in an alley, apparently the victim of neighborhood muggers. Cassidy, of course, had been identified as one of the victims in the explosion and fire.

Mulheisen remembered Davidson, a real loudmouthed creep. He realized now that Helen must have taken over Davidson's tobacco business. Deane said that was so, but that the word was that Davidson had been forced out, or sold out well beforehand. As far as he knew, LaDonna Detroit was legit.

Mulheisen asked about Roman Yakovich. Any rumors? No. But then, Roman had more or less retired when his boss was hit. No one ever saw him anymore. Andy would ask around, though.

In a mischievous mood, Mulheisen called Schwartz's office and identified himself as Badgerri, asking for an appointment. The receptionist didn't hesitate. She made the appointment, asking only if it was for any particular problem or just a checkup.

"Just a checkup," Mulheisen told her. "I thought I should. How long has it been?"

She checked and said it had been two months. He was due. The doctor would want to know how his blood pressure medication was doing. In fact, they probably ought to do another blood panel, so he shouldn't eat or drink anything but water after midnight before his appointment.

Mulheisen said in that case not to schedule the appointment just yet, he'd have to see when a good time would be, then thanked her and hung up. He sat for a long while, contemplating the circumstance of two men, closely related in age and background, one of them until fairly recently so notoriously obese that he was generally called the Fat Man, while the other was just as

fat and was said to be on a weight-losing regime. And both of them
lately being attended by the same doctor. Is that coincidence? He
considered the possibility that a man who has successfully dealt
with a personal health problem like obesity might be eager to help
out an old friend with the same problem. Like a reformed alco-
holic sponsoring an old fellow drunk at A.A., maybe. Except that
this old pal—one of the worst assholes in Christendom, a man
whom nobody, not even a notorious Samaritan like DiEbola, would
dream of assisting out of an open latrine he might have tumbled
into—had disappeared from public view . . . at about the time he
had been treated to medical care by Brother DiEbola. Too much
coincidence for Mulheisen. These guys were disappearing into the
woods like . . . like Indians, like Le Pesant. Another "bad bear,"
or was it "malicious bear"?

He called Brennan at the medical examiner's office and asked
what would be the difficulty of switching medical records, where
both patients were treated by the same doctor.

"You mean physically switching them? Gee, what a primitive
concept! You'd have to break into the offices, transfer records, fake
some, probably. And then there's the records on the computers.
You'd have to be computer literate, Mul. It'd be a laborious, time-
consuming bit of business. But, oh sure, it could be done." There
was a silence, then he mused, "It could work. The thing about doctors, they're very jealous of their record keeping. If something is in
a file, the doctor would be insistent that it was no mistake. In such
a case, the physician would prove to be a terrific ally if you were
trying to say one guy is who you want him to be. And the thing is,
you don't have to be absolutely ironclad about this, as long as the
big important details are covered. I assume you're still scratching
at the DiEbola evidence."

Mulheisen said he was. He speculated for Brennan that if, as
he said, the "big important details" pointed toward one identifica-

tion, then a smattering of noncorroborative evidence would be waved aside.

"Providing," Brennan expanded, "that A, there's no serious doubt or suspicion of faked evidence, and B, no single item surfaces that conclusively rules out the desired identification. If you've got that, Mul, you're on base."

Mulheisen felt it was worth pursuing. He called the legal guys and explained why he'd need a warrant. They said it sounded vague, but doable. They'd get right on it.

He put that out of his mind and went back to studying his notes. He focused especially on the Porky White story. DiEbola's version was fascinating. It was an obvious fabrication, even if it wasn't clear whether it was intended to deceive or an unconscious dream fiction: displacing the dead Arthur White with a nameless child, a defenseless victim, and distancing himself from the event while being able to describe the frightening, nightmarish scene, via a secondhand account. It could be a work of imagination, certainly. A child who had known Porky White, who might in fact have been frightened of him, could have devised this nightmare. Mulheisen was familiar with some psychology, and he thought he recognized some timeworn themes, such as guilt, the sexual associations. He supposed that a child who had been afraid of Porky White might have felt guilt as a price of relief at his disappearance. Or it might be a veiled fear that he might not really be dead, or . . .

He gave that kind of speculation up. For one thing, the body hadn't been found at the time. As far as children of the period knew, Porky had simply run away. The expected reaction would be guilt-less relief. Psychological speculation, especially when you had little hard evidence and couldn't interview the parties involved, was a great waste of time. It was bound to be wrong. He didn't doubt that kids might have had bad dreams about Porky White's disappearance, but so what?

He found himself humming the tune "Mairzy Doats." As he recalled, the nonsense verse was repeated in plain language, revealing the code. "Mairzy doats and dozey doats, and little lambsy divey" became "Mares eat oats and does eat oats, and little lambs eat ivy." "A kiddle-dee-divey too" finished out as "A kid will eat ivy, too, / Wouldn't you?" Amusing—once. When repeated endlessly, it quickly became tiresome.

A goofy thing to name a boat, though. He knew about boats, having grown up on the river. People gave them dumb names, sometimes. It was like vanity license plates, he supposed, without the restriction of space. People named them to reflect some jokey notion, like the expense—*Me'n the Bank*. Or a favored identification: *Serb-a-Rite* had been Big Sid's boat, he recalled, presumably a play on *sybarite*. Or they named them after their wife or girlfriend. He wondered if Humphrey had ever had a girlfriend, one named Ivy.

Suddenly, he recalled that Helen had mentioned that Humphrey had nourished a crush on a little girl. Perhaps.

He called Helen. She was skeptical, to say the least. To the best of her knowledge Humphrey had never mentioned anyone named Ivy.

"While I've got you on the line," he said, thinking about Brennan's notion of the difficulty of switching medical records, "was Humphrey what you would call computer literate?"

"Humphrey was a computer bore," she said. "He got into it late, but in a big way. I think he even took a private course from some guy, some whiz. No, I don't remember the guy's name. It was before I spent much time with him. He'd sometimes be up half the night fooling around on-line. He was a real nut for it. Maybe it was the bad dreams, afraid to go to sleep. He seemed apologetic about it, or do I mean regretful? He said it was eating into his reading. That's what that bunker of his was all about, I suspect. He had all kinds of computer equipment down there."

Unfortunately, of course, Mulheisen realized, all those computers had been destroyed in the explosion and fire. It would have been interesting to see what was on them. He wondered if the hard drives had been at all salvageable. He didn't know much about that kind of thing, but he thought he could find out. Of course, if Humphrey had staged the whole thing, he'd certainly have erased anything useful. But it was worth checking.

The other thing worth checking, he thought, was school records. Just out of curiosity. He supposed somewhere there would be a record of Humphrey's classmates. Perhaps there was a little girl named Ivy. The name seemed familiar to him, but he guessed it was from recalling the song lyrics.

It was too late for that today. He'd found out a lot. Too much, really. He had to digest it.

Happily, he also had Becky's special osso buco to digest. After dinner he set about shelving his books in his new library. He'd never had a library before, so much shelf space! Inevitably, he dug out White's *The Middle Ground*. He reread the account of Le Pesant with profound interest. He was struck anew by the treatment of the problem of murder. This notion of the differentiation between the killing of an enemy—i.e, an enemy of the group to which one belonged—versus the killing of a "friend," someone not an enemy of the group . . . it was difficult to comprehend.

How could any society treat the latter so lightly? Any society he'd ever heard of considered that kind of killing particularly heinous, a betrayal of friendship, trust, striking at the very heart of the social contract.

No, he saw that he misunderstood it. It wasn't that the Algonquians took it lightly. They killed their enemies without compunction or sentiment and expected to be slain by them, if caught in a weaker position. That wasn't particularly different from the traditional notion of the criminal inculpability of soldiers in battle. What was different was they absolutely rejected the concept of capital punishment for civil crimes, for murder. One man is slain; why should another valuable life be taken? What compensation was that? And yet, he had no doubt that there had been psychotics, murderers, among them. How did they deal with that?

A man like DiEbola, now, what was his ethic? He apparently killed at will, dispatching whomever he judged to be inconvenient for him. As far as Mulheisen could tell, DiEbola was quite conscienceless about it. Although . . . he was troubled by dreams. Possibly he was mad. Possibly his crimes were catching up to him. If what Helen had told him was true, DiEbola had become fascinated of late with his earliest experiences. Mulheisen couldn't help feeling there was something to this, that there was a significance to the Porky White episode. If he had been involved in that death, what a boon it would be to him if he could cover that body, or resurrect it, as the Algonquians saw it. What a concept!

Mulheisen had perceived no inclination on Becky's part toward further exploring their cohabitation. He went to bed thoughtfully, without tension.

17

Ontario

It was raining hard when Mulheisen got up, and it was still raining when he got to the precinct and called the Roman Catholic archdiocese educational offices. A very helpful woman supplied him with the information that Umberto Gagliano had attended their schools in Oakland County and, later, in Wayne County, from 1940 through 1950, after which he seemed to have dropped out. She was even able to locate class lists from the grade school, but there had been no little girl named Ivy in any of those rather small classes. She looked, as well, at classes a year or two on either side of Umberto's: no luck.

This was disappointing, but Mulheisen reasoned that Umberto's little girlfriend could just as well have attended public school. Through the Oakland County school district, with the help of yet another amiable official, he settled on Starr Primary School as the most likely place. If that didn't work, he was prepared to try private schools. It wasn't necessary. In 1944 and 1945, a girl named Ivy White had attended fourth and fifth grades.

Of course, he thought. Porky White's sister. He should have recognized it yesterday. Still, what did it mean? Just another connection to the White family, but they were neighbors, after all. Perhaps there was no more to it.

In the fall of 1945, her records had been transferred to a public school system in Peterborough, Ontario. This was way the hell the other side of Toronto—a little far to pursue a nebulous link, he thought.

The legal office called. They had his warrant. With the company of Detective Maki, Mulheisen visited Dr. Schwartz's offices. Within minutes they found enough questionable entries and irregularities in the files of Humphrey DiEbola and Angelo Badgerri to arouse the suspicions of even Dr. Schwartz. Mulheisen impounded the files and took them downtown to Brennan at the Wayne County medical examiner's office. Even a cursory glance convinced Brennan that the files had been tampered with. He would reopen the file on the corpse they'd identified as DiEbola, this time armed with data on Badgerri.

Mulheisen left him to make a definite determination, but he was now convinced, himself. He returned to the precinct and called Jimmy Go. The trucker was not in, but his secretary said she'd try to get hold of him on his cell phone. He called within minutes. From the sound of it, he was in a dump truck in high gear. He was clearly pleased at Mulheisen's news, but he was content to say "I told you so!"

Mulheisen warned him that the next step would be the hardest. Just because the evidence had been confused didn't mean that DiEbola was alive. People had died in that basement. One of them could have been Humphrey, regardless of the attempt to veil his identity. More to the point: if DiEbola was alive, where was he?

Jimmy Go was eager to know what Mulheisen's next moves would be. He seemed oblivious to Mulheisen's statement that the case was still in the hands of the FBI. Mulheisen assured him that he himself would pursue DiEbola as the no-longer-believed-to-be-deceased suspect in the murder of Pablo Ortega, whose body had washed up in Mulheisen's precinct.

"Atta boy!" Jimmy Go yelled over the roar of traffic. "Keep me posted, Mul! I'll make it worthwhile to you!"

Mulheisen didn't bother to respond to this artless bribery offer. He said Jimmy Go could read about it in the papers, if he was successful. For now, he had to do a lot more research into DiEbola's past.

"All I meant was, if you need any help," Jimmy Go said, "you can count on me."

Mulheisen thanked him and went back to work. One of the things that had interested him was the boat. What role had it played in DiEbola's plan? Like any Detroit policeman, Mulheisen had not only followed the case in the media but had supplemented that information by talking to other, official sources. By now he had seen the FBI report. The accepted scenario of the investigation had seen DiEbola as the victim of an assassination. Obviously, it had not gone well. At least one of the putative assassins, the security guard John Nicolette, had disappeared and was assumed to have died in the explosion of the *Kiddle-Dee-Divey*, although no bodies had been recovered. It was assumed that his original role would have been to let the killers into the grounds. That part of the assassins' plan had gone awry, it seemed, when Nicolette was invited to play cards with DiEbola. Questioning of the other guards had established that: Nicolette had informed the gate man of where he was going.

Mulheisen had thought that was a shaky assumption on the part of the investigators, but he hadn't considered it very deeply, as long as the original scenario seemed to hold up. Now Nicolette's role and the problem of access looked more interesting. It was thought that the assassins had gained access to the DiEbola estate via the lake, after they'd discovered the change in security plans. (Conceivably, they were notified hurriedly by Nicolette.) Why hadn't the conspirators just canceled and hoped for a better occasion?

The FBI had speculated that the change had been offset by the ad-vantage of having a co-conspirator, Nicolette, on the spot.

A stolen rowboat had been found, smashed at its mooring at the dock. Obviously, that was how they got in, or so the grand theory went. No abandoned vehicle had been found, but the assassins must have been dropped off, made their way along the canal path, where they stole the rowboat and simply rowed out to the lake and on to DiEbola's. No one had seen the boat being rowed, but it was fairly late at night. Presumably, they had always planned to escape via the *Kiddle-Dee-Divey*, which was conveniently moored and ready to use—perhaps another benefit of Nicolette's collusion.

Now, with the indication that DiEbola had attempted to confuse identification of the bodies, a new scenario was required. Two bodies had been found in the basement, neither of them intact. One of them was presumed to be Humphrey DiEbola, the other a small-time mobster named Matty Cassidy. It was thought that Cassidy was the key, somehow. He'd been allied to one of DiEbola's less-than-supportive henchmen. The missing figure was Nicolette. He had some tenuous marital connections, but there was no reason to see him as a conspirator, Mulheisen thought. He was still missing. Who else had been down there? There was ballistic evidence from at least three guns. If one of the bodies was Badgerri, that meant a cozy four-handed poker game. The FBI had established fingerprints on two weapons found at the scene, and they matched with prints they had earlier established as DiEbola's: prints derived not from files, since there were none, but from household sources, like drinking glasses, cups, doorknobs. But what if DiEbola had planted those? The FBI presumably had Badgerri's prints—he had a long record—but they'd never had any reason to try to match them with the prints found at the scene.

Mulheisen presumed that DiEbola must have intended to use the *Kiddle-Dee-Divey* himself. Why? The obvious answer: to escape

Jon A. Jackson

to Canada. The international border here was notoriously porous. He might have laid plans to fly out of Canada to some other destination. Or he might still be in Canada. A standard check of the airlines showed nothing, but Mulheisen had expected little from that.

And now, of course, another possibility raised its head. Say that DiEbola had escaped an assassination attempt, or even that he had staged the attempt himself, to make it appear he was dead. It was possible that he had died when the boat blew up. As yet, no sign of bodies had been found, and given the passage of a couple of weeks, it looked like none would be found. Was this just another subterfuge, to conceal the true nature of the plan? Had the assassins or, more likely, DiEbola destroyed the boat to close another channel of investigation? Had they, or he, then gone on in yet another boat? This seemed possible, even likely.

Mulheisen stared out through rain-blurred windows, pondering. It all seemed so speculative. Why bother with the boat at all? It just led the investigators on, provided them with another track. Very likely, it was a false trail. DiEbola was an intelligent man, a truly devious man. He had almost miraculously avoided arrest for decades. He probably could have simply packed his bags and taken a plane to anywhere in the world. Such a course would inevitably have been discovered, and pursuit would continue. Mulheisen, for instance, had been prepared to make an arrest on the basis of evidence he had discovered in the Hoffa investigation. Possibly, the FBI and other agencies were similarly poised to act.

DiEbola must have known that his long performance was about to end. He'd seen his fellow mobsters falling left and right, lately, to FBI investigations. Mulheisen couldn't help feeling that DiEbola had known that he, Mulheisen, was very close. No flight was likely to take him beyond the reach of the investigators, Mulheisen included.

It made sense to stage the death scene, if that is what had happened. Mulheisen now believed it. If that performance played as planned it could well have convinced everyone that DiEbola was dead. He couldn't help thinking about the farce that Cadillac had staged for Le Pesant. End of case. And here it had almost succeeded. But why the boat? Could this be one of those unconscious blunders that even the brilliant criminal makes? But where did it lead?

It led to Canada. That was a very large place, the second-largest nation in the world, geographically speaking. Not many people, however. It wasn't hopeless. He did have another, nebulous, lead to Canada.

What the heck, he thought. He called Peterborough and got through to the school system. Ivy White had graduated from school there. Her records had been sent on to McGill. The university in Montreal, in turn, said that Ivy White had graduated in 1958, in a premed program. Her records had been forwarded to the University of Michigan, in Ann Arbor. She had graduated from there with a medical degree in four years. She had interned at Henry Ford Hospital, in Detroit.

She had spent the early 1960s as a staff surgeon at Henry Ford. Having just looked at DiEbola's medical records, Mulheisen did not recall any instance of him ever being hospitalized, though it may have simply escaped his notice. But it was quite possible that someone DiEbola knew had been a patient there, very likely, in fact. He could have bumped into Ivy White there while visiting someone. Mulheisen was encouraged.

The physician's placement service gave him a link to Ontario, to an indigenous peoples community in the far north, up beyond Sioux Lookout. He groaned. This was getting pretty far afield. As long as Ivy White was in Detroit, he had nourished hopes for this line of investigation. But, what the heck, it had taken him only an hour or two to find out this much: there was a telephone up there, wasn't there?

There was. And for the first time he talked to someone who had actually known Ivy White. Dr. Ivy White, the beloved doctor who had delivered a couple of generations of babies, taken out appendixes, and "cured more ills than a whole tribe of stinkin' med'cine men," according to a garrulous gentleman named Ronnie Heavy Man, who'd answered the phone. This amiable fellow who said scathing things in a laughing voice was willing to inform any and all that "Indi'n med'cines no damn good. 'N' this new quack, Weatherby, or whatever he calls hisself, why he don't know pus from snot. If you could only send Doc White back, why . . ."

Mulheisen finally got from him the immensely gratifying news that Doc White had relocated, "down below." She had returned to southern Ontario to care for her aged mother, who was dying of cancer. It was hoped that once the old lady kicked off, Doc White would come back to Little Loon River Camp, and "The sooner the better—not to wish the old bag an early death, but."

The place Ivy White had gone to was an island in Lake Huron, off the Bruce Peninsula. Mulheisen looked it up on his map. He estimated it was a good day's drive from Detroit. Up to Port Huron, over toward Owen Sound and hang a left. Drive clear out to Tobermory and get a boat out to Shitepoke Island.

He looked in his agency manual. There was an office of the Royal Canadian Mounted Police on the peninsula. A Sergeant McPherson answered. He was happy to hear from Sergeant Mulheisen of the Detroit Police. Yes, indeed, he knew Dr. White. A very nice lady, eh? She lived on "Shypoke" Island. Her mother had died several weeks back. Well, by golly, it was Boxing Day, or thereabouts, now he thought of it. More like half a year, eh? Time flies.

Mulheisen mentally supplied the "Eh?"

What could Sergeant McPherson say about Dr. White? She was about fifty years old, but if Sergeant Mulheisen thought it was more like sixty, he supposed it was possible. Damned fine-looking woman for sixty, he'd say. She had spent many years among the people, up in the blackfly country. Helluva woman. He heard she was going back. He hoped not. She did some work locally and it was a damned good thing for the islanders to have a doctor.

There were probably a couple hundred people out there. Most of 'em old-timers. You know how it is, eh? Kids go off to "Taronna, Monreyall." But now there was an influx of yuppie-types, from "Taronna," even New York. They come in the summer, first, eh? Then they find they can manage their stocks and whatnot on-line, so why live in the city? But it creates problems, eh? The yuppies have money, fancy goods, and they want special things like good coffee, good bread, better groceries, eh? It creates a theft situation, some resentment, tax problems. Gotta build a better dock, better roads for their Jeep Cherokees, more ferry service, whatnot. And they want environmental regulations tightened, more enforcement. No off-season shooting of ducks and geese and whatnot. Eh?

Mulheisen considered calling Ivy White, but then, maybe that wasn't such a good idea. A personal interview would be much better. He went home to pack. Becky was not in a good mood. Nothing serious, just a little grouchy. She asked where he was off to, but he didn't have time to fill her in. He was eager to get going. When would he be back? He didn't know. She seemed annoyed by his incommunicativeness.

He left feeling a little uneasy about her, about the arrangement. But he couldn't think about it. It was still raining. And when he crossed the Peace Bridge, at Port Huron, into Ontario, the rain seemed to get harder. He got as far as Kincardine, on the Lake Huron shore. It was wonderful country, what he could see of it—a dark, wet, north country. He'd always liked that.

It was still raining in the morning. He'd slept in a decent motor inn at the harbor. He enjoyed the sense of being in a foreign country that was, after all, not very foreign. Just different enough to make him aware that he wasn't in Michigan. The country was much like the Michigan lake country, but more sparsely populated, it seemed. Small houses, different signs for things, but still some familiar American-style signs for food and gas. The people seemed vaguely British, what he saw of them while buying gas or eating in the restaurant. It was not quite as *modern*, somehow, as America, not so corporate-captive. He liked that.

The peninsula became more wooded the farther north he drove. It was a tourist destination, but it was early in the season and there was little traffic. Also, the rain had obviously depressed the trade. He saw a few disconsolate families, cars filled with outdoor gear and children staring mournfully out of streaky windows. Others seemed underdressed, in shorts, with wet jackets, waiting under storefront canopies. But the locals didn't seem upset by what now appeared to Mulheisen like quite a lot of incessant rain. They were in sweaters and rain gear, rubber Wellington boots, talking in normal, more or less cheerful voices.

He had arranged to meet Sergeant McPherson in a roadside cafe, along Highway 6. It was steamy inside. McPherson was chatting to the locals. He was a pleasant man with sandy hair and a mustache. He wore rain gear like the rest of them.

"Dr. White's still up there, all right," he told Mulheisen. "I didn't contact her, as you requested. No word of anyone unusual on the island. You'll want to stay at the inn, it's an old hotel. They have vacancies, though, I checked. They're used to a certain amount of tourist traffic, mostly bird-watchers and the like, eh? There's a ferry service from Tobermory, goes twice a day, six and six, on the hour. It's about ten miles offshore, so it takes, oh, a half hour or more, depending on the weather and the sea. They'll carry your car, but the island's only three miles long, so you wouldn't need it. Dr. White's place is only a short walk from the harbor. You got any boots, or a hat?"

Mulheisen's hat was a soft, cotton one. It was soaked just running from the car to the cafe, five steps. McPherson said he could get some gear at a store in Tobermory. He advised him to buy rain pants as well.

"There's a ferry to Manitoulin Island," McPherson said, "don't take that one. Take the little ferry."

"Bird-watchers, eh?" Mulheisen said. "My mother has probably been here. What do they have?"

"Shitepokes, I guess," McPherson said. "That's a kind of heron, a green one. Or is it a cormorant? And gulls, of course. Oh, and orchids. There are supposed to be a lot of orchids. About forty different kinds, eh?"

Mulheisen found the ferry. He had plenty of time to buy a waterproof rain hat, a very nice green jacket that shed water like a mallard, the much-recommended rain pants, and some green rubber boots. It was pretty pricey, considering that he'd probably never wear this gear again. Fancy, breathable, high-tech fabric. He decided not to take the car. The boat ride was brisk, the lake being more than a little choppy, despite what the laughing, fresh-faced ferry girls claimed. He found it necessary to hang on to something when he ventured from his seat in the little cabin where they served coffee.

The boat could carry several vehicles, Mulheisen saw. He talked to the captain, a big fellow with a once-handsome face, now ruined by hard living. He was no doubt competent and friendly enough, but conversation had that tentative feel. He was looking forward to the tavern at "Shypoke," but determined to be the sober captain until he was safely at the dock. Mulheisen didn't want to reveal his purpose, but he wanted to know if anyone who looked

like DiEbola had come across in the past couple of weeks. No one
of that description. They talked boats a bit, engines, especially Gray-
Marines, which led to Detroit, where they were made. A little chat
about the recent Stanley Cup playoffs and the Red Wings' shocking
failure.

No, Captain Grosvenor hadn't seen a fellow of about sixty,
dark hair. He would have seen him, all right, if he'd gone out to
"Shypoke," because this was the only way to get there. He'd seen
one car with Michigan plates last week, but it was a pickup truck, a
carpenter who was doing some work for one of the new people. He'd
finished putting in some cabinets and had left already.

It was only a hundred yards or so up the sand-gritted concrete road from the dock to the Shypoke Inn. It was pouring rain,
still, and fairly dark. Mulheisen lugged his bag, appreciating the
waterproof gear. The inn was a white clapboard affair, vaguely sum-
mery looking, despite the rain. Lots of flowering pots dangled from
the ceiling of the covered porch that ran the length of the front.
It appeared to have, perhaps, a dozen rooms. Only half were
occupied.

The proprietress was an affable middle-aged woman who wore
a sweater against the chill and jeans tucked into rubber boots, like
everyone else. She said her name was Jean. She had the fresh, hearty
face of nearly everyone he'd seen. McPherson had warned him that
islanders were a little odd—"They refer to the rest of the world as
off-islanders, eh?"—but Jean seemed like any innkeeper. Busy, but
friendly. She wasn't interested in his business at all. Probably she
thought he had no business, had just come out here to soak up the,
well, the fresh rain. Evidently, the whole off-island world coveted
the delights of "Shypoke" Island.

"Dinner will be up in about twenty minutes," she told him,
"but we serve till nine. It's very good. My sister, Janice, is the cook.

Tonight we have her planked whitefish. You'll like it." This was said with genial authority.

Four of the other guests were huddled in the parlor, around the fireplace, nursing hot drinks that surely contained alcohol. Mulheisen's room was upstairs, overlooking the harbor. A large white gull was sitting on the porch roof, just outside his window. It didn't mind the rain. The room had a full-sized bed that sat up high on a brass frame. It seemed a little soft, but comfortable enough. It featured a patchwork quilt and plenty of extra blankets. There was that familiar musty odor of the seashore. A shelf with a good stock of mystery novels. A good reading lamp. A small bath with a tub on legs and a curtain that could be pulled so that the shower, which rose up in a neat plumbing arrangement from the faucet, didn't spray all over everything.

Mulheisen had time for a cigar, if he could manage it in the rain. He took his .38 Airweight with him, if only because the door had only an unsecure-seeming skeleton-key lock. He'd bought his rain hat with an eye toward its broad brim shielding a cigar from the rain. He was gratified that it worked. He smoked a LaDonna as he trudged up the street. There was sand on all surfaces, a slightly disagreeable sensation underfoot. But shortly he came to the end of the finished surfaces anyway and walked on sandy paths through very wet and dense underbrush that by itself would have soaked him to his hips, even if it wasn't pouring buckets, except that he was completely sheathed in rain gear. He was grateful for the breathable fabric, and the pants were indispensable.

He found Dr. White's house without difficulty, after about ten minutes of hiking. McPherson had said it was easy to walk to, and it was. It stood off the sandy road, on a bluff facing out toward the lake, perhaps fifty feet above the shore. It was just a cottage, like all the others he'd seen. Apparently, from conversation he'd overheard, the new people had built some modern extravagances, but he hadn't seen them. This was white clapboard, with a broad overhanging roof that was shingled with mossy cedar shakes. Windows with little panes. Cottagey. Overgrown, of course, with lilacs, roses, and other shrubs that thrived in great profusion here. Doubtless, the famous orchids hid in the damp understory.

The sign was not a faded wooden one, such as he'd seen on others—declaring ROSE HAVEN and DEW REST. But there was an arrow, pointing to a side entry, that said SURGERY. There were lights shining through the curtains, but he could not see any sign of life. Smoke rose from the chimney and was baffled about by the shore breeze. Fog was moving in. He puffed his cigar and returned to the excellent planked whitefish, served with a buttery wine sauce. The same four people he'd seen earlier cheered up with dinner and tried to converse, saying they were from "Taronna," but he wasn't having any of that. He went to bed and slept. It rained and pounded deliciously outside the window, and he slept like the Old Man.

In the morning, the rain had tapered off to something more like a heavy mist. It was still solidly overcast, but the hotel people seemed to regard it as a nice day. After eating half of a breakfast that, if entirely ingested, would have disabled him for the day, he set off for the beach. It was cool, but perfectly walkable. He smoked a LaDonna as he strolled. There were several old rusting turtleback fish tugs, anchored, and numerous souvenirs of the now vanished fishing life, net floats and marine gear, lying about.

The lake was a metallic gray and tumbling. Large ships could be seen at a distance, tankers and ore boats. Gulls wheeled about, crying. Small groups of ducks were driving along at a distance. He didn't see anything that looked like a shitepoke, but there were small shorebirds that scurried ahead of him, peeping plaintively, fluttering onward when he got too close. He walked along the hard-packed sand, well past the bluffs on which the doctor's cottage perched. There was a track of sorts up to the cottage, mostly sand, but here and there reinforced with cedar steps. He decided to finish his cigar before attempting it. His walk took him around a long curve where great black and gray boulders stood offshore in the gravelly, stony lake bed. When he turned about and headed back he realized he'd walked farther than he'd thought. In the distance, he could see a dark, burly figure slowly climbing up the path. By the time he was halfway closer, the figure had disappeared over the top.

It took his breath climbing up the path, the sand shifting underfoot, except where there was a step or two. At last he stood at the top. He had to stand and catch his breath. The cottage was just a few feet beyond the breast of the bluff, too close for his taste. It had a glassed-in porch, decorated with marine bric-a-brac, nets, floats, wooden decoys, pieces of driftwood and weathered glass.

He went around to the surgery door and pulled a bell chain. He could hear the bell tinkle inside. After a brief wait, the door opened. A pleasant, weathered-looking lady of fifty-five-plus stood there. She had short, gray hair, a little mussed. She looked at him through glasses with large lenses in modern, sporty-looking frames. She wore wool Royal Stewart plaid slacks and a matching red sweater set. Over this, a white lab coat, unbuttoned.

"Dr. White?" he said, and when she nodded, he introduced himself. "Detective Sergeant Mulheisen, Detroit police force."

She looked wary. "What's the problem?"

He said he wanted to talk to her. "You're not ill?" she said. When he shook his head, she said, "I'm sorry, I'm busy just now. You'll have to come back later."

"Oh. You have a patient?"

She hesitated, then said, firmly, "Yes, I do. What is it about?"

"It's kind of complicated," he said. He realized now that to someone unacquainted with the details of the case, his story and questions would seem, well, far-fetched. But he had not wanted to risk contacting her in advance. "It's about a man named Humphrey DiEbola. You knew him as Umberto Gagliano, a long time ago, when you were children."

"I see," she said. She stood very stiffly, the door only partly opened. He could not be sure, but he felt that she was not quite open with him. She was a woman of considerable poise, however. He could not determine just how reserved she was, or what might be the cause. She didn't seem afraid, exactly, but she was very intent. "I knew him," she said.

"When was the last time you saw him?"

"I'm not sure. Why do you ask?"

"Did you meet him in Detroit? When you were adults, I mean. At Henry Ford Hospital?"

"I may have," she said. "What of it? That was a long time ago, thirty years."

"Then you know that he is known these days as Humphrey DiEbola," Mulheisen said. "He's a well-known Detroit mobster."

She didn't respond to that. Just looked down at him. It was beginning to rain harder now. Where he was standing there was no shelter, except for his rain gear, of course. The rain was swirling about the house in the wind off the lake.

He leaned to one side to look into the hallway. She was not going to invite him in, he saw. But of more interest, on the little entry table, where one might toss keys or gloves, was a familiar-looking cigar box. He had been given a similar box by Helen Sedlacek.

"It's important that we talk," Mulheisen said.

"What about?" she said, not conceding an inch to his interest. She didn't seem very friendly, not like what he'd expected: the beloved doctor of the north woods, ministering to poor indigenous peoples.

"Has DiEbola contacted you? Lately?"

"I'm sorry, I have a patient." She started to close the door.

"Dr. White! DiEbola is a dangerous man," Mulheisen said. "If he has contacted you, it could be very serious. Deadly serious."

"Are you staying at the inn?" she asked. "I'll come and see you this evening. About eight o'clock." She closed the door.

18

Payback

Joe Service knew this conversation was inevitable, but that didn't mean he had to like it. It was particularly ominous that the colonel had insisted on holding the little conclave at the boat they had provided for him. Joe was supposed to have returned the boat, but he was supposed to have done a lot of things that he hadn't done. Dinah Schwind had tried to defend him to the others, but even her patience needed relief.

It was pouring rain, which provided for maximum security—nobody was down at the marina on a night like this. The boat was docked at the Saint Clair Flats Boatyard, not far from the restaurant where Joe and Dinah had met earlier. It was also not far from Mulheisen's mother's house, but none of them were aware of that. It had just seemed a convenient moorage to Joe. The Sea Ray, a pretty sleek powerboat, had a tight Cordura canopy that buttoned up well.

The colonel sniffed as he came aboard. "You living here?"

"It's as good as any place," Joe said.

The colonel had brought along a guy whom he introduced as Pollak. He was also a member of the Lucani, the colonel said. Acker and Collins had other business, he said.

"I thought you were just a tight little outfit," Joe said, "four or five of you. How many Lucani are there?"

"Just six," the colonel said. "Seven, counting you."

"Well, don't leave me out," Joe said.

Pollak was a tall, blond man with a battered face. He looked like some kind of agent, once you were told he was an agent; until then, he looked like a hockey player. With Pollak, Schwind, and the colonel aboard, the Sea Ray was cramped. Joe provided the beer.

The colonel said he was disappointed that Joe hadn't come around after DiEbola had been hit. He had some money coming for that nice little piece of work, and they had more work for him. "We know how insistent you are on collecting," the colonel said.

"Yeah, well, I didn't think I could ask for payment," Joe said, "seeing as I didn't do anything."

The colonel was good at hiding his disappointment that his ploy hadn't worked. He frowned and said, "You didn't hit him, then? We thought you had. The FBI, of course, was convinced it was an internal thing. Well, you read the papers."

"I read the papers," Joe said, "but I don't necessarily believe them. Still, maybe it was like they say. But it wasn't me. So you don't owe me anything. As for more work, what have you got? I'm available."

The colonel and his friends didn't say anything for a long moment. Finally, the colonel said, "We were thinking something out of the country, maybe."

"Great," Joe said. "Whereabouts? Someplace sunny, I hope. South America?"

"Closer, actually," the colonel said. He seemed to have made up his mind. "Canada."

"Really?" Joe said. "What's in Canada?"

"Humphrey DiEbola," said Schwind.

They all watched Joe. He looked puzzled for a moment, then he nodded. "So," he said, "the Fat Man pulled a fast one. That guy's quick on his feet. It's like a polka party, isn't it? They have these dances, around here, you know. It's like a marathon, or something. All these big fat guys and their babushkas, wheeling around on the floor, bumping into each other. It gets pretty dangerous toward the end. The band starts playing faster and faster, 'Roll Out the Barrel,' that kind of stuff. The last guy standing is the big cheese, I guess. Or the big pickle in the barrel. Who knows? I went to one a couple nights ago, in Hamtramck. Pretty funny."

They all agreed it was funny. Not that any of them were laughing. They had found out, somehow, that Mulheisen had gone to Canada. A little judicious checking—it hadn't been difficult— had revealed that he'd gone to an island off the Bruce Peninsula. They couldn't be positive, but it looked like Mulheisen was onto something. Whether it was DiEbola himself or just a lead to him, they weren't sure. But there was a woman on the island who had, evidently, some connection.

Joe shook his head, marveling. "The guy is something," he said. "We're all convinced that Humphrey went down, but Mulheisen doesn't believe it. So, why should I go to Canada? If Mulheisen finds him, he'll bring him back."

"We want you to go and make sure," the colonel said. "Take Pollak with you. Mulheisen could have problems, if not with DiEbola, then with extradition. This one looks like a freebie, to us."

"How's that?" Joe asked. "I'm not into freebies."

"We didn't mean it in that sense," the colonel said. "You'll get your fee."

"Which is?"

"Whatever you can recover from DiEbola. And before you ask, let's say fifty grand, if you can't recover anything."

"A hundred," Joe said.

The colonel shrugged. "All right, a hundred. But believe me, the man clearly didn't leave his little mess in the basement without taking along a nice cushion. As far as we're concerned, it's all yours. It could be quite a bit. We know he managed to send a lot out of the country beforehand, and we think we can recover some of that. But he'll have a bundle with him."

Joe managed to look enthusiastic, but he calculated that they must have some other plans. They wouldn't let him keep everything that DiEbola had taken with him. Maybe that was why Pollak was along. "You said a freebie," he reminded them. "What does that mean?"

"Why, the man is presumed dead. Killed by his old buddies. That's the official line. You can just make sure it's true."

Joe looked at Dinah. She gazed back calmly. "I'm not a hired killer," he said to her. "I told you that. The thing with Echeverria was an accident. I never intended to take out Humphrey. That wasn't the deal, you know."

"No, but we figured you had," the colonel said. "Probably the situation got out of hand and you did the best you could, that's what it looked like. And then, you didn't come around, didn't correct our misunderstanding. A suspicious person might think you were involved, somehow."

"In the escape?" Joe said. "I didn't know anything about it. I was keeping tabs on him, through Helen. She seemed to think something was afoot, but she didn't know what it was. The best I could figure, he had some grand reorganization in the works. It looked like something might break and I'd get my chance. But I wasn't going to pop him. I figured once I could see which way it was going to break, I could set him up for you. If you want, I'll still do it."

"It'd be cleaner and easier if you just ran up there in your boat— this is your boat, Joe. Nice boat. And if DiEbola's up there you could show us, once and for all, that you're a team player. Joe

Seven." The colonel was calm and logical. That was the deal. "If you don't want to be on the team, fine. You're on your own."

Joe knew what that meant. It meant he would be fair game to anyone, and the Lucani would provide the direction to whoever came after him.

"I'll go get him," Joe said, "if he's there. You can do what you want when you've got him."

"Pollak will go with you," the colonel said. He wasn't accepting any refusals.

Joe knew what that meant. Pollak was set to ice Humphrey, if need be. And then, who knows? Maybe he'd ice Joe, too. These guys were in the direct-action business. Well, it looked like the complaint window was closed, Joe thought. He'd just have to play his position as the game unfolded. He peered out through the plastic side curtains. The rain was dancing on the deck.

"Not much of a night for a boat ride," he said. "Maybe we should wait till tomorrow, you could get us up there in a chopper, we could rent a boat."

"No," the colonel said firmly. "No choppers. No flying through international airways. No renting of boats. You can run up there, just a couple of fishermen. The Coast Guard doesn't bother. You find the island, find DiEbola. Our information is, he's at a house right near shore. Pollak's got the poop."

An hour later they were in the channel. It was a hell of a run, Joe thought, but it wasn't as if he didn't know the way. He'd brought Humphrey; now the problem was to pretend not to be familiar with the run. More than two hundred miles, the bulk of it across the open sea of Lake Huron, in pitch-black, pouring rain. But the seas were not heavy, the boat was powerful—he had a 205-horsepower MerCruiser, inboard/out, with a four-barrel carb. It took plenty of fuel, but he had gassed up, including the extra tanks on deck.

The navigation was uncomplicated. Once past Point Edward they would be out in the lake. It was mainly a matter of keeping an eye out for lake shipping. Joe figured they could cruise moderately through the night, through the Saint Clair River channel, and by daylight they would be well out in the lake. If the winds didn't get contrary, they should reach the island well before dark. They wouldn't want to be there any sooner.

According to Pollak, Mulheisen had already reached the island. They reckoned he wouldn't approach the woman before the next day. Presumably, Mulheisen could not be sure that DiEbola was even there. For that matter, neither could they. But Mulheisen would have to be a little cautious; a direct approach might be dangerous.

Joe was extremely interested in knowing how they had gotten their information and what it consisted of. Pollak, a man who didn't like to talk much, obviously was aware of Joe's keen interest and knew how much to reveal. Through a variety of sources they had become aware that Mulheisen had blown open the FBI investigation. As they understood it, he had learned that DiEbola had boldly faked the evidence of his death by breaking into a doctor's office and manipulating files. It appeared that the body identified as DiEbola's was really one Angelo Badgerri, a longtime associate of DiEbola's. Apparently, however, the authorities were still clinging to the idea that DiEbola had been the target of an assassination attempt.

It was amazing, Joe thought, how difficult it was for investigators to abandon a scenario once it had been established and agreed upon. This tendency had produced a modified scenario: DiEbola had planned to bolt but was nearly thwarted in his attempt, by an untimely attack by old enemies—or perhaps the mob knew he was bolting and that was why they had tried to hit him. They believed that Mulheisen had ferreted out a connection with an old girlfriend, one Ivy White, now a semiretired doctor living on Shitepoke Island.

DiEbola was presumed to have staged a fake boat explosion and then continued onward by switching to another boat.

This was the touchy part. If Pollak was not conning him, they assumed that DiEbola had provided himself with that other boat and was now at the island. No one had reported him there, but the doctor was known to be on the island. She had continued to see a few patients in the past two weeks, but that didn't mean that DiEbola wasn't present. She rarely went out, anyway, it seemed, and not at all, lately.

Joe and Pollak dined on sandwiches brought aboard by the colonel. Their coffee was soon gone, but they had beer and soft drinks. They took the wheel by turns, sleeping as best as they could in the small bunks forward. Pollak was in communication with the colonel by radio. The colonel informed them that Mulheisen was on the island, that he might have already visited the doctor.

At one point, trying to make conversation as they pounded along through the dark, Joe asked if Pollak was a Pole. There were dual seats, both of them the high, con type, comfortable enough. They could look out through the windshield over the deck. Joe had turned down the glow of the instrument lights, so they wouldn't interfere with their watch for shipping. It was damned bad visibility, so they had to keep alert.

Pollak said he was American. No Polish ancestry. Joe asked if he were Catholic. He wasn't. No denomination. Joe asked if he was a baseball fan. He wasn't. He didn't follow professional sports. Also, he volunteered, he didn't watch TV, hadn't read any good books, and never went to the movies.

"You eat, don't you?" Joe asked. "What's your favorite food?"

"Spaghetti," Pollak said.

"Great," Joe said. "I love spaghetti. What's your favorite?"

"Chef Boyardee. With meatballs."

That shut Joe up. He had been wondering if there was any good reason, should the occasion arise, to kill this bastard. It appeared there was.

They still had good fuel supplies, but they'd have to get more to make it back the way they had come. Pollak said they could run ashore at a village on the mainland, maybe even Tobermory, to get gas and food. It was still raining, but there were intermittent periods when it stopped, followed by heavier downpours and now some wind. The lake was kicking up. The Sea Ray, however, was taking it very well.

They got fuel in Tobermory, with little difficulty, and bought beer. They were fishermen, as anyone could see from the gear lying on the seats aft. They headed back out.

"What's the plan?" Joe asked.

"It's simple as hell," Pollak said. He was loading a Heckler & Koch MP5A3. "We'll beach below the house, walk up, and reconnoiter. If our man is there and no one's around, we grab him and go."

"What a plan," Joe said, smiling. "And what if?"

"We'll have to see when we get there, Joe. If Mulheisen's around, we'll cool it. If DiEbola's not there . . ." He shrugged. "We don't interfere with the lady. If Mulheisen's got him, we better discuss it with the colonel." He nodded toward the little handheld radio.

"How about if he doesn't want to go with us, puts up a fight, is armed, has help?" Joe asked.

They were motoring rather slowly now, angling in toward the island. Pollak had already pointed out the house, sitting up on the bluff and not very visible, thanks to heavy foliage. Joe knew the house all right, but appeared not to.

"We don't want a firefight," Pollak said. "It depends on what we see when we get up there. You about ready? You armed?"

Joe was armed. He had a .38 automatic, a nice Smith & Wesson he'd always liked. He slipped a couple of extra clips into the pocket of his rain parka.

They would move up as close as they could. Joe knew they could run the boat onto a sandy beach, thanks to the tilt function of the inboard/outboard engine, but he couldn't say as much. At any rate, in his previous run he had simply dropped Humphrey and Roman off. For the kind of operation they were envisioning, it wouldn't do to leave the boat beached. It might be difficult to get off. They agreed it would be better to anchor somewhere near the path up the cliffs.

There was no tide to speak of on these lakes, as oceanic as they might seem, so there was no danger of being stranded. There was also very little surf running, which helped. It would have been nice to dock, but it wasn't in the cards. The nearest dock was at the village, and they weren't going there.

Joe suggested anchoring among some of the larger rocks. That might be possible. They cruised along the shore. The best spot they could find for that was more or less ideal, but it was a good half mile from the spot where they would have to descend with DiEbola. Pollak decided that was all right. If DiEbola was mobile—that is, if they didn't wound him in the extraction—he could surely walk the half mile in the dark. And the boat would be much more secure than if it were left to wash in the weak surf. The alternative was to take a line ashore and anchor that way, and there was always the possibility that the boat would get beached and prove difficult to shove off.

It was getting dark. Rain was falling softly but steadily. There was a wonderful fresh smell of pines in the air. Joe nosed the Sea Ray in among some large rocks. It was quite secure here, in a gentle heave and pull. If the wind and the sea kicked up—which certainly looked likely—the boat might get scratched a little, but it was quite protected among these boulders. He could loop a line around a crag on either side. Best of all, they could hop out onto the rocks and, if they didn't slip and fall and skin their shins, they could leap to shore without getting very wet.

They set off.

They could see Roman standing in the kitchen, just staring at nothing. He was listening to something, conceivably. But he stood with his hands hanging at his sides. He was dressed in his usual dark suit, now rather wrinkled and baggy. A woman came into the room dressed in rain gear, obviously the doctor. She talked to Roman for a moment, gesturing toward the front of the house. Roman nodded. She left.

19

Qui Vive

Mulheisen trudged back to the village through the pouring rain. He went to the little tavern, the Shamrock Pub. It was next to the Mercantile, part of the same white clapboard building. It had living quarters above it. The bartender was Casey Gallagher, also the proprietor of the "Merc," as Mulheisen had already learned to call the store. The two enterprises shared an arched passageway with old-fashioned swinging tavern doors. Gallagher moved from one location to the other to take care of customers.

Mulheisen had a welcome double shot of Jack Daniel's, at a hearty five dollars American. He hadn't been drinking much lately, for some reason. It tasted good. There was nobody else in the bar, which was just a long room with a jukebox and several old framed photos of sailboats and fishing tugs on the walls, a pressed-tin ceiling. When there were no customers in the Merc, Casey stayed to chat. Casey was a wiry fellow of middle age with a mustache. He was happy to talk about hockey. He was a Toronto Maple Leafs fan. He was delighted that the Red Wings had thought they'd bought the Stanley Cup, paying far too much for players like Shanahan and Fedorov, to say nothing of Chelios, only to fall in the second round.

The Leafs had battled to the third round, at least, on a quarter of the payroll.

No, he hadn't seen any Detroiters around, although it was early in the season. They'd show up when the weather got warm. Mostly fishermen, boaters. Sure, he knew Doc White, helluva woman. Her folks had lived out here, off-islanders, from down below. They'd retired here. The old man had been a factory worker, at Massey-Ferguson, in Hamilton. Been gone about five years, and now the old lady had died. He hoped Doc White would stick around, not go back up to the Indians, as was rumored.

"Not much of a practice for her out here," Mulheisen ventured.

"Oh, I don't know. She's about retirement age herself, eh?" Casey observed. "She's got plenty to do. Besides the surgery, she's on-line, you know. She consults with some of these tribes up north. She can do that from here, advise the resident nurse, or paramedical people, you know. Not bad, eh? She can live in a healthy place like 'Shypoke' 'stead of the blackfly country, and do her doctoring on-line."

Mulheisen agreed that was quite a deal. He went back to the inn for a bowl of chowder and read an interesting book that Jean gave him, on the history of the lake country, the *coureurs de bois*, the independent fur traders. He wished he had thought to bring the book on Le Pesant. The story fascinated him, with its bizarre resonance in the DiEbola case. He reflected that, like the Algonquians, DiEbola seemed to live by an entirely different code from the conventional notion of justice. Perhaps that was unfair to the Indians, however. They were not, after all, people without a conscience, without a recognizable moral code. Quite the opposite. Whereas DiEbola, from what Mulheisen knew of him, was a man whose code, if he could be said to have one, was strictly personal, a law unto himself. For him, the concept of crime was apparently irrelevant: he did what he wanted.

He was confident that DiEbola had at least been here, and might still be. He had no idea why and he wasn't too concerned.

He hadn't a warrant for his arrest, but he didn't consider that a problem. No doubt he could call McPherson when and if documents seemed necessary.

In these and other thoughts he spent a pleasant afternoon. He hadn't taken much time to relax lately, he realized. He contemplated his recent living adjustments in Detroit, wondered if he'd made a mistake moving in with Becky. Complications. One minute she chided him for calling to say he wouldn't be home, the next she wanted to be informed about his movements. But it was interesting, he thought. He'd been getting stale, no social life. No sex life, either. This was definitely an improvement on that score. But who knew what lay down that road?

He supposed he'd also made a mistake in coming up here, if this turned out to be only a stopover visit on DiEbola's flight. A waste of time, wild-goose chase. Still, the woman had obviously been in contact with DiEbola. She might give some hint about where he'd gone next. That would be worth something. He imagined that they had established some kind of on-line relationship, if what Helen had told him about DiEbola's interest in the Internet was pertinent. The modern thing. What a world, he thought: a mobster meets his childhood crush again, on-line. He had no idea, really, what such a relationship entailed. He'd read about so-called chat rooms, but what were they? Lonely people sitting at a computer late at night, typing messages to one another, discussing topics of interest. He'd heard there were even Web sites for hockey fans, discussing the latest trades, that sort of thing. It sounded pitiful. Still, if you were on an island in Lake Huron, or up in the bush, the Net must seem like a window on the world.

Dr. Ivy White showed up on time. She wore a dress and her hair was brushed, although it was a little disheveled from the rain hat she'd taken off on entering. She had even put on some makeup. She wore her Wellingtons, however.

They sat in the lounge. Other guests were playing cards. Mulheisen and the doctor were served coffee. The conversation got off on a more comfortable tack than earlier, at the house. She quickly confirmed that she had been in communication with DiEbola on the Net. She called him Bert, which it seemed had been his name of choice in his youth. She claimed to be familiar with his reputation, but she also asserted that it was undeserved.

To Ivy White, Bert was a misunderstood man. He was bright, a talented entrepreneur and businessman who had survived a rocky youth to achieve success. Given his background and the milieu in which he'd grown up, it was not surprising that he'd had some difficulties with the law, early on. But he had risen above that, she felt. She didn't expect Mulheisen to believe her, she said. A policeman was bound to believe that young toughs never really reformed. But in her experience among the indigenous peoples, she'd seen first-hand a paradigm of how the greater society can affect, initially, expectations among the underprivileged and, later, through its misunderstanding of their different attitudes and behavior, the sense of self-worth of those same individuals.

In simpler terms, she said, the tribal people she'd worked with had struggled constantly with this problem. It had been a revelation to her, she said. The dominant society wanted everybody to conform, she saw. When they persisted in pursuing their traditional activities they were treated as outlaws. And even when they chose to play the white man's game, their accomplishments were denigrated. She thought that something like that had been Bert's burden, as well. But he'd risen above it. He'd carved out his own, unique niche and style.

Mulheisen hardly knew where to begin. He'd rarely encountered anyone so naive. It was all well and good, he said, to talk about different cultural values, discrimination, and so on. He went along with a lot of those notions himself, maybe most of them. But few societies, he said, accept blatantly criminal behavior as proper, tolerable, or even justified. A society that did that was a criminal society, he said. Mindful of his recent reading, he said that he understood that the indigenous peoples had a different way of dealing with aberrant behavior than modern Western cultures, but he reckoned they were no more tolerant of crime, especially violent crime. When it came to protecting their society and culture, they did deal with it.

But he didn't want to get into a philosophical or sociological discussion, he said. He just wanted to caution her about accepting Bert's version of his activities uncritically.

"You seem to think that DiEbola is just an ordinary businessman," he said, "maybe a little rough, or tough, but essentially one who contributes to the general economy, providing jobs, capital, and so on. I have evidence of a different kind of activity. Until very recently, this man sat at the very top of a criminal combine in Detroit and the surrounding area. He oversaw activities like drug dealing, prostitution, massive organized theft, loan-sharking, intimidation of ordinary citizens to obtain payments to avoid physical harm. And at the heart of it all is murder. That's what drives it all. They murder people for, among other reasons, the benefit of enforcing all other activities."

"I'm not so naive as you think," Dr. White said. "Those activities exist in all complex societies. There are always those who perform those activities. But I can't believe that Bert is a ruthless murderer, some kind of fiend. He may have transgressed, to some degree. People who hope to survive in those societies have to make accommodations. You can only hope that you don't have to compromise too much."

They went on in this vein for some time, rather spiritedly, until Mulheisen tired of the academic argument and simply showed his cards. "I have evidence that your Bert murdered at least half a dozen other men either personally or with the assistance of accomplices. He was there. He ordered deaths. In a couple of cases, at least, I'm sure he did the murder himself."

"I don't believe it," she said.

"Why is it so difficult to believe? If you came to Detroit, I could show you the evidence. What do I have to do to make you think otherwise?"

"I've seen him," she blurted out. "I've talked to him. He's wounded. The people who did those things want to kill him, because he opposed them. He's fleeing for his life. I have to help him."

20

Radio Silence

Joe explained to Pollak that he knew Roman. He would go in and find out what was going on. In the meantime, maybe Pollak should follow the doctor, see what she was up to.

"There's only one place she can go," Pollak said, "to the village. Must be she's going to see Mulheisen. Let's go in and see if DiEbola's here."

But Joe argued against that. "Why do that? No point in showing yourself to Roman, if DiEbola's not around. Besides, maybe she's got a nurse here, or a housekeeper. You can keep an eye on the path, warn me if the doc comes back."

Pollak thought about that for a moment, then said, "She'll be going to the hotel, or some such place, won't she? I can't exactly walk in and stand around unnoticed. Folks'll want to know where I came from."

"It can't be that small an island," Joe pointed out. "What the hell, you're supposed to be some kind of superagent. Figure it out!"

Pollak stubbornly said, "I'll just see where she goes. I'll be back toot sweet." He took off down the trail.

Joe slipped into the house as quickly as he could. Roman confronted him in the hallway, his massive revolver in hand. But as soon as he recognized Joe his face lit up.

"Joe! You come back! The boss'll be happy."

"How is he?" Joe asked.

"No good, Joe." Roman shook his head grimly. "He ain't gonna make it."

"The wound?"

Roman nodded. "What you doin' here?"

"I've got to see him," Joe said. "The feds are onto him. He's got to get out of here."

Roman shook his head. "Don't t'ink so, Joe. He's in here." He led Joe to the door of the bedroom.

Joe stopped. "Roman, there's a guy with me. He went down to the town, to make sure the doctor was out of the way. He's a fed, Roman. He thinks I'm cooperating. If he comes back, don't make a fuss, but keep an eye on him, okay?"

"Joe, you ain't wit' the feds?"

"No, no, don't worry. It's just a gag. Just keep an eye on him, all right?"

Humphrey was in the guest bedroom, downstairs. He was in bed, a large one with a brass bedstead. The doctor had rigged an I.V. for him. He didn't look good. His eyes were red and his mouth appeared dry, he had a yellowish tinge of jaundice. Joe was shocked. When he'd dropped him off he'd been stiff and sore, needing Roman's help, but he certainly hadn't looked like this.

"Slim," he called to him, "it's me, Joe. What's the prob, guy? You don't look so good."

Humphrey opened his eyes. They were yellow. "Joe," he said, hoarsely, "how you doin', kid? Ain't this the shits? That fuckin' Mongelo, he killed me. Or maybe it was the guard, John. That ricochet. How's Helen? She okay?"

"She's fine, Slim. But you don't look so good. Listen, I got kind of boxed in by the feds. One of them's here. I had to bring him. Sorry."

"It don't matter, kid." Humphrey closed his eyes. He groaned as if to himself. He made an effort and said, "I shouldn't have come. It was a dumb idea. A little unfinished business. I thought Ivy deserved. . . . But she ain't the same broad, Joe. I don't know what I thought." He moved his head slightly, in a negative way. "She's wacko," he said, after a moment. "Plus, she ain't exactly Ivy. She's . . . old." He made a gurgling noise, as if laughing. Then he groaned.

"Slim, take it easy," Joe said. "Listen, I got the boat. I can get you out of here. It'll be a hassle, but we could split, maybe go some warm place, lots of sun. You'll get better. There's doctors."

"What about the fed?" Humphrey said.

"I don't know, I'll take care of him."

"You're a good kid," Humphrey said, "but I don't think I'm goin' nowhere."

Joe heard a noise in the hall. He straightened up. Pollak came into the room, pushing Roman ahead of him. He had Roman's revolver in one hand, the Heckler & Koch in the other.

"Stand over there," Pollak said to Roman. Then he came over to the bed and looked down at DiEbola. "Well, the big boss," he said, matter-of-factly. "Looks like he's in a bad way."

"He can't be moved, not by us, anyway," Joe said. "We'll have to get a chopper or something in here."

Pollak shook his head. "That won't be necessary," he said. He stuffed Roman's pistol into his coat pocket, then checked the safety on the H&K.

Humphrey looked at the agent, then looked at Joe.

Joe lifted a hand, as if to halt Pollak. "Just a minute," he said.

"Sure, Joe," Pollak said reasonably. He rested the muzzle of the submachine gun on his free arm. "We've got a minute. What's on your mind? You got a problem here?"

"This looks a little weird," Joe said. "I mean, what's the doc gonna say when she comes back here and finds him?"

"Well, if she doesn't come back too soon, I don't see a problem," the agent said. He talked as if DiEbola were not listening.

"What about Roman?" Joe said.

Pollak looked at Roman, standing at the foot of the bed, watching the scene impassively. "I tell you what," Pollak said. "Actually, this is good. Here." He hauled Roman's gun out of his pocket and held it out toward Joe. As he did so, the barrel of the H&K came up, covering Joe. "Go ahead, take it," he said. "You can pop the monster with it, then pop him." He gestured at Roman with the H&K. "It'll look like . . . well, who knows what it'll look like? Let the mounties figure it out."

Joe took the bulky revolver from him. "What if the doc comes back before we get out of here?" he said. "She might have Mulheisen with her."

"Well, if we stand around here talking much longer . . ." Pollak said. "But let's hope she doesn't. Three bodies are already too many."

Joe wasn't sure if he'd heard that right. Three bodies? Did he mean to include Dr. White, anyway? Or was it a slip? Was there some other third body? He didn't want to debate this point. He laid the revolver down on the bed.

"I don't think so," Joe said.

Pollak shrugged. "Whatever. I can do it."

Humphrey scrabbled weakly at the pistol on his blanket. Pollak hastily reached to stop him.

It was a dreamlike moment for Joe—a very familiar dream. As if in slow motion Joe found his automatic in his hand. This time he didn't even think but shot the agent in the face. The bullet struck Pollak in the center of his forehead.

The dead man spun backward, knocking into a lamp, a chair. But imperturbably, Roman strode around the bed and caught the corpse, still upright. He snatched a towel from a nearby stand and wrapped it quickly and neatly about the man's head.

Joe blinked and glanced down at Humphrey. They looked at each other, amazed. Then Joe walked casually around the bed and helped Roman hold the body upright. "I got 'im, Joe," Roman said, and began to drag the body toward the door, his arms wrapped about the man's upper torso.

Joe stuffed his gun in one pocket, bent, and retrieved the H&K. When he went to the bed and picked up Roman's heavy revolver he looked at Humphrey. His mouth was ajar. "Jeez," Humphrey croaked. "Ivy'll shit."

Joe laughed. "I'll straighten it up," he said. "Be right back." He and Roman hauled the body outside and over to the cliff.

"I got 'im," Roman said. "It's easier this way." He hoisted the body onto his shoulders and started down the path.

Joe returned to the bedroom and very quickly set things aright. There was no blood that he could see. Roman had moved so quickly. But the room still reeked of gunfire.

"Open a window," Humphrey said.

"You think?"

"It'll be okay. You better git goin'."

Joe opened a window. The curtains billowed in, so he lowered it halfway. He looked to Humphrey. "That all right?"

"It's fine," Humphrey said. "Thanks, kid."

"I'm outta here, Slim," Joe said. "Take care."

Humphrey grasped his hand. "You too. Take care of Helen. And Roman. Get outta here." His hand dropped to the cover.

Joe caught up with Roman halfway down the steep path. Together they lugged the body down to the beach, battered by the wind and rain, cursing every step of the way. On the beach they attempted to carry him more or less upright, gripping an arm around their shoulders, but Joe was enough shorter than Roman that it proved too clumsy. Finally, Roman once again simply hoisted the man onto his shoulders in the fireman's carry and hauled him to the boat. There they managed to manhandle the corpse onto the boat, getting thoroughly wet in the process.

"You know, Roman," Joe said, "there's no point in going back up there. You've done all you could for Humphrey. Better than you did for Big Sid. This makes up for it."

Roman nodded.

"Helen's going to need a guy like you," Joe said. "Cast off."

When they were out on the pounding lake, Roman said, "Whatta you going to do, Joe?"

"When we get out a little farther, this guy goes to sleep with the fishes," Joe said. "I'll explain it to his friends, somehow. Or not." His eye fell on the radio that Pollak had used to contact the colonel. He picked it up, stepped back out of the sheltering bridge canopy, and hurled it into the choppy lake.

21

Requiem

"**W**here is he?"

"He's at my place," Dr. White said. "He's not well."

"Not well? You mean he's ill?"

"He was shot," she explained. "It was a ricochet. He narrowly escaped being murdered." It appeared that she was convinced by the physical evidence that DiEbola's story was true. He had told her that he'd discovered that some individuals in his enterprise were engaged in criminal activities. When he tried to put a stop to it, they had tried to kill him. She knew it was more complex than that, she said, but that was essentially the case. She was convinced.

Mulheisen listened to this with something between amusement and outrage. He insisted on seeing DiEbola. After a brief resistance—"He's much too weak"—she acquiesced.

As they walked through the rain she told Mulheisen that Humphrey had, in fact, asked about him.

"About me?" Mulheisen was surprised. "He knows I'm here?"

"No, I didn't tell him you were here. I didn't want to upset him. But I think he's been expecting you. Or, not exactly. What he said, several times, was 'Is Mulheisen here?' He seems to think that you are after him. That you're pursuing him."

"He's got that right," Mulheisen said. "How bad is he?"

"He's very close. To death, I mean. I wanted to have him airlifted off the island, to a hospital, but he wouldn't hear of it. He feels safe here. I think he fears that if he went to a hospital his enemies would soon discover his whereabouts and kill him. Apparently, these gangsters have some kind of ubiquitous network. Nothing escapes them."

"What exactly is wrong with him?" Mulheisen asked.

Dr. White explained that when DiEbola had arrived he was already weakened from loss of blood and shock. The blood loss wasn't critical, she had determined, and he seemed to perk up once he was made comfortable. But she soon saw that the wound was more serious than it had seemed. He hadn't been struck by a bullet directly, but only a ricochet fragment. However, it had perforated the abdominal membrane, and although she had cleaned it, there seemed to be a low-grade infection of some sort. The bullet may have picked up a contaminant en route—perhaps it had passed through another's flesh; she couldn't tell. She had some experience in these things, having treated many wounds, particularly hunting wounds. They could be benign at first and then, unexpectedly, turn nasty.

As time went on he would first rally to the point of getting out of bed, being quite cheerful, and then, soon after, lapse back. She had the feeling now, she said, that for one reason or another, he had taken a fatalistic view of his injuries and didn't believe he could recover. As a consequence, everything seemed to worsen: his fever rose, he was retaining fluids, his systems seemed to be failing. She did not have any fancy equipment; she hadn't come here to practice medicine, although she saw a few patients. She thought he could be helped—or could have been helped—at any modestly equipped hospital. But he would have none of that.

"For fear of exposing himself?" Mulheisen asked.

She stopped in the path. It was very dark. "It's more than that. I think he's disappointed," she said. "In me."

Mulheisen didn't get it. "How could you disappoint him?"

"Perhaps I've gotten it wrong," she said. "He's disappointed that he can't . . . I don't know . . . make amends. He can't atone."

"Atone for what?"

The doctor shrugged helplessly in the rain. "I really don't know. He seems to feel some responsibility toward my brother, Arthur, who died tragically when we were youngsters. I've tried to argue him out of it," she said, as they pushed on through the rain, which was now being driven hard by wind. "He persists in feeling that he was to blame."

Mulheisen told her he had informed himself about the case. He wondered what role DiEbola could have played in it. She had no idea. It was his imagination, she thought. But they had arrived.

Mulheisen was grateful to be out of the storm. He asked if DiEbola was alone.

"I don't have a nurse, if that's what you mean," she said quickly, hanging up their rain gear. "He's in here." She showed him into the guest room. The doctor went immediately to the open window. "Who—" she started to say.

DiEbola opened his eyes. "Leave it open," he croaked. "I like the air. I like to hear the rain."

The doctor hesitated, then lowered the sash until the window was nearly closed.

DiEbola frowned at the other person in the room, but then he realized who was there. His face took on a look of surprise, then he managed a ghastly grin, his lips curling back on his teeth. He had lost weight, and his features, always quite strong, were more pronounced: the nose more beaky, the forehead looming. Only his lips, normally rather red and sensuous, seemed thinner, almost bloodless.

"Mul!" he rasped. For an instant he seemed frightened. Perhaps a pang? But then he relaxed. "It's you," he said. "I was wondering if you'd make it." His voice was little more than a croak. "In time for the wake," he added.

Mulheisen looked to Dr. White. "We'd better get him out of here," he said.

"No," DiEbola said. He shook his head slightly, as if it hurt to move. "I'll stay right here. It won't be long."

Mulheisen ignored him. He started for the door, but stopped when DiEbola called to him.

"Mul," DiEbola croaked, "come and sit down. I got a lot to tell you." He waved feebly at Dr. White. "Wait outside," he said.

Mulheisen caught her by the arm. "Get on to the hospital," he said quietly. "I'm sure you know the procedure. I need to talk to him." Then he went to the bedside and pulled up a chair.

"Dumbest things happen," DiEbola said. "I never dreamed a place like this." He waved a thin hand weakly. "The jumping-off place. I need a token, it looks like, to cross over. You got a token, Mul? A dime?" He turned his palm up.

Mulheisen fumbled in his pocket for a coin. He placed a nickel in DiEbola's hand. "Sure, Humphrey, but what brings you here? I'd have thought you'd retire in Vegas, or maybe Rio. Not out in the woods, on the Lakes."

"Me too," DiEbola said. "Never saw myself croaking in the woods. I wanted to see Ivy, talk about old times. You get my age, Mul, everybody you knew is gone."

"Especially in your trade," Mulheisen said mildly. "You made a lot of them disappear, yourself. So, what was all that business in the bunker?"

"The bunker?" DiEbola seemed confused. Or maybe exhausted. He was silent for a while, eyes closed. When he replied, finally, it wasn't clear at first what bunker he was talking about. "Shou'n't have

gone into the bunker," he said. "Funny," he went on, after a long
moment, "Carmie went down there too, but Carmie never let it bug
him."

"Carmie?" Mulheisen said. "Carmine? What did Carmine do?"

"He went in the hole," DiEbola said. "Shou'n't have done it."

Dr. White came in and whispered to Mulheisen. "I'll have
to go down to the village. The phone's out."

"I'll go," Mulheisen said, getting up.

"No, you stay," she said. "I won't be long."

When she was gone, DiEbola said, "Good. We can talk." His
face took on a crafty look. "We went in Porky's fort, Mul."

"Yes?" Mulheisen was beginning to get the drift. "You and
Carmine? What happened?"

"Porky caught us. He'd a killed us," DiEbola whispered.
"Wasn't my fault, I swear. We left him there. We covered him up.
Nobody ever knew."

Mulheisen nodded. They sat silently, listening to the wind
howl and buffet the house, the rain pelting against the window.
Mulheisen sniffed. It smelled funny in here. He supposed it was the
medicine, perhaps the infection. But it smelled like cordite, over-
laden with a damp mustiness. Maybe it was sulfur, he mused: the
Devil come to get his favorite.

"But it bothered you," he prompted DiEbola.

"Not Carmie," DiEbola said. "He never gave it a thought.
Never mentioned it again. I almost forgot. I been dreaming about
it, though. I kept seeing him."

"The Boogey Man," Mulheisen said, quietly.

"You know about him," DiEbola said. He seemed comforted
to know that Mulheisen understood.

"Oh yes," Mulheisen said.

"I thought I forgot," DiEbola said. "But then he showed up.
We didn't do anything so bad, did we? He'd a killed *us*. Not my fault."

Mulheisen said, "Nobody ever blamed you for that."

"That's how it works," DiEbola said. "Luck and hard work, nobody can pin nothin' on you. Cover him up. Covered everything, after that. Ever' candy bar, ever' muscled buck." He paused. The effort was too much. When he could speak again, he said: "You know what, Mul? It gets to be too much. You can't hide all them bodies."

"Why did you come here?" Mulheisen asked. "What does this have to do with Ivy?"

"I owed her, Mul."

Mulheisen considered that. Then he said, "What did you owe her? What could you do for her? Remind her of a tragedy she got over fifty years ago? No, Humphrey. You came for yourself."

Humphrey tried to nod, but it was too hard. "Sure," he said. "I thought I could explain it to her. She'd understand."

"Maybe she'd forgive you," Mulheisen suggested.

Humphrey smiled. "She's wacko, Mul. She don't know from shit."

"No. She's a good woman," Mulheisen said.

"Sure." Humphrey didn't want to argue. "S'all my fault. You can't blame nobody but me, Mul. The girl didn't have nothing to do with it. Helen. She ain't done nothing wrong. I kept her out of the bad stuff. She liked playing at La Donna, but it wasn't happening.

"Ivy . . . she don't know nothing about me. I found her on the Internet! Accident! Fooling around one night, just 'surfing,' and I found this site up in the bush. Dr. Ivy White. I started E-mailing her. Her ma got cancer and she said she was coming down here, I figured it was a sign. I'd close up shop and come over. She didn't exactly welcome me, but she didn't say don't come. Thought I could make it up to her. Dumb idea. You got that coin?"

"I gave you the coin."

DiEbola lifted his hand, saw the nickel. "Fuckin' nickel? That enough?"

"It's enough," Mulheisen said. DiEbola's fist closed on it, then he closed his eyes. "Need this for the ferryman," he said.

"We have to get you out of here," Mulheisen said. "Dr. White is getting a Mercy Flight helicopter in. You don't have to just lie here and die."

"I don't? Looks like it to me," Humphrey said. "It's just like in Mac, you know."

"Mac?"

"Machiavelli. The Prince. His Prince, Borgia, didn't know when to quit. Not me. Hurts though."

DiEbola struggled to sit up, but he groaned and fell back. Dr. White returned. Mulheisen went into the hall to talk to her. She said the hospital would try to get the chopper out here, but it didn't look good. The weather was really kicking up. The RCMP would send a boat, for all the good that would do.

While she tended to DiEbola, Mulheisen stepped outside for some fresh air. Up here on the bluff, the wind roared, thrashing the limbs of the pines furiously. The rain pelted, paused, then came at you from another direction. Mulheisen retreated to the house.

The doctor had given DiEbola an injection of something, to ease his pain. He was breathing more calmly than he had been. He lay with his eyes closed, but he wasn't sleeping. Mulheisen beckoned Dr. White out of the room.

"How long can he last?" he asked.

Dr. White said she thought he was pretty close to the end. But one couldn't tell. She'd had patients worse than DiEbola hold out for days. But he didn't seem to want to hold out. She thought he'd be dead before the chopper or anybody else got there. They heard a noise; he was calling.

"Sit down, Mul," DiEbola said. He waved his clenched fist at the chair, pointing with a bony finger. Mulheisen sat down. Dr.

White fussed about the I.V. "Leave it, Ivy," DiEbola said. She sighed and retreated to a chair on the other side of the room.

"Mul, talk to me. What's goin' on in town?"

"Nothing's going on, Humphrey. Town's quiet, now that you're gone."

"Tell me a story," DiEbola demanded.

"I don't know any stories," Mulheisen said. He stared at the dying man impassively.

"Sure you do," DiEbola said. His eyelids lifted. He gazed at Mulheisen. "Never know what you're thinkin'." After a moment, he begged, "A story. Some of those cop stories."

Mulheisen thought for a moment, then hitched closer. "I heard this funny story. First murder in Detroit." He related the whole tale of Le Pesant. Humphrey seemed to enjoy it. He smiled, even tried to laugh.

Suddenly his eyes opened wide. They looked bright. "You know what? That was me. I covered the body, then I raised it up."

Mulheisen stared at him.

"I was Porky," DiEbola said. He shifted his head, wondering. "I wish I knew."

He lay back and that was it. Mulheisen stared down at the body. One minute it was a man, alive, thinking. The next, nothing.

Dr. White came to the bedside. She lifted an eyelid, felt his pulse, then laid his hands on his breast. She looked over at Mulheisen and said, "He was an impressive man, but so strange."

"You don't know how strange," Mulheisen said.

"It's funny," she said, "I can hardly remember Arthur, my brother. I haven't even looked at a picture of him in years. He's always been this kind of brutish figure to me. He wasn't nice. But when I think of him, he's always fifteen, but somehow older than me. He was like that for Bert, too," she said. Then she sighed and smoothed back the hair on the brow of the corpse. "Poor man," she said.

Mulheisen nodded, as if in agreement. Privately, he thought, Not like Le Pesant, after all. Not a real chief, willing to assume a burden for his people. Just a shrunken fat man who didn't survive the storm.